IMAGERY IN SPORT

TONY MORRIS, PhD
School of Human Movement, Recreation, and Performance
and Centre for Ageing, Rehabilitation, Exercise and Sport
Victoria University

MICHAEL SPITTLE, PhD
School of Human Movement and Sport Sciences
University of Ballarat

ANTHONY P. WATT, PhD
School of Education
and Centre for Ageing, Rehabilitation, Exercise and Sport
Victoria University

**HUMAN
KINETICS**

Library of Congress Cataloging-in-Publication Data

Morris, Tony, 1950-
  Imagery in sport / Tony Morris, Michael Spittle, Athony P. Watt.
    p. cm.
  Includes bibliographical references and index.
  ISBN 0-7360-3752-7 (hardcover)
  1. Sports--Psychological aspects. 2. Imagery (Psychology) I. Spittle, Michael, 1971- II. Watt, Anthony P., 1959- III. Title.
  GV706.4.M675 2005
  796.01--dc22

2005005755

ISBN: 0-7360-3752-7

Acquisitions Editors: Amy N. Clocksin and Myles Schrag; **Developmental Editor:** Renee Thomas Pyrtel; **Assistant Editors:** Ann M. Augspurger and Bethany J. Bentley; **Copyeditor:** Cheryl Ossola; **Proofreader:** Sarah Wiseman; **Indexer:** Betty Frizzéll; **Permission Manager:** Dalene Reeder; **Graphic Designer:** Nancy Rasmus; **Graphic Artist:** Denise Lowry; **Photo Manager:** Kelly Huff; **Cover Designer:** Keith Blomberg; **Photographer (cover):** Comstock Images; **Photographs (interior):** © Human Kinetics, unless otherwise noted; **Art Manager:** Kelly Hendren; **Illustrator:** Denise Lowry; **Printer:** Edwards Brothers

Printed in the United States of America   10   9   8   7   6   5   4   3   2   1

Human Kinetics
Web site: www.HumanKinetics.com

United States: Human Kinetics, P.O. Box 5076, Champaign, IL 61825-5076
800-747-4457
e-mail: humank@hkusa.com

Canada: Human Kinetics, 475 Devonshire Road Unit 100, Windsor, ON N8Y 2L5
800-465-7301 (in Canada only)
e-mail: orders@hkcanada.com

Europe: Human Kinetics, 107 Bradford Road, Stanningley, Leeds LS28 6AT, United Kingdom
+44 (0) 113 255 5665
e-mail: hk@hkeurope.com

Australia: Human Kinetics, 57A Price Avenue, Lower Mitcham, South Australia 5062
08 8277 1555
e-mail: liaw@hkaustralia.com

New Zealand: Human Kinetics, Division of Sports Distributors NZ Ltd.
P.O. Box 300 226 Albany, North Shore City, Auckland
0064 9 448 1207
e-mail: info@humankinetics.co.nz

Contents

PREFACE

Studies have shown that almost all elite athletes intentionally employ imagery. Further, most sport psychologists systematically apply imagery in their work with sport performers (e.g., De Francesco and Burke 1997; Gould, Tammen, Murphy, and May 1989; Martin, Moritz, and Hall 1999; Rushall and Lippman 1998). Automatically generated, imagery is ubiquitous in sport and life. Although it is still not clear why, imagery frequently predicts behavior: Imaging disaster or success at work, in relationships, or in sport often leads to that outcome. Taking control of our imaginations is vital if we are to manage our behavior effectively, particularly in sport. Athletes, coaches, and most important, the experts who guide sport performers and their mentors in using psychological processes need to have the best information available to ensure effective application of techniques like imagery. We believe that only our imaginations limit their own potential, as long as knowledge guides the application of imagery.

The amount of literature on imagery is vast, and recently the body of published work on imagery in sport has grown rapidly—so why do we need a text like this one? The reason is that much of the writing about imagery in sport has been condensed into book chapters, (e.g., Gould, Damarjian, and Greenleaf 2002; Hall 2001; Morris, Spittle, and Perry, 2004; Murphy and Martin 2002; Vealey and Greenleaf 2001; Weinberg and Gould 1999). Hall (1998) presented a book chapter that focused specifically on the measurement of imagery ability and imagery use. Although these chapters are excellent summaries, they are, of necessity, restricted in breadth and depth. Imagery in sport has been the focus of only one book, *Imagery in Sports and Physical Performance*, which is limited in scope and is now more than a decade old (Sheikh and Korn 1994). Although it presented a rich array of experts writing about aspects of imagery, the authors focused on their own perspectives, so the book did not address all aspects of imagery in sport and included a substantial amount of duplication.

Sport psychology periodicals that focus on imagery, such as the *Journal of Mental Imagery,* and the proceedings of major sport psychology conferences present new research on aspects of imagery and its new applications (e.g., Eton, Gilner, and Munz 1998; Hall, Mack, Paivio, and Hausenblas 1998; Moritz, Hall, Martin, and Vadocz 1996; Murphy 1994; Spittle and Morris 1999a, b, 2000; Vadocz, Hall, and Moritz 1997; Watt and Morris 1999a, b, 2000). However, gaining access to all of this specialist literature is not easy, and even the most devout scholar would find it difficult to keep abreast of the proliferation of written knowledge in every area of psychology. We must rely on those who have specialized in the study of particular topics to bring our attention to the critical issues and the essential reading. Review articles in journals do this to some extent, but, again, they tend to have a narrow focus and limited depth (e.g., Martin, Moritz, and Hall 1999; Murphy 1994).

Clearly, although many writers and researchers in sport and sport psychology address various aspects of imagery, no single source offers a comprehensive look at it. We believe that the growing cohorts of sport psychologists, researchers, teachers, and students in our field, as well as coaches and athletes, would benefit from such a text. Therefore, in this book, we address the breadth of what researchers and practitioners in sport psychology know about imagery in sport, and we treat each issue in depth. In developing the book, we considered current theories and research on imagery and its application in sport.

In presenting this large body of information, we had three more goals. First, our explanations must help readers understand the material. We want to encourage practicing and trainee sport psychologists to become familiar with current knowledge about imagery and to learn to view it with a critical eye. Some of the theories and research are complex, but we have taken care to define terms and present clear explanations. To help readers understand the sometimes complex theoretical conceptions, we have included examples from everyday sport contexts. Second, we have presented evaluations of the material. In our view, not all the writing on imagery is useful, relevant, or accurate, so by providing readers with information about theories, research, and practice relating to imagery, they can judge it for themselves. We also evaluate the work based on our experience in the field. Third, we want to provide practicing sport psychologists with guidelines and strategies for using imagery. Understanding theories and research related to imagery ultimately must lead to its practice.

In writing a book that addresses all currently understood and practiced aspects of imagery in the context of sport, we hope to stimulate our colleagues and the sport psychology researchers of the future to take up the challenge of investigating imagery in sport. At the same time we are giving sport psychology practitioners information they can work with. Imagery is a fascinating process, and we still have much to learn about it. What we will discover could change how people prepare for and engage in sport at all ages and at every level. Nonetheless, our understanding of the imagery process, and particularly its application in the sport context, has increased dramatically in the past three decades. Researchers and practitioners are generating information on imagery faster than ever. We hope that *Imagery in Sport* will help sport psychologists use imagery to greatest effect for the personal growth and experience of the athletes with whom they work.

ACKNOWLEDGMENTS

Imagery in Sport has been a labor of love for its three authors. Bringing it to fruition would not have been possible if not for the support, advice, and forbearance of a range of people, whom we wish to acknowledge and thank.

First, we would like to express our deepest gratitude to our families for their understanding of our frequent absences from family life, as we worked on the manuscript and the various stages of production of the book that followed. We hope that those who are nearest and dearest to us will benefit from the satisfaction we have with completion of a massive task, which we believe has been well done.

Timely completion of the book would not have been possible without the assistance of our colleagues who made important contributions to several crucial chapters at a time when we were sinking under a deluge of academic work of all kinds. Thus, to Michelle Walsh, Cadeyrn Gaskin, and Scott Fletcher, our appreciation for their excellent contributions to *Imagery in Sport*.

We were all very pleased with the manuscript that emerged from our hard work, but it did represent a view from a group of scholars who had worked together for a number of years. Thus, it was important to have a critical eye cast over the manuscript by an independent expert in the field. We are most grateful to Professor Craig Hall for performing that review. Craig is without question the most prolific researcher on the topic of imagery in sport. His comments on the manuscript helped us greatly to refine it and to ensure that the book provided a balanced picture of research and practice on imagery in both sport and exercise.

A number of people at Human Kinetics deserve mention for the support and guidance they gave us as we struggled with the substantial challenge of encapsulating all we think has been learned about imagery in the context of sport into one text. Amy Clocksin deserves the highest accolade. She encouraged and patiently nudged us along the path during the most difficult period we had in writing productively on the book. Without Amy's understanding and determination, the book would never have emerged. Myles Shrag helped us through the final phase of readying the book for publication in a good-humoured way that was refreshing at that stage. Renee Thomas Pyrtel has been a well-organised, friendly persona on the end of the e-mail, guiding us along tracks that were untrodden by us, as the book went through the final editing stages. Her contribution has certainly been of great importance to the final product.

Our thanks also go to all the other staff at Human Kinetics who handled specific elements of the production of *Imagery in Sport*. We don't always know their names, but we appreciate their efforts so much.

Finally, we would like to thank all our colleagues and students at Victoria University's School of Human Movement Recreation and Performance and School of Education, and the University of Ballarat for giving us the time and freedom to work on this project. We trust that those colleagues will look at this achievement with some pride because it was within the nurturing environments they created that we were able to cultivate the rich growth that is *Imagery in Sport*.

To all these people and to many others, we extend our heartfelt thanks.

Tony Morris, Michael Spittle, and Tony Watt

PART I

Understanding Imagery in Sport

In the first part of *Imagery in Sport,* three chapters introduce and define the concept of imagery and discuss its role in sport. Chapter 1 provides an introduction to the concept of imagery. In it, we explain how imagery has become a major focus of research in sport psychology as well as a principal component of psychological skills training in sport. We also describe the structure and content of the rest of the book. Definitions and conceptualizations of imagery, with particular reference to sport, constitute the focus of attention in chapter 2. We discuss the distinction between imagery and related terms and look briefly at some specific aspects of imagery. We close part I with a chapter on theories of imagery. This is a vast field, so we concentrate on those theories that have been applied to sport, even if only in a minor way. We also briefly consider some of the research that compares different theories or tests specific ones.

CHAPTER 1

INTRODUCTION: THE POWER OF IMAGINATION

What is the power of imagination? We all create and recall experiences mentally. For example, an employee rehearses how she will ask her boss for a raise, imagining how she will dress in her most businesslike suit and stand confidently in front of the boss's large, mahogany desk, with its smell of beeswax polish. She hears herself speaking slowly, quietly, and clearly, listing her skills and accomplishments that merit increased remuneration. Or, yesterday's bridegroom remembers standing in front of the wedding guests in their brightly colored, new outfits as he made his speech in a shaky and unusually throaty voice. He senses again how dry his mouth felt as he spoke. He recalls the words he used in welcoming the guests to the celebration, lauding the bride, and thanking emotional parents (hearing echoes of his mother sobbing happily). He relives the embarrassment he felt when he knocked over a tall champagne flute as he waved his hands excitedly, as if conducting his own speech. He feels the rap of his hand against the glass, hears the tinkle it made as it hit a saucer on its way down, and senses the cool moisture of the champagne on the back of his hand. In fact, just from reading these descriptions you might be experiencing some of the sights, sounds, smells, and bodily sensations that these experiences evoked in others.

Athletes frequently experience such mental episodes (e.g., Hall 2001; Martin, Moritz, and Hall 1999; Rotella, Boyce, Allyson, and Savis 1998; Rushall and Lippman 1998). Many sport performers generate detailed and precise images intentionally. A tennis player who is about to compete on the center court at Wimbledon might be able to generate a vivid image of the venue, picturing the dark-green walls, smelling the freshly mowed grass, and hearing the applause of the spectators as he moves around on that hallowed turf. He can feel the sensation in his muscles as he plays his shots powerfully and accurately. He sees his opponent stretching, struggling to reach the probing drives, and hears his gasps of frustration when his desperate effort results in yet another netted shot. Our Wimbledon star feels in control already!

In contrast, athletes often create or remember negative performance experiences, despite their desire to obliterate them from their thoughts. For example, a gymnast preparing for the Olympics repeatedly relives the fall from the beam that cost her a medal at last year's world championships. She does not imagine the whole routine, just the moves leading up to the back somersault that spelled disaster. She experiences once again the slight slip of her right foot at takeoff, her effort to adjust during the somersault itself, and the pain as her left foot missed its intended landing spot on the beam by just a few millimeters—enough for her foot to slide off the beam and her ankle to crash painfully against its edge. She vividly recalls the gasp of the crowd as she tumbled to the mat and the sinking feeling as she realized that her first medal at this level had evaporated during that final discipline, which had always been her best. Although the gymnast has performed the routine many times in practice since that competition, she has avoided that back somersault when possible. When forced to go through the whole routine, she rushes that element and performs it poorly. Her confidence in the routine is low, and she cannot stop replaying the fall in her head.

Experiences like these have the power to raise performers to the pinnacle of their sport or to make chumps out of champions. They often happen spontaneously. Switching them on or off at will is difficult, but under conscious control they can be powerful allies.

Imagery is the mental creation or re-creation of sensory experiences that appear to the person imagining them to be similar to the actual event (Suinn 1993). We constantly relive past experiences and imagine wished-for events, in pictures, sounds, smells—in fact, with all our senses. We can also experience the same emotions as those that the real event generated, which can lead to changes in physiological indicators such as heart rate, respiration, or muscle tension. *In other words, an imaginary event can provoke real-life emotional and physiological responses.*

With practice, we can manipulate our imagination to preview upcoming events, as the tennis player did. We can review things that have already happened, sometimes intentionally but often when we would rather not, as in the example of the gymnast's unwanted imagery of her biggest disaster. We can "replay" these imagery experiences in real time (at the same speed that they occurred) or we can slow them down. And, as the gymnastics example shows, we can imagine only part of an event— although we would prefer it to be that part where we performed at our best! Taking full advantage of the amazing flexibility of imagery, we can zoom in on specific aspects of the action or pull back to see more of what was happening around us or to observe the event from different angles. Similarly, we can focus on one sense modality, such as the kinesthetic sense, for example, how our fingers and wrist feel as we imagine bowling a leg-spin ball in cricket or pitching a curve ball in baseball. Sometimes, especially when we consciously control the imagery, we call these experiences daydreams. On other occasions, they can be nightmares, such as when an athlete imagines missing the final shot that would have won the championship. The most important point to understand about imagery is that athletes can learn to use it systematically to aid performance, reduce anxiety, increase confidence, enhance endurance, speed recovery from injury or heavy exercise, and much more.

POWER OF IMAGERY

Imagination is terrifically powerful. By mentally rehearsing a routine before a major competition, athletes can prepare themselves to achieve their optimal performance when it counts most. By imagining playing at their peak, athletes can build their confidence for a match. Imagery can also help a performer through a tough injury layoff by shifting attention away from the injury onto the mental rehearsal of sport skills. Knowing that research supports the value of imagery for maintaining skill level when physical practice is not possible can help motivate an athlete during recovery. When physical practice is not possible, such as during travel, imagery can provide athletes with a way to practice. It allows them to review previous strokes or movements so they can correct errors. It is difficult to think of anything else that has as much potential to enhance or destroy not only performance outcomes but the entire experience of sport.

Not all imagery has a positive impact, however. In some cases, imagery can stop fully recovered athletes from reproducing their preinjury form because they repeatedly imagine themselves breaking down at the point of maximum effort. What we imagine can make us anxious or confident, determine our focus during play, motivate us to extra effort, or convince us that all is lost.

But athletes who bring the power of their imaginations under control can use it for personal improvement. Research indicates that elite athletes, their coaches, and sport psychologists employ imagery more than any other performance-enhancement technique (De Francesco and Burke 1997; Gould, Tammen, Murphy, and May 1989; Hall and Rodgers 1989). It also shows that imagery is a highly complex process that we must understand well if we are to optimize its benefits (e.g., Hall 2001;

Martin et al. 1999; Morris, Spittle, and Perry 2004; Murphy and Martin 2002). For example, Woolfolk, Parrish, and Murphy (1985) found that when experienced golfers used positive imagery of putting (they imagined their shots dropping into the hole), they gave performances superior to those of golfers who did not image at all. Golfers in their study who were instructed to use negative imagery (to imagine their putts missing the hole) produced performances inferior to the no-imagery golfers.

Often we can improve performance, reduce anxiety, or enhance focus simply by eradicating negative imagery. This is not as easy as it sounds, however. To use imagery effectively, most athletes need training that is based on information about how imagery works, under which conditions it works best, and how personal factors affect the process. Understanding of imagery processes within the sport context has greatly increased since sport psychologists first examined imagery in the 1970s. The knowledge gained is the result of research conducted in the sport context, combined with a vast increase in the systematic use of imagery by athletes under the supervision of sport psychologists (e.g., Hall 2001; Murphy and Martin 2002). Nevertheless, we know less about imagery than what remains to be discovered.

Many questions about the effective use of imagery in sport contexts remain unanswered. Should athletes perform their imagery rehearsal in quiet environments, where they can focus on the experience, or is it more effective to use imagery in the sport environment, so that they learn to concentrate despite all the distractions present in the minutes before competition? Should they learn to image predominantly in one sense modality, such as vision, or is using all the sense modalities more effective? Does the choice of sense modality depend on which senses are used in the actual sport context? Is the athlete's imagery perspective important? Should performers image as if they were inside their bodies all the time (called an *internal imagery perspective*) or are there times when it is best for them to image as if they were watching themselves on a video (an *external imagery perspective*)?

For sport psychologists, questions about how to implement imagery techniques abound. Should they identify which senses and perspectives each athlete uses and develop scripts to match those perspectives, or should they train athletes to image using the perspective that research has determined is best for that sport skill? Is it most effective to use imagery in real time, by slowing things down, or by speeding the action up? Should imagery always include all aspects of the actual sport context, or can it be useful to extract key elements of the sport skill and image them free from the context? Can imagery be enhanced by external aids, such as video clips of the performer doing the task well or biofeedback from the muscles showing whether the skill is being performed correctly in biomechanical terms? Is it productive to experience emotion during imagery? If so, should the emotion be positive, because it might lead to positive emotion during actual performance, or negative, so that athletes image themselves playing well despite being anxious? Perhaps they need to use both types of imagery, to cope with stressful situations and reduce typical stress levels by associating performance with positive mood states.

At this time, sport psychologists do not have convincing answers for many of these questions (Hall 2001; Morris et al., 2004; Murphy and Martin 2002). Research and practical experience suggest some responses, yet controlled experiments and experiential evidence often do not come to the same conclusions. As the body of research on imagery increases, it becomes clear that many issues cannot be resolved with a simple yes or no. Sport psychology researchers frequently find that answers depend on a wide range of personal and environmental factors.

Despite continued increases in imagery use by athletes, much of its potential for application in sport remains to be discovered, for several reasons. One explanation is that research on imagery in sport, particularly on how it works, has been limited. Such research is not attractive because imagery is an internal thought process that cannot be measured directly. Thus designing research on the mechanisms by which imagery works requires a lot of imagination! Another reason is that few major research programs exist in which a group addresses a specific imagery issue through a set of studies. Instead, research has been piecemeal, with many sport psychologists undertaking a single study that provides limited information. Often researchers examine an idiosyncratic issue in the imagery domain, then move on to another area of sport psychology research (Morris et al., 2004).

Until recently, little applied research on imagery in sport existed. Although sport psychology researchers regularly conducted laboratory studies concerning the effects of imagery (or mental practice) on movement, few of them examined whether the practice enhanced performance in actual sport competition. Sport psychology practitioners based the growing use of imagery among athletes on anecdotes and largely unsubstantiated recommendations in applied sport psychology texts. The study by Gould et al. (1989) raised awareness that many sport psychologists use imagery techniques with athletes and coaches, yet such practice was based on little data. During the last decade, recognition of this gap in the literature has stimulated more research on which imagery techniques are effective, particularly in the actual sport context.

Sport psychologists are paying increasingly more attention to the imagery process. They have explored how to describe imagery and how it works in the sport context (e.g., Hall 2001; Martin, Moritz, and Hall 1999; Murphy 1994; Murphy and Martin 2002; Suinn 1993). They have investigated which kinds of imagery athletes use (e.g., Hall et al.

1990; Spittle and Morris 1998), their goals for using it (Hall 2001), which personal and situational factors facilitate or obstruct the process (e.g., Eton, Gilner, and Munz 1998; Spittle and Morris 1998; White and Hardy 1995), and whether studying psychophysiological variables will increase understanding of imagery (e.g., Collins and Hale 1997).

For their part, researchers have developed measures to help sport psychologists assess the imagery process in sport (Hall, Mack, Paivio, and Hausenblas 1998; Hall, Rodgers, and Barr 1990; Watt and Morris 1999a, b, 2000). They have studied whether imagery can enhance or hinder sport performance (Callery and Morris 1993, 1997a; Shambrook and Bull 1996) and its effect on confidence, anxiety, motivation, attention, and other psychological factors (Callery and Morris 1997b; Lee 1990). By combining the information gained from research with athletes' experiences using imagery, writers have proposed principles for using imagery effectively and developed imagery scripts and programs. Often, imagery-related issues are included in books on applied sport psychology or mental training (e.g., Bull 1991; Hodge 1994; Lynch and Scott 1999; Syer and Connolly 1987; Ungerleider 1996; Weinberg 1988).

CHALLENGES, THEORY, AND RESEARCH ON IMAGERY

The difficulties encountered in producing a comprehensive reflection of imagery in sport and physical activity include the wide range of topics in imagery research and the great variety of situations to which imagery can be applied. In addition, researchers have used different paradigms to address the same topic, while practitioners have implemented imagery programs to address the same situation based on a number of psychological models. In examining the breadth of imagery research and practice, we can see that a systematic approach has rarely been sustained over a substantial sequence of studies or applications. Thus, the challenge that faced us when we decided to write a book on imagery was to organize the book in a manner that would clearly reflect the breadth and complexity of research and practice on imagery in sport. At the same time, this great variety of study and application of imagery in sport has created the need for this kind of text. Because students, teachers, researchers, and practitioners find it difficult to conceptualize the whole field of imagery, they need one source that takes a comprehensive look at the research and practice of imagery in sport. We hope that this book will be that source. (See figure 1.1 for the primary questions addressed in this book.)

Here at the outset, we must be clear about the state of the theories and research from which this book draws. Developing theories about the way imagery works has not been easy, because unlike what happens to a soccer

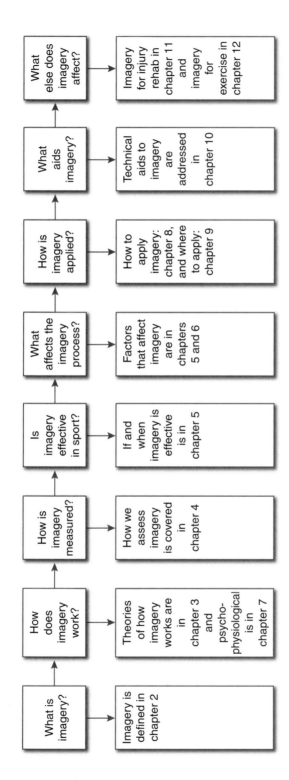

Figure 1.1 Questions about imagery in sport addressed in this book.

9

ball when it is kicked in different ways, imagery is not an observable process. When sport performers face stressful situations, we can record changes in their heart rates or the electrical activity in their skin to help us understand the impact of such experiences on arousal levels, but measuring the effects of imagery is much more difficult. Theories about imagery tend to be abstract, like the process, making them difficult to test. In general, research has relied on asking people about their imagery experiences; however, self-reports are notoriously unreliable.

Two approaches that have attempted to avoid the pitfalls in using self-reports are: (a) studies that infer aspects of imagery by monitoring observable occurrences when a person is instructed to imagine something, and (b) the measurement of brain activity during imagery. An early and potent example of the former approach was the study of electrical activity in the muscles that Jacobson (1930a, b, c, d) argued provided evidence supporting his psychoneuromuscular theory of imagery. This work was widely cited and periodically repeated over several decades (see chapter 3) before it was recognized that such electrical activity could well be a by-product of imagery that contributes nothing to learning or performance. Similarly, when people are instructed to use imagery, we can say little more about the resulting electrical activity in the brain than that it is a concomitant of imagery. In fact, we don't know for sure what people are doing when we instruct them to imagine hitting a tennis serve or shooting a basket.

However, we hasten to add that researchers' efforts to examine imagery have been ingenious and have enhanced our knowledge in a host of ways. Researching imagery is a difficult job. Perhaps for this reason, the research on imagery in sport appears fragmented, with few topics that have been thoroughly studied. The efforts to test psychoneuromuscular theory against symbolic learning theory (see chapter 3), the examination of Suinn's (1976a) visuomotor behavior rehearsal (see chapter 5), and Hall's (2001) recent work on imagery use in sport and exercise (see chapter 12) are rare examples of areas that show a concerted effort in terms of published studies of research on imagery. The list of researchers who have dedicated their careers to understanding imagery or, perhaps more practically, one element of imagery, is a very short one. Many psychologists dip into imagery research, and some researchers come back to imagery every now and again, but who besides Hall has published research on imagery consistently over a 15- or 20-year period?

The range of topics addressed and variety of methods seem almost as numerous as the list of researchers. We have encountered experimental studies, field studies, case studies, single-case design studies, interview studies, psychophysiological studies, questionnaire-based studies, studies involving correlations or regressions, and a few that have applied structural equation modeling. But in the study of imagery in sport and exercise, you rarely find researchers who address one important issue intensively over an extended period of time. Again, the best (and probably the only) example of this is the work of Hall and his colleagues on imagery use in sport and exercise (see chapters 4 and 12). Those of us in this field need more concerted efforts like Hall's if we are to fully understand imagery.

Another constraint on imagery research in sport is the lack of psychometrically validated measures of imagery's relevant aspects. Once again, Hall's work on the Sport Imagery Questionnaire (SIQ; Hall et al. 1998) has provided a promising measure of imagery use. Researchers do need to be careful, of course, not to fall into the trap of thinking that the imagery used, even by elite performers, in any particular situation is necessarily the most effective. Imagery use might be influenced by experience or have personal and situational antecedents that are not related to efficacy. Now that we have a measure, investigating such issues is possible.

Probably more important to our understanding of various aspects of imagery than the measurement of imagery *use* is the reliable and valid measurement of imagery *ability*. Much of the research on imagery in sport has not monitored ability, possibly because no psychometrically validated sport-specific measure exists. Unless imagery ability is taken into account, such studies cannot conclude that a particular type of imagery or context in which it is conducted is superior to another. The reason is that differences in outcomes of imagery use could be related to differences in ability between participants in various research conditions. A recent, promising measure, the Sport Imagery Ability Measure (SIAM; Watt et al. 2001), could provide a check that will reduce the chance that research results in unwarranted conclusions (see chapter 4).

Until a thorough understanding of imagery emerges, systematic research programs that examine one aspect of it in a variety of ways are needed. In addition, research on imagery must focus on issues that will increase knowledge rather than repeat what is already known. In particular, we propose that substantial evidence indicates that imagery works in a range of sport contexts. Imagery can enhance learning, performance, confidence, and motivation, reduce stress and anxiety, and facilitate recovery from injury, among other benefits. We need more research on how imagery works, because by understanding the mechanisms we will be able to predict and control its use, even in untested circumstances. Research should also more systematically examine *successful* imagery, investigating key personal and situational variables that affect the process. We should also aim to conduct more intervention studies in realistic contexts. Whether the tasks involve learning or performance, training or competition, the objective of imagery should be meaningful for the participants. Further, the imagery should be practiced in the environment in which it would normally be used, and the outcomes should be goals that have value for the participants. Research is a precious resource. Every study involves large investments of the participants' time and effort. We should focus our best efforts on designing studies that will produce meaningful information. Unfortunately, the history of research on imagery in sport is littered with examples that fail to do so. We hope that this book will help future researchers avoid some of the pitfalls that have snared their predecessors.

CHAPTER 2

DEFINITIONS: WHAT IS IMAGERY?

The primary goals of this chapter are to describe and analyze the major imagery definitions and conceptualizations within both cognitive and sport psychology, and to present a working definition of the construct from a sport-oriented perspective. Defining mental imagery is a difficult task. Consequently, extensive debate about its characteristics and qualities continues both within and between the various fields of psychology.

Currently, only limited consensus exists as to which conceptualizations represent accurate descriptions of the imaginal experience. Richardson (1983) concluded, after analyzing a large collection of existing definitions, that the term "imagery" is ubiquitous and is used both to describe and explain. He suggested that it typically referred to "either a class of inferred cognitive constructs or processes, or a class of more or less percept-like experience" (p. 36). Recently, theorists have presented models of the imagery construct, rather than narrative detail, as a method for clarifying the process. The definitions and conceptualizations considered in this chapter focus primarily on the cognitive processes associated with mental imagery from both a general psychological perspective and from within the sport psychology domain, with specific reference to the terms "imagery ability" and "imagery use."

DEFINITIONS FROM COGNITIVE PSYCHOLOGY

Within the field of cognitive psychology, descriptions of mental imagery lack consistency in terms of the features that constitute the process. The focus of each definition seems to vary depending on the purpose for which the imagery description is used. Finke (1989), whose work examined information retrieval using mental images, defined mental imagery as "the mental invention or re-creation of an experience that in at least some respects resembles the experience of actually perceiving an object or an event, either in conjunction with, or in the absence of, direct sensory stimulation" (p. 2). Paivio (1971), also working within the field of learning and memory, proposed a description oriented toward neurological functioning within which imagery is "used to refer to a memory code or associative mediator that provides spatially parallel information that can mediate overt responses without necessarily being consciously experienced as a visual image" (pp. 135-136). Richardson (1994) suggested that this definition intended to contrast the verbal and visual aspects of imaginal processing emphasized within Paivio's dual-code theory of imagery functioning. (The theory assumes the existence of two cognitive subsystems, one for the representation and processing of nonverbal objects or events, such as imagery, and the other dealing with language.) Contrasts based on use, observed within the existing set of imagery definitions, restrict the utility of certain descriptions and can cause confusion in adopting a single conceptualization for research.

Other researchers have provided operational definitions of imagery in developing imagery theory. Lang (1979a) offered a bioinformational theory that described imagery in the context of the brain's information-processing abilities, defining an image as "a finite information structure which can be reduced to specific propositional units" (p. 109). Subsequent examination of Lang's theory leads to the description of imagery as a process in which networks of stimulus and response propositions that are stored as coded information in the long-term memory are activated (Hecker and Kaczor 1988). Lang (1979b) originally suggested that images are strictly controlled by "a finite propositional structure (and not the analogue representation suggested by phenomenology)" (p. 495). Lang also presented substantial research evidence derived from examining the key elements of his initial conceptualization of imagery.

Dean and Morris (2003) recently reevaluated the conceptualizations of Kosslyn (e.g., Kosslyn 1980, 1994) and Farah (1984), which outline imagery as a process best characterized as a collection of abilities They suggested that the Kosslyn definition of an image is the "end product of a collection of differentiated constructive processes. The surface properties of this image (our phenomenological experience) are a reflection of both the results of these processes and the properties of a structure he refers to as the visual buffer" (Dean and Morris 2003, 247). The key observable characteristics of the visual buffer are resolution and spatial extent. Kosslyn (1980) detailed three broad classes of the imagery process: image formation, maintenance, and transformation. The empirical analysis of the framework of any representation of mental imagery is an important aspect of developing accurate definitions of the construct. Both the Lang and Kosslyn frameworks are good examples of conceptualizations that are still being examined, in a broad range of studies, in an effort to gather evidence to support the efficacy of their descriptions of the imagery phenomenon.

Anderson (1981a) also presented an operational, or working, definition, but from the perspective of imagery assessment rather than theory development. "'Imaginary experiences' will refer, at a minimum, to awareness of sensory-like qualities in the absence of environmental stimuli appropriate to the sensation. This will usually involve awareness of visual qualities, but not always. Along with the minimum requirement of sensory awareness, imaginary experiences may also include thought segments that are part of, or that occur in the context of, the imaginal sensory awareness" (p. 151).

Formulation of the Anderson definition involved the assumption that imagery is a constructive behavior, actively undertaken. Anderson was quite clear in pointing out that the primary role of the definition was to aid the practitioner and investigator in designing and selecting appropriate instruments for imaginal assessment.

Of the existing definitions, the classic description of mental imagery formulated by Richardson (1969) is the one most regularly referred to in discussions of the imagery phenomenon. The developmental basis of the definition was within the field of general psychology, but it has also been consistently acknowledged in sport psychology literature (e.g., Janssen and Sheikh 1994; Martin, Moritz, and Hall 1999; Murphy and Jowdy 1992; Murphy and Martin 2002; Perry and Morris 1995). In addition, this definition, or one or more of its composite elements, has served as a starting point for various imagery studies (e.g., George 1986; O'Halloran and Gauvin 1994) and constituted a base for more elaborate discussions of imagery functioning (e.g., Martin et al. 1999; Murphy and Jowdy 1992; Murphy and Martin 2002). The definition has lost little relevance or validity in the 30 years since its creation. Richardson (1969) stated that "mental imagery refers to (1) all those quasi-sensory and quasi-perceptual experiences of which (2) we are self-consciously aware and which (3) exist for us in the absence of those stimulus conditions that are known to produce their genuine sensory or perceptual counterparts, and which

(4) may be expected to have different consequences from their sensory or perceptual counterparts" (pp. 2-3).

Murphy and Martin (2002) considered Richardson's explanation to be of great value in examining imagery functioning and outlined three key features of the definition that are relevant to interpreting the process within a sport-oriented context. The first feature is the mimicking of the sensory or perceptual experience, such as the "feeling of movement." The second is that the individual is conscious of the experience, purposefully generating an image—for example, of a familiar sporting venue. The third is that the experience occurs without known stimulus antecedents; in other words, no track or competitors need be present in imagining an athletic event. Perry and Morris (1995) suggested that the Richardson definition does not adequately distinguish imagery from other cognitive processes. For example, Murphy and Jowdy (1992) interpreted the reference to conscious awareness within the definition as highlighting a differentiation of imagery from dreaming and daydreaming. Perry and Morris (1995) argued that daydreaming typically occurs in a fully conscious state. They suggested that focusing on the concept of volitional control of the images is a more appropriate way to differentiate imagery from dreaming states. Generally, Richardson's definition is sufficiently complex and flexible to allow for its use as a descriptor of the key characteristics of images experienced within the context of sport.

DEFINITIONS FROM SPORT PSYCHOLOGY

Unfortunately, many definitions of imagery derived from sport psychology literature have tended to focus on only limited aspects of this ubiquitous mental experience. Moran (1993), in examining imagery assessment in sport, referred to two simple definitions of the term. The first, presented by Matlin (1989), described imagery as a procedure for mentally representing things that are not physically present. The second definition, developed by Solso (1991), described it as "a mental representation of a non-present object or event" (p. 267). Moran (1993) extended these descriptions by emphasizing that imagery should include not only the visual sense but multiple sensory inputs. Such a belief contrasts with a tendency in areas of the sport psychology literature, even in relatively recent texts (Cox 1998; Wann 1997), in which the definition of imagery concentrates on the visual perspective only, through terms such as "visualization," "mental picture," or "the mind's eye" (Morris 1997). Hardy, Jones, and Gould (1996) avoided this problem by focusing on the sensorial nature of imagery, describing the term "as a symbolic sensory experience that may occur in any sensory mode" (p. 28). Murphy (1994) proposed a definition that highlighted the memorial aspects of the process, suggesting that it relied on the recollection of stored sensory experiences, which may be recalled in the absence of external stimuli. Although these definitions provide a basic foundation for describing the process, they have tended to oversimplify a complex concept of substantial importance within sport psychology.

Vealey and Walter (1993) and Vealey and Greenleaf (1998, 2001) also produced a simple functional definition: "Imagery may be defined as using all the senses to re-create or create an experience in the mind" (Vealey and Greenleaf 2001, 248). This definition, however, is best understood when considered in conjunction with Vealey and Greenleaf's extended discussion of the three key characteristics associated with sport-oriented imagery. These elements are in part derived from the definition and include (a) imagery as re-creating or creating an experience, (b) imagery as a polysensory experience, and (c) imagery as the absence of external stimuli. Although Vealey and Greenleaf's definition is distinct from Richardson's (1969) in terms of time and context, their conceptualization still refers to several important elements derived from his definition (e.g., polysensory, absence of stimuli). It is, however, their emphasis on the re-creation and creation of the imaginal experience and their presentation of a sport-oriented conceptual framework that distinguishes this conceptualization from others.

Denis (1985) formulated a definition that highlighted the dynamic and creative properties of images:

> Imagery is a psychological activity which evokes the physical characteristics of an absent object (either permanently or temporarily absent from our perceptual field). It is worth emphasizing here that imagery is not restricted to recollection of the appearance of static objects, but it extends to moving objects, objects undergoing transformations, in other words, to dynamic events. The scope of imagery is not limited to recalling objects or events that have been perceived in the past (recent or distant past), but imagery also refers to objects or events that have not yet been accomplished. Imagery allows people to anticipate future (or even purely theoretical) events. (pp. 4S-5S)

Denis' definition has proved popular, specifically through its alignment with the extensive imagery research work of Craig Hall and his colleagues (e.g., Hall 1998, 2001). The definition is useful in how it considers the image's specific properties, its possible uses, and the involvement of other cognitive processes, such as memory. The detailed nature of this definition provides a substantial basis for a framework for the examination of individual differences in the dimensional and sensorial characteristics of imagery.

Several authors (e.g., Murphy and Jowdy 1992; Murphy and Martin 2002; Perry and Morris 1995) have distinguished between commonly used terms relating to imagery within sport psychology research. The terms regularly used with the least discrimination are "imagery," "mental practice," "mental rehearsal," "visualization," and "imagery rehearsal."

Mental practice, according to Corbin, is the "repetition of a task, without observable movement, with the specific intent of learning" (1972, 94). Mental practice may not use imagery at all; it could include nonimage-based strategies such as verbal rehearsal or self-talk. For the purposes of this book, a distinction originally outlined by Murphy and Jowdy (1992) and discussed again in Murphy and Martin (2002) provides a critical differentiating framework. It defines imagery as a mental process and mental practice as a nonphysical rehearsal or practice technique used by athletes. Aligned with this distinction is the definition of mental rehearsal as "the employment of imagery to mentally practice an act" (Hardy et al. 1996, 28). The emphasis here is also on mental rehearsal as a technique rather than imagery as a process.

Within an applied sport psychology context, Suinn (1976a, 1983, 1993) used the term "imagery" in relation to his procedure known as visuomotor behavior rehearsal (VMBR):

> The imagery of visuomotor behavior rehearsal apparently is more than sheer imagination. It is a well-controlled copy of experience, a sort of body-thinking similar to the powerful illusion of certain dreams at night. Perhaps the major difference between such dreams and VMBR is that the imagery rehearsal is subject to conscious control. (Suinn 1976a, 41)

Another important component of Suinn's analysis of the imagery construct is the multimodal nature of visuomotor behavior rehearsal and its relation to mental experiences. Suinn (1993, 499) proposed that VMBR is "a covert activity whereby a person experiences sensory-motor sensations that reintegrate reality experiences, and which include neuromuscular, physiological, and emotional involvement."

Additional important elements of Suinn's (1984) VMBR program are that the process of imagery is holistic and multisensory, involving the reintegration of experiences derived from visual, auditory, tactile, kinesthetic, and emotional cues (Murphy 1990). The process also involves the specific use of imagery by individuals in rehearsing for sport activities (Murphy 1994). As a form of imagery rehearsal, VMBR has proved to be adequately detailed, systematically analyzed, and a popular technique within sport psychology practice. As an imagery conceptualization, the quality and depth of the description of VMBR facilitates the incorporation of pertinent content in the design of measures that examine a broad range of imagery abilities.

Recently, Simons (2000) presented an excellent analysis of the process of using imagery as a psychological-skills training technique. The information relevant to his definition of imagery emanated from his conclusions about the manner in which athletes process imagery. Simons described the process as follows:

> Imagery is intriguing for its close relationship to perception and action. It is such a rich memory system, matching the complexity of information presented by the environment and contained in the execution of motor skills. Images bind personal thoughts and emotions to experience, and they have qualities far beyond simple stimulus/response propositions. . . . Imagery can be creative, allowing one to experience attitudes and actions mentally in ways that have not yet been encountered in real performance. (p. 92)

Simons' description of sport-oriented imagery highlights many of the important characteristics of the conceptualizations outlined previously. Future imagery investigations must align applied interpretations of the phenomenon with those definitions formulated from research findings and theory analysis.

WORKING DEFINITION OF SPORT IMAGERY

For the purpose of this text, it seems appropriate to formulate a complete definition of sport imagery to aid in interpreting and evaluating the theory and research presented. The following definition compiles specific elements of relevance from the definitions of Richardson (1969) and Denis (1985), the conceptualizations of Suinn (1976a, 1983, 1993) and Vealey and colleagues (Vealey and Walter 1993; Vealey and Greenleaf 1998, 2001), and the applied interpretation of Simons (2000). It emphasizes the nature of mental imagery in relation to involvement in sport.

> *Imagery, in the context of sport, may be considered as the creation or re-creation of an experience generated from memorial information, involving quasi-sensorial, quasi-perceptual, and quasi-affective characteristics, that is under the volitional control of the imager, and which may occur in the absence of the real stimulus antecedents normally associated with the actual experience.*

This definition is not unique when examined on the basis of its individual elements; however, what is distinctive is the combination of key components of existing definitions into an operational framework that is relevant to the exploration of the construct of sport imagery.

OPERATIONAL DEFINITIONS OF IMAGERY ABILITY AND IMAGERY USE

The two skills most regularly examined in the context of sport imagery are imagery ability and imagery use. Both have received substantial examination within sport psychology and are discussed extensively in this text. Operational definitions of these characteristics will clarify the use of these terms in subsequent chapters.

Imagery-ability questionnaires typically examine self-reported quality of imagery. As such, they are not, in the strictest sense, tests of ability. Hall and Martin (1997) and Hall (1998) supported the use of the term "ability" (as distinct from skill) in the assessment context, on the basis that all people have the capacity to generate and use images, "but not to the same degree" (Hall 1998, 165). Research and applied work on imagery training indicates that imagery abilities can be improved, which is a characteristic of skills, not abilities. It has become conventional, however, to refer to the self-reported assessment of the qualities of imagery as "imagery ability" (e.g., Ahsen 1997; Hall 1998; Hall and Martin 1997). Morris (1997) defined imagery ability as "an individual's capability of forming vivid, controllable images and retaining them for sufficient time to effect the desired imagery rehearsal" (p. 37). Hardy et al. (1996) defined it as the "performers' ability to form vivid images and also to control their images" (p. 28). More recently, Watt, Spittle, and Morris (2002) stated that "imagery ability represents the capacity of the individual to create images, and is typically evaluated in terms of generational, sensorial, and emotional qualities" (p. 1). These definitions share the same basic characteristics of imagery ability in relation to creation and assessment. The term is typically used in the context of measuring this attribute in athletes.

The definition of imagery use has also received only minimal attention. Hall and colleagues have proposed broader conceptualizations of the construct but as yet have not provided a specific description. Watt, Spittle, and Morris (2002) proposed a simple definition: "Imagery use is the manner in which people image themselves in ways that can lead to learning and developing skills and can facilitate performance of those skills. It is normally assessed in terms of its cognitive and motivational attributes" (p. 1). Murphy and Martin (2002) provided a descriptive outline of imagery use in relation to their overview of Martin, Moritz, and Hall's (1999) applied model of imagery use in sport. They proposed that imagery use is an athlete's "use of imagery to achieve a variety of cognitive, behavioral, and affective changes. Another important feature of this model is that it centers on imagery content (i.e., what the athlete images) as a key determinant of these changes" (p. 418). Like "imagery ability," "imagery use" is a term that has been developed in relation to its measurement; consequently definitions will highlight those characteristics that the measures of the attribute evaluate.

CONCEPTUALIZATIONS FROM SPORT PSYCHOLOGY

Over the last decade, high-quality conceptualizations have been developed specifically in relation to sport imagery. As yet few of them have undergone rigorous empirical analysis; however, the support they receive from practitioners in the field suggests that appropriate investigations of their theoretical merit and construct strength will become more common in the near future. Those of greatest conceptual viability are

applied model of imagery use in sport (AMIUS),

PETTLEP model,

four Ws of sport imagery,

imagery content model,

three-level model of sport imagery, and

sport imagery ability model.

We address each of these models in the following sections.

APPLIED MODEL OF IMAGERY USE IN SPORT

An important underlying element of the AMIUS is Paivio's (1985) functional analysis of imagery in relation to behavior mediation. Paivio suggested a 2×2 imagery model in which categories are derived from combinations of the dimensions of cognitive and motivational processing relationships and the dimensions of general and specific behavioral goal achievement. The dimensions are distinguishable based on image content.

As an outcome of their extensive involvement in the field of sport and movement imagery, Hall and colleagues have provided sport-oriented descriptions of these dimensional classifications (Hall 1998, 2001; Hall, Mack, Paivio, and Hausenblas 1998; Martin et al. 1999). Martin et al. (1999) summarized and extended the original four Paivio categories into five classes of imagery use: (a) cognitive general (CG)—imagery related to competitive strategies; (b) cognitive specific (CS)—imagery directed toward skill development or production; (c) motivational general arousal (MG-A)—imagery related to arousal, relaxation, and competitive anxiety; (d) motivational general mastery (MG-M)—imagery representative of effective coping and confidence in challenging situations; and (e) motivational specific (MS)—imagery that represents specific goals and goal-oriented behavior.

Martin et al. (1999) stated that the basis for the model centered on the "type of imagery used by the athlete (i.e., the function or purpose that imagery is serving) as a determinant of cognitive, affective, and behavioral outcomes" (p. 249). Consequently, the model comprises four components representative of this description (see figure 2.1): the type of imagery used (e.g., MG-A, CS), outcomes of imagery use (e.g., modifying cognitions, strategy rehearsal), imagery ability, and the sport situation (e.g., training, competition).

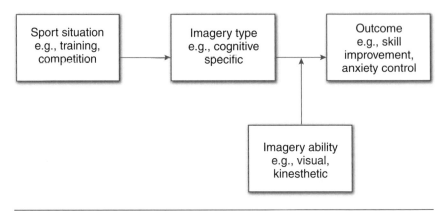

Figure 2.1 Model of imagery use in relation to sport.
Based on Martin et al. 1999.

PETTLEP MODEL

In response to perceived problems in implementing programs involving motor imagery, Holmes and Collins (2001) proposed a model for optimizing the efficacy of these interventions (see figure 2.2). Holmes and Collins (2002) outlined the model's structure, which comprises "physical, environment, task, timing, learning, emotion, and perspective (PETTLEP) elements derived from neuroscientific functional equivalence literature, empirical studies in our own laboratories, and clients' detailed personal experiences of those factors that relate to the construction of effective motor-imagery scripts" (p. 127).

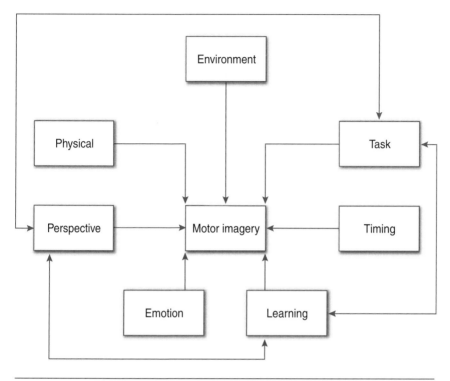

Figure 2.2 PETTLEP model of motor imagery.
Based on Holmes and Collins 2001.

Weinberg and Gould (2003) provided a summary of specific factors detailed by Holmes and Collins (2001, 2002) to consider in relation to each of the elements. *Physical* relates to the physical nature of imagery a performer may generate. Athletes must determine if their need is for the approximation of motor programs, arousal orientation, or use of relaxation techniques. *Environment* implies that the performer requires the use of stimulus materials (e.g., scripts, video, photos) that are personalized and multisensory and that mimic the environments typical of motor performance. *Task* requires that the imagery represents the nature of the skill to be performed, the ability level of the performer, and perspective. *Timing* concerns the importance of the imagery being performed in real time. *Learning* focuses on the need for imagery content to be reviewed and modified as new skills are learned. *Emotion* refers to the necessity for performers to include an emotional component in their images. *Perspective* provides guidance in the prioritization of internal imagery; however, depending on the activity, including external imagery may be an appropriate strategy for the performer.

Four *W*s of Imagery Use

In a recent representation of imagery use presented by Munroe, Giacobbi, Hall, and Weinberg (2000), a simple format categorized key aspects of how athletes incorporate imagery into their involvement in sport. They proposed that by responding to the following four questions a broader understanding of sport imagery might be acquired: *Where* is imagery used? *When* is imagery used? *Why* is imagery used? and *What* is being imaged? Hence, the "four *W*s."

Where relates to the context of imagery use within training and performance activities, with recent evidence indicating that athletes employ imagery in the competition environment more regularly than in the practice situation (Munroe et al. 2000).

When refers to the timing of imagery use. This is determined in relation to scheduling factors, such as within or outside of physical practice or training time; before, during, or after competition; or as a component of rehabilitation.

Why represents the functional aspects of imagery use. Munroe et al. (2000) have incorporated the Martin et al. (1999) cognitive and motivational structure of imagery use (described earlier) as a representation of the functional aspects relating to why athletes image.

What athletes image constitutes the most detailed element of the Munroe et al. model. They proposed that a content- and qualitative-based structure of sport imagery most appropriately represents the "what" of imagery use. The six key categories of content include sessions, effectiveness, nature of imagery, surroundings, type of imagery, and controllability. Subcategories relate more to specific qualitative and processing aspects of imagery, such as sensory involvement, image generation, image manipulation, emotional states, and perspective. Munroe et al. presented a summary model (see figure 2.3) of their analysis of interviews with athletes concerning the use characteristics of the imagery they incorporate within training and competition.

Three-Level Model of Imagery Use in Sport

A recent conceptualization proposed by two well-credentialed imagery researchers is the Murphy and Martin (2002) three-level model of imagery in sport (see figure 2.4). Although initial review of it suggests an overly simplified design, the supporting documentation Murphy and Martin provide is a detailed amalgamation of relevant theory and research. Briefly, the model describes three levels: (a) nature of imagery, (b) use of imagery to achieve goals, and (c) meaning of the image to the athlete.

Level 1 concerns the nature of the construct and represents an overview of the physiological and cognitive processes associated with

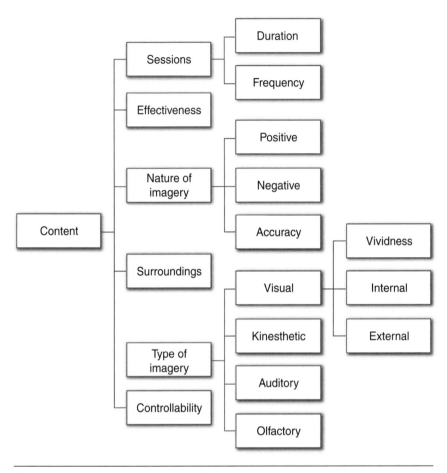

Figure 2.3 Model of the content of imagery.

Based on Munroe et al. 2000.

imagery. Level 2 deals with both the general use of imagery by athletes and how incorporating imagery within mental preparation affects performance. In Level 3 Murphy and Martin expand on the work of Ahsen (1984) by describing the role of image meaning in the context of sport imagery. This level has yet to be fully explored by researchers interested in examining the imagery construct in relation to sport. Murphy and Martin also discussed the importance of an interlinking between levels, which is highlighted by their comment that "the three-level model suggests that a more useful strategy is to use the concepts being studied in Level 1 research as a basis for understanding how athletes use imagery to control and manage athletic performance" (p. 412), which represents level 2 analysis. Level 3 is then interlinked with levels 1 and 2 on the

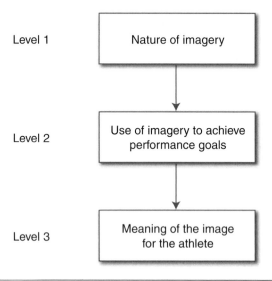

Figure 2.4 Three-level model of imagery use in sport.

Based on Murphy and Martin 2002.

basis that it is experiential activity associated with the meaning that the physiological, cognitive, and use aspects of imagery have for the individual. This blending of knowledge would also extend to an enhanced understanding of the role of image meaning when examined in the context of areas such as processing and use. Overall, the model represents a tool for uniting the vast array of theoretical and empirical information regarding imagery into a framework that, through its simplicity, may assist in analyzing such a complex construct as imagery.

Sport Imagery Ability Model

Based on their research using the Sport Imagery Ability Measure (SIAM), Watt and Morris (1998a, 1999a, 2001) have formulated a model of imagery ability in relation to sport (figure 2.5) (Watt, Morris, and Andersen 2004). The basic model constitutes a three-tier framework, with a general imagery-ability factor leading to image generation, feeling, and single-sense factors, and a third stage that details individual dimension, sense modality, and emotion characteristics.

The third-stage characteristics include the image-generation components of vividness, control, duration, ease, and speed in combination with the visual sense modality. The preceding characteristics represent a latent factor formulated on the proposition that visual images may create the base from which to evaluate the dimensional qualities of

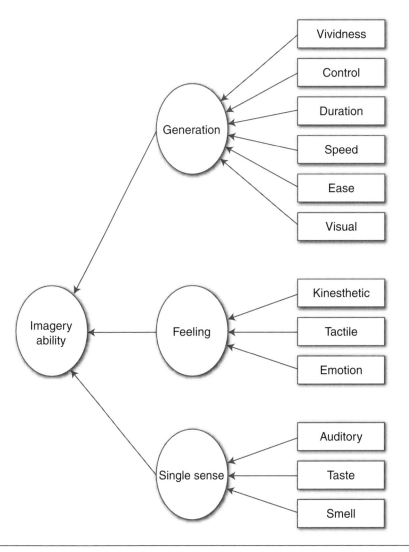

Figure 2.5 Model of imagery ability in relation to sport.

Based on Watt et al. 2004.

sport imagery. Two more latent factors, the SIAM's tactile, kinesthetic, and emotion subscales and auditory, olfactory, and gustatory subscales, formed the rest of the model's basis. The second latent factor represents those image characteristics associated with diffuse body-feeling states. The third represents the nonvisual senses associated with somatic type sensory organs. This grouping of variables represents imagery characteristics that appeared to have the strongest conceptual clarity according to analyses of data from a wide age range, both genders, several cultural groups, and a broad set of performance levels and sport activities. Confirmatory factor analysis was used to test variations of this structure, particularly with respect to the positioning of the visual modality and the experience of emotion. The identification and confirmation of ability as a second-order factor still requires additional analyses. As with the imagery-use model discussed earlier (Martin et al. 1999), this conceptualization is presented as an initial framework for the ongoing analysis and description of the structure of sport imagery ability.

CONCLUSIONS

The definition and conceptualization of the imagery construct in relation to sport remains an ongoing challenge for researchers and theorists. A recent resurgence in interest in the task is apparent; however, limited liaisons between the various investigative cohorts may restrict the formulation of accepted definitions of sport imagery constructs.

Ongoing research in both imagery ability and use may garner support for the Watt and Morris definition of sport imagery. This will also enhance the Hall et al. definition of imagery use and the Watt and Morris description of imagery ability. Because both definitions are associated with conceptual models and assessment devices, their confirmation as accurate representations of sport imagery constructs will certainly lie in the targeted use of the measures for the purposes of ongoing theoretical development.

A review of several other recent conceptualizations reveals the researchers' efforts to generate a suitable framework from which to explore how imagery operates in sport. Conceptualizations such as sport imagery use, PETTLEP, and imagery content models represent viable representations that further research will refine and confirm. The Murphy and Martin (2002) model of imagery in sport establishes a base from which to categorize theories and evidence about the imagery's operation and involvement in athletic performance.

Efforts to extend the explanation of the imagery construct within sport psychology are progressing positively. For a long time, too few theorists were prepared to propose definitions or construct models. Thus, perhaps undeservedly, they sustained the misconception that describing imagery was too difficult a task. Although the various conceptualizations reflect a reasonable degree of divergence, increased information sharing and interaction between research groups should lead to a more succinct set of descriptors for sport imagery.

CHAPTER 3

THEORIES: HOW DOES IMAGERY WORK?

This chapter explores the explanations offered by researchers and theorists for the effects of imagery on motor-skill performance and sport performance. These theories aid us in understanding why imagery operates the way it does and provide practitioners with a basis for using it effectively. They also might help us understand how imagining hitting a perfect tennis forehand, sinking a free throw, or crossing the finish line first can actually help us to successfully complete these tasks. It could be because it helps us plan our movements or because it strengthens motor patterns through kinesthetic feedback. Or perhaps imagery prepares us for action or pumps us up or gives us confidence to perform. Perhaps imagining performance activates the same neural paths as in motor preparation and this improves synaptic efficiency. This chapter on the major theories about how imagery works examines these ideas and more. Table 3.1 provides a summary of each theory.

We first examine early theories of mental practice that sport psychologists have used to explain the effects of imagery. These theories have not adequately explained the effects of imagery as it is used in applied sport psychology; therefore sport psychologists have sought out alternative explanations and turned to general psychology for ideas. As a result, several alternative conceptualizations for how imagery might enhance sports performance have evolved. So far, however, little direct research has been done on these explanations in sport. This chapter reviews several of these explanations, divided into categories: theories with a cognitive basis, such as the dual-code, bioinformational, and triple-code theories; those that emphasize

Table 3.1 Theories and Models of Imagery in Sport

Authors	Name of theory or model	Major concepts
Carpenter (1894) Jacobson (1930a, b, c , d, 1931a, b, c) Richardson (1967) Start and Richardson (1964)	Psychoneuromuscular theory	Imagery enhances performance by producing minute muscle innervations that are identical in pattern to actual execution, providing neuromuscular feedback that allows adjustment to the movement pattern.
Sackett (1934)	Symbolic learning theory	Imagery provides the opportunity to rehearse the sequence of movements and thus help the learner symbolically code these patterns in the central nervous system.
Paivio (1975)	Dual-code theory	Information in memory can be stored as one of two independent codes (an image or a word), either of which can result in recall.
Lang (1977)	Bioinformational theory	Images are propositional structures. There are 3 main classes of propositions: stimulus (the scene), response (the response to the scene), and meaning (interpretation of the events).
Ahsen (1984)	Triple-code theory (ISM)	Imagery has 3 important components: the image (I), the somatic response (S), and the meaning of the image (M).

References	Theory	Explanation
Grouios (1992) Hale (1994)	Gross framework or insight theory	Imagery helps the learner get a general idea or the "whole" of the skill rather than the details of the movement. Learning results from insight rather than gradual improvement.
Schmidt (1982)	Attention-arousal set theory	Imagery functions as a preparatory set that assists the athlete in achieving an optimal arousal level prior to performance.
Bandura (1977a, b) Budney et al. (1994) Grouios (1992) Perry and Morris (1995)	Self-efficacy/self-confidence theories	Imagery increases the athlete's success expectations and this increases performance.
Paivio (1985)	Motivational explanations	Imagery plays a motivational and cognitive role in enhancing performance.
Farah (1989) Finke (1980, 1985) Finke and Shephard (1986) Jeannerod (1994, 1995)	Functional equivalence theories	Imagery and perception or imagery and movement recruit common central nervous system structures and processes, but during imagery execution is blocked.

psychological states such as motivation or self-confidence/self-efficacy; and arousal-attention set explanations. Another possible explanation, based largely on neurophysiological evidence that researchers have only recently recorded, is that motor imagery and motor preparation are functionally equivalent. This chapter describes the main elements of each theory, reviews research related to it (with an emphasis on studies in the context of sport), and assesses its viability as an explanation of the performance-enhancing effects of imagery. It also discusses the current status of imagery theory.

EARLY THEORIES OF MENTAL PRACTICE

Studies by Jacobsen (1931a) and Sackett (1934) have led to a large amount of research examining the efficacy of mental practice (MP). As outlined in chapter 2, MP refers to "the repetition of a task, without observable movement, with the specific intent of learning" (Corbin 1972, 94). It generally involves using imagery or some other cognitive process to repetitively practice a skill. Many MP studies have used just one session, typically half an hour or less, with instructions that emphasize "thinking about" the task or "picturing oneself" doing it (Perry and Morris 1995). Researchers have conducted most MP studies using analogue tasks designed for use in the laboratory and developed so that participants will not be familiar with them, which is very different from how imagery is used in an applied sport setting. There, the sport psychologist generally provides skilled performers (who are often very familiar with the skill being imagined) with several sessions of detailed imagery training, utilizing many of the strategies described in chapter 8, and for reasons other than skill acquisition, such as motivation and self-confidence (see chapter 9). These studies usually utilize a pre- and posttest design that compares performance changes due to MP with one, two, or all of three other conditions: physical practice (PP), no practice (NP), and a combination of mental practice and physical practice (PP/MP). Several reviews of the effects of MP on skill acquisition have concluded that MP is typically more effective than NP and less effective than PP (Driskell et al. 1994; Feltz and Landers 1983; Feltz, Landers, and Becker 1988; Grouios 1992; Weinberg 1982).

Literature in sport psychology has generated two major theoretical explanations for the effects of mental practice: psychoneuromuscular explanations (Corbin 1972; Jacobson 1931a, b, c; Richardson 1967b; Schmidt and Lee 1999) and the symbolic learning theory (Sackett 1934). These theories have been examined for almost 70 years without determining what occurs during imagery to enhance performance (e.g., Harris and Robinson 1986; Morrisett 1956; Shaw 1938). Murphy (1990) suggested that this is because these early theories were developed to

EXAMPLES OF TYPICAL MENTAL PRACTICE STUDIES

A study by Hird, Landers, Thomas, and Horan (1991) compared varying ratios of MP and PP on performance of a pegboard (cognitive) and rotary pursuit (motor) task. The pegboard task required the 36 male and 36 female participants to place as many round and square pegs in the appropriate place in the pegboard as they could in 60 seconds. The rotary pursuit task required participants to maintain contact between a target spot on a spinning disk and a handheld wand. In this study the target moved in a circular pattern at 45 rpm for 15 seconds. There were six different practice conditions: 100% PP; 75% PP, 25% MP; 50% PP, 50% MP; 25% PP, 75% MP; 100% MP; and a control condition (NP), which consisted of a different type of activity. Participants completed seven practice sessions with four trials per session on the pegboard task and eight trials per session on the rotary pursuit task. Results revealed that MP was better than NP, and as the relative proportion of PP increased, performance increased. Performance effects were greater on the cognitive task than on the motor task.

McBride and Rothstein (1979) conducted a study that compared the effects of mental and physical practice on learning and retaining open and closed skills. The participants, 120 high school girls, hit a solid Wiffle ball with a table-tennis bat at a concentric-circles target with a nondominant forehand stroke. For the closed skill, the ball was placed on a batting tee; for the open skill a ball was dropped down a curved tube at a 45° angle every 10 sec. After performing a pretest, the participants were randomly assigned to an MP, PP, or PP-and-MP condition and practiced in those conditions for three days. Each participant practiced the skill 40 times each day. McBride and Rothstein recorded accuracy scores in blocks of 10 trials during acquisition, testing, and retention, reporting that participants performed the closed skill more accurately than the open skill. However, the effects of the type of practice appeared to be similar for open and closed skills: MP was not as effective as PP, and PP was not as effective as combined PP and MP.

explain why MP might work, which makes them part of a model of MP, not mental imagery. The theories provide contrasting views, with one proposing a neuromuscular or "motor" explanation (psychoneuromuscular theory) and the other a cognitive explanation (symbolic learning theory) for the effects of MP.

PSYCHONEUROMUSCULAR THEORY

The psychoneuromuscular theory evolved largely out of the ideomotor principle, originally proposed as far back as 1855 by Carpenter (1894). This principle suggests that during imagery localized muscular activity occurs, which is weaker in magnitude but identical in pattern to muscle activation during actual physical performance of the task.

Start and Richardson (1964) and Richardson (1967b) were the first researchers to develop a psychoneuromuscular explanation of MP, based on early psychophysiological studies such as those by Jacobson (1930a, b, c, d, 1931a, b, c), Shaw (1938, 1940), and Allers and Scheminsky (1926), but others have proposed similar explanations (Corbin 1972; Schmidt and Lee 1999). These psychoneuromuscular theories propose that the efficacy of imagery rehearsal (IR) of a motor task is due to feedback that results from the minute muscle innervations (identical in pattern to those that occur during actual execution) that occur when an individual imagines performing a motor skill. This feedback enables adjustments in motor behavior (Corbin 1972) or facilitates the rate at which the performer activates mental nodes representing the desired motor behavior during overt performance (MacKay 1981). When skills are performed overtly (PP), performers receive feedback, both visual (e.g., knowledge of results and performance) and kinesthetic (e.g., body position, muscular tension, tactile feelings), that allows them to evaluate performance. For example, in trial-and-error learning, performers receive sensory and perceptual information from the Golgi tendon organs, which is fed back to the premotor cortex, so that they can adjust for the next performance. The principle of feedback is well supported for overt practice and, according to psychoneuromuscular theories, is applicable to MP (Hale 1994).

Evidence in support of the psychoneuromuscular hypothesis includes early studies that found electrical activation in the muscles involved in the task being imaged (e.g., Allers and Scheminsky 1926; Jacobson 1930a, b, c, d, 1931a, b; Shaw 1940). Jacobson conducted a number of studies with various imaginal and actual activities, such as bending the arm, sweeping, and performing a biceps curl. He concluded that muscle activity specific to the muscles involved occurred during imagination, but at a considerably lower level than during actual movement.

To demonstrate the psychoneuromuscular theory, theorists need evidence of task-specific muscle activation rather than general activation of the body. Some researchers have suggested that the response is limited to the specific muscles involved in the activity being imagined (e.g., Bird 1984; Hale 1982; Harris and Robinson 1986); others have not (e.g., Shaw 1938). For example, Shaw described increased muscular activity in most muscle groups during imagery of various tasks. These action potentials were concomitant with the activities; however, no evidence was found of localization to the muscle groups involved in such activities.

To investigate whether electromyographic (EMG) activity during imagery (mental training) is task specific, Wehner, Vogt, and Stadler (1984) measured EMG activity of the biceps synchronously to a paced contour-tracking task. They assigned participants to paced contour-tracking (active), mental training, or control groups. They found similar time and frequency characteristics in the mental-training EMGs and the active-training EMGs, but not in the control group. This, according to Wehner et al., indicates that the EMG during mental training is task specific in its frequency distribution.

In a recent study, Slade, Landers, and Martin (2002) compared EMG activity patterns in both the active and passive arms during actual and imagined dumbbell curls. EMG activity increased during imagery in the active arm compared to rest and the passive arm, but it did not mirror that of actual performance. Thus, research is not conclusive that muscle activity during imaginary practice is localized to the specific muscles involved in the activity being imagined. The increased activity could be a general increase in readiness for performance or a by-product of central processes. Also, the methodologies employed in the studies to support such psychoneuromuscular explanations are problematic. For example, the data measured to date has been limited to amplitude measures of EMG, not factors such as frequency and duration of EMG, which would be necessary to prove a "mirror hypothesis" (Hale 1994). In addition, Hale suggested that it might be impossible to ensure that participants instructed to image "are not consciously minutely tensing the muscles used in the task and producing localized efference" (p. 78). Even if we accept that this muscle activity is localized, to provide strong evidence for the psychoneuromuscular theory, researchers must go a step further and show that performance improvements result from neuromuscular feedback from that activity. That is, they would need to show that performance facilitation was greater under conditions of "mirrored" muscle innervation. To date, the researchers who have examined muscle innervation during imagery have not monitored performance. Researchers have yet to devise studies that can meet these requirements.

Another concern about the psychoneuromuscular theory is that research seems to indicate that cognitive processing rather than neuromuscular feedback is a more likely explanation for the efficacy of MP and imagery. For instance, research (e.g., Ryan and Simons 1981, 1983), as well as reviews of MP and imagery literature (e.g., Driskell, Copper, and Moran 1994; Feltz and Landers 1983; Feltz, Landers, and Becker 1988), suggest that cognitive rather than strength tasks benefit most from imagery.

SYMBOLIC LEARNING THEORY

Sackett (1934) suggested that imagery of a task presents the imager with the opportunity to rehearse the sequence of movements as symbolic components of the task. That is, movement patterns are symbolically coded in the central nervous system, and imagery assists in coding movements into symbols that make the movement easier to perform. Repetitive mental practice could focus attention on key cues within the skill, reinforcing those cues and allowing the construction of sub-conscious perceptual-motor plans or schemas in the premotor cortex. Consequently, according to this theory, imagery or MP facilitates only the cognitive aspects of a skill, such as movement timing, sequencing, and planning. Sackett proposed that cognitive skills are more easily coded than strength or motor tasks and so should respond better to imagery. To support this theory, research should demonstrate that imagery is more effective with primarily cognitive tasks and less effective with primarily motor tasks. In addition, motor-learning theorists (e.g., Fitts and Posner 1967; Gentile 1972, 1987, 2000) have suggested that early stages of learning are primarily cognitive. Thus, if the benefits of imagery are primarily cognitive (working out how the skill should be done), imagery should benefit performers in early stages of learning more than in later stages.

Sackett (1934) demonstrated that mental rehearsal improved performance on a finger maze (a largely cognitive task). Other research (e.g., Minas 1980; Morrisett 1956; Ryan and Simons 1981, 1983; Wrisberg and Ragsdale 1979) has supported symbolic learning theory by showing that mental rehearsal facilitated cognitive more than motor performance. Feltz and Landers (1983) and Feltz et al. (1988), in a meta-analysis of the MP literature, concluded that the data seem to support the symbolic learning theory, largely because of the stronger effects of MP on cognitive as opposed to strength tasks. Driskell et al. (1994) also supported this position in a later meta-analysis of the MP literature, when they found a stronger effect on cognitive than physical tasks. Other supporting evidence for the symbolic learning theory includes studies by Kohl and Roenker (1980, 1983), who showed that bilateral transfer occurred even when participants performed the training task with the contralateral limb, using imagery. Bilateral transfer refers to a situation when practice (in this case, imagery practice) with one limb enhances the rate of learning with the other limb on the same task. Johnson (1982) further demonstrated that imagining movements biased later performance when the participant completed a visual-interference task. Johnson's findings support the symbolic learning theory because he had hypothesized that images of movements would be primarily visual (Denis 1985).

Athletes at various skill levels have reported using imagery (Hall, Rodgers, and Barr 1990), and the literature has not demonstrated that those at different levels reap different benefits from using imagery. However, individuals at various levels do appear to respond favorably to imagery or MP. For example, Wrisberg and Ragsdale (1979) investigated the effect of imagery on motor-skill learning as a function of the amount of physical practice the participants had experienced. They introduced imagery either early or later in the learning process and found its facilitative effects increased as a function of decreasing the amount of physical practice experienced. Ziegler (1987) also found that groups with the least basketball experience showed greater improvement in foul shooting.

An opposing view states that experienced performers find imagery more effective because they have a stronger, more accurate image of correct performance of the skill (Blair, Hall, and Leyshon 1993; Woolfolk, Parrish, and Murphy 1985). Several studies (e.g., Blair et al. 1993; Clark 1960; Corbin 1967a, b; Isaac 1992; Noel 1980) support this position. Feltz and Landers (1983), in their meta-analysis of the imagery literature, calculated an effect size based on participants' experience with the task and discovered no significant differences between more experienced and novice participants when averaged across tasks varying in cognitive elements. Feltz and Landers found a slightly larger effect size for more experienced participants, although that of novices was also large. Feltz and Landers concluded that the effects of MP occur in both early and later stages of learning. Driskell et al. (1994), in their meta-analytic review of MP literature, found no significant difference between the performance gains of novice and experienced participants in imagery studies. The data indicated a moderate and significant effect for both novice and experienced participants. They did, however, find an experience by task type interaction when they classified skills as being high in cognitive or physical components. For novice participants, the results indicated a stronger effect of MP for cognitive tasks than physical tasks. For experienced participants, there was no significant difference between cognitive and physical tasks. Driskell et al. argued that experienced participants benefit equally from MP on cognitive and physical tasks, whereas novice participants benefit more from MP on cognitive than on physical tasks.

The symbolic learning theory has problems and fails to answer certain questions. For example, it does not predict that imagery will enhance performance of motor and strength tasks. Reviews such as the meta-analysis of Driskell et al. (1994), however, have found an effect on physical tasks, albeit a smaller one than on more cognitive tasks. Hale (1994) stated that researchers have not tested the theory in a single study that compares tasks at both ends of the cognitive–motor continuum. He further suggested that if participants were more familiar with practicing in a cognitive rather than a motor or kinesthetic mode, evidence would be biased toward support of a cognitive explanation for imagery effects.

Also, several studies have found that imagery facilitated performance in experienced participants with well-established movement patterns, which is a difficult result for symbolic learning theory to explain (Hecker and Kaczor 1988).

The two early theories, the psychoneuromuscular hypothesis and symbolic learning theory, do not adequately explain how imagery influences performance. As stated earlier, Murphy (1994) attributes this to the fact that these theories were developed specifically to explain skill learning and MP effects. They have concentrated on explaining why MP might work, which makes them part of the MP model. Imagery in sport psychology is used in a much wider range of applications today, including influencing psychological variables (affect, cognition, conation) as outlined in chapters 5, 8, and 9. To explain how imagery influences performance, Murphy (1994) and Murphy and Jowdy (1992) suggest looking beyond the field of sport psychology toward cognitive science, which would investigate the nature of imagery.

COGNITIVE THEORIES OF IMAGERY

Cognitive psychologists have offered promising explanations for the effects of imagery, which are only gradually being investigated by sport psychologists. Cognitive psychology refers to the study of the processes by which people transform, reduce, elaborate, store, recover, and use sensory input (Neisser 1976). This definition has several implications. Inclusion of the term "sensory input" implies that cognition begins with input entering our information-processing system. "Transformation" implies that our representation of the world is not merely a passive copy of our physical surroundings but an active reconstruction that we can reduce or elaborate on. The terms "storage" and "recovery," of course, refer to memory. "Use" is possibly the most important part of Neisser's definition, because after we have perceived, stored, and recovered information, we must be able to use it effectively to make decisions, solve problems, or complete tasks or skills. We also use our memories to produce imagery, so how we process and store images is important in understanding how imagery works from a cognitive perspective.

Cognitive psychologists have proposed various models of imagery experience. The most popular approach to understanding mental processes such as imagery is an information-processing one, which includes several stages during which information is acquired, stored, retrieved, and used. Thus, in this approach, how imagery is used in this process and how images are stored in memory are important. Early cognitive psychologists tended to emphasize serial, or step-by-step, processing of information. For example, in shooting a basketball free throw, a player might first analyze the problem (look at the hoop and judge distance), then formulate a plan (how hard to shoot), then solve the problem (shoot the ball). Today, many cognitive psychologists emphasize parallel processing, whereby multiple mental processes occur all at once. For example, in basketball, a player dribbles the ball, scans the court, and makes decisions on whether to pass or shoot the ball all at the same time. In this view, verbal and visual information can be processed at the same time. In one model of imagery, Paivio (1971, 1975, 1986) proposed that we store information both verbally and visually in a complementary fashion. The form of representation we use depends on how the information is presented (verbally or nonverbally) and the imagery value of the information to be remembered. Concrete words that are high in imagery value seem to favor visual representation; for example, "ball," "shoe," "bat," and "football stadium." Abstract words, such as "truth," "motivation," and "kindness," are less likely to be stored visually because we have no images that we consistently associate with them.

Although evidence exists that we store some memories separately as images or words, an alternative view is that much of our memory is based on a network of abstract representations tied to meanings rather than sensory or verbal information (Dworetsky 1988). Storing information by its meaning, rather than in a verbal or visual code, means it must be stored as a proposition rather than in its raw form. A proposition refers to "the smallest unit about which it makes sense to make the judgement true or false" (Anderson 1980, 102). The basic idea is that we store propositions (e.g., the boy kicks the soccer ball) that consist of nodes or ideas (e.g., ball, soccer, kicks, boy) that are linked by relationships between ideas. The more an athlete activates the links by cognitive rehearsal (e.g., imagery rehearsal) the stronger they become, and the more numerous the links or alternative routes are to a specific idea, the more likely the athlete is to recall it (e.g., the correct execution of the skill). Propositional theories argue that if we want to recall how something looked or was stated, we must first recall its meaning and then reconstruct the actual sensory or verbal representation. One sport-related theory that uses a propositional representation of imagery is Lang's (1977) bioinformational theory. First, however, we will look in more detail at Paivio's theory, which proposes we store information in verbal as well as imaginal forms.

DUAL-CODE THEORY

Paivio's (1975) dual-code theory suggests that images are effective in learning because they provide two independent memory codes, either of which can result in recall. For example, if we store both the word "ball" and an image of a ball, we can retrieve the ball from memory as either an image or a word. Similarly, it might be possible to learn movement sequences both verbally and through images. For example, a gymnast might remember her floor routine as an image or verbally, as a sequence of words. Evidence suggests that the two memory codes are independent—we can forget one code without forgetting the other (Paivio 1975). Thus, having two memory codes gives us a better chance of remembering an item. Marschark and Hunt (1989) highlighted a major criticism of dual-code theory, which is that it functions only in situations in which people focus on relational information (such as in paired associate learning, in which a person learns to associate or pair one stimulus or item with a different item or response). Some examples are learning the association between a word and its definition, or in sport, the association between a foul in basketball and shooting free throws or between the angle of approach to a soccer goal and the size of the target. Even so, the restricted uses are still fairly large since many learning activities require us to learn associations between items, such as in learning rules, movement schemas, tactics, and strategies. One criticism of the research on dual-code theory is its focus on visual imagery (e.g., pictures), which is a very narrow conception of imagery as it occurs in sport (Murphy and Jowdy 1992).

We now turn to two clinically based cognitive theories of imagery, Lang's bioinformational theory and Ahsen's triple-code theory, which consider two aspects of imagery that are important to sport, psychophysiology and meaning.

BIOINFORMATIONAL THEORY

Bioinformational theory, a cognitive hypothesis, uses an information-processing model of imagery stored as propositions but considers the psychophysiology of imagery. Lang (1977) originally developed this theory to increase the understanding of research into phobias and anxiety disorders, by combining the perspectives of information-processing theory and psychophysiology. However, because Lang's theory is aimed at analyzing fear and emotional imagery, it may not be readily applicable to sport. Lang described image processing and storage and argued that affective images are best conceptualized as propositional structures rather than as reperceived raw sensory representations. One way to conceptualize propositional storage is to consider it similar to a digital TV code—the code is processed and then displayed as a picture rather than as an analogue wave (which is essentially a copy of the picture). Lang suggested that the units abstracted and interpreted during perception are stored in long-term memory (LTM) in abstract form and must be processed and linked to generate an experience of an image.

According to Lang, images contain two main classes of propositions: stimulus and response. Stimulus propositions describe the content of the scene to be imagined. They describe specific features of stimuli, for example, "a heavy, wooden baseball bat." Response propositions describe the response to the scene. They are modality-specific assertions about behavior, such as verbal responses, overt motor acts, and physiological responses (for example, "tensing my biceps").

Lang argued that learning and performance involve linking appropriate stimulus and response propositions and that the process of imagery allows strengthening of these links. Thus, quality imagery should include feelings (such as fear, anxiety, anger, and elation) as well as physical symptoms (such as fatigue, perspiration, and tension), because these physiological and emotional reactions generally accompany actual performance. Lang proposed that an individual gains more control and hence improves performance by modifying responses to given situations through imagery. For example, Lang's work with fear and the techniques of desensitization and flooding indicates that the more realistic and frightening the scene and the more fear the imagery produces, the better the person will cope with the real fearful situation. Therefore, applied sport psychologists would be advised to include response propositions in imagery scripts to assist athletes in processing the entire network and producing physiological responses that lead to overt behavior changes.

Support for the bioinformational theory comes from a number of sources. Several nonsport studies support the prediction that the type of propositions in the image structure will determine efferent flow (e.g., Carroll, Mazilier, and Merian 1982; Lang 1979; Lang, Kozak, Miller, Levin, and McLean 1980; Lang, Levin, Miller, and Kozak 1983; Mermecz and Melamed 1984; Miller, Levin, Kozak, Cook, McLean, Carroll, and Lang 1981). This research has shown that response propositions elicit efferent activity, whereas stimulus propositions do not. Cuthbert, Vrana, and Bradley's (1991) review of this line of research supports the hypothesis that including response propositions in imagery scripts produces emotional outflow. And Lang has demonstrated with phobic patients that the greater the physiological responses to imagery, the greater the change in behavior (e.g., Lang, Melamed, and Hart 1970). However, no sport studies have tested this.

In sport psychology literature, support comes directly and indirectly from several studies. Research indicates that scripts that are weighted in response rather than stimulus propositions produce a greater efferent flow (Bakker, Boschker, and Chung 1996; Hale 1982; Hecker and Kaczor 1988). However, most research in sport psychology has not linked physiological data to performance.

Indirect support for Lang's predictions comes from the internal and external perspective and muscle-innervation studies. Researchers (e.g., Budney, Murphy, and Woolfolk 1994; Hale 1982, 1994; Janssen and Sheikh 1994) have suggested that stimulus and response propositions may be functionally similar to internal and external imagery perspectives (see chapter 2 for definitions and chapter 6 for research). They suggest that internal imagery enhances response-proposition processing because the imagery is of performing rather than watching the skill. According to this conception, internal imagery contains many response propositions because the imagers experience it from a first-person perspective (as if they were present and performing the movement), which emphasizes kinesthetic and muscular sensations. External imagery would consist mainly of stimulus propositions "because the sense modality is constrained to a third-person visual perspective during processing" (Hale 1994, 89). But it must be stressed that internal and external imagery and stimulus and response propositions are not the same thing. (This issue is addressed in greater detail in chapter 6.)

Hale (1982) and Harris and Robinson (1986) found that internal imagery produces more EMG activity than does an external perspective. Other motor research also indicates that internal imagery produces localized muscular efference (e.g., Bird 1984; Jacobson 1931a, b, c; Suinn 1976a; Wehner et al. 1984). It seems likely, however, that the description of response information given in the instructions to the participant is more important to producing efferent flow than the perspective. For instance, simply telling someone to imagine from a first-person perspective is not likely to produce as much efferent flow as telling them to "feel the movement," "experience all the sensations," and so on. A nonsport study looking at imagery of fearful and neutral situations by Bauer and Craighead (1979) supports this. Bauer and Craighead compared manipulations of stimulus or response imagery and manipulations of imagery perspective (first or third person). They found differences only as a result of changing response and stimulus processing, with response propositions producing greater activation of heart rate and skin conductance. In the motor domain, Hale's (1982) and Bakker, Boschker, and Chung's (1996) findings support the claim that response propositions produce greater activation than stimulus propositions. For more discussion of the psychophysiological responses during imagery, see chapter 7.

A possible basis of support for Lang's bioinformational theory comes from the suggestion that experienced athletes may benefit more from imagery than novice performers (e.g., Feltz and Landers 1983; Hall and Erffmeyer 1983; Noel 1980; Weinberg 1982). Because they have had greater exposure to these feelings and situations, experienced athletes may produce stronger reactions to imagery of anxiety or muscular movement than novices. Less experienced athletes may have trouble producing response propositions or might even produce harmful ones that would inhibit performance.

For this theory to be credible in the movement domain, more research in sport, especially in the applied sport setting, is required, as well as studies that link the theory to performance outcome and not merely efferent activity. In the applied sport setting, one of the main concerns with bioinformational theory is that the focus is on investigating differences between the effects of stimulus and response propositions on muscular activity. This does not seem to enhance understanding of the theory, since the whole bioinformational theory is not necessary to explain how different imagery scripts lead to different efferent activity and emotional reactions. What is needed in sport are studies that demonstrate that scripts weighted in response propositions elicit greater efferent activity, which is accompanied by improved performance, than scripts weighted in stimulus propositions.

Studies that have tried to link performance enhancement to stimulus and response propositions have found equivocal results. Ziegler (1987) could not find any significant difference in basketball free-throw shooting between groups using active (stimulus and response propositions) and passive (stimulus propositions) imagery. Kremer and Pressing (1998) found greater improvement in pistol-shooting performance for the group using stimulus-only propositions when compared to a group using stimulus-and-response propositions.

One recent study in sport that did provide support for Lang's model by linking stimulus and response propositions to sport performance was conducted by Smith, Holmes, Whitemore, Collins, and Devonport (2001). Novice hockey players were randomly assigned to stimulus proposition, response proposition, and control groups and were pre- and posttested on hockey penalty-flick performance. The response-proposition group improved performance significantly more than the stimulus-proposition group, who improved significantly more than the control group. Many theories ignore the aspect of Lang's theory that proposes that meaning propositions are important to the image. However, one cognitive theory with a strong meaning component is Ahsen's (1984) triple-code theory (ISM).

AHSEN'S TRIPLE-CODE THEORY

A cognitive model, the triple-code theory sets out three components of imagery that Ahsen proposed are important to understanding how it affects performance. The first component is the image itself (I), which Ahsen viewed as a centrally aroused, internal sensation that possesses all the attributes of actual sensation. The second component is the somatic response (S). Ahsen suggested that imagery causes psychophysiological changes in the body. The third component is the meaning of the image (M), which is ignored by most imagery models. Ahsen proposed that people bring their backgrounds and histories with them into imagery, so even if they receive the same imagery instructions, the experience will be different for each individual. For example, for a rower who imagines competing at the Olympics, the image might include the kinesthetic feel of running the blade through the water, the sound of the crowd, the vision of the other crews, and all the other sensory experiences of an Olympic final. The somatic response might be an increased heart rate as the imager begins to feel nervous, or it could be an increase in muscular activity, as reported in psychoneuromuscular explanations of imagery. The meaning of the image is crucial in this example. If the rower had been to the Olympics four years ago and performed poorly, the imagery experience would probably be different from that of an Olympic champion or someone who has never been to the Olympics. The meaning is also important because an athlete might use imagery of the same activity for different purposes, which could change its effect on performance. For example, a gymnast who imagines successfully completing a vault or floor routine might be concerned with the technical aspects of the skill, and so the imagery might enhance his cognitive planning of the execution (as in symbolic learning explanations). Another gymnast, imagining the same skill, might focus on the successful outcome, experiencing herself landing the vault or completing the routine and the emotions involved. In this case, she might improve performance by gaining confidence in her ability to clear the bar.

Ahsen suggested that psychologists need to take into account the meaning of the imagery. Other recommendations that can be derived from his theory are that research reports should describe the imagery script and sport psychologists must consider the participant's imagery experience. Also, because psychophysiological changes occur, researchers should consider psychophysiological measures and assess the meaning of the image to the individual to evaluate whether the image evokes other thoughts that may detract from optimal imagery. For example, in imaging a soccer penalty kick, if the imager allows other thoughts to interfere he could be distracted from the process of taking the penalty. If those thoughts are negative images of the penalty kick going over the crossbar, they could make the imagery experience detrimental to performance. Imagery instructions might guide the player to imagine placing the penalty kick into the corner of the goal, past the goalkeeper, and include specifics such as "watch the ball," "step into position," and "strike the ball firmly with the instep of your left foot just inside the left post." If instead the player imagines the goalkeeper staring at him, the aggression on his face, the crowd booing, and his teammates watching anxiously, he could imagine taking a poor penalty.

Researchers have found that just as positive imagery can lead to enhanced performance, negative imagery can produce performance decrements compared to no imagery (Woolfolk et al. 1985). In a study of dart throwing, Powell (1973) found that participants who imaged their darts landing near the center of a target performed better than participants who imaged their darts landing further away. In addition, Gregory, Cialdini, and Carpenter (1982), in a nonsport scenario, found that participants imagining unsuccessful events believed more strongly that these events would occur.

Ahsen's theory provides a useful framework for investigating imagery, but it does not explain the cognitive effects of imagery; that is, why tasks with a greater cognitive component seem to benefit more from imagery than tasks with a greater strength component. Ahsen developed the theory outside sport, and sport psychologists are only beginning to link it to the field.

GROSS FRAMEWORK OR INSIGHT THEORY

Grouios (1992) and Hale (1994) have identified two related approaches to the question of how imagery works: the gross framework and insight theories. These efforts to explain how imagery enhances performance are based on Gestalt psychology, a predecessor of cognitive psychology. Gestalt psychology is usually traced to the work of German psychologist Max Wertheimer (1880-1943), who collaborated with Kurt Koffka (1886-1941) and Wolfgang Kohler (1887-1967). Together they developed a school of psychology that emphasizes the understanding of "wholes" in their own right, rather than the parts that make up the whole. For example, they proposed that problem solving could not be explained simply in terms of automatic responses to stimuli. Instead, people can devise new ways of seeing problems that are not merely recombinations of old ways. The generation of a new way of seeing or doing things is called "insight"—the sudden discovery of the correct solution following a period of incorrect attempts based largely on trial and error. The factor that distinguishes insight from other forms of learning is the suddenness of the solution. Unlike solutions that occur through careful planning or small steps, insight solutions seem to occur in a flash.

Lawther (1968) advocated the gross framework theory as necessary for optimal motor learning to occur. The learner must be able to conceptualize the entirety, or gestalt, of the task in order to improve skill performance. Imagery rehearsal (IR) or MP could help the learner direct attention onto the general impression, or gross framework, of the skill rather than on the details of the movement. Theorists and researchers have often used this theory to explain why previous experience (vicarious or actual) seems to benefit the positive effects of MP. In this conception, performance improvements do not necessarily come in direct proportion to the length of time spent in practice. Rather, learning comes about with changes in behavior over time, resulting from insight. "Most individuals have experienced 'insightful' behavior after periods of practice" (Grouios

1992, 49). Prior to and during the improvement of performance, imagery may be necessary to provide the opportunity for behavioral changes resulting from insight. MP or IR would not ensure learning, but "would provide for a new perceptual organization through insight" (Grouios 1992, 49), for example, a beginner combining all aspects of a baseball swing (feet, hands, bat, head) with the arrival of the ball. Both the sporting domain and general imagery literature reveal a lack of research on gross framework or insight explanations of how imagery works to enhance performance. Research seems warranted, since this theory appears to be a reasonable explanation for some instances of performance enhancement through imagery. For example, a beginner learning a new skill can use imagery to zoom in on a specific aspect in a problem-solving way or to focus on the "whole" of the skill.

Psychological State Explanations

The cognitive theories provide a possible explanation of how imagery can enhance performance in sport; however, they have not been sufficiently researched or developed for sport. Other potential explanations by sport psychologists consider how imagery affects the athlete's psychological state. For example, imagery of winning an important match in front of a large crowd, or even simply performing a skill correctly, can affect the athlete's motivation, self-confidence, or arousal. Such effects then influence performance.

Attention-Arousal Set Theory

According to attention-arousal set theory, imagery functions as a preparatory set that assists the performer in achieving an optimal arousal level and thus peak performance. The attention-arousal set theory has not received any direct empirical support (Hecker and Kaczor 1988; Murphy, Woolfolk, and Budney 1998), but some research indirectly supports such a theory. Researchers (e.g., Hale 1982; Harris and Robinson 1986; Jacobson 1931a, b, c; Ryan, Blakeslee, and Furst 1986; Shaw 1940) have found low-level muscle innervations associated with imagery. Schmidt (1982) proposed that these innervations could be indications of the performer "preparing for the action, setting the arousal level, and generally getting prepared for good performance" (p. 520). The evidence does not provide adequate support for an attention-arousal explanation of imagery effects. One problem with this sort of explanation is that it does not adequately explain the facilitative effects of imagery-training programs that use imagery not only as a preperformance readiness tool but as a part of daily training (e.g., Blair, Hall, and Leyshon 1993; Shambrook and Bull 1996).

MOTIVATIONAL, SELF-EFFICACY, AND SELF-CONFIDENCE EXPLANATIONS

Performance differences between imagery (or MP) and control groups may be due to different motivation levels in these groups. Verbal instructions, demonstrations, and introductory educational statements about imagery and sessions of imagery can stimulate interest in the participants and make them motivated to perform, or create expectations of superior performance following imagery. Also, imagery programs often include an introductory session that attempts to ensure that athletes believe in imagery's facilitative effects. In investigating motivation levels as a possible explanation for imagery effects, studies need to compare performance effects from an imagery-training program on high- and low-motivation groups. The Driskell et al. (1994) meta-analysis of the MP literature suggested that the effects of MP were not due to a Hawthorne Effect (an unintended impact of the researcher or research design on the participants, especially in terms of their behavior). That is, with a Hawthorne Effect, change is due to a factor other than the independent variable (in this case, MP). The possibility of a Hawthorne Effect was suggested because of the condition in MP studies where a control group (NP) gets nothing and the MP group gets something. Driskell et al. examined this possibility by comparing studies that used a no-contact control group with studies using an equivalent control group (participants engage in some form of unrelated activity). They found no significant difference in the effects of MP in those studies.

Paivio (1985) proposed another motivational explanation of imagery that provides a framework for evaluating imagery. He emphasized the need to consider the task and function of memory and verbal mechanisms in IR. Paivio's framework is essentially a 2 × 2 factor model, in which imagery plays a motivational role and a cognitive role at a general or specific level. Research on Paivio's model has come recently through Hall and his colleagues (Hall 1998, 2001; Hall, Mack, Paivio, and Hausenblas 1998; Martin, Moritz, and Hall 1999), who designed the Sport Imagery Questionnaire (SIQ) to measure the 2 × 2 factors. The SIQ summarizes the classes of imagery as (a) cognitive general (CG), (b) cognitive specific (CS), (c) motivational general arousal (MG-A), (d) motivational general mastery (MG-M), and (e) motivational specific (MS). Research using this model suggests that athletes do engage in imagery for motivational functions (Callow and Hardy 1997; Salmon, Hall, and Haslam 1994; White and Hardy 1998). Refer to chapters 2 and 4 for additional discussion on the SIQ and Paivio's model.

Self-confidence or, more frequently, self-efficacy theory (Bandura 1977a, b) explains imagery's effect on performance (Budney et al. 1994; Grouios 1992; Perry and Morris 1995). Self-confidence in sport is probably the more widely understood concept, referring to people's perceptions of their overall capability in a sport context. Self-efficacy is task specific; it is a person's belief in his ability to perform a particular task. Thus, for example, we talk about a golfer's self-confidence in the sport, but we refer to the level of his self-efficacy in putting or, even more specifically, in short, downhill putts. According to Bandura, as we increase a task's specificity, we make the prediction from self-efficacy to behavior more accurate. The proposition developed from self-efficacy theory is that imagery increases a performer's success expectations, which leads to successful overt performance. Most of the research on the relationship between self-efficacy and performance is based on Bandura's (1969, 1977a, b) social learning theory, which suggests that expectations of success are based on past performance success, vicarious experience (modeling), verbal reinforcement, and emotional arousal.

Modeling is a process in which observers copy or reproduce behaviors or actions demonstrated by others. The idea is that imaging oneself performing a task successfully is similar to observing someone else perform the skill (modeling), or overtly performing the skill (past performance success), and therefore provides reinforcement and increased expectations of success. A considerable amount of literature suggests that increased self-efficacy leads to enhanced performance in sport (e.g., Feltz 1982; Feltz and Mugno 1983; McAuley 1985). Several studies on imagery in sport or motor skills have suggested that it can influence self-efficacy or self-confidence (e.g., Callery and Morris 1993, 1997a, b; Feltz and Reissinger 1990; Garza and Feltz 1998; Hale and Whitehouse 1998; Martin and Hall 1995; McKenzie and Howe 1997; She and Morris 1997; Short et al. 2002; Woolfolk, Murphy, Gottesfeld, and Aitken 1985), although few of them have tested causal links between imagery, self-efficacy, and performance. Other studies have been more equivocal in their findings about the relationship between imagery and self-efficacy (e.g., Callow and Hardy 1997; Moritz, Hall, Martin, and Vadocz 1996).

A series of studies by Callery and Morris investigated the relationship between imagery, self-efficacy, and sports performance. Callery and Morris (1993, 1997a) found that imagery training increased the self-efficacy and performance of elite professional Australian Football League (AFL) players in actual games. Similarly, She and Morris (1997) found increased performance, self-efficacy, and state sport confidence for baseball batters during a season-long imagery intervention. One issue for researchers is determining the relationship between imagery, self-efficacy, and performance. That is, does imagery affect self-efficacy, which then produces changes in performance, or does imagery affect both performance and self-efficacy directly? These relationships are illustrated in figure 3.1*a* and *b,* respectively. In an attempt to establish the links between imagery, self-efficacy, and performance, Callery and Morris (1997b) used structural equation modeling (SEM), using previous data (from Callery and Morris 1997a). The analysis showed a causal link between imagery and performance, as well as one between imagery and self-efficacy. No significant causal link between self-efficacy and performance was found, suggesting that although imagery affected both performance and self-efficacy, self-efficacy was not a mediator between imagery and performance. This seems to support the type of relationship shown in figure 3.1*b*.

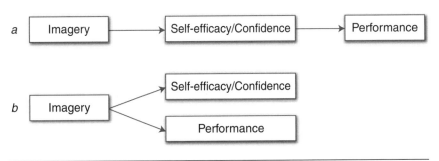

Figure 3.1 Models in which self-efficacy/confidence is *(a)* a mediator of the imagery–performance relationship and *(b)* an independent outcome of imagery.

Garza and Feltz (1998) found that MP improved figure-skating performance, self-efficacy, and self-confidence for competition. Hale and White-house (1998) used imagery-based interventions to manipulate an athlete's facilitative or debilitative appraisal of competitive anxiety. Measures of heart rate, anxiety (using the Competitive State Anxiety Inventory-2 [CSAI-2]), and direction of anxiety (using the Competitive State Anxiety Inventory-2 Directional [CSAI-2 D]) were collected from 24 experienced soccer players who underwent either "pressure" or "challenge" hypothetical game penalty-kick situations, re-created through audiotape and imagery. They found that imagery could manipulate intensity and directional anxiety responses. During the pressure situation, participants reported more cognitive and somatic anxiety and a lack of confidence, which they described as debilitating. In the challenge situation, participants reported less cognitive and somatic anxiety and more confidence, and they interpreted these emotions as facilitative. This suggests that imagery can affect athletes' self-confidence and self-efficacy and emphasizes the importance of imagery content in enhancing self-efficacy.

Martin and Hall (1995) assigned beginner golfers to one of three conditions: performance plus outcome imagery, performance imagery, or no imagery (control group). They hypothesized that imagery participants would spend more time practicing a golf-putting task and have higher self-efficacy than control participants. The basis for this was the belief that efficacy expectations determine persistence and effort in completing an activity (McAuley 1992). Martin and Hall also hypothesized that imagery may be a source of efficacy information that could influence intrinsic motivation to practice. Results indicated that participants in the performance-imagery group spent significantly more time practicing the putting task than participants in the control group did. Martin and Hall also found that imagery participants set higher goals for themselves, had more realistic self-expectations, and adhered to their training program more consistently. However, their study failed to support the hypothesis that imagery enhances motivation through efficacy mechanisms.

Moritz, Hall, Martin, and Vadocz (1996) and Callow and Hardy (1997) used the Sport Imagery Questionnaire to investigate the types of imagery associated with high sport confidence and self-efficacy of elite competitive roller skaters and netballers, respectively. Their results suggested that MG-M and CG imagery were more important than CS imagery in enhancing confidence. Thus, imagining specific sport skills (CS) may not be as important for sport confidence as imagining sport-related mastery experiences. To reconcile the findings of Moritz et al. and Callow and Hardy with those of Callery and Morris (1993, 1997a, b, c) and She and Morris (1997), we must acknowledge that any imagery experience can produce multiple effects. Thus, an imagery script that is intended to enhance performance by requiring performers to repeatedly image a correct or optimal performance involves success imagery, which would be expected to enhance confidence or self-efficacy. For instance, Abma, Fry, Li, and Relyea (2002) found that high-trait-confident track-and-field athletes used significantly more of each type of imagery (MG-M, MG-A, MS, CG, and CS) than low-trait-confident athletes.

Jones, Bray, Mace, MacRae, and Stockbridge (2002) investigated the impact of imagery involving MG-M and MG-A on self-efficacy, stress, and performance on novice female rock climbers. They found that the imagery scripts led to lower levels of reported stress and higher levels of confidence than a control condition. Interestingly, there was no difference in climbing performance for the imagery and control conditions, which suggests that imagery aimed at motivation affects both motivation and level of confidence but may not be directly associated with performance enhancement.

Self-efficacy or confidence explanations for imagery's effects have some research support in that imagery does seem to influence self-efficacy levels and performance (Callery and Morris 1997a; She and Morris 1997). However, Callery and Morris (1997b) did not find that self-efficacy was a mediator between imagery and performance. Additionally, self-efficacy and self-confidence theories do not explain the effects on cognitive skills as opposed to strength or motor tasks (e.g., Feltz and

Landers 1983), or the fine-grain muscle innervation that has occurred during imagery in some studies (e.g., Hale 1982; Harris and Robinson 1986; Jacobson 1931a, b, c, d). One explanation is that increased self-efficacy of a sport task may be an outcome of imagery, which occurs when the imagery that is experienced (as opposed to that which is scripted or instructed) includes imagining successful performance. This would explain why increased self-efficacy sometimes occurs during imagery intended for another purpose and why increases in self-efficacy are more likely outcomes of scripts that emphasize success.

An alternative explanation, which is related to motivational theories of imagery such as Paivio's, is that self-efficacy/self-confidence does not mediate the CS imagery–performance relationship (e.g., Callery and Morris 1997b), but MG-M imagery might do so (Moritz et al. 1996). This kind of explanation fits well with the Applied Model of Imagery Use in Sport (Martin, Moritz, and Hall 1999) reviewed in chapter 2, which suggests that imagery use should be matched with its desired outcome. For instance, imagery directed toward skill acquisition or performance (CS) will likely have an effect on those areas, whereas imagery directed at effective coping and confidence in challenging situations (MG-M) will affect motivation or confidence (which could influence skill acquisition and performance). That is, self-efficacy does not explain how imagery aimed at skill acquisition or performance (CS) influences sport performance, but it does help explain how imagery aimed at motivation or confidence (MG-M) affects performance.

More research on motivation and self-efficacy/self-confidence as frameworks for analyzing imagery effects is needed. However, the motivational and self-efficacy effects may be by-products rather than causes of performance change. Most sport psychologists would probably agree that athletes can affect their confidence, anxiety, mood, and emotions by using imagery; however, whether it affects behavior independent of these affective states seems to require more evidence. To investigate motivational and self-efficacy/self-confidence explanations, studies must compare imagery that is employed to affect motivation, self-confidence, or anxiety with imagery employed to affect performance directly. In these studies researchers would need to test for changes in the psychological variables and performance and determine whether they can be separated.

FUNCTIONAL EQUIVALENCE AND NEUROPHYSIOLOGICAL EXPLANATIONS

With the development of more sophisticated neurophysiological measures (such as positron emission tomography and regional cerebral blood flow scans) researchers in psychology have gained a greater understanding of the relationship between imagery and movement. In fact, research suggests that imagery and movement are very similar, and some researchers have gone so far as to suggest that motor imagery and motor preparation are functionally equivalent (e.g., Decety 1996a, b; Jeannerod 1994, 1995). The neurophysiology as well as the functional equivalence of imagery and movement is discussed in chapter 7, in the psychophysiological concomitants of imagery. This chapter will help readers understand how researchers have investigated functional equivalence. The brief description of functional equivalence and the major findings are offered here as a potential explanation of how imagery enhances sport performance.

The hypothesis of functional equivalence is that imagery and perception, and imagery and movement, recruit common structures or processes (Finke 1980, 1985; Finke and Shephard 1986). Basically, imagery enhances performance because imagery and performance are the same in their preparation, but during imagery execution is blocked. So imagery practice is like actual physical practice except that it does not involve the final execution of the motor commands (which are generated centrally, in the brain). The implication is that movement and imagery have similar functional outcomes. Researchers have addressed two forms of functional equivalence: visual imagery and visual perception, and motor imagery and motor preparation.

Neurophysiological studies can give clues as to whether imagery and perception are functionally equivalent. Support for the functional equivalence of visual imagery and perception from a psychophysiological standpoint is strong (Farah 1989; Jeannerod 1994). Many studies have found similar activation of occipital and inferior temporal regions during performance of visual-perception and visual-imagery tasks (e.g., Farah, Peronnet, Gonon, and Giard 1988; Goldenberg et al. 1989; Kosslyn et al. 1993; Peronnet and Farah 1989; Roland and Friberg 1985; Rosler, Heil, and Glowalla 1993; Stuss, Sarazin, Leech, and Picton 1983; Wijers, Otten, Feenstra, Mulder, and Mulder 1989). Tasks requiring motor imagery or nonimaginal thinking did not activate the same areas. Reviews have generally concluded that the research suggests a functional equivalence between visual imagery and visual perception (e.g., Annett 1986; Berthoz 1996; Decety 1996a, b; Holmes and Collins 2001; Jeannerod 1994).

Jeannerod (1994), in a substantial review of neurophysiological research on imagery, proposed that the similar neural substrate for visual imagery and visual perception could be translated to motor physiology. Jeannerod (1995) hypothesized that motor images have the same properties as those of the corresponding motor representations and therefore have the same functional relationship to the imagined movement and the same causal role in the generation of movement. Thus the benefits of motor imagery on motor execution would be due to increased traffic in the neural circuits responsible for improving synaptic efficacy in critical parts of the system, such as the cerebellum and basal ganglia. This, Jeannerod suggested, could result in an increased capacity to tune motor neuronal activity or sharpen coordination between agonist and antagonist muscle groups. According to this hypothesis, the peripheral EMG activity observed during imagery would be more of an effect rather than a cause of the learning process. This central explanation thus suggests that because the neurophysiological substrate is the same for both, learning by performing is not substantially different from learning through mental imagery.

Research supports Jeannerod's suggestion of a functional equivalence between motor imagery and motor preparation and planning. Research reviews (e.g., Annett 1996; Berthoz 1996; Decety 1996a, b; Jeannerod 1994) have concluded that psychophysiological measures support a common neural substrate for motor imagery and motor preparation. The supporting evidence comes from studies that utilized central measures of psychophysiological activity, which found that cortical activation during motor imagery occurs in areas related to motor control and that the activity follows a specific pattern that closely resembles action execution (e.g., Besteiner, Hollinger, Lindiner, Lang, and Berthoz 1995; Decety et al. 1994; Deecke 1996; Deiber et al. 1991; Fox, Pardo, Peterson, and Raichle 1987; Hallett, Fieldman, Cohen, Sadato, and Pascual-Leone 1995; Ingvar and Philipsson 1977; Naito and Matsumura 1994; Roland, Skinhoj, Lassen, and Larsen 1980; Stephan et al. 1995). These structures include the premotor cortex, lateral cerebellum, basal ganglia, dorsolateral prefrontal cortex, inferior frontal cortex, and posterior parietal cortex (Deiber et al. 1998; Grafton, Arbib, Fadiga, and Rizzolatti 1996; Mellet, Petit, Mazoyer, Denis, and Tzourio 1998; Parsons and Fox 1998). Additionally, peripheral cardiac, respiratory, and muscular measures suggest activation of motor pathways (e.g., Beyer, Weiss, Hansen, Wolf, and Seidel 1990; Bonnet, Decety, Jeannerod, and Requin 1997; Decety, Jeannerod, Durozard, and Baverel 1993; Decety, Jeannerod, Germain, and Pastene 1991; Decety, Sjoholm, Ryding, Stenberg, and Ingvar 1990; Hale 1982; Jacobson 1931a, b, c; Wang and Morgan 1992; Wehner, Vogt, and Stadler 1984; Yue and Cole 1992). These peripheral responses during imagery are reviewed in chapter 7.

Possibly the strongest evidence in support of the functional equivalence of motor imagery and motor preparation is the demonstration that the supplemental motor cortex is involved in motor imagery. Regional cerebral blood-flow studies suggest that the supplemental motor cortex is involved in assembling an established motor pattern (e.g., Roland, Larsen, Lassen, and Shinhoj 1980), and research has indicated that the supplemental motor cortex is also activated during the imagination of movement (e.g., Cunnington, Iansek, Bradshaw, and Phillips 1996; Decety, Sjoholm,

Ryding, Stenberg, and Ingvar 1990; Roland, Larsen, Lassen, and Shinhoj 1980; Ryding, Decety, Sjoholm, Stenberg, and Ingvar 1993; Stephan et al. 1995). Several studies have now gone further, suggesting that even the primary motor cortex may be active in imagery (e.g., Hallett, Fieldman, Cohen, Sadato, and Pascual-Leone 1995; Lang, Cheyne, Hollinger, Gerschlager, and Lindinger 1998; Lotze et al. 1999).

Studies finding that the timing of simulated movements is similar to that of actual movement also support functional equivalence theories (e.g., Decety, Jeannerod, and Prablanc 1989; Decety and Lindgren 1991; Georgopoulos and Massey 1987; Vogt 1995), as do interference studies that suggest that actual and imagined movements have similar biasing effects on recall (e.g., Boschker, Bakker, and Rietberg 2000; Engelkamp and Cohen 1991; Hall, Bernoties, and Schmidt 1995; Johnson 1982; Orliaguet and Coello 1998; Smith and Waller 1998; Vogt 1995). This is in line with research finding that MP and PP have similar practice effects (Gabriele, Lee, and Hall 1991; Gabriele, Hall, and Lee 1989).

Gabriele, Hall, and Lee (1989) took an interesting approach to studying the functional equivalence of imagery and movement by examining the contextual interference effect and whether it occurs in a similar way in MP as it does in PP. The contextual interference effect refers to the beneficial effect on learning a skill that occurs from random practice as opposed to blocked practice (Magill 2004; Schmidt and Lee 1999). In study 1, Gabriele, Hall, and Lee (1989) compared random and varied imagery practice of four movement patterns and found better retention on performance of the task as a result of random imagery practice than with blocked imagery practice, as would be expected for PP. Study 2 compared random imagery with random PP, random PP with a rest interval, and blocked PP. Random imagery practice was as effective as random PP for retention of the movement skill. This supports two ideas: that mental and physical practice use similar processes, and that many of the practice principles for PP might also apply to MP. See chapter 8 for a review of strategies for applying imagery in sport.

The functional equivalence of motor imagery and motor performance appears to be a potentially fruitful explanation of how imagery enhances motor skills, including sport performance. The functional equivalence of visual imagery and visual perception and of motor imagery and motor preparation may explain how imagery enhances sport performance. If they are the same, imagery is analogous to physically practicing a movement and is equivalent to actual physical practice in its motor preparation. The research indicates that imagining a motor act is similar to performing it; however, we have yet to produce studies using neurophysiological approaches that compare imagery of a complex movement or sport performance with actual performance of those activities. Research using timing and interference protocols with sport skills (as opposed to movement skills) is limited. We encourage sport psychologists to pursue research of this nature, utilizing both timing and interference protocols (especially neurophysiological approaches) with more complex sport skills.

CONCLUSIONS

None of the theories discussed in this chapter have sufficient research to support them as definitive theories of imagery functioning. Hall (2001) concluded his review of imagery theories by stating that a comprehensive theory covering all aspects of motor imagery is unlikely to be developed in the near future. Earlier, Janssen and Sheikh (1994) said, "It appears that while all theories have a kernel of truth, none of them, in its present state, is sufficiently developed or detailed with respect to sport psychology" (p. 6).

Perhaps the functioning of imagery combines several of these ideas. After all, in overt practice performers get feedback from the muscles, cognitively plan what they are going to do, gain confidence from viewing successful performance or performing the skill successfully, and feel motivated by performance success and their belief that imagery works. All of these factors could occur in imagery or MP. What the athlete gains from each imagery session may be determined by multiple factors, including what he intended the session to achieve, the emphasis of the imagery script, his preferences, and the nature of the task.

The idea of some form of functional equivalence between imagery and performance is promising. One implication is that just as skilled performance depends on many factors, so might imagery. Researchers might find examining the variables that affect performance to be a useful strategy in increasing understanding of how imagery works. Researchers might also look toward developing a model for sport that utilizes an information-processing approach coupled with functional-equivalence ideas, as Lang (1977) tried to do for emotional imagery with an information-processing model that included psychophysiological reactions. In an interesting discussion of the integration of imagery theories, Lavallee, Kremer, Moran, and Williams (2004) recommended an integrated model of MP that is based on functional-equivalence views of motor imagery but incorporates the strengths of neuromuscular, cognitive, and bioinformational views of imagery. They proposed that the concept that imagery is functionally equivalent to perception and motor preparation allows MP to be best understood as a "centrally mediated cognitive activity that mimics perceptual, motor, and certain emotional responses in the brain" (Lavallee et al. 2004, 40). They maintained that this concept integrates functional-equivalence views with psychoneuromuscular views (because MP activates neural activity, even though it is centrally regulated rather than peripherally important), cognitive views (because MP is mediated by a central representation), and the bioinformational approach (because it involves emotional reactions). This integrated view has some promise but lacks enough research to support it.

This chapter demonstrates that research support for the equivalence of motor imagery and perception and motor preparation is strong, but research on the functional equivalence of emotional responses in motor imagery is limited. In addition, although the research supporting a functional equivalence between motor imagery and perception and motor preparation is strong, little research exists on the functional equivalence of imagery of sport skills or imagery of sport performance, especially with neurophysiological measures (let alone the emotions during sport). We encourage those interested to investigate the lead of Lavallee et al. (2004) and their proposed integrated view. We also encourage theorists in the field to consider other approaches to integrating these theories into one comprehensive theory of imagery in sport. Since none of the theories discussed in this chapter can be considered a definitive theory of imagery functioning, we hope the quest continues.

PART II

Investigating Imagery in Sport

In part II of *Imagery in Sport* we take a detailed look at research on imagery, which we have divided into four chapters. Chapter 4 discusses the measurement of imagery in sport. It also discusses measures of imagery that originate in mainstream psychology, because only recently have sport psychologists developed sport-specific instruments to assess aspects of imagery. We address the main areas of research on imagery in sport in chapter 5. Cadeyrn Gaskin has made a noteworthy contribution to this chapter. To minimize repetition, chapter 5 focuses on research not covered elsewhere, which could give the misleading impression that research on imagery is limited in breadth and depth. However, throughout the book you will encounter the vast amount of research that has been conducted on imagery in sport.

We believe that including pertinent imagery research along with relevant conceptualizations increases comprehension, so part I included theory-related research (chapter 3) and measures-related research (chapter 4). Here in part II, chapters 6 and 7 cover research on imagery perspectives and psychophysiology, respectively. Chapter 6 reflects the substantial attention that sport psychologists have given to internal and external imagery perspectives in research and practice. Psychophysiology has long been linked to imagery, primarily because of the absence of any directly observable element of the imagery process. In chapter 7, we discuss the efforts to examine imagery through a variety of psychophysiological variables.

CHAPTER 4

IMAGERY-ABILITY AND IMAGERY-USE ASSESSMENT

Because imagery cannot be directly observed, assessing it presents a problem similar to those of many other mental processes in psychology (Perry and Morris 1995). Although measuring variations in imagery-influenced performance is possible, such measurements cannot be equated with the actual assessment of characteristics such as imagery ability. Anderson (1981a) acknowledged an additional concern: Due to the broad range of conscious activity represented within the imagery definition, the possibility of finding an all-purpose assessment procedure is limited.

Because of these inherent difficulties, the measurement of imagery ability has suffered from a lack of rigorous examination in both general and sport psychology (Perry and Morris 1995). Nevertheless, an extended history of imagery-ability assessment in relation to both motor and sport performance has resulted in a detailed collection of literature associated with its evaluation. Of equal importance within the context of sport and exercise psychology is the determination of the different ways in which athletes have described using imagery.

Imagery-assessment research has adopted a variety of conceptual and methodological approaches, but only a limited number of studies have taken the necessary steps to present sufficient evidence of a sound theoretical base and acceptable psychometrics (Moran 1993). Understanding the role of imagery in the sport domain requires an understanding of the assessable qualities of imagery, measurement techniques, and the characteristics of existing measures. This chapter describes those image attributes that have been examined as representations of individual differences in imagery ability and the most common assessment techniques and test formats. Next it reviews the existing measures of imagery ability, with a focus on the evidence relating to their theoretical basis and psychometrics status. Then comes detailed information regarding the newer area of imagery use by athletes, with a particular focus on the work of Hall, Paivio, and colleagues. The chapter concludes with a description of a possible framework of the procedures and measures considered most appropriate in sport-related assessment of imagery ability and use.

COMPONENTS OF IMAGERY ABILITY

Imagery-ability questionnaires typically examine self-reported quality of imagery. As such, they are not, in the strictest sense, tests of ability. Hall and Martin (1997) and Hall (1998) supported the use of the term "ability" in the assessment context (as distinct from "skill"), on the basis that all individuals seem to have the capacity to generate and use images, "but not to the same degree" (Hall 1998, 165). Research and applied work on imagery training indicated that imagery abilities can be improved, which is a characteristic of skills, not abilities. However, referring to the self-reported assessment of the qualities of imagery as "imagery ability" has become conventional (e.g., Ahsen 1997; Hall 1998; Hall and Martin 1997), so we will use this term throughout this chapter. As detailed earlier in this book, Morris (1997) defined imagery ability as "an individual's capability of forming vivid, controllable images and retaining them for sufficient time to effect the desired imagery rehearsal" (p. 37). Substantial support exists for the conceptual attention directed toward the three specific characteristics of imagery ability outlined in Morris' description. The conclusion drawn by many researchers was that the construct represents more than a single measurable factor (Dean and Morris 2003; Ernest 1977; Hall et al. 1985; Lequerica, Rapport, Axelrod, Telmet, and Whitman 2002; Munzert and Hackfort 1999; Richardson 1994; Richardson, J.T.E. 1988; Slee 1988; Sheehan, Ashton, and White 1983).

Imagery literature uses many terms to describe the characteristics that measures of imagery ability assess, such as "traits," "qualities," "dimensions," "aspects," "components," "competences," "properties," "processes," "parameters," and "modalities" (Ahsen 1993; Anderson 1981a; Dean and Morris 2003; Denis 1985; Hall 1998; Lequerica et al. 2002; Perry and Morris 1995; Munzert and Hackfort 1999; Richardson 1994; Tower 1981). Many of the studies and reviews that examined this area consistently discussed an assessment framework in which imagery ability comprised a specific set of dimensional and sensory modality components.

DIMENSIONS OF IMAGERY ABILITY

The two dimensions most regularly discussed are those of vividness and controllability (Denis 1985; Gould and Damarjian 1996; Lequerica et al. 2002; Moran 1993; Morris and Hampson 1983; Murphy and Martin 2002; Perry and Morris 1995; Richardson 1977, 1994; Richardson, J.T.E. 1999; Sheehan et al. 1983; Tower 1981; White et al. 1977). Moran (1993) described the first of these dimensions, vividness of an image, as "its clarity and 'sharpness' or sensory richness" (p. 158). Alternatively, Denis (1985) suggested that vividness "reflects the rate of activity of the mental processes underlying the experience of imagery" (p. 8S). Murphy and Jowdy (1992) referred to the self-report aspect of the dimension and how it reflects the reality of the image to the individual. Richardson (1994), in his elaborate analysis of vividness, outlined two important points. First, the dimension does not measure image-recall accuracy, and second, he suggested that it represents the percept-like content (cognitive cues) and feelings (affective cues) generated within an image. Although such a broad variation in the descriptions of vividness implies that it is yet to be defined in a manner fully accepted within psychology, its most consistently mentioned feature is that it assesses the reality of the imaginal experience, or as McLean and Richardson (1994) succinctly described it, the "lifelikeness" of an image.

The term "controllability" describes the "ease and accuracy with which an image can be transformed or manipulated in one's mind" (Moran 1993, 158). Denis (1985) referred to controllability from a cognitive-processing perspective and stated that imagery is "under the control of processes which regulate their [images'] current rate of activation and the possibility of their transformations" (p. 8S). Elaborating further, Denis suggested that control reflects the processing involved in refreshing an image and its maintenance over a certain period. Murphy (1994) also emphasized that control represents an individual's ability to influence image content.

Additional dimensions referred to in the literature include preference (Richardson 1994), exactness of reference, duration (Denis 1985), ease of generation (Hall et al. 1985; Tower 1981), ability to change (Munzert and Hackfort 1999), "unvividness" (Ahsen 1985), and orientation or perspective (McLean and Richardson 1994). Several of these are relevant to an understanding of the nature of imagery ability in the context of the physical and sport domains. Denis (1985) suggested that exactness of reference is important because it is necessary that the figural content of the image accurately depicts what it is supposed to refer to; for instance, the dimensions of the objects, the distance from the subject to the objects, the direction of the movement, its magnitude, etc. (p. 9S)

Duration is represented by the amount of time an image is clearly maintained in the mind from its initial generation until it disappears or is substantially modified (Denis 1985). The dimension of ease of generation represents the level of ease or difficulty in evoking an image (Hall et al. 1985; Tower 1981). The speed of formation of an image is a dimension that warrants investigation in determining the status of imagery skills. Currently only limited research and analytic discussion of the imagery process proposes the assessment of this attribute (Watt, Morris, and Andersen 2004). We contend, however, based on a perceived high level of validity, that speed of image generation represents a qualitative dimension that provides valuable evidence of imagery ability.

Several researchers have reported that examining the imagery perspective is important in understanding imagery ability (Hale 1994; Mumford and Hall 1985; McLean and Richardson 1994). "Unvividness," or weak imagery, was described by Ahsen (1985) as "not a sign of absence of imagery; rather, it is one of imagery's independent functional attributes" (p. 1). Ahsen claimed that the perceptual quality of all images is always imperfect to some degree, and that significant information is represented within the analysis of both complete and incomplete imagery detail. Perspective can be external (third person), as if watching oneself on video, or internal (first person), which involves experiencing the image as if in one's own body (Mahoney and Avener 1977). Recently Dean and Morris (2003) promoted the assessment of the imagery processes of formation, maintenance, and transformation, attributes derived from the broader image-properties work of Kosslyn (1980, 1994). As with vividness and control, some of the dimensions reviewed are already being assessed in existing imagery-ability measures. Additionally, several dimensions that are not currently being assessed should be included in future tests if they can provide information useful to the understanding of imagery.

MODALITIES OF IMAGERY ABILITY

Many authors have highlighted the need to involve all the senses (modalities) when using imagery rather than using only the visual modality (Bird and Cripe 1986; Janssen and Sheikh 1994; Vealey and Greenleaf 2001; Weinberg and Gould 2003). Ahsen (1995) has closely examined the interaction of vision with the other senses and stated that "imagery ability (like intelligence) is itself comprised of components and their functions; and to make it more difficult, other senses commingle with the visual cue" (p. 114). The assessment of imagery ability should, therefore, incorporate a range of sensory modalities, which may include visual, auditory, kinesthetic, olfactory, tactile, and gustatory senses (Ahsen 1995; Munzert and Hackfort 1999; Perry and Morris 1995; Richardson 1994; Sheehan et al. 1983; White et al. 1977).

The visual and kinesthetic modalities have received the most attention in examining imagery ability and motor performance (McLean and Richardson 1994), perhaps because the design of several of the existing imagery-ability measures incorporates the assessment of only the visual and kinesthetic modalities, or modifications that isolate these senses (Hall et al. 1985; Isaac, Marks, and Russell 1986). Such a trend reveals the emphasis that researchers placed on the visual and kinesthetic senses as the key characteristics of imagery in the motor domain. More recent discussions support the necessity to use multimodal imagery (Cox 2002; Gould, Damarjian, and Greenleaf 2002; Vealey and Greenleaf 2001) in the sport context.

Another characteristic that could be included as a component of imagery ability is the experience of emotion (Suinn 1993). Affective states such as emotion are typically aligned with the senses as an imaginal subcomponent rather than aligned with the dimensions (Vealey and Greenleaf 1998; Weinberg and Gould 2003). Vealey and Greenleaf (1998) suggested that in re-creating outstanding performance "athletes should feel the emotions associated with those experiences, such as elation, satisfaction, pride, and self-esteem" (p. 239). Based on the emphasis that several authors have placed on involving emotions in sport imagery, this characteristic is an appropriate variable to include in measuring imagery ability (e.g., Murphy and Martin 2002; Perry and Morris 1995; Suinn 1993; Weinberg and Gould 2003).

Ideally, the assessment of imagery ability requires a measure that examines the salient components used in producing images. Such a measure should include the dimensions of vividness, controllability, duration, ease, and speed of generation. Although evidence supporting the existence and independence of several of these dimensions is limited, the multidimensionality of the imagery phenomenon is a well-accepted proposition (e.g., Perry and Morris 1995; Richardson 1994). Investigations that target the full range of image-generation components could enhance understanding of the relationship between and uniqueness of dimensional descriptors. Additionally, the accepted phenomenological viewpoint (e.g., Perry and Morris 1995; Richardson 1994; Suinn 1993) supports the examination of specific sensory modalities such as vision, audition, touch, kinesthesis, olfaction, and gustation, plus the emotional concomitants of imagery. Consequently, this necessitates a multimodal approach to assessment to ensure the accurate representation of the sensory characteristics of sport imagery (Watt, Morris, and Andersen 2004).

CLASSIFICATION OF IMAGERY-ABILITY AND IMAGERY-USE MEASURES

Imagery ability is typically assessed from performance on a specific set of mental-ability tasks or from answers to questionnaires that require behavioral or emotive-imagery responses (Sheehan et al. 1983). Imagery-use measures typically incorporate a questionnaire format to determine when, where, and how (Hall 1998) people use imagery during their involvement in a particular performance or experience. The majority of the following section concentrates more on the assessment of imagery ability rather than imagery use because of its longer history in psychology.

No existing measure of imagery ability has yet achieved widespread acceptance as demonstrating content depth and cohesion and psychometric adequacy. Anderson (1981a) suggested that confusion exists in relation to the description of the constituents of imagery functioning. The complexity of the phenomenon has "spawned a number of procedures for assessing different dimensions of imaginal processes" (p. 149). Several researchers proposed that because of the varied nature of imagery skills, matching the measure to the task under examination is important (Anderson 1981a; Katz 1983; Paivio 1985; Tower 1981). Tower (1981) presented a summary of imagery measures used in general psychology that included the following categories: (a) self-report (questionnaire, interview, phenomenological), (b) projective, (c) behavioral, and (d) physiological. The foundations underlying these assessment approaches emanate from the test designers' "implicit or explicit assumptions about the nature and relevant dimensions of the processes and phenomenal products involved" (Anderson 1981a, 149). The two types of imagery measures used most regularly in sport psychology are classified as either objective or subjective in nature (Hall 1998; Hall et al. 1985; Moran 1993). An additional category of imagery assessment described by Sheehan et al. (1983) is termed the "experience-based measurement of imagery." This category represents the qualitative procedures that are used in examining imagery functioning.

OBJECTIVE MEASURES

Objective measures normally infer imagery ability from behavioral analysis of people's perceptual, cognitive, and spatial manipulation and control skills on specific tasks related to spatial visualization and transformation abilities (Lequerica et al. 2002; Vandenberg and Kuse 1978). The tests require individuals to mentally perform spatial manipulations of stimulus objects. Recently Dean and Morris (2003) stated that "spatial tests frequently require participants to manipulate abstract geometrical shapes of one type in a specific way. These shapes are black-and-white line drawings and are usually previously unseen" (p. 248). Finally, they must select the object in its correct orientation from a given set of alternatives (Hall et al. 1985). The responses are then evaluated against externally verifiable criteria, such as a correct answer (Lequerica et al. 2002).

Researchers have generally assumed that objective measures attempt to examine the control dimension of imagery ability (Lequerica et al. 2002; Moran 1993; Richardson 1977). Morris and Hampson (1983) considered that what imagery-ability objective measures assess is still not clear. Several authors have suggested that these tests could be representative of more general cognitive skills, such as memory, problem solving, or associative learning, that do not require the use of imagery (Hall et al. 1985; Moran 1993; Morris and Hampson 1983). Objective measures of imagery ability typically assess visual imagery and include no test of spatial abilities designed to examine the nonvisual senses (Heil 1984; Morris and Hampson 1983).

SUBJECTIVE MEASURES

Much more common in imagery-ability testing, particularly in the movement and sport domains, are questionnaires or self-report inventories. These tests are based on the assumption that the individual's subjective experience of the image "is of primary importance, rather than the match to any objective criterion, and that this experience is at a conscious level" (Tower 1981, 87). Respondents are usually required to report on specific characteristics, such as clarity of a descriptive image, for individual items that examine common experiences, such as hearing an ambulance siren or seeing a sunset. Another method involves participants generating an image described during the test and responding to a set of items that relate specifically to the outlined image. For example, four items might relate to a country scene that involves imagery of trees, a mountain, and a lake. One or more image scenarios may be presented in this kind of test. Response techniques have included 5- or 7-point Likert-type scales, visual analogue scales, yes-or-no or true-or-false response scales, semantic differential scales, or the selection of one response from a set of multiple-choice alternatives (Quilter, Band, and Miller 1999; Richardson 1994). Specific dimensions of imagery previously examined include vividness, controllability, perspective (internal versus external), presence, and ease (Hall 1998; Moran 1993; Perry and Morris 1995; Tower 1981; Vealey and Greenleaf 2001). Although some subjective tests have considered only one sense modality, usually the visual, several have examined both the visual and kinesthetic sensory modalities, with a small number of tests attempting to assess up to seven modalities (Hall et al. 1985; Kwekkeboom 2000; Sheehan 1967a; Switras 1978; Watt and Morris 2001). The self-report assessment of imagery use relies on the respondents detailing content in relation to their utilization of imagery "to achieve a variety of cognitive, behavioral, and affective changes" (Murphy and Martin 2002, 418) by rating characteristics such as ease or frequency of the usage of the various functional characteristics of imagery.

Reviews of imagery-ability assessment have detailed several criticisms of subjective measures (Anderson 1981a; Katz 1983; Lequerica et al. 2002; Moran 1993; Richardson 1994). Morris and Hampson (1983) pointed out the absence of an absolute standard for differentiating between responses to imagery items, such as rating an image's vividness or evaluating the ease of generating it. For example, how different is a rating of "perfectly clear and vivid" regarding the smell of freshly cut grass from a rating of "moderately clear and vivid" for the same imaginal experience? Additionally, research has not determined how greatly imagery questionnaires are affected by the unwanted error variance that results from faking responses, response leniency, or the influence of a social-desirability factor (LeBoutillier and Marks 2003; Richardson 1994; Richardson, J.T.E. 1999). Finally, most subjective measures rely on memory of objects or events in some manner; thus, the recency or frequency of experience of the imagined item may influence the quality of responses (Lequerica et al. 2002).

QUALITATIVE ASSESSMENT

The final method of imagery assessment reviewed concerns the examination of aspects of consciousness that directly reflect experiences (Sheehan et al. 1983). Ericsson and Simon (1993) described two forms of verbal reports that appropriately reflect cognitive processes such as imagery. First, concurrent verbalization (CV) involves "talk aloud" or "think aloud" reports in which the participants verbalize information as it enters their attention. The second type, retrospective verbalization (RV), is a report provided by the participant after the initial occurrence of the cognitive process. Of course, as Anderson (1981a) noted, all verbal reports are retrospective to some degree because participants describe what they were cognitively processing prior to the verbalization.

Anderson (1981a, b) presented reviews of a qualitative imagery-assessment procedure involving content analysis of verbal reports that described imaginal activities. The analysis system he detailed was developed with two theoretical perspectives of imagery processing in mind: the propositional interpretation of imaginal processing that represents key elements of theories proposed by Pylyshyn (1973) and Lang (1977), and Neisser's (1976) conceptualization of imagery as it relates to the nature of cognition and perception. Anderson's interpretation of these two imagery conceptualizations provided key elements in the creation of a framework for image-description analysis. More specifically, Anderson stated that "the amount and kind of information that is processed may be important dimensions of imaginal activity. One way of assessing these dimensions is by indexing the amount and kind of descriptive detail contained in narrative reports of imaginal activity" (1981a, 164).

Sheehan et al. (1983) have suggested that measures of this type, which tap people's real experiences, "may be more valid for measuring those aspects of cognition that characterize current everyday thinking" (p. 195). They outlined several advantages of these procedures, the first being that narrative or verbalization methods are sensitive in how they address the idiosyncratic aspects of participants' experiences and involve them in the measurement process. Second, the methodology attempts to examine recent memories, which, as the researchers point out, has more value than questionnaire measures "where items are relevant to memory of events that rarely have taken place in the immediate past" (p.195).

The disadvantages of verbalization procedures center on the assumptions made concerning the participants: one, that participants are thought to be articulate about the experiences they are asked to describe, and two, that they may require assistance to retrieve the generated images, which may bias their responses (Sheehan et al. 1983). Although this type of procedure has been infrequently discussed in the sport psychology literature (e.g., Spittle and Morris 1999a; Watt and Morris 2000), the methodologies described by Anderson (1981a), Ericsson and Simon (1993), and Sheehan et al. (1983) could provide interesting and useful adjuncts to self-report measures in examining mental imagery in the motor domain.

In determining which type of measure is most suitable for assessing imagery attributes, two important points warrant acknowledgement. First, Katz (1983) supports the use of subjective assessment because he believes that subjective measures are more directly associated with the construct of imagery than objective tests. Second, self-report material is considered a more appropriate representation of the experience or phenomenon of imagery. Katz (1983) also suggested that the response detail from self-report measures provides a more structured indication of ability than objective measures. Pylyshyn (1979) argued that spatial manipulations may be completed using skills not associated with imagery functioning.

Historically, the preferred assessment methodology in the motor domain has been the use of subjective tests (Hall 1998). Consequently, in developing new measures of sport imagery ability or use, researchers have focused on the incorporation of a subjective self-report design. The use of qualitative evaluation methodologies compared to the evaluation of imagery characteristics remains relatively limited in sport psychology (e.g., Moran and MacIntyre 1998; Munroe et al. 2000; Spittle and Morris 1999a). However, it appears that the procedures can provide valuable information pertaining to the imagery experience that are not available through either subjective or objective assessment techniques.

MEASURES OF IMAGERY USED IN SPORT PSYCHOLOGY

Interest in the area of imagery abilities and imagery use has prompted the development of a variety of assessment devices. Researchers have directed substantial effort toward the conceptualization, design, and psychometric evaluation of an interesting collection of measurement approaches. Reviews of these tests, presented in both the general and sport psychology literature, serve as a valuable base in examining measures used previously in sport psychology (Anderson 1981a; Hall 1998; Moran 1993; Ostrow 1996; Perry and Morris 1995; Richardson 1994; Richardson, J. T. E. 1999; White et al. 1977). The format, assessed imagery characteristics, and examples of the basic psychometric properties of these instruments are summarized in table 4.1a and b (see the end of this chapter, page 98) and discussed in greater detail in the following section.

TESTS OF IMAGERY ABILITY

Measures of imagery ability have been used over the last 40 years. Initially, tests developed for use in general psychology were adopted for use within sport psychology, to ascertain athletes' imagery skills. The need for more specialized instruments was recognized a couple of decades ago and has led to the construction of measures that evaluate movement-imagery abilities and several questionnaires that assess imagery characteristics with a sport-specific orientation. Here we review those measures that have been used in research and practice to assess imagery abilities within the human movement sciences.

BETTS QUESTIONNAIRE UPON MENTAL IMAGERY

The Betts (1909) Questionnaire Upon Mental Imagery (QMI) is a scale of 150 items that investigates imagery in seven major sensory modalities: visual, auditory, cutaneous, kinesthetic, gustatory, olfactory, and organic. Forty items pertain to the visual modality and 20 items to each of the other senses (except the organic modality, which has 10). Individuals attempt to generate images suggested by the items and rate the vividness of their imagery on the Betts 7-point rating scale, on which 7 means "no image present at all" and 1 means "perfectly clear and vivid." Betts did not provide a rationale for the distribution of items across modalities, and no reliability information appears to be available. In reviewing this measure, Moran (1993) stated that it is "the prototypical test of imagery vividness. Most of the other scales in this field adopt its Likert-style rating format (and sometimes borrow its items)" (p.161).

Sheehan (1967a) developed a shortened form of Betts' questionnaire, called the Questionnaire on Mental Imagery (SQMI). The revised test derived 35 items (5 per modality) from the original measure, and a correlation with the long version was reported as $r = .9$ (Sheehan, 1967a). Reliability has been consistently established, with typical findings such as an internal consistency of $r = .92$ (Quilter et al. 1999) to $r = .95$ (Juhasz 1972), and test–retest reliability of $r = .78$ over a 7-month interval (Sheehan 1967b). Several researchers have implied that evidence supports the test's convergent validity, because the SQMI correlates moderately with other imagery-ability measures (Kihlstrom, Glisky, Peterson, Harvey, and Rose 1991), including the Vividness of Visual Imagery Questionnaire ($r = .43$; Lorenz and Neisser 1985) and the Gordon Imagery Control Scale ($r = .56$; Lorenz and Neisser 1985). Sheehan (1967a) reported the determination of a homogenous factor structure (imagery vividness).

The SQMI has proven to be both reliable and popular, yet remains restricted because it evaluates only the dimension of vividness. The most current version of the SQMI is the randomized short Betts QMI developed by White, Ashton, and Law (1978). Modifications to the previous SQMI centered on two important areas: items previously presented in groups of five were presented independently, and White et al. (1978) randomized the format of individual items in an effort to reduce any response-set bias generated by grouping similar modality items. Only limited evidence of the reliability of this adaptation of the SQMI is available (Ashton and White 1980; White et al. 1978). Inferences of improved validity resulted from the analysis of a comparison between the original and randomized SQMI to highlight any gender differences. Ashton and White (1980) found that the substantial gender differences reported for the earlier version were reduced for the randomized version. They suggested that this test represents a measure of imagery vividness that is less contaminated by response biases.

VIVIDNESS OF VISUAL IMAGERY QUESTIONNAIRE

The Vividness of Visual Imagery Questionnaire (VVIQ) is a 16-item self-report inventory developed by Marks (1973) as an extension of the visual subscale of Betts' questionnaire. Participants are required to rate the vividness of their visual images on a scale from 1 ("perfectly clear, as vivid as normal vision") to 5 ("no image at all; you only know you are thinking of the object") on four different scenes, first with their eyes open and then with their eyes closed. The scenes examine the following topics: characteristics of a friend or relative, the weather, a local shop, and the country. Respondents can score 16 to 80 points; the lower the score, the better the self-rated imagery. Studies of the internal consistency of the VVIQ were reviewed by McKelvie (1995), who reported a mean alpha coefficient of $r = .89$. Eton, Gilner, and Munz (1998) reported internal consistencies of $r = .91$ and $r = .95$, for the two subscales. Test–retest reliability has also been reported as ranging from $r = .62$ (Eton et al. 1998) to $r = .86$ (Parrot and Strongman 1985), both over 2-week intervals. Evidence of criterion validity is typically generated by comparing VVIQ scores with a range of tasks, including self-reported imaging, cognitive–perceptual processing, and memory (McKelvie 1995). After analyzing available criterion-validity data, McKelvie reported a coefficient of $r = .27$ and concluded that evidence supports the VVIQ as a valid measure. Factor analysis has yielded a unitary factor pattern (Dowling 1973). Although the VVIQ is widely used, its assessment of only the vividness dimension in the visual modality in inferring imagery ability restricts its applicability within sport psychology. Ongoing questions about its stability over time and construct validity are also of concern (Chara and Hamm 1989; Eton et al. 1998).

GORDON TEST OF VISUAL IMAGERY CONTROL

The Gordon Test of Visual Imagery Control (GTVIC; Gordon 1949; Richardson 1969) is a self-report test designed to assess how well a person can manipulate and control an image. The test originally involved oral instructions, which preceded 11 questions relating to a suggested image (for example, a car, with questions addressing color and physical position). Participants answered either yes or no, depending on their ability to manipulate evoked visual images. Richardson (1969) modified this format by adding a 12th item and including a tripartite scoring scheme: "yes," "no," and "unsure." Richardson also suggested the use of written rather than oral instructions. Reliability data has been reported as internal consistency estimates of $r = .77$ to $r = .84$ (Hiscock 1978) and a split-half value of $r = .76$ (McKelvie and Gingras 1974). Stability over time has been represented by test–retest coefficients of $r = .84$, over a 3-week interval (McKelvie and Gingras 1974), and $r = .60$ to $r = .64$, over a 12-month period (White and Ashton 1976). A more current investigation reported that a 7-point Likert version of the GTVIC yielded a Cronbach's alpha of .88 (Lequerica et al. 2002). The GTVIC has not proven to be one-dimensional; it is generally represented by three or four factors of imagery control in factor-analytic studies (Ashton and White 1974; Morrison and White 1984; White and Ashton 1977). The test has been widely used and is reliable, but its assessment of general imagery ability is limited by its focus on controllability.

MENTAL ROTATIONS TEST

The Mental Rotations Test (MRT; Vandenberg and Kuse 1978) contains 20 items in 5 sets of 4 items. Each item consists of a criterion figure, two correct alternatives, and two incorrect ones. Correct alternatives are always identical to the criterion in structure, but are shown in a rotated position. For half the items in the test, the distracters are rotated mirror images of the criterion, while distracters in the other half are rotated images of one or two of the other criteria. The reliability of the test has been reported as test–retest coefficients of $r = .83$ and $r = .70$, over periods of 1 year, and a Kuder-Richardson value of $r = .88$. Convergent validity was supported through positive correlations with measures of spatial ability, and predictive validity is related to the significant correlation of the MRT with performance in World Cup canoe slalom racing (Moran 1993). Although reviewed by Moran (1993) as a test of mental imagery, the developers of the instrument have described it as a test of spatial visualization (Vandenberg and Kuse 1978), and for this reason its usefulness as a specific measure of the control dimension is difficult to support. Recent investigations using the MRT, however, specifically classified it as a spatial test aligned with imagery assessment (Dean and Morris 2003) and as an objective imagery-ability measure of the control dimension (Lequerica et al. 2002).

VIVIDNESS OF MOVEMENT IMAGERY QUESTIONNAIRE

The Vividness of Movement Imagery Questionnaire (VMIQ; Isaac, Marks, and Russell 1986) contains 24 items that measure the visual imagery of movement and the imagery of kinesthetic sensations associated with movement. Items examine participants' ability to image specified basic body movements and movements requiring precision and control in upright, unbalanced, and aerial situations. Participants are asked to rate the vividness of imagery for each item, both with respect to watching someone else and as if watching themselves. They respond to each item on a 5-point ordinal scale, which ranges from 1 ("perfectly clear and as vivid as normal vision") to 5 ("no image at all; you only know that you are thinking of the skill").

The VMIQ has a basic format that makes it relatively easy to administer to large groups. Eton et al. (1998) reported that alpha coefficients ranged from $r = .96$ ("other" subscale) to $r = .97$ (total scale). Recently Lequerica et al. (2002) reported very high internal-consistency values of $r = .95$ for the visual subscale and $r = .97$ for the kinesthetic subscale. A test–retest coefficient of $r = .76$ has been reported over a 3-week period (Isaac et al. 1986) and of $r = .62$ over a 2-week period (Eton et al. 1998). High ($r = .81$; Isaac et al. 1986) to moderate ($r = .60$; Eton et al. 1998) correlations with the VVIQ and Movement Imagery Questionnaire ($r = .58$; Hall and Martin 1997) form the basis of the minimal evidence of the measure's validity data.

Several studies used the VMIQ to examine individual differences in imagery abilities as a framework for generating criterion validity evidence. Both the Eton et al. (1998) and Isaac and Marks (1994) studies determined that scores on the VMIQ could distinguish between athlete groups of varying participation levels and nonathletes. In contrast, Williams and Isaac (1991) found that the VMIQ could not differentiate between people grouped on motor-skill-performance levels. (Chapter 5 includes a more detailed analysis of motor-skill and sport-performance research.)

The most recent revision of the VMIQ, the VMIQ Mark II, has only 18 items and includes a third rating score related to the kinesthetic sensation. Two items relating to the respondent's eye status (open or closed) during imagery and handedness (left, right, or both) are also included. The emphasis on direct reporting of kinesthetic imagery in the revised version may have resulted from a reported unitary (visual) factor structure for the original measure (Campos and Perez 1990). The single-dimensional component of this measure appears to be directly related to its adaptation from the VVIQ. Although it is limited in the number of modalities assessed (visual and kinesthetic), the VMIQ is a more relevant approach than other multimodal, general-imagery techniques in assessing movement-imagery ability in the context of sport psychology (Eton et al. 1998; Isaac et al. 1986).

MOVEMENT IMAGERY QUESTIONNAIRE

The Movement Imagery Questionnaire (MIQ; Hall et al. 1985) is completed over 4 phases and contains 18 items, 9 for the visual subscale and 9 for the kinesthetic subscale. Individuals are initially asked to read descriptions of various arm, leg, and full-body movements. Next, they physically perform the movement required for that particular item. The respondents then assume the starting position of the movement and are asked to image the movement either visually or kinesthetically (no movement is actually performed) and rate how easy or difficult it is to use that imagery. Individuals respond to each item using a 7-point rating scale, ranging from 1 ("very easy to picture or feel") to 7 ("very difficult to picture or feel"). The total score for each subscale extends from 9 (the high imagery limit) to 63 (the low imagery limit). Reliability has been reported as internal-consistency coefficients ranging from $r = .87$ to $r = .89$ (visual) and $r = .86$ to $r = .91$ (kinesthetic), in addition to a test–retest reliability of .83 for a 1-week interval (Atienza, Balaguer, and Garcia-Merita 1994; Hall et al. 1985; Lovell and Collins 2001).

A moderately high correlation of $r = .58$ was found between the test's visual and kinesthetic subscales, suggesting only a limited level of independence of the modalities. Hall et al. (1985) proposed that the correlation indicated "that visual and kinesthetic imagery of movement are related but separate measures" (p. 115). Exploratory factor analysis revealed a bifactorial (visual and kinesthetic) structure (Atienza et al. 1994). Evidence supporting the measure's predictive validity was gathered by comparing MIQ scores with participants' movement-pattern learning ability (Goss, Hall, Buckolz, and Fishburne 1986; Hall, Buckolz, and Fishburne 1989). The design of the test is sound, but administration is more difficult than a paper-and-pencil measure due to the physical-performance component. Overall, the test items appear more suitable to assessing imagery ability related to motor learning rather than sport performance.

Hall and Martin (1997) modified the MIQ to create the more compact revised version (MIQ-R). The primary goal of the revision was to reduce administration time and eliminate those items that some participants would refuse to physically perform (Hall 1998). Modifications included reducing the number of items from nine to four for each subscale, reversing the rating values so that higher scores relate to higher imagery ability, and rewording certain items to improve clarity (e.g., "hard" and "see" replaced "difficult" and "picture"). A number of studies have reported the psychometric properties of the MIQ-R to be very good. For example, Abma, Fry, Li, and Relyea (2002) found the internal consistency to be $r = .87$ for the visual and $r = .88$ for the kinesthetic. Moritz, Hall, Martin, and Vadocz (1996) reported a correlation between the visual and kinesthetic subscales of $r = .44$, a value that indicates improved modal uniqueness compared to that found for the subscales of the original version. However, Abma et al. (2002) found that the subscales were highly associated ($r = .66$). Hall and Martin (1997) suggested that the MIQ-R is a adequate revision of the MIQ because of the significant correlation ($r = .77$) between corresponding visual and kinesthetic subscales for each measure.

After investigating the relationship between the VMIQ, MIQ, and MIQ-R, Hall and Martin (1997) outlined a framework for the most effective applied and research usage of these three measures of movement-imagery ability. The VMIQ is best suited to large groups where space is limited and restricts the performance of physical movements. The MIQ-R is administered easily to individuals or small groups and examines both the visual and kinesthetic modalities. The MIQ is most appropriate for use with young, fit people when there is no time restriction on the test. Hall (1998) also suggested that using a combination of these measures may "provide a more complete assessment of imagery abilities" (p. 167).

SPORT IMAGERY QUESTIONNAIRE

The Sport Imagery Questionnaire (SIQ) is a self-report measure developed by Martens (1982) and modified by Vealey (1986), Vealey and Walter (1993), and Vealey and Greenleaf (1998). The test involves descriptions of four common sport-oriented scenes: (a) practicing alone, (b) practicing with others, (c) recalling a peak performance, and (d) playing in a contest. For each scene, time is allowed for image generation and then the vividness of visual, auditory, kinesthetic, and mood imagery are rated on a 5-point scale. The modified 28-item test examines imagery relevant to sport situations across (a) the three sensory modalities and mood characteristics from the original, (b) the dimensions of vividness and controllability, and (c) the visual imagery associated with the internal and external perspectives. Participants rate items related to modality and dimension on a 5-point scale with 1 representing "no image present" or "no control of image" and 5 representing an "extremely clear and vivid image" or "complete control of image." The items relating to internal and external imagery perspectives are also rated on a 5-point scale. At this point no reliability or validity data is available. Although the test has been widely used in applied sport psychology, its lack of psychometric properties makes the few research conclusions that are based on it questionable (Kenitzer and Briddell 1991; Thomas and Fogarty 1997). The multimodal, multidimensional design is sound and the four scenes are well described, but the test lacks any reference to generation and duration of image. It is useful in the applied setting because it provides information concerning relevant aspects of imagery ability; however, the perspective items are not typically considered indicators of the same class of imagery attribute. Unfortunately, the developer and subsequent revisers of the SIQ have failed to appropriately determine its qualities and efficacy in a scientific manner.

SPORT IMAGERY ABILITY MEASURE

The Sport Imagery Ability Measure (SIAM) developed by Watt and Morris (1998a, b) is a task-oriented, multimodal, multidimensional imagery-ability measure. Participants choose a sport-specific version of each of four generic sport-related scenes, then image each scene for 60 seconds. After imaging each scene, participants are instructed to respond to 12 items that assess five imagery dimensions (vividness, control, ease of generation, speed of generation, duration), involvement of six senses during imagery (visual, auditory, kinesthetic, olfactory, gustatory, tactile), and the experience of emotion. Participants are instructed to make their responses on 10 cm visual analogue scales (see figure 4.1). Each 10 cm line separates two opposing anchor statements (for example, "no feeling" and "very clear feeling" for the tactile modality). The test comprises 48 items. Twelve subscale scores are calculated by adding together the relevant dimension or sensory-item scores for the four scenes.

The Cronbach's alpha values for the SIAM indicated good to very good internal consistency with coefficients ranging from .66 (speed subscale) to .87 (gustatory subscale). Test–retest reliability results for 58 participants

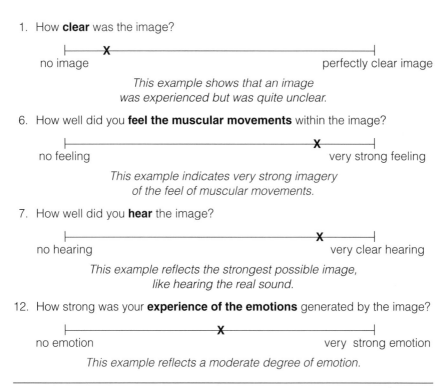

1. How **clear** was the image?

no image   perfectly clear image

*This example shows that an image
was experienced but was quite unclear.*

6. How well did you **feel the muscular movements** within the image?

no feeling   very strong feeling

*This example indicates very strong imagery
of the feel of muscular movements.*

7. How well did you **hear** the image?

no hearing   very clear hearing

*This example reflects the strongest possible image,
like hearing the real sound.*

12. How strong was your **experience of the emotions** generated by the image?

no emotion   very strong emotion

This example reflects a moderate degree of emotion.

Figure 4.1 Instructions for measures like the SIAM need to be detailed and clear. See the sidebar on page 76, "Administering the SIAM," for guidance.

over a 4-week interval revealed moderate to very good correlations for the specific subscales, varying from .41 for auditory to .76 for gustatory (Watt and Morris 1999a).

Construct validity of the SIAM has involved several investigations that have examined its factor structure and generated criterion along with convergent, discriminant, and concurrent evidence. To test the criterion validity of the revised SIAM, subscale differences between elite ($n =$ 272) and non-elite athletes ($n = 361$) were examined. The results of the independent samples t tests indicated significant differences between the groups for the vividness, control, visual, kinesthetic, and emotion subscales. Convergent and discriminant validity evidence was examined by comparing the SIAM with tests examining (a) self-reported general imagery, including vividness and control; (b) movement imagery; (c) objective imagery ability; and (d) nonimagery cognitive functioning. Small to moderate correlations (.27 to .48) were found for the SIAM control, vividness, visual, and kinesthetic subscales, with some of the related dimension and modality variables of the other imagery measures, thus, providing support for their convergent validity. Very low to small

Administering the Sport Imagery Ability Measure

The following instructions are provided to give readers an appreciation of the importance of a standardized procedure for administering psychological tests, primarily to aid comparison across tests administered in different sessions on different occasions, and also across a variety of athletes. The administration process needs to be clear so that athletes can understand what is required and follow the instructions with ease.

1. Welcome the athletes and briefly outline the reasons for administering a multimodal, multidimensional imagery questionnaire. For example, you might wish to examine characteristics associated with how athletes create images prior to implementing or developing their imagery-training program. More complete information relating to sport imagery should be provided at the completion of the test session.

2. Confirm the confidential nature of the session and encourage the athletes to relax and respond naturally in completing the imagery activities. Indicate that there are no right or wrong responses, because everyone images in their own way.

3. Wait for the athletes to be seated comfortably, distribute the questionnaire, and explain that noise should be kept to a minimum to help them focus on the task. Ask them to complete the personal information sheet and read carefully through the introduction page. Ensure that the instructions are clearly understood, particularly the placement of the intersection of the cross on the imagery-rating scale.

4. Allow the athletes time to ask questions about the questionnaire and the example on the introduction page.

5. Instruct the athletes that they should not turn the page when they finish reading through the introduction page. They should wait until the administrator asks them to do so.

6. Instruct the athletes that they will be asked to read through the description of each scene, then image it for 60 seconds, and finally respond to the 12 scales. When you feel the athletes have finished reading the scene description, allow 60 seconds for the imaging activity. A stopwatch should be used to time it.

7. After the athlete has read through the scene description, start and stop imagery for each scene using the following instruc-

tions: "Start imaging now," and after 60 seconds, "Stop imaging. Go ahead and complete the questions." Ensure that the athletes do not respond to the scales until the end of the 60-second imaging phase. Ask them to place their pens or pencils down to signal that they have finished marking their responses for that scene. Remind them not to turn the page. When they have finished responding, tell them, "Turn the page and read the next scene."

8. If the athletes seem comfortable with the general instructions, ask them to complete the practice "fitness" scene under assessment conditions (follow steps 6 and 7). Then encourage them to ask questions if they are still unsure of any task requirements.

9. Ask the athletes if they are ready to continue. If so, tell them to turn the page and read the next scene. Steps 6 and 7 should be followed for each of the remaining scenes.

10. Provide advice and support at any time during the imagery-assessment session, but avoid directing the athletes.

11. On completion, thank the athletes for participating and remind them to feel free to ask questions or make comments about the measure.

12. Summarize the purpose of the exercise and set a time to discuss the athletes' responses and how they might relate to their future use of sport imagery or participation in an imagery-training program. For example, if an athlete reports that he cannot control an image, he might need specific exercises to develop this ability. In the follow-up session with the athletes following completion of the SIAM, discuss their responses in relation to specific areas, such as vividness or kinesthetic imagery, which they could benefit from targeting in an imagery-training program.

correlations (.01 to .20) were typically reported between the SIAM subscales and (a) the cognitive-ability measures and (b) unrelated dimension and modality variables of the other imagery measures, supporting the discriminant validity of the SIAM. Concurrent validation involved comparing the SIAM's subscale scores with data from a qualitative analysis of the athletes' verbal reports of the sport imagery. Small to very small insignificant correlations were found between the two measures for all modalities for the total sample, providing only limited support for the SIAM's validity.

Exploratory factor analysis on the subscale totals showed a clear two-factor structure, with nonvisual sense modalities as one factor and dimensions plus vision as the other. The emotion subscale did not load above .5 on either factor. The factor structure was subsequently examined with structural-equation modeling. Confirmatory factor analysis supported a three-factor (single sense, generational, and feeling) model. Based on these findings, the SIAM appears suitable for use in assessing sport imagery ability in both research and applied settings (Watt and Morris 1997, 1999a, b, 2000, 2001).

CONCLUSIONS ON TESTS OF IMAGERY ABILITY

Although many of the tests described are used in both research and applied situations, no single measure is ideal for use in imagery-ability or imagery-use assessment in sport psychology. A look at several design problems provides insight into those areas that should be addressed in developing or revising measures. First, a lack of conformity across measures in the selection of modalities and dimensions to be evaluated indicates ambiguity in the definition of imagery ability. Second, variations in question styles, item numbers, and response formats highlight a need for test designers to continue to analyze existing measures when determining the question-and-response framework for new measures. (These components generally determine the time required to complete the measure and its ease of administration.) Third, reliability data appears adequate, but validity data for some of the measures is insufficient (which is of concern due to the regularity with which some of these measures are used in research). Finding a major factor that supports the rationale for and longevity of the use of these imagery-ability measures is difficult. In fact, certain tests appear sound in design but have been used minimally in research and practice, whereas other tests that lack basic psychometric properties are preferred in applied settings or investigative situations.

TESTS OF IMAGERY USE

Moran (1993) suggested that an intensive study should be undertaken of why athletes employ imagery in training and competition. These purposes could then be used to validate new tests, which should help validate the construct of imagery in sport. The examination of the use of imagery by athletes has included questionnaires, interviews, and anecdotal reports. Questionnaires have either been general in nature, asking about various psychological skills including imagery, or aimed specifically at imagery use. Mahoney and Avener (1977) surveyed elite athletes using a general questionnaire, which included material on imagery use. This led to several replication studies, such as those by

Meyers, Cooke, Cullen, and Liles (1979), Highlen and Bennett (1979), Rotella, Gansneder, Ojala, and Billing (1980), and Doyle and Landers (1980), which have been the basis for much of the research into imagery perspectives.

The Mahoney and Avener (1977) questionnaire was a general instrument that inquired about aspects of personality, self-concept, and training and competition strategies. It contained 53 items, most of which used an 11-point Likert-type scale. Participants rated such things as the frequency and type of dreams they had, their anxiety leading up to performance, attention given to various factors, their frequency of self-talk, their attributions for success and failure, and their imagery. The four imagery items probed frequency of imagery use in training and competition, difficulty in controlling imagery, imagery clarity, and perspective use. Mahoney and Avener did not provide any psychometrics of the questionnaire.

One other general approach, again by Mahoney, is the Psychological Skills Inventory for Sports (PSIS; Mahoney, Gabriel, and Perkins 1987). Mahoney et al. aimed at identifying skills that differentiate elite and non-elite athletes. The original PSIS measured five psychological skills (anxiety, concentration, self-confidence, team emphasis, and mental preparation). It consisted of 51 true-or-false items, and 5 of the mental-preparation items concerned mental imagery. Mahoney (1989) later modified the PSIS, which became known as the PSIS R-5. It consisted of 45 Likert-scale items rated from 0 ("strongly disagree") to 4 ("strongly agree"), measuring six psychological areas (anxiety control, concentration, confidence, motivation, team focus, and mental preparation).

Researchers have used the PSIS R-5 in some studies (e.g., Mahoney 1989; White 1993), but authors have questioned its use (e.g., Chartrand, Jowdy, and Danish 1992). Mahoney (1989) reported internal consistency (coefficient alpha) of $r = .64$, and split-half reliability of $r = .57$ for the whole scale, which are quite low values in psychometric terms. Validity was also a problem, because non-elite athletes sometimes scored higher than elite athletes. Chartrand et al. administered the PSIS R-5 to 340 intercollegiate athletes in various sports to assess its psychometric properties. They found that the internal consistency for each scale was low and that the mental-preparation scale, including imagery, was well below an acceptable level, with an alpha coefficient of $r = -.34$. Chartrand et al. also concluded that the mental-preparation scale is conceptually ambiguous, because some of the items correlated negatively with each other. In addition, a confirmatory factor analysis showed that the data did not fit the predicted six factors.

The Imagery Use Questionnaire (IUQ; Hall, Rodgers, and Barr 1990) is designed specifically to investigate the use of imagery by athletes. Hall and his colleagues have used the IUQ and its variations in several studies (e.g., Barr and Hall 1992; Hall et al. 1990; Rodgers, Hall, and Buckolz 1991; Weinberg, Butt, Knight, Burke, and Jackson 2003). The IUQ consists of 35 Likert-scale items ranging from 1 ("never" or "very difficult") to 7 ("always" or "very easy"). There are two yes-or-no responses. Hall (1998) reported that the IUQ has had no psychometric evaluation. Sport-specific versions of it have been developed and used in research, including the IUQ for Rowing (Barr and Hall 1992), the IUQ for Figure Skating (Rodgers et al. 1991), and a major modification, the IUQ for Soccer Players (IUQ-SP; Salmon et al. 1994). Barr and Hall (1992) reported that they formulated questions on the IUQ in part based on previous imagery-use questions asked of high-performance athletes (Mahoney and Avener 1977; Rotella et al. 1980). The IUQ for Rowing and IUQ for Figure Skating both seem to be reliable tests of imagery use with test–retest values ranging from $r = .65$ to $r = .95$ (Hall 1998). Recently, Weinberg et al. (2003) reported a high alpha reliability of $r = .90$ for a shortened version of the IUQ, which incorporated only frequency items.

Salmon et al. (1994) developed the IUQ-SP to investigate the motivational function of imagery and its actual use by soccer players. The IUQ-SP has four sections covering demographic details, general imagery use, motivational and cognitive functions of imagery based on Paivio's (1985) model, and auditory imagery. The functions section classified four types of imagery based on image content: cognitive general (CG), cognitive specific (CS), motivational general (MG), and motivational specific (MS). Salmon et al. reported internal consistency, assessed by alpha coefficients, of .75 for CG, .85 for CS, .82 for MS, and .76 for MG. Using a corrected-item total correlation (CIT) minimum of .4, only 2 of 34 coefficients failed. Additionally, the data fit the model using a principal-components exploratory factor analysis (assuming four factors and using varimax rotation).

The IUQ-SP was soccer specific, so Hall, Mack, Paivio, and Hausenblas (1998) developed the Sport Imagery Questionnaire (SIQ) as a more general instrument to examine the cognitive and motivational functions of imagery (see figure 4.2). The result is an instrument with five subscales: CS, CG, MS, MG-A (MG-arousal), and MG-M (MG-mastery). (Details about the functional basis of each subscale are in chapter 2.) Hall et al. (1998) reported that internal consistencies for each subscale were acceptable, with alpha coefficients greater than .7 for all subscales and all items loaded on their appropriate factor (criterion level > .40). Munroe, Hall, Simms, and Weinberg (1998) confirmed the structure of the SIQ, finding adequate internal consistency (Cronbach's alpha coefficients ranged from .68 to .87) and interscale correlations ranging between .28 and .73. Abma et al. (2002) found internal consistencies similar to the original SIQ development study (Martens), with values ranging from .68 (MG-A) to .90 (MS).

Rarely   Often

   1   2   3   4   5   6   7

1. I make up new strategies in my head. _____

2. I image the atmosphere of winning a championship (e.g., the excitement that follows a win). _____

3. I image giving 100% during an event or game. _____

4. I can re-create in my head the emotions I feel before I compete. _____

5. I image alternative strategies in case my event or game plan fails. _____

6. I image myself handling the stress and excitement of competitions and remaining calm. _____

7. I image other athletes congratulating me on a good performance. _____

8. I can consistently control the image of physical skill. _____

Figure 4.2 Sample of items and response scale from the SIQ.

Construct validity has been partially established through the generation of both predictive and criterion evidence. First, Hall et al. (1998) used regression analyses to determine which function of imagery use predicted performance at three levels of competition (high school, varsity, national) for a sample of 217 male and female athletes. Their results indicated that the cognitive functions of imagery were more likely to predict the performance of lower-level athletes. In contrast, the motivational functions of imagery predicted the performance of athletes who competed at higher levels. Second, Weinberg et al. (2003) reported a greater motivational function of imagery for individual athletes when compared with team athletes. Sport confidence was used as a discriminating criterion, and differences were found in all five subscales between high- and low-sport-confident athletes (Abma et al. 2002). A recent confirmatory factor analysis did not support the 30-item, 5-factor model (Watt, Spittle, Jaakkola, and Morris 2003). The SIQ is used regularly in research and applied areas; however, this examination of its factor structure suggests that minor modifications are required. After it is revised, further psychometric evaluation should fully establish the Hall et al. (1998) conceptualization of the cognitive and motivational functions of imagery use.

PSYCHOMETRIC ISSUES

Within the field of sport psychology, the problems related to imagery-ability and imagery-use assessment are similar to those experienced in all areas of psychology when examining social-psychological variables. Gauvin and Russell (1993) stated,

> Despite the considerable effort that has been directed toward test and scale development and recent attempts to provide instrumentation guidelines, many researchers are still grappling with the often difficult task of achieving reliable and valid measurement in sport and exercise settings. (p. 891)

This situation appears to exist due to a lack of continuous reevaluation of test instruments (Gauvin and Russell 1993) and because, quite often, the statistical methods used to show evidence of reliability and validity are poor (Schutz and Gessoroli 1993). The primary outcome of these measurement-based problems is the limited development of useful measures to evaluate imagery-related phenomena. Such minimal progress also inhibits the substantiation and expansion of current theoretical perspectives of imagery functioning (Mahoney and Epstein 1981; Murphy and Martin 2002).

Several of the important psychometric issues concerning imagery-ability and imagery-use assessment are the substantiation of reliability and the presentation of evidence to support the construct validity of existing measures and those under development. This section summarizes the procedural characteristics and reporting of these essential measurement characteristics, in relation to imagery tests.

RELIABILITY

Generally, the tests outlined previously have provided appropriate initial reliability data. For the more established measures, consistent replication of relevant reliability data has been a vital component of ongoing psychometric evaluations (e.g., McKelvie 1994; Richardson 1994). Evidence of reliability has normally been presented as one or more of test–retest, parallel or alternative forms, split-half, Kuder-Richardson-20, or Cronbach's alpha coefficients. In the majority of reported cases, the data appears satisfactory, equaling or exceeding a minimum criterion level of $r = .7$ as suggested by experts in psychometrics, such as Kerlinger (1986) and Nunnally (1978). McKelvie (1994) suggested that evaluating the evidence of reliability in relation to test–retest coefficients for imagery measures may necessitate a less stringent application of this value, depending on interval period and the type of measure. Schutz (1998) noted that the use of the parallel-forms methodology has been limited in psychology research because of the difficulty in constructing suitable matching measures. As a result, researchers have relied on the test–retest and internal-consistency methods in determining a measure's reliability. Sheehan et al. (1983) concluded that "studies on the reliability of the imagery-ability measures . . . continue to reveal that self-report inventories are reliable and stable in the scores they yield within subjects and on the same subjects who are retested" (p. 204).

Item analysis is a statistical procedure used to understand why a particular measure displays a specific level of reliability (Murphy and Davidshofer 1994). The primary value of item analysis centers on maximizing the measurement characteristics of a test by identifying and eliminating items that do not adequately assess the variable under investigation (Murphy and Davidshofer 1994). Tenenbaum and Fogarty (1998) have described the two most common scale-item analysis procedures used in developing measures in sport psychology. One, the corrected-item–total correlation, provides information about the relationship between a single item and the total scale score; another, the "alpha if item deleted" statistic, indicates an item's contribution to the overall internal consistency of the scale. Unfortunately, attempts to gather information relating to item analyses of existing imagery-ability measures proved difficult. Of the measures reviewed previously, only one discussed how this procedure was undertaken in the development of the test or questionnaire. The developers of the MIQ, Hall et al. (1985), provided a useful description of the item-analysis procedures incorporated in the initial phase of test construction, which resulted in a reduction in the number of items from 28 to 18. Future measures of imagery ability must be scrutinized at the individual-item level and the results suitably described and reported.

An additional psychometric property closely related to item analysis is item variability, or skewness. Previous research has shown that imagery-ability measures have tended to be skewed toward the upper end of the response scale (Hiscock 1978; Kihlstrom et al. 1991; Sheehan 1967a). Kihlstrom et al. (1991) surmised that the majority of questionnaire respondents are "claiming to experience at least moderately vivid images, and vanishingly few subjects reporting no imagery at all" (p. 134). Sheehan (1967a) reported a similar finding during his initial investigations of the SQMI and concluded that relatively few individuals lack the capacity to generate the images contained within imagery-ability measures. More specifically, findings have highlighted the substantial negative skew for individual items with respect to dimension (e.g., vividness and control), and a contrasting directional distribution in the analysis of individual modality. Item scores for both the VMIQ and the MIQ typically are negatively skewed. Hall and Martin (1997) reported a mean score for the visual subscale items of the MIQ of 2.07, equating to an approximate scale response of "easy to see." Eton et al. (1998) found that on a 5-point scale, varsity athletes had a mean item score for the VMIQ of 2.04 ("clear and reasonably vivid"). Nonathletes registered a mean item score of 2.39, which falls between the response-scale anchors of "clear and reasonably vivid" and "moderately clear and vivid." These findings suggest that practitioners using these tests should carefully consider how items are devised in order to ensure the most appropriate distribution of item scores.

Analysis of an imagery measure's reliability is a fundamental component of its development. The procedures relating to item analysis, collection of reliability data, and review of item-score distribution should follow accepted psychometric methodologies. Only when researchers can demonstrate the reliability of imagery-ability and imagery-use measures will it be appropriate to draw conclusions based on the evidence they generate.

VALIDITY

The complexities surrounding the issue of test validity are interrelated with the primary difficulties of all psychological measurement: assessing that a test measures what it purports to measure and determining whether the data derived from the measure are useful in making decisions concerning the construct of interest (Murphy and Davidshofer 1994). Kaplan and Saccuzzo (1997) have provided a simple definition of validity that highlights the relationship of measurement and meaning. They stated that "validity can be defined as the agreement between a test score or measure and the quality it is believed to measure" (p. 131).

In examining validation strategies and procedures, several authors of books relating to psychological assessment have referred to a 1985 text, Standards for Educational and Psychological Testing, published by a joint committee of the American Education Research Association, the American Psychological Association, and the National Council on Measurement in Education (Anastasi and Urbina 1997; Kaplan and Saccuzzo 1997; Murphy and Davidshofer 1994). The committee's findings in relation to a definition of validity were summarized by Kaplan and Saccuzzo (1997), who described validity as inferential evidence of test scores made up of three types of evidence: content related, criterion related, and construct related.

All of the authors referred to in the previous paragraph made particular reference to the specific nature of construct validity. They drew similar conclusions, inferring that construct validation is a procedure that includes all other types of validation activities. Each piece of evidence gathered in the development and analysis of a measure contributes to the establishment of construct validity. Most recently, Marsh (1998) has described a construct validation approach with respect to measurement in sport and exercise psychology that is based on the concept that theory, measurement, empirical research, and practice interact in such a manner that ignoring one component will affect the accuracy of evidence derived from another. Marsh (1998) defined the ideal validation process as one:

> in which theory and practice are used to develop a measure,
> empirical research is used to test the theory and the measure,

both the theory and the measure are revised in relation to research, new research is conducted to test these refinements, and theory and research are used to inform practice. (p. xvi)

As detailed earlier, establishing the construct validity of psychological measures involves assembling evidence that adequately defines the meaning of the test or instrument (Kaplan and Saccuzzo 1997). The accumulation of this evidence necessitates applying a range of statistical and experimental methodologies. Murphy and Davidshofer (1994) outlined three procedures, beyond those related to reliability and content validity, that appear most appropriate in considering the construct validation of imagery-ability measures. The first method is to show the relationship between the test of interest and other tests or behavioral measures. Marsh (1998), describing an important feature of this process, stated that "two measures of the same construct should be substantially correlated with each other (evidence for convergent validity) and less correlated with measures of different constructs (evidence for divergent validity)" (p. xvii). Typically, procedures involve comparing measurement approaches, such as self-report questionnaires and opinion surveys, or correlating scale scores derived from subjective and objective tests of the construct. The results of different techniques of data collection, such as quantitative and qualitative procedures, also warrant comparison (Marsh 1998).

The second procedure, factor analysis, provides an important insight into the construct characteristics represented in the responses to a given measure. Murphy and Davidshofer (1994) outlined that this procedure involves analyzing test scores to determine the relationship between derived or predicted factors and the items or subscales of an assessment device. The goal is to show that the resultant or a priori factors accurately represent the construct of interest.

The final methodology used in establishing an instrument's construct validity involves experimental manipulation of the selected construct and interpreting responses to the measure in relation to the manipulation (Murphy and Davidshofer 1994). For example, if previous research and theory suggests that a certain intervention will result in specific changes in participants' responses or behaviors, the extent to which the measure can substantiate the predicted changes provides evidence for its construct validity.

Evidence Related to the Construct Validation of Imagery Measurement

Substantial research has provided evidence relevant to the construct validity of existing measures of imagery. This section overviews studies that have examined (a) the relationship between imagery measures (e.g., subjective and objective) and between them and other psychological and psychophysiological variables, (b) their factor structure, and (c) experimental manipulations designed to assess specific psychometric characteristics. (Research examined in relation to experimental investigations is covered in chapter 5.) This section highlights the psychometric characteristics, qualities, and weaknesses of certain measures as evidence that sport-oriented imagery measures are the most appropriate imagery-assessment tools in sport psychology research and practice.

RELATIONSHIP BETWEEN IMAGERY-ABILITY MEASURES

The examination of intertest correlations between imagery measures is primarily undertaken to gather convergent and discriminant evidence as part of the construct validation process. Analyzing the relationships between the tests as complete measures or subscales typically generates this data. Several reviewers have provided critical analysis of a substantial portion of the existing research on comparisons of imagery measures (Ernest 1977; Hall 1998; Lequerica et al. 2002; Moran 1993; Richardson 1994; Sheehan et al. 1983; Watt 2003; White et al. 1977). These authors presented summaries of the evidence relating to the assessment of imagery ability and imagery use, with respect to the uniqueness of characteristics, dimensions and modalities examined, and the nature of imagery as measured by self-report and objective tests.

GENERAL SUBJECTIVE MEASURES

The most detailed of these reviews, by Richardson (1994), summarized 25 studies that correlated two or more of seven imagery measures that assessed one or more of the dimensions of vividness, controllability, or preference. The relationships of primary interest to the field are those involving the SQMI, GTVIC, and VVIQ. Mixed-gender samples ranged in participant number from 18 to 208, and the reported correlations between the measures varied from $r = -.06$ to $r = .81$. The mean correlation between the SQMI and VVIQ was $r = .48$, between the SQMI and GTVIC was $r = .36$, and between the GTVIC and the VVIQ was $r = .37$. These findings indicated that measures of vividness have shown larger correlations with each other than the moderate relationships reported between measures of vividness and control. Evidence such as this suggests that support, although limited, exists for the independence of the two dimensions. Other researchers have also drawn this type of conclusion (Ernest 1977; White et al. 1977; Wolmer, Laor, and Toren 1999). Following his review of mental-imagery measures used with athletes, Moran (1993) questioned their purity on the basis of similar correlation values and stated that "the imagery dimensions of vividness and controllability are neither conceptually nor empirically distinguishable" (p. 161).

OBJECTIVE MEASURES

Resolving the confusion in interpreting the relationship between subjective self-report measures and objective imagery-ability tests has been important in several correlational studies and research reviews (Dean and Morris 2003; Di Vesta, Ingersoll, and Sunshine 1971; Ernest 1977; Hiscock 1978; Lequerica et al. 2002; Lorenz and Neisser 1985; Richardson 1977). As mentioned previously, objective measures often include subtests of spatial relations or visualization, derived from measures such as the Differential Aptitude Test (DAT; Bennett, Seashore, and Wesman 1966) and the Minnesota Paper Form Board Test (MPFB; Likert and Quasha 1970). The information generated through this type of research provides a broader base for understanding assessment of the imagery construct. Specific multiple-test studies that analyze the relationships between imagery constructs must ensure that the findings are examined as outlined by Sheehan et al. (1983), who stated that "the data need to define for us not only the relationship among the various measures, but how the measures converge (or diverge) with respect to the underlying process that is being assumed" (p. 193).

The general findings from administering a battery of imagery measures is that subjective and objective measures correlate significantly among themselves (Hiscock 1978; Lequerica et al. 2002; Lorenz and Neisser 1985; Richardson 1977), but the two test types tend to be weakly intercorrelated (Dean and Morris 2003; Katz 1983; Morris and Hampson 1983). Interestingly, Sheenan at al. (1983) suggested that objective measures provide an adjunct data set that supplements responses from subjective measures. Hiscock (1978) reported correlational data for a mixed-gender sample of 79 psychology undergraduates that showed that the SQMI (visual) and GTVIC are not strongly associated with the MPFB ($r = -.09$ and $-.06$). Recently, Lequerica et al. (2002) analyzed the degree of association of the MRT with the GTVIC, VMIQ, MIQ-visual, and MIQ-kinesthetic. For a sample of 80 university participants, insignificant correlations of the self-report measures with the MRT of $r = .02$, -15, $-.16$, and $-.07$, respectively, were found.

The evidence presented in the previous paragraph helps substantiate the argument that subjective and objective imagery-ability tests are unrelated (Hall 1998; Moran 1993). Each type of instrument either measures a different construct or assesses orthogonal aspects of imagery ability (Katz 1983; Morris and Hampson 1983). Various researchers have suggested possibilities about the basis of this ambiguous relationship. First, Katz (1983) described neurological evidence that indicates that the measures operationalize different parts of the brain. Second, Morris and Hampson (1983) and Moran (1993) presented similar frameworks that purport that self-report measures are related to generation or representation abilities, whereas objective tests assess transformation or processing skills.

More recently, Dean and Morris (2003) analyzed the relationship between the VVIQ and the MRT and reported a very low correlation of $r = -.04$. In the next phase of the study the authors created their own self-report measure in which the stimuli for the dimensional ratings (e.g., vividness, clarity, ease) were diagrams used in the MRT. Interestingly, more than half of the correlations were found to be significant and ranged from $r = -.01$ to .37. The researchers suggested that the content of imagery measures plays a critical role in determining the level of association between tests of differing imagery constructs. As yet, no definitive conclusion can be drawn about the nature of the difference between subjective and objective measures; therefore, the relationship warrants investigation in future assessments of sport-related imagery attributes.

MOVEMENT-BASED AND SPORT-ORIENTED MEASURES

Over the last decade, tests designed to assess movement-based and sport-oriented imagery abilities have undergone the same kinds of convergent and discriminant evaluations as the more general imagery-ability instruments have (Eton et al. 1998; Lequerica et al. 2002; Isaac and Marks 1994; Watt and Morris 2000). Although certain similarities have been acknowledged between movement imagery and imaging in a sport context, not all the developers of measures with a specific sport-based orientation have presented validity evidence related to the associations between their measures and other imagery- and nonimagery-based variables.

Several documented studies report correlational data for the VMIQ and other measures of imagery ability (e.g., Campos and Perez 1988; Isaac et al. 1986). The initial development study of the VMIQ, using a sample of 170 university and 50 high school physical education students, detailed a large correlation with the VVIQ ($r = .81$) as evidence of convergent validity (Isaac et al. 1986). Perry and Morris (1995) suggested that this high level of shared variance could be due in part to a similarity in format and response methodology.

In subsequent studies investigating the relationship between the VMIQ and the VVIQ, Isaac and Marks (1994) found that for a sample of 547 participants ranging in age from 7 to 78 years, the correlation was substantially lower ($r = .35$) than the value reported by Isaac et al. (1986). The most recent study involved a group of 125 university students of varying degrees of athletic ability. Eton et al. (1998) found a correlation of $r = .60$ between the two vividness measures. These relationship variations suggest that variables such as age and athletic ability may influence the response patterns. Additionally, sample-size differences could also affect the value of the measure relationships.

Campos and Perez (1988) compared the VMIQ with imagery measures other than the VVIQ: the Individual Differences Questionnaire (IDQ; Paivio 1971) and the Mental Imagery Questionnaire (MEIQ; Farthing,

Venturino, and Brown 1983). The IDQ is an 86-item true-false measure designed to assess visual imaginal and verbal thinking habits and skills. The MEIQ is a 20-item, 2-part test that examines the dimensions of vividness, ease, and absorption related to visual experiences and personal behavior. The relationships of key interest were between the VMIQ and (a) the imagery subscale of the IDQ, $r = -.34$, and (b) the vividness dimension, $r = -.51$, and (c) the ease dimension, $r = .43$, for the visual scenes of the MEIQ. Lequerica et al. (2002) reported correlations between the GTVIC and the VMIQ of $r = .72$ for the visual subscale and $r = .29$ for the kinesthetic subscale. The high value for the visual subscale may suggest a link between the measures on the basis of the visual modality and the perception that the VMIQ, although described as a vividness measure, may also evaluate control. These data in general, and in conjunction with the VVIQ evidence, contribute to the proposition that the VMIQ assesses a different attribute of imagery, movement imagery,than the more general types of measures (Campos and Perez 1988; Isaac et al. 1986). The degree of variation in the correlations between the VMIQ and the VVIQ, the fact that the original intertest correlation of $r = .81$ is higher than the test–retest correlation of $r = .76$ (Isaac et al. 1986), and the strong association with the GTVIC (Lequerica et al. 2002) highlight evidence that contradicts the measure's validity as a pure indicator of vividness of movement-imagery ability (Perry and Morris 1995; Richardson 1994).

The second measure of movement-imagery ability mentioned, the MIQ, also suffers from insufficient intertest correlational evidence (Moran 1993). Data describing the relationship between the MIQ and other imagery-ability measures was not included in the original development report (Hall et al. 1985), and was only recently generated with the revision of the questionnaire (Hall and Martin 1997). Correlating material was not presented in two multiple-test examinations of athletes' imagery abilities that included the MIQ as one of the measures (Jopson et al. 1989; Young-Overby 1990). This type of data, if made available, would significantly contribute to understanding the MIQ's function as an imagery measure in assessing movement- or sport-related imaging (Murphy and Jowdy 1992).

Correlational data presented by Hall et al. (1985) for a sample of 80 university physical education students showed that the visual and kinesthetic subscales ($r = .58$) assessed related but separate aspects of movement imagery. More recently, Hall and Martin (1997) examined the relationship between the MIQ and the VVIQ and VMIQ for a sample of 44 physical education students. The correlations between the measures were $r = .58$ and $r = .54$, respectively. Separate correlations for the VMIQ and the visual and kinesthetic MIQ subscales, $r = .65$ and $r = .49$, were reported. Hall and Martin stated that "the kinesthetic subscale of the MIQ is tapping a component of imagery that the VMIQ does not capture"

(p. 146). Also, the large correlation of $r = .78$ found between the VMIQ and the VVIQ, similar to that presented by Isaac et al. (1986), suggests that the VMIQ is substantially more oriented to examining visual rather than kinesthetic imagery. Unfortunately, the authors did not present correlations between the VVIQ and either the MIQ or its subscales, or the correlation between the MIQ subscales. The inconsistency in the presentation of correlations between the MIQ and other general subjective or objective imagery-ability measures must be addressed in considering the validity of this well-designed and highly reliable instrument.

Lequerica et al. (2002) recently presented correlations between the visual and kinesthetic subscales of the MIQ-R and the VMIQ. Similar subscales showed a moderate level of association, $r = .52$ for the visual and $r = .56$ for the kinesthetic. The confusing issue here, however, is the level of association between dissimilar modalities, which for the two combinations of visual and kinesthetic subscales were $r = .47$ and $r = .31$, values not substantially smaller than the similar correlations. Again, this finding suggests that ongoing work is needed to facilitate the independence of attributes assessed within movement-imagery measures.

Scores from two well-known sport psychology measures, the State Sport Confidence Inventory (SSCI; Vealey 1986) and the Competitive State Anxiety Inventory-2 (CSAI-2; Martens, Burton, Vealey, Bump, and Smith 1990), have been compared with scores from both subscales of the MIQ. Moritz et al. (1996) reported, for a sample of 57 elite roller skaters, small significant correlations between the SSCI and the kinesthetic ($r = .34$) and visual ($r = .35$) subscales of the MIQ-R. Moritz et al. noted that the high-sport-confident athletes reported higher movement-imagery scores and inferred a potential mediating effect of these abilities on sport confidence. More recently, Abma et al. (2002) also reported only small correlations of $r = .20$ for both subscales of the MIQ-R and an alternative sport-confidence measure, the Trait Sport Confidence Inventory (TSCI; Vealey 1986).

Another similar study, conducted by Vadocz, Hall, and Moritz (1997), investigated the interaction of competitive anxiety (CSAI-2) and imagery ability. It was found, for the same sample, that visual-imagery ability was significantly correlated with both cognitive anxiety ($r = -.29$) and somatic anxiety ($r = .27$), but kinesthetic-imagery ability was correlated with the anxiety variables at a near-0 level. Vadocz et al. proposed that visual-imagery ability may assist the athlete to control the visual content of images in a manner that regulates anxiety levels. This is possible with respect to cognitive anxiety, where the negative correlation indicated that stronger visual-movement imagery was related to lower state anxiety. However, the positive correlation of somatic anxiety and visual-imagery ability and the very small correlations found for kinesthetic-imagery ability suggest that the association of anxiety variables and imaging abilities is unclear. Generally, the minimal size of the relationships examined between either psychological variable and subscales of the MIQ-R, and the authors' limited discussion of these interactions, support the arguments that movement-imagery ability is relatively independent of other assessable sport-related psychological characteristics.

Watt and Morris (2000) reported on a study to determine the convergent and discriminant characteristics of the revised SIAM. Convergent and discriminant validity evidence was examined by comparing the SIAM with tests examining (a) self-reported general imagery, including vividness and control, (b) movement imagery, (c) objective imagery ability, and (d) nonimagery cognitive functioning. Individual SIAM subscale scores were correlated with subscale and total scores of the following measures: Shortened Form of the Questionnaire on Mental Imagery (SQMI), Vividness of Movement Imagery Questionnaire-II (VMIQ), Gordon Test of Visual Imagery Control (GTVIC), and Multidimensional Aptitude Battery (MAB—Spatial Ability and Verbal Comprehension). A group of 466 participants recruited from high schools, university physical education courses, and elite sport groups completed the six measures over two sessions. Small to moderate correlations (.27 to .48) were found between the SIAM control, vividness, visual, and kinesthetic subscales and some of the related dimension and modality variables of the other imagery measures, which supports the convergent validity of these SIAM subscales. Very low to small correlations (.01 to .20) were typically reported between the SIAM subscales and (a) the cognitive ability measures and (b) unrelated dimension and modality variables of the other imagery measures, which supports the discriminant validity of the SIAM. In spite of the small correlations found between SIAM subscales and other imagery measures, the findings were generally representative of the predicted pattern of relationships and typical associations reported in relation to the other measures. It is difficult to generate clear support of the independence of modalities and dimensions examined in these types of multimodal, multidimensional imagery questionnaires.

MEASURES OF IMAGERY USE

Substantially fewer investigations have examined the relationships between nonimagery variables and imagery-use (as opposed to imagery-ability) measures. Although various versions of the IUQ were used in research in conjunction with other psychological measures, no association data was reported (e.g., Rodgers et al. 1991; Weinberg et al. 2003). This lack of comparative evidence and other critical psychometric data may account for the decline in use of the questionnaire.

Fortunately, several studies have examined both the within-scale relationships of the SIQ and the level of subscale associations with other imagery measures and nonimagery psychological attributes. Abma et al.

(2002) reported that significant correlations between the motivation and cognitive subscales of the SIQ ranged from $r = .51$ (CS and MS) to $r = .78$ (MG-M and CG). In an earlier study, Vadocz et al. (1997) found smaller subscale correlations ranging from $r = .33$ (CG and MS) to $r = .63$ (CS and CG). Using a modified version of the SIQ (17 items instead of 30), Beauchamp, Bray, and Albinson (2002) reported smaller values for the subscale relationships: $r = .17$ (CG and MS) to $r = .56$ (MS and MG-A). These findings highlight inconsistency in the pattern of subscale relationships. Consequently, as with the assessment of imagery attributes in general, creating relatively independent attributes that operate effectively as distinct subscales remains a challenge for test developers.

The SIQ has also been analyzed in terms of its relationships with the MIQ-R and other popular sport psychology questionnaires. In another component of the Abma et al. (2002) study, the authors found that the correlations were higher between the SIQ subscales and the TSCI, a measure of trait sport confidence ($r = .31$ to $.59$), than those reported for the SIQ subscales and the MIQ-R subscales ($r = -.05$ to $.33$). Vadocz et al. (1996) found a similar pattern of relationships with the SIQ and the MIQ-R and CSAI (a measure of sport anxiety), where no clear distinction in the SIQ correlation values indicated convergence between the imagery measures and divergence with the anxiety measure. Overall, information derived from examining these results suggests that further work is required to gain a clearer understanding of the relationship of imagery use and imagery ability, as well as how these imagery attributes are different from other psychological variables often examined in the context of athletic performance.

A primary goal in the use and development of imagery measures should be to present convergent and divergent evidence that supports their validity. The research examined in this section demonstrated the independence of the imagery-ability tests from other psychological variables, but it did not present strong evidence for the validation of imagery-use measures. In addition to highlighting the uniqueness of a score from a given imagery measure, researchers must endeavor to provide information about the possible links between nonimagery cognitive processes and the ability to generate and use images. More specifically, investigations within sport psychology require psychometrically sound, sport-oriented measures of imagery that can facilitate the generation of accurate evidence regarding the relationships between various cognitive operations.

FACTOR STRUCTURE

A critical procedure in generating psychometric evidence for the validation of any measure is examining its factor structure. Many imagery-ability questionnaires have been factor analyzed with the primary goal of defining a factor structure that supports the researcher's proposed theoretical framework. Researchers examining those measures that assess only one or two modalities or dimensions, such as the VVIQ, VMIQ, and MIQ, have reported factor-analysis results that clearly support their original design (Atienza et al. 1994; Campos and Perez 1990). Unfortunately, researchers who analyze measures that attempt to assess a larger number of dimensions or modalities have been unable to consistently support a multidimensional or multimodal factor structure (Lane 1977; Switras 1978; White, Ashton, and Law 1974). In addition, investigators who have examined the factor structure of imagery measures given as part of a multiple test battery have reported results that highlight both a single, general imagery-ability factor and an associated multiple-modality or dimensional factor structure (Hiscock 1978; Kihlstrom et al. 1991; Richardson 1994). As yet, only limited work has examined the factor structure of existing measures of imagery use, such as the SIQ.

The primary focus of several factorial studies was the examination of the construct structure of well-established, single-dimension, single-modality imagery-ability measures. Factor analyses demonstrated that all items of the VVIQ load on a single vividness factor (Dowling 1973; Marks 1973), and that the similarly designed items of the VMIQ also represent a simple unitary structure (Campos and Perez 1990). Isaac et al. (1986) reported the correlation between the two measures as $r = .81$. These results indicated that very little distinguishes the items that represent movement or visual imagery within these measures. Analysis of the factor structure of the GTVIC has resulted in four distinct factors being clearly interpretable (White and Ashton 1977). In their original analysis of the GTVIC, using a large sample of 1,562 psychology students, Ashton and White (1974) reported finding three factors but considered their interpretation, in relation to loadings of test items, to be impossible. Two methodological inadequacies, a conservative factor-extraction procedure and the use of orthogonal rotation, were considered the cause of a lack of clarity in the factor structure in this analysis. White and Ashton (1977) reanalyzed the original data using a new sample of 532 students, oblique rotation, and factor extraction that produced four factors: movement, misfortune, color, and stationary image. The authors' recommendations centered around further examining the uniqueness of these four factors and increasing the number of items representing each factor construct.

Imagery-ability measures constructed to assess multiple modalities have been factor analyzed with mixed results. Depending on which factor-analysis procedures were used to examine the SQMI, White et al. (1974) reported that, for the original larger sample in the Ashton and White (1974) GTVIC study, a general imagery factor was revealed by using principal-components extraction before rotation. Following orthogonal and oblique rotations, seven specific sensory factors were found, and after a second-order analysis of the oblique factor pattern, a general imagery factor was revealed once again. A second bipolar factor also resulted from the latter analysis, which accounted for 9% of the variance and had positive loadings on the two mechanical senses of touch and kinesthesis, and negative loadings for the chemically sensitive modalities of smell and taste. In a later study, White, Ashton, and Law (1978) modified the SQMI's format, with the restriction that no items of the same modality should follow each other. An oblique factor analysis undertaken on this data produced a 5-factor structure with items related to the specific senses loading in the following arrangement: smell and taste on factor 1, kinesthesis on factor 2, vision on factor 3, organic on factor 4, and hearing and touch on factor 5. The authors believed that randomizing the SQMI might produce a more accurate representation of factor structure than the earlier version of the SQMI did. Following a principal-components analysis with orthogonal rotation on SQMI data from 2,083 psychology students, Kihlstrom et al. (1991) reported that the seven senses examined existed as distinct factors. Atienza et al. (1994) examined the factor structure of the MIQ using the maximum-likelihood method with oblique rotation. Results supported a visual and kinesthetic two-factorial structure. The authors concluded that these findings supported the usefulness of the MIQ as a measure of the vividness of movement imagery, yet individual items require participants to report on the ease or difficulty of their imaging and not its clarity.

Richardson (1994) constructed a correlation matrix between seven imagery self-report questionnaires, based on the data collected in 24 smaller studies involving the intercorrelation of imagery test scores. The resultant 7×7 matrix was analyzed using both principal-components analysis and principal-axis extraction with orthogonal and oblique rotations. Richardson found that both the VVIQ and SQMI loaded highly on the first of three factors revealed, using principal-components analysis. He labeled this factor "vividness." Under all analysis methods, the VVIQ, SQMI, and GTVIC loaded on the third factor reported, subsequently defined as controllability. Again, this evidence from the evaluation of the factor structure of existing imagery measures makes it difficult to support the proposal that vividness and control are two conceptually distinct imagery dimensions (Richardson 1994).

The typical factor-structure analyses of imagery-ability measures have relied on exploratory methods. Studies pertaining to the use of more rigorous statistical techniques, such as structural-equation modeling, specifically confirmatory factor analysis (CFA), appear infrequently in the imagery research literature. Few published investigations have discussed the factor structure of an imagery-ability measure on the basis of an a priori interpretation of its dimensional or modal content. Babin and Burns (1998) detailed the confirmatory factor analysis of an untitled 14-item scale designed to measure communication-evoked mental imagery. The term "communication-evoked mental imagery" is derived from consumer and marketing studies in which imagery is associated with the degree and character of "mental imagery triggered by particular advertising stimulus" (Babin and Burns 1998, 262). They proposed, following a principal-components analysis and subsequent reduction of a larger item pool, the a priori existence of three dimensions: vividness (eight items), quantity (three items), and elaboration (three items). Specific details of the 3-factor model-testing procedure reported for a sample of 251 students included the following fit index values: comparative fit index of .91, a root-mean-squared error of approximation of .09, and a nonnormed fit index of .91. Internal consistency estimates for vividness, quantity, and elaboration were $r = .94$, $r = .87$, and $r = .79$, respectively.

This factor structure and reliability data support an imagery-ability conceptualization that provides a psychometrically adequate basis for the ongoing investigation of this cognitive process. Minor modification of the measure could enable its use in a wide variety of contexts within which these dimension types (e.g., vividness, elaboration) are believed to operate. The test developers noted that the scale would benefit from additional revision, specifically suggesting that factors based on only three items may be unstable or of limited reliability in model testing. In the overall context of analyzing the factor structure of imagery abilities, Babin and Burns' research provides an excellent example of best-practice procedures that warrant adoption in the development and revision of tests in this area.

Examination of the factor structure of sport-imagery measures using the CFA procedure has been observed only minimally in sport psychology research. Recently, Watt and Morris and colleagues (Watt et al. 2001; Watt, Spittle, Jakkola, and Morris 2003) have evaluated the factor structure of both the SIAM and the SIQ. Several multimodal, multidimensional factor models of the SIAM were examined with structural-equation modeling. A model based on individual items of the measure did not result in a good fit, so models constructed using the subscale scores as observed variables were evaluated. A two-factor model derived from earlier exploratory factor analysis (Watt and Morris 1999a) did not reflect strong indices of fit. Three alternative models representative of possible structures of sport-imagery ability were created, and analysis resulted in broadly acceptable fit data based on comparison with the fit indices suggested in recent reputable texts on multivariate analysis techniques (e.g., Pedhazur and Schmelkin 1991) and the review of recent articles related to measure development in sport psychology (e.g., Conroy, Motl, and Hall 2000). Following final evaluation of the fit data and a logical review of the model structure, it was decided that the greatest conceptual coherence as a representation of sport imagery ability was found in the 3-factor model involving (a) the auditory sense grouped with the other single-organ senses of taste and smell, (b) a visual sense and dimensions factor, and (c) a bodily feeling factor incorporating kinesthetic, tactile, and emotion scores. The SIAM model appears to demonstrate sufficiently robust levels of fit to justify its continuing development (see table 4.2).

Table 4.2 Goodness of Fit Indices for SIAM and SIQ CFA Models for Total, English-Speaking, and Finnish Samples

Model	$\chi^2/(df)$	AGFI	NFI	CFI	TLI	RMSEA	Model description
M1: SIAM	8.63	.81	.92	.92	.90	.12	3 factor— generation, feeling, and single sense
English-SIAM	5.97	.76	.89	.91	.88	.13	
Finnish-SIAM	3.60	.81	.90	.93	.91	.11	
M2: SIQ	3.30	.82	.77	.82	.81	.07	5 factor— matching subscales
English-SIQ	2.45	.77	.70	.79	.77	.07	
Finnish-SIQ	2.17	.77	.70	.81	.79	.07	

Results of a CFA pertaining to the SIQ have not provided strong support for the developers' (Hall et al. 1998) original exploratory five-factor structure. Watt et al. (2003) examined the measure's factor structure using data obtained from a sample of 275 athletes with a range of sport backgrounds. The first model evaluated, which used 30 items as observed variables and only cognitive and motivational latent factors, did not result in a good fit. The primary model of the SIQ (M2, with 30 items and 5 factors) resulted in an equivocal set of indices. Several alternative models with different items removed on the bases of high modification indices and standardized residual covariances resulted in improved fit. These analyses of factor-structure models indicate that the SIQ data is close to supporting a proposed representation of sport-imagery use. Evidence generated from examining this set of models indicates that modification of the original 30 items rather than the 5-factor structure appears to be warranted. Unfortunately, the SIQ developers have yet to present data associated with the psychometrically more rigorous examination of factor structure that is possible by using CFA methods.

CONCLUSIONS

The structural conceptualization underlying measures of imagery ability and imagery use has varied considerably. There are unimodal, unidimensional tests such as the VVIQ, VMIQ, and GTVIC; multimodal, unidimensional questionnaires such as the VMIQ-II, SQMI, and MIQ; and multiscale measures of imagery use such as the SIQ. As yet, only one psychometrically validated, multimodal, multidimensional ability measure has exhibited any significant usage beyond its developmental research: the SIAM.

In relation to imagery use, ongoing reliability and validity evidence for the SIQ is being generated to substantiate its psychometric status. Practitioners and researchers have demonstrated a preference for subjective measures over both objective and qualitative assessment techniques, although recent findings support consideration of the latter methods in the context of evaluating sport-imagery attributes (e.g., Dean and Morris 2003; Munroe et al. 2000). In addition, confusion remains about the factor structures of imagery-ability and imagery-use measures, particularly those that purport to be multiscale, multimodal, or multidimensional. Future investigations of factor structure would benefit from applying current measure-development procedures that have been proposed and applied in both general (e.g., Reise, Waller, and Comrey 2000) and sport psychology (e.g., Conroy et al. 2000).

Finally, of the preferred instruments that evaluate sport imagery, the SIQ is in regular use in both the research and applied areas; however, examination of its factor structure suggests that minor modifications are required. Once the revisions are complete, further SEM should fully validate the Hall et al. (1998) conceptualization of the cognitive and motivational functions of imagery use. As for the SIAM, its generational, feeling, and single-sense framework requires further development. In addition, the incorporation of items associated with meaning, as recently discussed by Murphy (2002), may contribute to ongoing improvements in imagery-ability conceptualizations, and as a consequence, imagery processing.

Table 4.1a Overview of Existing Imagery Measures, Part A

Scale	Modalities	Dimensions	Question style	No. of items and format
Questionnaire Upon Mental Imagery (QMI), Betts (1909)	Visual, auditory, cutaneous, kinesthetic, gustatory, olfactory, organic	Vividness	Generate common image per item	150—Likert
Shortened Questionnaire Upon Mental Imagery (SQMI), Sheehan (1967)	Visual, auditory, cutaneous, kinesthetic, gustatory, olfactory, organic	Vividness	Generate common image per item	35—Likert
Survey of Mental Imagery (SMI), Switras (1978)	Visual, auditory, olfactory, gustatory, tactile, somathetic, kinesthetic	Vividness, controllability	N/A	86—Likert
Vividness of Visual Imagery Questionnaire (VVIQ), Marks (1973)	Visual	Vividness	Generate images about 4 set scenes	16—Likert
Vividness of Movement Imagery Questionnaire (VMIQ), saac, Marks, and Russell (1986)	Visual, kinesthetic	Vividness	Generate basic movement image per item	24—Likert
Vividness of Movement Imagery Questionnaire-II (VMIQ-II), Isaac (1995)	Visual, kinesthetic	Vividness	Generate basic movement image per item	18—Likert 2—tick the box
Movement Imagery Questionnaire (MIQ), Hall and Pongrac (1983)	Visual, kinesthetic	Vividness, ease of imagining	Generate/rate a movement image after rehearsal	18—Likert

Test	Modality	Dimension	Task	Response format
Movement Imagery Questionnaire-Revised (MIQ-R), Hall and Martin (1997)	Visual, kinesthetic	Vividness, ease of imagining	Generate/rate a movement image after rehearsal	8—Likert
Gordon Test of Visual Imagery Control (GTVIC), Gordon (1949), Richardson (1969)	Visual	Controllability	Generate and manipulate set images	12—yes, no, or unsure
Individual Differences Questionnaire (IDQ), Paivio (1971)	Visual	Vividness, preference	Respond to items relating to use of imagery	86—true or false
Mental Rotations Test (MRT), Vandenberg and Kuse (1978)	Visual	Controllability	Manipulation of a criterion figure	20—choice of pictorial alternatives
Sport Imagery Questionnaire (SIQ), Vealey and Walter (1993)	Visual, auditory, kinesthetic, emotional	Vividness, controllability, perspective	Generate/rate images for 4 sport scenes	20—Likert 4—yes or no
Sport Imagery Ability Measure (SIAM), Watt and Morris (1999)	Visual, auditory, kinesthetic, tactile, olfactory, gustatory, and emotional	Vividness, controllability ease, speed, and duration	Generate/rate images for 4 sport scenes	48—visual analogue using opposing anchors
Imagery Use Questionnaire (IUQ), Hall, Rodgers, and Barr, (1990)	Visual, kinesthetic, tactile, and emotional	Vividness, controllability, ease, and perspective	Rate statements about how, when, and what imagery is used	35—Likert 2—yes or no
Sport Imagery Questionnaire (SIQ), Hall, Mack, Paivio, and Hausenblas (1998)	Visual and kinesthetic	Cognitive and motivational functions of imagery use	Rate statements about imagery types' frequency of use	30—Likert

Table 4.1b Overview of Existing Imagery Measures, Part B

Scale	Reliability	Validity	Usage	Comments
QMI	Subscale correlations: .4 to .78	Expected single general factor	General psychology before SQMI developed	Prototypical test of imagery vividness
SQMI	Internal consistency: –.95 Test–retest: –.78	Homogenous factorial structure	General and sport psychology (extensive)	Restricted by assessment of vividness dimension only
SMI	Internal consistency: –.68 to .95 Parallel form: –.91	Factor analysis. 7-factor structure	General and sport psychology (minimal)	Good basic design but minimal research usage
VVIQ	Internal consistency: .83 to .95 Test–retest: .62 to .87	Construct, predictive, and convergent. Single-dimension factor structure	General and sport psychology (extensive)	Widely used but limited by single dimension/modality format
VMIQ	Internal consistency: .96 Test–retest: .76	Convergent	Sport psychology (continued)	More appropriate for sport but limited rationale for design
VMIQ-II	None reported	None reported	Sport psychology (continued)	Development of original with emphasis on kinesthetic modality
MIQ	Internal consistency: .87 Test–retest: .83	Predictive; 2-dimension factor structure	Sport psychology (continued)	More related to motor learning than sport imagery

Measure	Reliability	Validity	Use	Description
MIQ-R	None reported	Convergent as represented by $r = .7$ (MIQ)	Sport psychology (continued)	Simplified version of original related to motor skills
IDQ	Internal consistency: .80 imagery, .83 verbal	Factor structure supports subscales	General psychology (limited)	Compares modes of cognitive processing in one measure
GTVIC	Split-half: .76; Test–retest: .84	Convergent as represented by $r = .42$ (QMI) and $r = .67$ (VVIQ)	General and sport psychology (extensive)	Widely used but restricted by assessing control in one modality
MRT	Test–retest: .7 to .83; Kuder-Richardson: .88	Convergent as represented by positive correlation with DAT-Spatial	General and sport psychology (minimal)	More a test of spatial visualization than imagery
SIQ	None reported	None reported	Sport psychology (research minimal, widely used in practice)	Basic design very good but limited psychometric evaluation
SIAM	Internal consistency: .66 to .87; Test–retest: .41 to .76	Convergent and discriminant, compared with other measures; criterion and 3-factor structure	Sport psychology (research minimal, increasing use in practice)	Most recent and psychometrically developed sport-oriented measure of imagery ability
IUQ	Test–retest: .7 to .83	None reported	Limited use in research and practice	Earliest version of a larger set of imagery-use measures
SIQ	Internal consistency: .87	Criterion and 5-factor structure	Extensive use in research and practice	Currently most advanced and well-developed measure of sport-imagery use

CHAPTER 5

IMAGERY RESEARCH

WITH CADEYRN GASKIN OF VICTORIA UNIVERSITY, MELBOURNE

Because it is one of the most common tools used by sport psychologists, imagery has been the subject of many research investigations. The foremost question that sport psychology researchers have sought to answer is "Does imagery work?" If imagery is effective, then it would be valuable to know which factors may enhance or detract from the efficacy of the process. From a practical perspective, knowing the optimal amount of imagery that is needed to bring about changes in performance would be helpful. This chapter focuses on research on these key issues only. For this reason, the chapter might appear rather brief for the main research chapter on a topic that we claim has been extensively studied in sport. This is because we have decided to report research related to other aspects of imagery in the chapters on those topics. Research on the examination of theories, the validation of measures, and the psychophysiological concomitants of injury is covered in chapters 3, 4, and 7, respectively. In addition, even though imagery perspective is a variable that affects imagery effectiveness, research on it is substantial enough to warrant separate treatment (see chapter 6). Imagery research in the contexts of injury rehabilitation and exercise is addressed in chapters 11 and 12, respectively. This chapter provides a synthesis of research that has focused on answering the key questions "Does imagery work?" and "What influences the effectiveness of imagery in sport?" before commenting on the quality of research in this field.

DOES IMAGERY WORK?

Research concerning the efficacy of imagery may be divided into its effects on performance (behavior) and psychological variables (affect, cognition, conation). This section highlights studies that have reported on imagery's efficacy in bringing about changes in behavior, thoughts, and feelings. The research on whether imagery works is summarized in table 5.1 (see page 121), which lists the design and results of studies, dividing the research by the general method or paradigm used.

IMAGERY AND PERFORMANCE

Most imagery research has concerned the effect of the cognitive rehearsal of sport skills on subsequent performance (Hall 2001). Early meta-analyses (Feltz and Landers 1983; Hinshaw 1991) concluded that mental practice was more effective than no practice for improving subsequent performance of a motor skill. In Hinshaw's meta-analysis, the overall effect size for mental practice over no practice was .68 (SD = .11).

The validity of these meta-analyses was weakened by the inclusion in them of studies on different forms of mental practice. The meta-analyses typically combined effects from studies that used various forms of mental practice (e.g., imagery, self-talk, relaxation) to arrive at one overall effect size. To illustrate this point, the development of rich images of skill execution is potentially very different from thinking through the steps needed to execute the skill or imagining a top performer executing the skill. It follows, then, that these different forms of mental practice could have dissimilar effects on performance. As discussed in chapters 2, 3, and 8, current imagery research usually involves detailed scripts that focus on achieving particular outcomes and various aids to effectiveness, such as training in imagery use and repeated rehearsal. Earlier mental-practice research was not as rigorous in this regard. Examples of imagery scripts for use in an applied context are presented in chapter 9 on pages 217, 224, and 226. Imagery scripts used in research tend to be limited by the requirement for tight control (see "An Imagery Script Used in a Specific Research Context"). Because elaborate imagery scripts involve many variables that could affect the development or enhancement of sports skills, imagery's value to skill execution remains of interest to researchers.

Imagery is not superior, however, to physical practice for increasing motor-skill performance (Hird, Landers, Thomas, and Horan 1991). The research of Hird et al. showed that physical practice was the most effective at improving performance on pegboard and pursuit rotor tasks. Combinations of physical and mental practice were progressively less effective with decreases in physical practice and increases in mental

An Imagery Script Used in a Specific Research Context

In the validation of the Sport Imagery Ability Measure (SIAM; see chapter 4), a study was conducted to examine its construct validity. State water-polo squad players were instructed to follow the instructions given in an imagery script that described a number of common water-polo situations. The script was developed in discussion with the state coach and included references to all the sense modalities and emotion. Players were instructed to talk aloud about their imagery as they performed it, a technique called concurrent verbalization. They were also encouraged to describe the quality of their imagery, such as its clarity, duration of images, and ease with which images were generated. Participants completed the SIAM on a separate occasion. The aim was to determine whether the content of the players' descriptions corresponded to their self-reported imagery-ability strengths and weaknesses, according to the SIAM. Here is the detailed imagery script.

1. Shooting Maneuver

   "You are situated at the opposition 4 m line to the left of goal and in line with the post. You tread water vigorously directly in front of your opponent, who is marking you closely. You lift up out of the water to receive a clean pass from a player to your right who was calling out to you. You swim back slightly and raise the ball out of the water above your head. The goalie looks toward you and moves into a defensive position to the left of goal. You shoot the ball powerfully over the top of your opponent to the top right corner of the goal and it smashes into the back of the net. Your teammates are pleased that your shot for goal is successful."

2. Passing Maneuver

   "You are swimming quite quickly with a big splash, the ball just in front of your face. You move from your back line to the centerline toward an opponent who is swimming rapidly in your direction. An unmarked teammate situated to your left, in a good scoring position, is calling out loudly for the ball. You manage to release a perfect straight pass and the ball lands cleanly in the outstretched right hand of your teammate, just as the opposition reaches you and forces you

   (continued)

(continued)

vigorously under the water. Your teammate then shoots for goal and scores. Teammates yell their congratulations for the successful shot."

3. Chase-and-Steal Maneuver

"An open opposition player is waving his arms and yelling for the ball to your left. He receives a wet pass just over the centerline, and then swims very quickly toward an open goal. You must change direction and start swimming as fast as you can toward this player. You chase really hard and catch up to him and prepare to tackle him. As you struggle for the ball, water splashes in your face. You are still able to legally steal the ball from directly out of his hand just as he is about to pass it off. You have successfully stopped an important opposition scoring opportunity."

4. Defensive Block Maneuver

"The opposition players are passing the ball to each other just outside the 4 m line and are preparing to shoot for goal. The scores are tied, with 60 sec to go in the game. There is a lot of noise from spectators and players in both offense and defense as they struggle for position. You see your opponent receive a beautiful backhand pass and you swim in front of her, just below the 2 m line. The player lifts herself out of the water and fakes a shot. You stay focused on her and continue to pressure her in defense. She lifts the ball out of the water again, ready to release a powerful shot. You lunge toward her and successfully block the shot. The ball bounces off your hands with a loud 'whack,' straight to one of your teammates to your left."

practice. The drawbacks of this study, however, were that different time periods were used for each task and that the two tasks were different, so it was not simply a matter of the pegboard task requiring greater cognition. For people untrained in imagery who are able to practice physically, however, it would seem unwise to replace physical practice with mental practice.

Like much imagery research, the Hird et al. (1991) study was conducted in a laboratory setting. Savoy and Beitel (1996) examined imagery in an applied setting, investigating its effect on mean foul-shot percentages during the regular season and postseason play (35 games). Although the study had methodological problems that weaken its validity, the research warrants attention because it is one of the few imagery studies to investigate imagery's efficacy in the field.

In this study, the participants were 10 players on a nationally ranked collegiate women's basketball team. An ABABAB design was used. During the first intervention (B1), participants were asked to image 20 successful basketball foul shots each night, for 20 out of 30 days, and to keep an imagery log. The number of successful shots in games increased by 18% compared with the baseline period (A1), during which the participants used only physical practice. In the second period of physical practice only, performance decreased 7.7%. The imagery program was reinstated (B2), but this time a sport psychologist conducted the imagery training for 20 min, 3 times per week. During this period (B2), the mean foul-shooting success rate fell a further 2%. Although there was no increase in performance, the intervention arguably stopped a downward trend in performance, which could have been due to increased pressure during the end of the regular season. The imagery intervention was stopped at the start of the postseason play. During the start of the postseason competition (A3), the foul-shooting success rate dropped 11%, to a level below the original baseline (A1). Contributing factors to this drop in performance were the cessation of the imagery intervention, the players' unfamiliarity with the change in competitive situation, and the absence of the sport psychologist. The imagery program was resumed (B3) with an emphasis on imaging, despite verbal distractions from opposition players. In this final period, foul-shot success increased by 10%.

Although the study lacked experimental rigor because of its design, and some of the changes in performance did not reach statistical significance because of low power, the results suggest that imagery did affect foul-shot percentages and that further research and practical application of imagery is warranted.

The study was confounded, however, because the increases in performance may have been due to the Hawthorne Effect rather than the effect of the imagery treatment. That is, the participants may have expected their performances to improve during the imagery-treatment periods, and that expectation of improvement may have been sufficient to produce changes in performance. Although Savoy and Beitel (1996) found that foul-shooting percentage was higher in the second period of no intervention (A2) than in the first period (A1), the drop in performance in the third period of no intervention (A3), below even the preintervention level, casts doubt over the imagery treatment's efficacy.

The internal validity problems associated with the single-case design, however, are insufficient reason to cease using this method in imagery research. Bryan (1987) has argued that the single-case, multiple-baseline design is particularly appropriate for the study of applied sport psychology. To be confident that an increase in performance was not due to the

Hawthorne Effect, researchers need to demonstrate a sustained increase in performance over baseline levels following the administration of an imagery intervention.

Research using a single-case, multiple-baseline design has demonstrated that imagery has enhanced performance in elite Australian Rules football (Callery and Morris 1993, 1997c), baseball (She and Morris 1997), and basketball (Shambrook and Bull 1996). In the first Callery and Morris (1993) study, imagery was used to enhance performance of the ball-disposal-by-foot skill (an important part of Australian Rules football) over most of a competitive season. The first week of the intervention was devoted to introducing imagery to each player and practicing imaging during five sessions. In subsequent weeks, each player did three 20-min imagery-rehearsal sessions per week, in which the ball-disposal-by-foot skill was imaged. Of the 10 participants, 5 demonstrated clear and sustained improvement in their disposals during matches, 3 showed a trend toward improvement, and 2 showed no change in performance. Callery and Morris reported that of the two players who did not improve, one had a recurrent injury that disrupted his performance and the other had a major slump in match performance, with the result that he rarely gained possession of the ball.

Figure 5.1 illustrates the standard way of presenting results of single-case design studies, with the data from the first study by Callery and Morris (1993). For each participant, performance is plotted week by week on an individual graph. The vertical line represents the point at which the intervention was introduced for each player. Note how some graphs peak immediately after the imagery program was introduced, then level off. It is reasonable to assume that those peaks reflect a component of the Hawthorne Effect. However, the pattern after the peak often remains relatively stable at a level above the baseline, which probably reflects a genuine effect of imagery rehearsal.

Imagery can enhance performance in both novices and experts (Blair, Hall, and Leyshon 1993). Blair et al. designed a soccer task that involved dribbling, passing, and shooting segments. The intervention involved both cognitive-specific and cognitive-general imagery and was conducted over a 6-week period, with sessions held biweekly for 15 min each time. Although no changes in performance accuracy were found, larger reductions in task completion times were recorded for the imagery participants than for the control subjects. This finding makes sense because the task was timed, so participants focused on speed rather than increasing accuracy.

Imagery may be useful for enhancing physiologic training transfer (Van Gyn, Wenger, and Gaul 1990). Van Gyn et al. tested participants' peak power on a cycle ergometer and in a 40 m sprint, then assigned them to one of four conditions: imagery training, power training, imagery-plus-power training, and a no-imagery and no-power-training control.

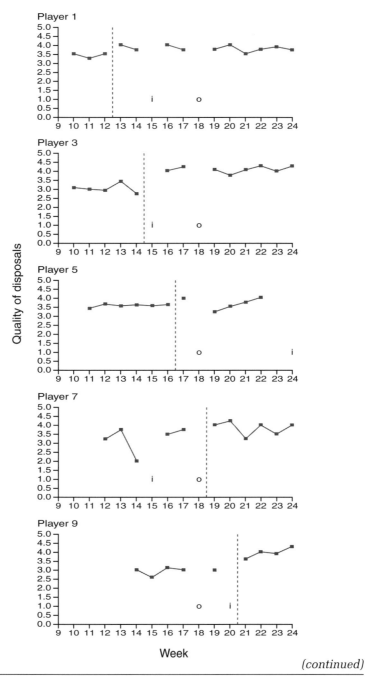

Figure 5.1 Quality of the 10 players' disposals in each week. The vertical dashed line represents the time at which the intervention was started. The letters "i" and "o" represent games missed due to injury and weeks where no games were played, respectively.

(continued)

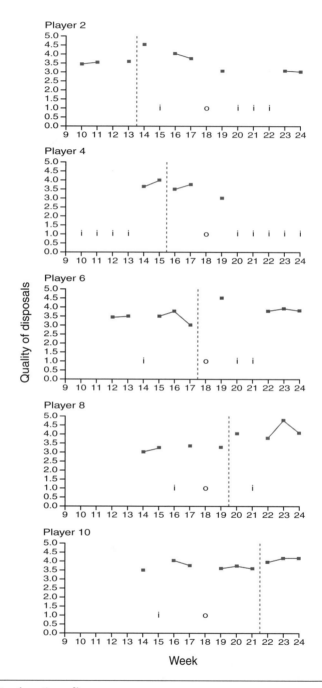

Figure 5.1 *(continued)*

Participants in the imagery conditions were instructed in the use of imagery and met with the researchers 3 times per week throughout the 6-week program, to perform cognitive-specific imagery. (They imaged performing a 40 m sprint, followed by recovery jogging.) Participants in the power-training conditions performed three sessions per week on the cycle ergometer. Both power-training groups demonstrated substantial increases in peak power on the cycle ergometer. Only participants in the imagery-plus-power-training condition, however, showed similar increases in 40 m sprint times. Participants in the imagery-only and power-training conditions showed only marginal changes in performance, suggesting that the combination of nonspecific training with performance-specific imagery can increase performance in the specific task. This finding could have useful application when physical training for a specific task is not possible (e.g., because of weather or lack of access to facilities), but it is practical to train the relevant physiological systems (for example, in the gym) and link that training to competitive performance through imagery.

Brief imagery sessions have been shown to be effective in enhancing grip strength (Elko and Ostrow 1992; Perkins, Wilson, and Kerr 2001). In the Elko and Ostrow study, participants used three mental-preparation strategies (preparatory arousal, imagery, counting backwards) before gripping a hand dynamometer. Grip strength was greater after performing cognitive-specific imagery (i.e., visualizing themselves squeezing the hand dynamometer as hard as possible) than when participants counted backward prior to the test of grip strength. This result is in concordance with that of Murphy, Woolfolk, and Budney (1988), who found that emotive imagery (i.e., anger and fear) was ineffective in bringing about changes in grip strength. Relaxation imagery, however, reduced grip strength.

Visuomotor behavioral rehearsal (VMBR) training is a performance-enhancing program that has three components: progressive muscle relaxation, imagery practice of the sport skill, and imagery practice incorporating the context in which the skill is intended to be used (Suinn 1972a, b, 1976a, 1977). The premise behind this program is that anxiety may interfere with athletes' abilities to perform during competition. In VMBR training, imagery under normal conditions is combined with a physical-relaxation technique and the practicing of imagery under stressful conditions in an attempt to improve the quality of imagery under competitive conditions and, therefore, enhance performance.

The effectiveness of VMBR in increasing performance has been demonstrated in several sports, including karate (Seabourne, Weinberg, and Jackson 1984; Weinberg, Seabourne, and Jackson 1981, 1982), pistol marksmanship (E.G. Hall and Hardy 1991), and tennis (Noel 1980). VMBR training is also effective in reducing state anxiety (Seabourne et al. 1984). In the Seabourne et al. study, students in two university karate classes participated, with one class receiving VMBR training ($n = 18$) and the other class receiving a placebo of memorizing Chinese writings ($n = 26$). Both classes met 3 times per week for 16 weeks, and, following the initial introduction to their cognitive technique in the first session, practiced the technique with their instructor during each session as well as at home. Performance was evaluated and anxiety measured during the 5th, 10th, and 16th weeks of the classes. The results showed a greater increase in performance for the students doing VMBR training than for those receiving the placebo. State anxiety decreased over the three measurement periods for the students in the VMBR group, whereas it marginally increased for placebo recipients.

In a more recent study, Lorh and Scogin (1998) have shown that VMBR is effective when self-administered. The researchers gave half of their sample of 36 collegiate athletes a brief orientation to the VMBR package, which included a training manual, a relaxation audiotape, and a visualization videotape. The remaining participants formed the control and were given the package after the research had been completed. The self-administered training lasted 18 days, and focused on relaxation (days 1 to 5), visualization of successfully competing (days 6 to 11), and putting the skills together to enhance performance (days 12 to 18). Because the athletes were participating in a variety of sports, the performance measure was a composite score derived from their self-ratings and their coaches' or trainers' ratings of their performances. Performance was rated using five 11-point Likert-scale items. Using this performance measure, Lorh and Scogin found a much larger percentage difference between pre- and posttest performance for the athletes who used VMBR than for those athletes who were not doing the program at that stage ($d = 1.74$).

Other interesting findings from the Lorh and Scogin (1998) study relate to the athletes' perceptions of their performances and the effect of the intervention on anxiety and imagery quality. At the end of the intervention, athletes who did the VMBR program subjectively rated both their mental and actual performance higher than the athletes who formed the control ($ds = 1.46$ and 1.13, respectively), had lower competition anxiety ($d = 1.49$), and rated the quality of imagery more highly ($d = 1.33$). These findings support those in other studies (e.g., Seabourne et al. 1984) and suggest that imagery may not only have a positive direct effect on performance, it may also assist performance through a number of psychological variables. It is this relationship between imagery and psychological variables that will now be explored.

Imagery and Psychological Variables

In addition to the large amount of work that explores imagery and physical performance, researchers have examined the effect of imagery on psychological variables. This section highlights research in this area, and table 5.2 (page 125) summarizes the results of the studies that have utilized psychological variables.

Studies have shown that competitive anxiety can be manipulated through imagery in order to improve performance (Carter and Kelly 1997; Hale and Whitehouse 1998; Page, Sime, and Nordell 1999). Page et al. found that imagery was effective in changing intercollegiate female swimmers' perceptions of their competitive anxiety. The swimmers' competitive anxiety, as measured by the Competitive State Anxiety Inventory-2 (CSAI-2; Martens, Burton, Vealey, Bump, and Smith 1990), and their perception of that anxiety, as measured by the Competitive Anxiety Perception Scale (CAPS; Murray 1989), were determined prior to competition before an imagery intervention, and then again prior to competition following the intervention. The participants took part in a 30-min imagery session and were requested to practice the imagery between the session and the next competition. Although little change in cognitive anxiety and somatic anxiety was noted, positive changes occurred in the swimmers' self-confidence along with larger positive changes in their perceptions of the anxiety.

Martin and Hall (1995) demonstrated an association between imagery and motivation. These researchers conducted a study of 39 beginner golfers to investigate whether the use of mental imagery would affect intrinsic motivation to perform a golf-putting task. The participants were divided into three groups: performance plus outcome imagery, performance imagery, and a no-imagery control. In this instance, motivation was inferred from the length of time that participants voluntarily spent practicing putting and a measure of intrinsic motivation: the Task Reaction Questionnaire (TRQ; Mayo 1977). When participants were asked to achieve researcher-set goals, differences were found between groups (performance-plus-outcome imagery, performance imagery, and no imagery) in terms of the time voluntarily spent practicing. The performance-imagery participants, who focused on how they performed the skill, practiced longer than the other two groups; however, the groups showed no differences in terms of their TRQ scores. Although no group achieved the researcher-set goals, the performance-plus-outcome-imagery group, which imaged both their behavior and the result, consistently improved their performances. The other two groups' performances were inconsistent. The improvements in performance of the performance-plus-outcome-imagery group, which were in line with their own established goals of doing as well as or better than they had previously, could explain why this group did not practice longer. The findings encourage further investigation of how imagery can affect motivation.

Imagery has been effective in increasing self-efficacy for a motor task (McKenzie and Howe 1997), for a muscular-endurance task (Feltz and

Riessinger 1990), and for sport skills at an elite level (Callery and Morris 1997a, c; She and Morris 1997). Using a single-subject, multiple-baseline design, Callery and Morris conducted 20-min imagery-rehearsal sessions 3 times per week with 8 elite Australian Rules football players over a competitive season. The players imaged themselves getting to front-and-center positions during games. For all players, both performance and front-and-center self-efficacy were higher during the treatment phase than they had been throughout the preceding baseline phase.

In a similar single-case, multiple-baseline study, She and Morris (1997) found that an imagery program for nine male elite baseball players was effective in improving their batting averages, self-efficacy relating to batting, and the state self-confidence in their batting ability. Three players clearly showed an improvement in their batting averages, two had batting averages that tended toward improvement, two had no change, and two had a decline in batting averages. In regard to self-efficacy, five players improved, one had a trend toward improvement, and three showed no change. Similar results were found for state self-confidence, with five players improving their confidence and four showing no change. Only one player showed no improvement on any of the measures, which may have been due to recurring injuries and an accompanying lack of form.

The frequency with which netball players use various types of imagery has been linked with their confidence of performing successfully in a game (Callow and Hardy 2001). In the Callow and Hardy study, two samples of netball players were used: one each from higher-ranked and lower-ranked counties. For the players from the higher-ranked county, greater confidence of performing successfully was associated with more frequent use of motivational-specific (i.e., goal-oriented) imagery. For those from the lower-ranked county, greater confidence was related to more frequent use of motivational-general-mastery imagery (i.e., mastering a skill in a competitive situation), cognitive-general imagery (i.e., game strategy), and motivational-general-arousal imagery (i.e., psyching up). More research is needed to determine whether imagery can increase confidence levels and whether athletic ability might influence the effectiveness of an imagery treatment.

In summary, the evidence produced thus far supports the use of imagery to benefit performance. Research has shown that imagery can produce better performance outcomes and have a positive effect on anxiety, motivation, and self-efficacy. It is encouraging that researchers are taking their studies from the laboratory to the field. Many of the earlier studies were conducted in settings that did not emulate the contexts in which athletes perform and which involved tasks that are irrelevant to sport (i.e., they have low ecological validity). Recently, the number of studies that have examined elite or skilled athletes performing in competition, using imagery-rehearsal programs like those employed by practitioners, has increased. Researchers in the future should seriously consider these factors in the design of their studies.

WHICH FACTORS INFLUENCE THE EFFECTIVENESS OF IMAGERY?

The effect of an imagery program on individual performance may be influenced by a number of factors. This section highlights factors that can increase or decrease the effectiveness of imagery.

Studies have shown that the speed at which skills are imaged may be different from the speed at which they are physically executed (Boschker, Bakker, and Rietberg 2000; Calmels and Fournier 2001; Orliaguet and Coello 1998). Calmels and Fournier found that twelve gymnasts imaged a routine, and each of the six acrobatic and choreographic stages that comprised it, at a faster rate than they actually performed them. Factors that may have contributed to these differences are the time constraints that gymnasts normally have on their preroutine preparation, the intended function of the imagery (i.e., cognitive or motivational), and the perceived task difficulty. The duration of the imagery was longer for the more technically difficult stages.

The findings of the Orliaguet and Coello (1998) study, in which imagery and actual golf-putting speed were assessed, suggest that the results of other studies using short-duration movement imagery need to be reexamined. In the actual performance of a golf putt, the duration of the skill is consistent ($\approx$250 milliseconds) regardless of the targeted distance, whereas the amplitude of the movement increases with greater distance to the target. Orliaguet and Coello found, however, that study participants took longer to image the skill with increasing target distance (the only imaging timed was the skill execution, not imagery of the time the ball took to travel to the hole). This finding means that, with increasing target distance, the imaged skill was progressively out of phase with actual performance.

The detrimental effect that incorrect imagery speed may have on performance was illustrated in the Boschker et al. (2000) study. These researchers had participants perform a motor sequence at their preferred speed, and at double and half that speed. Participants were then assigned to one of six treatment groups that practiced or imaged the sequence at a fast or slow pace or did not practice the sequence. The results showed that retroactive interference occurred, with the slow-practicing and slow-imaging participants recording slower performance times in the retention test than in the baseline test, and the fast-practicing and fast-imaging participants recording faster performance times in the retention test than in the baseline test.

The success of an imagery intervention to reduce anxiety may depend on the personal characteristics of the athlete. A study by Carter and Kelly (1997) demonstrated that, following paradoxical imagery (i.e., imagery of performing while feeling anxious and doubtful), high-reactant basketball players (i.e., those players with a tendency to offset pressure or restrictions placed on them with the aim of protecting their personal freedom) had lower somatic state anxiety and higher state self-confidence than did low-reactant players. This finding suggests that high-reactant athletes who wish to lower their anxiety levels may benefit more from defiance-based imagery than the commonly used compliance-based imagery. There was little difference in free-throw performance, however.

Goal orientation is another personal characteristic that may influence the efficacy of imagery (Cumming, Hall, Harwood, and Gammage 2002). Researchers in sport have examined two kinds: task orientation and ego orientation (Chi 2004; Duda 1989, 1992). Task orientation refers to a perspective in which athletes aim to demonstrate ability in comparison to their own previous performance. Task-oriented athletes show their ability by mastering tasks, principally by performing skills more effectively than they have before in practice or competition. Thus, task-oriented athletes do not place high priority on whether they win or lose. Ego orientation is based on the demonstration of ability in comparison to others. Thus, high ability is demonstrated by defeating other athletes. For ego-oriented athletes, winning is central to showing high ability. As a consequence, high ego-oriented athletes are likely to drop out of a sport when they lose persistently (because they are showing low ability, which they want to avoid), while high task-oriented athletes will persist in the face of defeat as long as they perceive that they are improving.

Although the preceding description refers to high task- or ego-oriented athletes, research has shown that task and ego orientation are orthogonal; that is, they are independent of each other. This means that athletes can score high, moderate, or low on both task and ego orientation, as well as high on one and low on the other (Chi and Duda 1995; Duda and White 1992). In particular, elite athletes often score high on task and ego orientation. Cumming et al. found a relationship between the goal-orientation profiles of swimmers, who were competing at three different levels at a provincial championship, and their use of imagery functions. Although swimmers with different goal-orientation profiles used imagery differently, they did not vary greatly in their amounts of task or goal orientation or imagery use. Swimmers who had moderate task and low ego orientations used task-mastery imagery more frequently (i.e., cognitive specific, cognitive general, motivational general mastery) than those with low task and moderate ego orientations. Those swimmers with moderate task and high ego orientations tended to use more motivational imagery than others did.

Imagery content would seem pertinent to increasing the efficacy of the treatment; however, it has not received much research attention. Lee (1990) provided some evidence of this effect by finding that task-relevant imagery increased sit-up performance more than task-irrelevant imagery or no imagery. The changes in performance were minimal, however, which was probably a reflection of the duration of the imagery intervention (30 sec).

Just as positive imagery may enhance performance, negative (Taylor and Shaw 2002; Woolfolk, Murphy, Gottesfeld, and Aitken 1985) and suppressive (Beilock, Afremow, Rabe, and Carr 2001) images have been found to be detrimental to performance. In a competitive golf situation, Taylor and Shaw asked skilled and unskilled participants to execute putts under each of three conditions: positive-outcome imagery, negative-outcome imagery, and no imagery. Greater putting error was recorded for the negative-outcome imagery condition than for either of the other two conditions, and there was no difference between the positive-outcome imagery and no-imagery conditions. For skilled golfers, there was a mean difference in golf-putting error of 11.3 cm between the positive- and negative-outcome imagery conditions. Confidence, as assessed by a single item before each putt, was lower following the negative-imagery condition than the two others.

The efficacy of imagery may be affected by the stage of learning at which it is used (Bohan, Pharmer, and Stokes 1999; Feltz and Landers 1983). In their meta-analysis, Feltz and Landers found no significant difference between the efficacy of imagery for participants who were novice or experienced at the skill being measured in the respective studies. There was large variability, however, in the magnitudes of change as a result of imagery. This finding means that regardless of participant experience, studies showed large differences in the efficacy of the intervention. Some of this variation can probably be attributed to the fact that the meta-analysis focused on mental practice in general rather than on imagery per se. In a more recent study, Bohan et al. investigated the effect that imagery has on the performance of a target-acquisition computer task. The efficacy of the imagery treatment (20 imaged trials of the task) was greatest for the participants who were in the earliest phase of learning and least for the most experienced participants. Given that evidence suggests that imagery can assist the performances of both novice and experienced athletes (Blair et al., 1993), research is needed to determine how imagery may be most effectively used by athletes at varying ability levels.

In summary, various factors have been found to influence the efficacy of imagery treatment, such as imaging speed and content and personal characteristics of the athlete. Research in this area should continue in order to provide guidance to practitioners on the most effective ways to deliver imagery treatments.

HOW MUCH IMAGERY IS ENOUGH?

Although dose-response effects have been found for physical practice (Hird et al. 1991), Landers (1999) reported that determining the optimal number of mental-practice trials remains a matter of guesswork. Dose-response effects are the relationship of dosage of some kind of treatment (e.g., imagery) to the affective, conative, cognitive, or behavioral effect produced. Contrary to the idea of dose-response, Etnier and Landers (1996) found that individuals in groups that were instructed to use mental practice for either 1 or 3 min improved task performance more than those in groups that practiced for 5 or 7 min or did no mental practice.

Little guidance is provided by the literature about the desirable number of imagery sessions, length of sessions, and number of trials (i.e., number of imagery sequences) per session. In their meta-analysis of the effects of mental practice on performance, Feltz and Landers (1983) reported no significant relationship between the number of mental-practice sessions and performance. In regard to session length, the largest effects for mental practice occurred when sessions were less than 1 min long; however, similar effects have resulted from mental practice of motor tasks from 15 to 25 min. These findings were supported by Hinshaw's (1991) meta-analysis, which found that sessions of less than or equal to 1 min and those between 10 and 15 min were most effective in increasing performance. Fewer than six trials were required to achieve large effects on cognitive tasks, whereas a greater number of trials or minutes were required to produce similar results on motor or strength tasks (Feltz and Landers 1983). Hinshaw found that 15 to 25 trials yielded the largest effects on performance. There seems to be great potential for further examination of dose-response effects of imagery use.

IS IMAGERY RESEARCH IN ITS OWN LITTLE DREAM WORLD?

Investigating the operation of psychological processes such as imagery and their effect on sport performance is not a simple task. Imagery occurs inside athletes' heads, so researchers cannot directly observe it; instead, they have to infer its effect through athletes' self-reports (e.g., completion of questionnaires or descriptions of the experience) or behavior changes (e.g., improved performance on the relevant task).

Still, researchers should endeavor to design studies that minimize threats to internal and external validity. Simply put, internal validity refers to the extent to which the change in the variables measured (e.g., performance) can be attributed to the treatment (i.e., imagery) rather than to unrelated factors (e.g., the effect of physical practice). External validity is the extent to which research findings may be generalized to other settings. For example, a study that focuses on using imagery to improve a skill in an applied setting would have high external validity to sport situations, whereas a novel physical task performed in the laboratory would have low external validity.

Although this review of research on imagery in sport has highlighted studies that were based on sound research principles, we have included some with inherent design weaknesses. Various authors (e.g., Goginsky and Collins 1996; Moran 1993) have provided critiques of the research methods used in imagery studies. Areas of concern include a lack of conceptual clarity, manipulation checks, and appropriate methods to investigate a clear research question. A pertinent example of a lack of conceptual clarity is an inadequate distinction between imagery and mental practice. Some earlier studies used the term "imagery" to describe what was in fact mental practice. (See chapter 2 for a discussion of these terms.) Such deficiencies in a study can make it difficult for practitioners to judge the efficacy of imagery and for researchers to build on the earlier work.

Because researchers cannot directly observe the imagery process, manipulation checks are necessary to make sure the participants imaged what they were meant to. The specific questions asked in a manipulation check depend on the research design. Researchers may want to know how clear the imagery was, how often it was used outside the researcher-run sessions, and how easy it was for participants to follow the imagery instructions during the sessions. Unfortunately, no manipulation check can guard against participants who, for whatever reason, do not perform the imagery as instructed, but merely go along with the researcher's wishes (whether perceived or expressed) during completion of tasks.

To answer a given research question, the use of appropriate methods is imperative. Unfortunately, researchers in the past have used designs that confuse the situation by having nonequivalent groups, using inappropriate measures of the variables of interest, not examining competing hypotheses, and so forth.

Statistical weaknesses are still evident in many studies, despite the teachings of Shutz and Gessaroli (1993). They are particularly common in studies that use experimental designs, especially the inappropriate use of univariate tests to follow a significant multiple analysis of variance (Bird and Hadzi-Pavlovic 1983; Huberty and Morris 1989), incorrect testing for differences between groups in a pretest and posttest design (Huck and McLean 1975), and the failure to report and comment on effect sizes (Cohen 1990, 1994; Speed and Andersen 2000).

Research design, which is frequently a contentious issue, is particularly important in studying a process like imagery, which is not directly observable (e.g., Hale, Holmes, Smith, Fowler, and Collins 2003; Landers

2003). Hopefully the design of studies will continue to improve in the future so that imagery's effect on performance and the factors that affect this relationship can be more clearly elucidated.

CONCLUSIONS

A great deal of research effort has been dedicated to understanding imagery and its application in sport situations. The results have generally supported the view that imagery can produce changes in physical performance and in psychological variables that may affect sport performance. Various factors, such as imagery speed and content, have been suggested as influences on the efficacy of imagery. How much imagery is optimal to bring about changes in performance is still an important research question. Although exceptions do exist, most research has been conducted over short periods, in a laboratory setting, with participants who are not particularly skilled in imagery use. Greater research attention should be applied to investigating imagery use in the field, particularly directed to understanding how, when, and why imagery affects sports performance, as well as its effects on the thoughts, emotions, and motivations that accompany this performance.

Table 5.1 Summary of Research on Imagery and Performance

Study	Activity	Participants	Findings
Meta-analyses			
Feltz and Landers (1983)	Various	146 effect sizes from 60 studies	Mental practice was more effective than no practice.
Hinshaw (1991)	Various	44 effect sizes from 21 studies	Mental practice was more effective than no practice.
Single-case studies			
Savoy and Beitel (1996)	Basketball foul shooting during games	Elite collegiate female basketball players ($n = 10$, $M_{age} = 20.3$)	Imagery was associated with improvements in foul-shooting percentages.
Single-subject, multiple-baseline studies			
Callery and Morris (1993)	Ball disposal by foot in Australian Rules football	Elite male players ($n = 10$) ages 18–27	Imagery improved performance in 5 of 10 cases, with a trend toward improvement in 3 cases.
Callery and Morris (1997c)	Front and center in Australian Rules football	Elite male players ($n = 8$) ages 18–26	Imagery improved performance during the treatment period.
Shambrook and Bull (1996)	Basketball foul shooting	Female varsity basketball players who had played for at least 5 years ($n = 4$, $M_{age} = 20.3$)	Consistent improvement in performance with imagery in 1 of 4 participants

(continued)

Table 5.1 *(continued)*

Study	Activity	Participants	Findings
She and Morris (1997)	Baseball batting	Elite and sub-elite Australian state male players ($n = 9$, $M_{age} = 30.3$)	Imagery improved standardized batting averages for 3 of 9 players (trend toward improvement for 2 other players). Improvement in standardized expert ratings in 5 players.
Experiments			
Blair et al. (1993)	Soccer drill	Female soccer players ($M_{age} = 20.0$) from a varsity soccer team ($n = 22$) and an introductory soccer class ($n = 22$)	Imagery enhanced performance for both novices and experts.
E.C. Hall and Hardy (1991)	Pistol marksmanship	Males ($n = 15$) and females ($n = 15$), ages 18–23, enrolled in beginner's classes in pistol marksmanship at a university	VMBR was superior to transcendental meditation and a no-intervention control at increasing performance.
Elko and Ostrow (1992)	Gripping a hand dynamometer	Older males ($n = 15$, $M_{age} = 59.9$), older females ($n = 15$, $M_{age} = 60.3$), younger males ($n = 15$, $M_{age} = 22.1$), and younger females ($n = 15$, $M_{age} = 21.0$)	Grip strength was greater after performing imagery than when participants counted backward prior to the grip-strength test.
Hird et al. (1991)	Pegboard and pursuit rotor tasks	Male ($n = 36$) and female ($n = 36$) undergraduate students enrolled in physical education classes	Physical practice was superior to mental practice for people untrained in mental practice.

Study	Activity	Task	Participants	Findings
Lorh and Scogin (1998)	Athletics		Male ($n = 17$) and female ($n = 19$) collegiate athletes	Self-administered VMBR training was effective in increasing performance over a no-intervention control.
Murphy et al. (1988)	Gripping a hand dynamometer		Male college undergraduates ($n = 24$)	Relaxation imagery reduced grip strength. Fear and anger imagery did not increase grip strength.
Noel (1980)	Tennis serving during a tournament		Male ($n = 14$, $M_{age} = 28.6$) tennis players recruited during a local tournament	The percentage of good first serves was greater for players using VMBR training than for those receiving no intervention.
Perkins et al. (2001)	Gripping a hand dynamometer		Elite male ($n = 22$) and female ($n = 6$) athletes ($M_{age} = 20.3$) involved in predominantly explosive sports	Grip strength was greater when arousal was high and positive than when high and negative or neutral.
Seabourne et al. (1984)	Karate		Males ($n = 18$) and females ($n = 26$), ages 18–24, enrolled in 16-week-long karate classes at a university	Performance was greater for students using VMBR training than for those receiving a placebo.
Van Gyn et al. (1990)	Power training on cycle ergometer		Male ($n = 19$) and female ($n = 21$) undergraduate students taking a physical education fitness class	Imagery enhanced the physiological transfer of power training on the cycle ergometer to the 40 m sprint.
Weinberg et al. (1981)	Karate		Males ($n = 32$) ages 18–24, enrolled in a karate club	Sparring performance was better for participants using VMBR than for participants using relaxation only, imagery only, or an attention placebo. No differences for skill or combinations.

(continued)

Table 5.1 *(continued)*

Study	Activity	Participants	Findings
Weinberg et al. (1982)	Karate	Experiment 1: Males ($n = 18$) ages 18–24, enrolled in a karate club Experiment 2: Males ($n = 14$) enrolled in a karate club	Experiment 1: Participants who received VMBR training over 6 weeks did not differ in performance from those who received VMBR in the last session only. Experiment 2: Participants who received VMBR training over 6 weeks showed superior performance to those who received VMBR in the last session only.

Table 5.2 Summary of Research on Imagery and Psychological Variables

Study	Psychological variable	Participants	Findings
Correlation			
Callow and Hardy (2001)	Confidence	Female county netball players ($n = 123$) who had played for at least 2 years	For high-standard netball players, goal-achievement-oriented imagery was a predictor of confidence. For low-standard players, mastery imagery and game-strategy imagery were predictors of confidence, and imagery of the emotions associated with playing negatively contributed to confidence.
Experiments			
Carter and Kelly (1997)	Competitive anxiety	Male ($n = 43$) and female ($n = 30$) intramural university basketball players ($M_{age} = 19.8$)	High-reactant athletes had lower somatic state anxiety and higher state self-confidence, when given a paradoxical imagery treatment, than low-reactant athletes. No differences seen in anxiety when the two groups were given a confidence-imagery treatment.
Feltz and Riessinger (1990)	Self-efficacy	College males ($n = 60$) and females ($n = 60$)	Participants in the mastery-imagery-plus-feedback group had higher self-efficacy on a competitive muscular-endurance task than did participants in the feedback-only and control conditions.
Hale and Whitehouse (1998)	Competitive anxiety	Male soccer players ($n = 24$, $M_{age} = 21.5$)	Imagery of a challenging situation produced less cognitive anxiety, less somatic anxiety, and greater self-confidence than did imagery of a pressure situation.

(continued)

Table 5.2 *(continued)*

Study	Psychological variable	Participants	Findings
Martin and Hall (1995)	Motivation	Males ($n = 15$) and females ($n = 24$) from a university community ($M_{age} = 27.2$)	Performance-imagery group participants practiced for longer than those in the performance-plus-outcome imagery and no-imagery groups.
Page et al. (1999)	Competitive anxiety	Elite female intercollegiate swimmers ($n = 40$, $M_{age} = 20.1$)	Imagery produced positive changes in swimmers' perceptions of anxiety. No changes in cognitive or somatic anxiety. Self-confidence improved.
Single-subject, multiple-baseline studies			
Callery and Morris (1997c)	Self-efficacy	Elite male Australian Rules football players ($n = 8$) ages 18–26	Front-and-center self-efficacy in Australian Rules was higher during the imagery treatment.
McKenzie and Howe (1997)	Self-efficacy	Male ($n = 3$) and female ($n = 3$) college students ages 22–33	Imagery was effective in improving dart-throwing self-efficacy for participants who had high imagery ability, dart-throwing experience, relaxation and imagery experience prior to the research, and who believed the treatment would be effective.
She and Morris (1997)	Self-efficacy	Elite and sub-elite Australian state male baseball players ($n = 9$, $M_{age} = 30.3$)	Imagery treatment improved batting self-efficacy in baseball.

CHAPTER 6

IMAGERY PERSPECTIVES

As chapter 5 demonstrated, imagery is an important cognitive process that is widely used in sport. Research that helps us understand how to use imagery more effectively is, thus, of value to sport psychologists. Imagery perspective has received attention in the sport psychology literature, yet its most efficacious use is unclear. If using one perspective for a particular situation is more effective than another, then this information is important to applied sport psychologists who use imagery with athletes. Could it be that imaging from one's own viewpoint (internal imagery) assists performance effectively because it resembles actual physical performance and creates kinesthetic feedback? Or perhaps imagery from a third-person perspective, like watching a TV replay (external imagery), provides athletes with feedback on correct movement execution and spatial aspects of a task.

Sport psychologists have, perhaps erroneously or at least without strong research support, proposed that internal imagery is superior to external imagery for performance enhancement (Cox 2002), often because of its expected close relationship with kinesthetic sensation (Callow and Hardy 2004). But Hardy (1997) questioned the recommendation that performers should use internal rather than external visual imagery. Perhaps the most effective type of imagery for performance enhancement is that which provides the most useful information. Human movement is based on information about the environment and a person's location in it and his relationship to objects in that environment (Haywood and Getchell 2001). For instance, in soccer, when passing the ball, players see the location of the ball and other players and feel the positions of their bodies in relation to the ball. They feel where their legs are and how hard and fast they are moving. The players integrate and use this information to decide where, when, and how hard to pass the ball. Thus imagery can be useful in skill learning and performance if it provides information to enhance skill practice.

Several researchers have suggested that the type of task might mediate the imagery perspective–performance relationship and determine which type of imagery will be most useful (Annett 1995; Hardy and Callow 1999; Harris 1986; McLean and Richardson 1994; Spittle and Morris 2000). Information in imagery could come from an internal or external perspective and also be based on visual or kinesthetic information. This chapter examines these sources of information in imagery. We first consider what visual and kinesthetic imagery and internal and external imagery are and the confusion that surrounds them. Then we review research that has investigated imagery modality and imagery perspectives in sport.

DEFINITIONS OF IMAGERY MODALITY AND IMAGERY PERSPECTIVES

The literature reflects frequent confusion about the distinction between imagery perspective and imagery modality (Hardy 1997). Here we define the terms "visual imagery," "kinesthetic imagery," "internal imagery," and "external imagery" and distinguish between imagery modality and imagery perspective.

IMAGERY MODALITY: VISUAL AND KINESTHETIC IMAGERY

Skilled performers in sport receive and process large amounts of information quickly and accurately to monitor and make adjustments to their performance (Schmidt and Wrisberg 2004). They use this sensory information to plan their actions and regulate their performance. Motor control, or the regulation of movement, relies heavily on the use of sensory information (Schmidt and Lee 1999). That is, successful learning and performance often depend on how effectively the performer detects, perceives, and uses important sensory information. Two sources of sensory information are particularly important in motor performance: visual and kinesthetic information. Thus researchers in imagery in sport who have focused on imagery ability and modality have targeted visual and kinesthetic imagery (Murphy and Martin 2002).

"Vision" refers to information that relates to the perceptual experience of seeing, so visual imagery is related to the visual processing of information. In the imagery literature, visual imagery is synonymous with "seeing" movement or being instructed to "picture" or "visualize" it. Kinesthetic information refers to sensory information from receptors throughout the body about body-part location and movement, the nature of objects with which the body comes into contact, and movement of the muscles, tendons, and joints (Schmidt and Wrisberg 2004). So kinesthetic imagery pertains to this sensory experience. In the sport psychology and imagery literature, kinesthetic imagery is "still loosely defined as the feel of the movement" (Callow and Hardy 2004, 168) and is synonymous with the "feel" of the movement or instructions to "feel" the movement.

IMAGERY PERSPECTIVE: INTERNAL AND EXTERNAL IMAGERY

Mahoney and Avener (1977) defined perspective in terms of whether an image is internal or external. Internal imagery "requires an approximation of the real-life phenomenology such that the person actually imagines being inside his or her body and experiences those sensations which might be expected in the actual situation" (p. 137). In external imagery "a person views himself from the perspective of an external observer (much like in home movies)" (p. 137). For example, in imaging kicking a ball from an internal perspective, the imager would see the ball at his feet and his attention would be on the ball as his foot draws back to strike it. From an external perspective, the imager would be outside his body and would see his movement from a third-person viewpoint. Thus, just as visual and kinesthetic imagery refer to different sources of information, internal and external imagery refer to different sources of information and a first-person or third-person perspective. Examples of imagery scripts that emphasize internal and external imagery are presented in the sidebar on the next page.

One of the limitations of the research and our understanding of perspective and sense modality in imagery is the apparent confusion between modality and perspectives. For instance, Cox (1998) expressed this confusion when he stated that "internal imagery is considered to be primarily kinesthetic in nature, as opposed to visual" (p. 176) and that "external imagery is considered to be primarily visual in nature" (p. 176). One reason that internal imagery has been proposed to be superior to external imagery for performance enhancement is the assumption that it has a stronger association with kinesthetic imagery (Callow and Hardy 2004). Weinberg (1982) and Janssen and Sheikh (1994) both stated that internal imagery is sometimes called kinesthetic imagery, but this is confusing the two terms.

Researchers have found that participants are able to form kinesthetic images equally well with either imagery perspective (Gates, DePalma, and Shelley 2003; Glisky, Williams, and Kihlstrom 1996; Hardy and Callow 1999; White and Hardy 1995), and more recent research even suggests that for some tasks, kinesthetic imagery may have a stronger

Examples of Internal and External Imagery

To see the difference in perspective between internal and external imagery, consider the following two examples describing the first 50 m of a freestyle swimming race.

Internal Imagery

"Imagine that the official is calling your event. You are standing on the blocks. You can see this with your own eyes. You look down at your feet and see your toes on the blocks. You glance across to the competitors on your left and right from behind your goggles, taking time to adjust your swim cap and goggles. The starter issues the command 'On your marks!' and you bend forward in the track start position and focus forward toward the water. At the sound of the beep you take off and see the water approaching. With a strong, powerful, and streamlined dive, you enter the water and it immerses your body. You look ahead and toward the surface and take a strong kick to drive you forward and upward toward the surface. As you break the surface you begin to take some powerful strokes and kick hard. The water glides over your skin as you move through the water with speed. With your peripheral vision you notice the swimmer in the lane next to you is level with you. You concentrate harder on each stroke. Ahead you are approaching the first turn. You come to the wall, focusing clearly on the surface in front of you so that you make a good, powerful turn. You start the turn, throwing your legs over your head and pushing hard into a tight streamline. You kick hard and surface again. . . ."

External Imagery

"Imagine that the official is calling your event. You can see yourself standing on the blocks in your suit. It is like you are watching yourself on TV. The other competitors are on their blocks alongside you as you adjust your cap and goggles. The starter commands, 'On your marks!' and you and all the competitors bend forward in the start position. You are in the track start position. At the sound of the beep you and the field take off into the air. With a strong, powerful, and streamlined dive, you enter the water. You are completely immersed. All you can see of yourself is your streamlined form under the water. You emerge from the water and break the surface in equal first with the other swimmers. You take some strong, powerful strokes and kick hard. You are gliding through the water as you move with speed. The swimmers in the lanes next to you are level with you as you come toward the first turn. As you reach the wall you start the turn. You flip over, pushing hard against the wall as you are submerged. Your body underwater makes a tight streamline and at the same time all the other competitors are underwater. Your head breaks the surface first and you are in the lead. . . ."

association with external imagery than with internal imagery (Callow and Hardy 2004). The terms "internal" and "kinesthetic" are not synonymous; they refer to different aspects of imagery. "Imagery perspective" refers to whether the imagery is experienced from inside or outside of the body, not to which sense modality or modalities are used. According to Denis (1985), it is not acceptable to equate the dimensions of internal and external imagery and visual and kinesthetic imagery, nor to state that first-person experience has only kinesthetic components and visual images are involved only in third-person experience.

A recent study by Callow and Hardy (2004) has attempted to explore the relationship between imagery perspective and imagery modality. Callow and Hardy (2004) completed two studies where participants completed the VMIQ (Isaac et al. 1986) to measure internal and external imagery and the MIQ (Hall et al., 1985) to measure visual and kinesthetic imagery. They found no significant correlation between imagery perspectives and imagery modality in study 1, but in study 2 external visual imagery was significantly correlated with kinesthetic imagery, whereas internal visual imagery was not. Callow and Hardy (2004) concluded that these studies offered tentative evidence that for movements in which form is important, kinesthetic imagery has a stronger association with external rather than internal visual imagery. It should be noted that the VMIQ was not developed as a measure of imagery perspectives and has not been validated for this use. Replication of this research using a measure like the SIAM (see chapter 4) to assess internal and external imagery perspectives would be of interest.

The confusion and debate in the literature might, in part, be due to Mahoney and Avener's (1977) original definitions of internal and external imagery. Collins and Hale (1997) and Collins, Smith, and Hale (1998) have expressed a contrasting view on the distinction between internal and external imagery and visual and kinesthetic imagery from the one in this chapter and from others, such as Hardy and Callow (1999). They suggested that many people frequently switch perspectives during the performance of a complex task, such as a sport skill. They argued that switching imagery perspective is like watching a demonstration and then trying to perform the movement that was demonstrated, which could be a superior strategy to a single imagery perspective. In relation to the perspective–modality debate, Collins et al. maintained that first external, then kinesthetic is the actual perspective sequence employed by learners. Holmes and Collins (2001) suggested that advanced performers might process an external visual perspective in parallel with kinesthetic imagery, but even they must switch between perspectives in order to be consciously aware of them, due to the mono-task nature of attention. The speed of switching might be so fast that they are reported as occurring simultaneously. Holmes and Collins argued that whether external visual imagery and kinesthetic imagery are considered to occur together (Hardy and Callow 1999) or as conscious and unconscious elements that must be switched between (Holmes and Collins 2001), they are related to the same motor representation and are therefore important. The point is that external visual imagery can be used with kinesthetic imagery to enhance the imagery experience.

What is most important to understand is that kinesthetic and internal imagery are not the same, and visual and external imagery are not the same. In this chapter, we use the terms "imagery perspective" and "internal and external imagery" to refer to whether imagery is experienced from inside or outside of the body (first or third person), and "visual and kinesthetic imagery" to refer to the two major sense modalities through which an athlete experiences the world.

VISUAL AND KINESTHETIC IMAGERY RESEARCH

Visual and kinesthetic imagery have been the subjects of much research; nevertheless, very little is known about the relationship between these two modalities (Callow and Hardy 2004). In addition, no systematic comparison of visual and kinesthetic imagery in the motor or sport domain has been done (Hall 2001; Hall, Schmidt, Durand, and Buckolz 1994), so their comparative effects on motor and sport skills are not well established (Farahat, Ille, and Thon 2004). However, several studies provide information about the impact of visual and kinesthetic imagery. For instance, studies that have investigated imagery ability or use have compared more- or less-skilled athletes on visual and kinesthetic imagery, and some recent studies have compared visual and kinesthetic imagery on simple movement tasks. Also, evidence of the distinction between visual and kinesthetic imagery has arisen from functional-equivalence and psychophysiological studies.

PSYCHOPHYSIOLOGICAL STUDIES

Psychophysiological and interference studies on functional-equivalence views of imagery have supported a distinction between visual and motor (kinesthetic) imagery (see chapter 3). Interference studies have suggested that visual tasks interfere with visual imagery, and motor or kinesthetic tasks interfere with motor or kinesthetic imagery, supporting the idea that visual imagery and vision use similar processes, as do kinesthetic imagery and kinesthesis (e.g., Boschker, Bakker, and Rietberg 2000; Engelkamp and Cohen 1991; Hall, Bernoties, and Schmidt 1995; Johnson 1982; Orliaguet and Coello 1998; Smyth and Waller 1998; Vogt 1995).

In an example of an interference study comparing visual and kinesthetic imagery, Smyth and Waller (1998) investigated imagery of rock climbing. Participants were asked to imagine two different rock-climbing tasks, one that relied more on visual information (vertical route) and one that relied more on kinesthetic information (horizontal route). Results indicated that a visual interference task caused the vertical route to take longer to complete and that a kinesthetic interference task caused the horizontal route to take longer to complete.

Research using psychophysiological measures has suggested that visual imagery activates visual neural pathways and motor or kinesthetic imagery activates motor neural pathways (Jeannerod 1994; Annett 1986; Berthoz 1996; Decety 1996a, b; Farah 1989; Holmes and Collins 2001). This research includes peripheral psychophysiological studies as well as those on central processes in the nervous system. Some of the psychophysiological studies have directly compared visual and kinesthetic imagery, for instance, the classic studies by Jacobson (1930a, b, c, d, 1931a, b, c). This series of studies is important in the development of psychoneuromuscular theories of imagery and in research on internal and external imagery. The literature often reports that Jacobson conducted an experiment on performing a biceps curl, but he did much more than that. He did extensive research on muscular activity during imagery and found that muscular activity during imagination of such activities as bending the forearm, lifting a weight (biceps curl), sweeping, and climbing a rope was greater than muscular activity at rest and was located in the specific muscles involved with the imagined activity. In one study, Jacobson (1931a) found that when participants were asked to *visualize* performing a biceps curl, eye activity increased, and when they were asked to *imagine* experiencing a biceps curl, localized biceps muscle activity occurred. Jacobson (1930d) reported that participants responded differently to the two instructions "Imagine bending the right arm" and "Visually imagine bending the right arm," with the former instruction resulting in activity in the right arm muscles and the latter resulting in eye-muscle activity.

Marks and Isaac (1995) collected electroencephalogram (EEG) data while participants performed visual imagery of the first four items of the VVIQ and movement imagery of the first four items of the VMIQ, and during performance and imagery of two motor tasks, finger touching and fist clenching. They concluded that visual imagery was associated with alpha attenuation in the left posterior cortex with the vivid imagery group. Motor imagery had the opposite effect, with alpha enhancement in vivid imagers, the greatest difference occurring in the left posterior region.

Davidson and Schwartz (1977) assessed the patterning of occipital and sensorimotor EEG activation during self-generated visual and kinesthetic imagery. The researchers asked participants to imagine, in separate trials, a flashing light (visual imagery), a tapping sensation on the right arm (kinesthetic imagery), and both the light and tapping together. The results indicated that visual imagery elicited greater relative occipital activation than kinesthetic imagery. The researchers found no difference in overall alpha activity. Davidson and Schwartz concluded that these findings suggested that imagery in different modalities elicits specific changes in the sensory regions of the brain that are responsible for processing information in the relevant modalities.

IMAGERY ABILITY AND USE STUDIES

Studies on imagery ability and use may give clues to the relationship between imagery modality and performance. As discussed in chapter 4, imagery ability in the sport and motor domain is often operational-ized as visual and kinesthetic imagery ability (Martin, Moritz, and Hall 1999; Murphy and Martin 2002). Research examining the relationship between imagery ability and sport or motor-skill performance indicates that better imagers tend to perform better (Murphy and Martin 2002). Therefore, a combination of visual and kinesthetic imagery is probably an effective approach to take in imagery training. Studies have suggested that kinesthetic imagery ability is positively related to performance in high-level athletes (e.g., Orlick and Partington 1988; Vadocz, Hall, and Moritz 1997). In addition, kinesthetic and visual imagery seem to be positively related to learning a motor skill (Isaac 1992; Goss, Hall, Buckolz, and Fishburne 1986; Ryan and Simons 1981, 1982). For instance, Goss, Hall, Buckolz, and Fishburne (1986) classified participants as high visual, high kinesthetic; high visual, low kinesthetic; or low visual, low kinesthetic imagers on the MIQ, then compared how they learned a movement pattern using imagery. The high visual, high kinesthetic imagers acquired the movement best, and the low visual, low kinesthetic imagers acquired it the least. Ryan and Simons (1982) compared the effects of mental practice (MP) and physical practice (PP) on learning to balance on a stabilometer. The results suggested that PP was more effective than MP, but MP was more effective than no practice. For MP, they found that participants with strong visual images or kinesthetic images improved more than those with weak ones.

Visual and kinesthetic imagery ability seem important in the learning and performing of motor and sport skills. If they are, then improving these abilities would seem a reasonable goal for people who use imagery to enhance sport performance. Very little research has been conducted on whether improvement can be achieved by imagery training in sport, and more is needed, especially on kinesthetic imagery ability. One study by Rodgers, Hall, and Buckolz (1991) suggested that imagery ability can be improved. In this study, figure skaters reported significant improvements on the MIQ after a 16-week imagery-training program.

In terms of imagery use, it appears that both elite and lower-level performers use visual and kinesthetic imagery extensively. Some evidence indicates that better performers use more kinesthetic imagery than lower-level performers and that modality use could be influenced by the type of task being imagined, but these are tentative conclusions given the limited comparison studies of visual and kinesthetic imagery in sport. Research using the Imagery Use Questionnaire (IUQ; Barr and Hall 1992; Hall, Rodgers, and Barr 1990; Salmon, Hall, and Haslam 1994; Spittle and Morris 1999a, b, 2000) suggests that elite and non-elite athletes in a variety of sports use visual and kinesthetic imagery extensively. Hall et al. (1990) found extensive use of both forms by athletes from a range of sports, including American football, ice hockey, soccer, squash, gymnastics, and figure skating. Hall et al. reported that the gymnasts and figure skaters tended to use more kinesthetic imagery than the football and soccer players, suggesting that task type might influence the choice of imagery modality. Barr and Hall (1992) found that elite rowers reported more kinesthetic imagery than novice rowers. In a study of high-level canoe slalom athletes, kinesthetic imagery was reported more often than visual imagery (Moran and McIntyre 1998).

PERFORMANCE STUDIES

Studies investigating the impact of visual and kinesthetic imagery on performance of motor skills seem to indicate that the nature of the task might affect the imagery's efficacy for learning and performance, although the research so far has utilized only simple motor skills, not more complex sport skills. For instance, Fery (2003) conducted two studies comparing visual and kinesthetic imagery for learning tracing and drawing tasks. Fery concluded that in initial learning, the kinesthetic and visual imagery groups performed better than the control group and the visual group performed better on form, but the kinesthetic group was more effective in learning proprioceptive elements and duration of movement. Similarly, Farahat, Ille, and Thon (2004) compared visual and kinesthetic imagery for learning to produce a graphic form using a stylus. Four conditions were used: visual model and visual imagery, kinesthetic model and kinesthetic imagery, visual model and no imagery, and kinesthetic imagery and no model. All groups improved performance, and the imagery groups improved more than the no-imagery groups. The visual imagery group performed the movement better than the kinesthetic imagery group at retention, but not at the end of learning. Thus, visual and kinesthetic imagery had differential effects on learning the movement pattern.

One study that used a sport skill was conducted by Fery and Morizot (2000), who compared visual and kinesthetic imagery (MP) and modeling in learning a tennis serve. Modeling involved a demonstration of the skill either visually (participants watched) or kinesthetically (participants were blindfolded and manually guided). They compared four conditions: kinesthetic modeling and kinesthetic imagery, visual modeling and visual imagery, kinesthetic modeling and no imagery, and visual modeling and no imagery. Results indicated that imagery was effective. The kinesthetic imagery was more effective than the visual imagery on learning the speed and form of the tennis serve, but there was no difference in learning precision.

Overall, the research on visual and kinesthetic imagery in sport suggests that they are distinct modalities and so may serve different purposes and provide different information in imagery. Both appear to be important in imagery in sport, and their effectiveness may depend on the imagery's purpose and the nature of the task being imagined. Using both visual and kinesthetic imagery to add to the information developed in imagery is recommended.

Internal and External Imagery Research

One feature of imagery that has been examined extensively in sport is perspective. Research on internal and external imagery has adopted several approaches, including psychophysiological studies, surveys of ability and use, and performance studies.

Psychophysiological Studies

The psychophysiological research on internal and external imagery described in this chapter includes studies using peripheral measures, such as muscular (EMG), ocular (electrooculographical, or EOG), and peripheral autonomic responses, and those that have measured brain activity during imagery through the use of central measures such as EEG, positron emission tomography (PET scan), regional cerebral blood flow (rCBf), and functional magnetic resonance imaging (fMRI). The research on central measures tends to focus on simple motor activity, not sport skills, and so might not translate readily to the sport domain. In addition, in many of the central and peripheral studies, the distinction between internal and external imagery and kinesthetic and visual imagery has been confused, so that instructions for internal imagery emphasize kinesthetic sensations and external instructions emphasize visual sensations (Hardy 1997). Thus, it is no surprise that kinesthetic internal imagery produces greater muscular activity than nonkinesthetic external imagery.

Jacobson's (1930a, b, c, d, 1931a, b, c) studies on visual and kinesthetic imagery instigated psychophysiological research into imagery perspectives. It must be emphasized again that the instructions used by Jacobson emphasized sensory modality rather than internal and external perspective. Unfortunately, many of the psychophysiological studies that have followed have confounded the distinction between internal and external imagery and visual and kinesthetic imagery by following Jacobson's research. For instance, Hale (1982) attempted to replicate Jacobson's (1931a) site-specific findings using internal and external imagery. Hale recorded EMG activity in the biceps and EOG activity of the dominant eye during imagery of a dumbbell curl. In the internal condition, instructions were to "*imagine* what it *feels* like in your biceps to lift the 25 lb dumbbell" (our italics). In the external condition, instructions were to "*visualize* what it *looks* like to lift the 25 lb dumbbell" (our italics). The problem here, again, is confounding of the internal and external and visual and kinesthetic instructions. Hale found that internal imagery produced significantly more biceps activity than external imagery. There was no significant effect on EOG activity. In a replication of Hale's (1982) study, Vigus and Williams (1987, as cited in Hale 1994) measured EMG activity of dominant biceps and triceps and nondominant triceps during imagery rehearsal in both perspectives of a biceps curl, but found no significant differences for perspective.

Harris and Robinson (1986) investigated muscular innervation during internal and external imagery with karate athletes. Internal imagery instructions were to experience *feelings* and sensations associated with executing the task, whereas external instructions were to *see* themselves executing the task (as though watching a videotape). Internal imagery produced more EMG activity than external imagery. Harris and Robinson also reported a lack of control in maintaining the desired perspective, with over 61% of participants switching perspective, according to self-report measures. Advanced students favored internal imagery (77.8%) more than beginners (50%), whereas a larger number of advanced students (55.6%) than beginners (27.8%) reported switching from external to internal imagery during testing. Harris and Robinson suggested that the existence of a stable imagery perspective is unlikely due to the number of reports of switching (usually from external to internal).

As part of her paper on mental practice of volleyball skills, Shick (1970) measured anterior deltoid and tibialis anterior EMG activity in addition to EOG activity. Shick reported that, in describing the serve, most participants seemed to be "watching themselves (or another figure) in the form of a complete entity entirely separate from their own bodies" (p. 90), which is an external perspective. In describing the wall volley, most of the participants "mentioned the total body in the initial stance; once the action of the volleying had begun the image was quite different, in that they then described the image in terms of only what one would see if she were to actually take the wall volley test" (p. 90), indicating a shift from an initial external perspective to an internal one. Shick did not identify any EMG or EOG pattern.

Wang and Morgan (1992) examined the effect of internal and external imagery of dumbbell curls on the psychophysiological responses of oxygen consumption (VO_2), ventilatory minute volume (VE), respiratory rate (RR), respiratory exchange ratio (RER), heart rate (HR), systolic blood pressure (SBP), and diastolic blood pressure (DBP). They randomly assigned undergraduate and graduate students to perform either internal imagery, external imagery, or rest (control). The internal-imagery instructions directed participants "to *imagine* that your arm muscles are contracting, your heart is beating, and your breathing is changing. In other words, try to recall all the physical sensations that you *experienced* while actually lifting the dumbbells" (p. 169 [our italics]). The external instructions asked participants, "Can you *see* yourself sitting here and lifting the dumbbells?" (p. 169 [our italics]). No mention was made of any physical sensations; the only sense mentioned was sight, again confounding imagery perspective and sense modality. Wang and Morgan concluded that the results did not demonstrate a significant difference between internal and external imagery; however, "the psychophysiological responses to internal imagery resemble actual exercise more than external imagery" (p. 167). This seems like a surprising conclusion, since the only difference found between internal and external imagery across more than eight measures was in VE. Wang and Morgan reported difficulty in maintaining the instructed perspective.

Studies have also shown increased muscular activity when using an internal perspective, but they have not compared it with an external perspective. For instance, Suinn (1976a), in an anecdotal report of an imagery exercise with an alpine skier, described how the skier's leg muscle EMG during imagery from an internal perspective "mirrored" the downhill course being imagined. Bird (1984) conducted a series of case studies investigating imagery of five athletes who participated in equestrian, rowing, breaststroke swimming, water skiing, and basketball. Results indicated an increase in EMG activity for all participants during imagery of their sporting activity. Bird documented that participants reported the ability to image internally. No explanation was given, however, of how this was tested, nor were any manipulation checks provided to test maintenance of imagery perspective in test trials. Oishi, Kimura, Yasukawa, Yoneda, and Maeshima (1994) investigated motor neuron excitability and autonomic reactions during imagery of speed-skating sprints by elite skaters. Oishi et al. encouraged participants to use internal imagery and found that skin-conductance response (SCR), HR, and RR were significantly active during imagery.

The peripheral-measures studies appear to demonstrate greater physiological activity for internal than external imagery. This must be considered in light of the suggestion that the effect could be due to the instructions given in these studies. Researchers seem to have used more kinesthetic instructions in internal imagery scripts than in external imagery scripts. These studies may have simply shown that visual and kinesthetic imagery are physiologically distinct. Psychophysiological studies that actually manipulate internal and external imagery are needed to prove whether the perspectives are physiologically distinct. Many imagery-perspective studies have also failed to use adequate manipulation checks to ensure that participants used the perspective as instructed. In addition, the studies have not measured performance changes, so whether this greater activity is beneficial for performance is also unclear.

Central measures of psychophysiological activity of the brain during imagery also have a long history, but none have specifically investigated internal versus external imagery (Hale 1994). Studies have investigated what their authors have suggested is analogous to either internal or external imagery, but the instructions are not adequately delineated. For instance, Williams, Rippon, Stone, and Annett (1995) conducted two experiments using EEG to investigate imagery of the first 12 statements from the VMIQ. According to Williams et al., each statement takes a first-person, or internal, perspective ("imagine yourself") and a third-person, or external, perspective ("imagine someone else"). However, once again this is not true imagery-perspective distinction; the instructions might not be enough to manipulate the two perspectives. Williams et al. anticipated possible differences between internal and external perspectives in activating motor and visuospatial areas of the cortex, depending on the perspective taken during imagery. They found no differences. Alternatively, many of the studies have compared the often confounded aspects of imagery such as visual, kinesthetic, and motor, rather than imagery perspectives. This has led several of the papers reviewed to equate motor imagery with internal imagery and visual imagery with external imagery, and thus provide suggestions for psychophysiological responses in internal or external imagery that may not be accurate (e.g., Decety 1996a, b; Jeannerod 1994, 1995). Again, studies are required that employ internal and external imagery protocols rather than inferring perspective from visual or motor imagery instructions.

IMAGERY ABILITY AND USE STUDIES

Numerous questionnaire studies have assessed internal and external imagery, usually as part of a general psychological-skills inventory measuring several aspects of psychological preparation or as part of a general imagery-use questionnaire. Often the imagery perspective is addressed with one question that asks participants whether they usually use an internal or external perspective, and researchers have often compared "successful" and "less successful" performers based on this one question.

Mahoney and Avener's (1977) study of elite gymnasts instigated research into imagery perspective in the sport domain. In an exploratory study, Mahoney and Avener found that successful gymnasts tended to use internal imagery more than external imagery, based on a self-report questionnaire. Subsequent studies have attempted to replicate Mahoney and Avener's findings but have found mixed results. The Mahoney-Avener questionnaire may be partly to blame for the equivocal findings because it has not been validated and does not have the sole aim of determining imagery-perspective use. In fact, it covers a large range of psychological factors and cognitive strategies, with only 4 of the 53 items relating specifically to imagery use. Of those that do, only one addresses imagery perspective.

Researchers who have used the Mahoney-Avener questionnaire include Meyers, Cooke, Cullen, and Liles (1979), who found that less- and more-skilled racquetball players did not differ in the use of imagery perspectives. Similarly, Highlen and Bennett (1979) assessed wrestlers attempting to qualify for the 1980 World Games Canadian squad and found that reported imagery perspective use did not correlate with final selection classification for the team. Rotella, Gansneder, Ojala, and Billing (1980) investigated downhill skiing with the Mahoney-Avener questionnaire and the Coping and Attentional Inventory (CAI), which they developed for the study. Rotella et al. found that imagery questions on the Mahoney-Avener inventory did not correlate highly with ranking. The CAI, however, indicated that the more successful skiers reported more internal images and the less successful skiers developed more external images. Doyle and Landers (1980) found that international-level (elite) pistol and rifle shooters used predominantly internal imagery, whereas state- and junior-level (sub-elite) shooters used a mixture of internal and external imagery.

Other questionnaires have also been used to assess imagery-perspective ability and use in sport. For instance, Mahoney, Gabriel, and Perkins (1987), using the Psychological Skills Inventory for Sports (PSIS), conducted another general assessment of psychological skills in sport and concluded that elite athletes used internal and kinesthetic imagery more than non-elite athletes do. In a study with gymnasts, using the

PSIS, Jopson, Henschen, and Schultz (1989) found that junior elite gymnasts reported using more kinesthetic and significantly more external imagery than junior competitors. Suinn and Andrews (1981) surveyed elite alpine skiers and found no trends based on internal and external perspective. Carpinter and Cratty (1983) collected interview data, and Cratty reported that 13 out of 21 male university water-polo players (62%) responded that they usually used internal imagery. However, no significant relationships were found between type of imagery reported and coaches' ratings of ability and motivation intensity.

Olympic athletes have also been surveyed on imagery-perspective use. For instance, in a study of 235 Canadian Olympic athletes by Orlick and Partington (1988), the qualitative analysis of interviews suggested that the athletes "had developed an inside view" (p. 113). Smith (1983, as cited in Smith 1987) found that only 17% of Olympic gymnasts reported imagining from an internal perspective, 39% reported imagining from an external perspective, and the rest (44%) used a combination of both. This is an interesting finding, coming so soon after the Mahoney and Avener study, also with Olympic gymnasts. Jowdy, Murphy, and Durtschi (1989), in a survey of elite athletes and coaches, found that a majority indicated a preference for internal imagery and that imagery perspective fluctuates. In a survey of 1988 U.S. Olympic trials track-and-field athletes by Ungerleider and Golding (1991), 34.3% reported that they saw themselves from both perspectives, 35% reported an inside view, and 30.7% reported an outside view. Significantly, the Olympians reported a more external perspective than non-Olympians and a stronger physical sensation associated with that imagery. The authors suggested that this might indicate that imagery-perspective requirements may differ depending on the event.

The Imagery Use Questionnaire (IUQ; Hall, Rodgers, and Barr 1990) has been used in a number of studies to assess imagery use; it also asks about imagery-perspective use. Hall et al. investigated the use of imagery by athletes in six sports: American football, ice hockey, soccer, squash, gymnastics, and figure skating. Athletes reported that they used internal and external visual perspectives equally. Spittle and Morris (1999a, b, 2000) have used the IUQ as a pretest of imagery perspective use in a series of studies on imagery perspective and found that participants with a range of sport experiences reported more use of internal than external imagery.

Barr and Hall (1992) administered the IUQ for Rowing to 348 rowers at high school, college, and national team levels. Rowers reported more frequent use of an internal than an external visual perspective, although no statistical analysis of this difference was conducted. Younger rowers adopted an external visual perspective more than older rowers. In opposition to this, Rodgers et al. (1991), in a training study covered in more detail later in this chapter, found that at pretest junior figure skaters had a higher rating on external visual imagery than internal kinesthetic imagery. The internal kinesthetic rating was higher than that for internal visual imagery.

In a study investigating the motivational function and the actual use of imagery by soccer players, Salmon, Hall, and Haslam (1994) administered the IUQ for Soccer Players (IUQ-SP) to a large sample of male and female national, provincial, and local-level soccer players. The players generally reported higher use of internal than external imagery; however, on both internal and external imagery the ratings for national and provincial players was significantly higher than for local players.

The questionnaire research has provided mixed information on the relationship between imagery perspectives and their use by elite athletes. Of the Mahoney and Avener replication studies, only Mahoney and Avener (1977) and Doyle and Landers (1980) found internal imagery to be associated with more successful performance or performers. Other replication studies did not differentiate between performance level and perspective use (e.g., Meyers et al. 1979; Highlen and Bennett 1979; Rotella et al. 1980). Other questionnaire studies have also provided mixed findings, with the more successful athletes reporting adopting both perspectives or higher use of external imagery (Ungerleider and Golding 1991). The IUQ studies found no difference between internal and external imagery use (e.g., Hall et al. 1990), nor a preference for internal imagery (e.g., Barr and Hall 1992; Salmon et al. 1994). Salmon et al., however, also found high ratings on external imagery, suggesting that soccer players used both perspectives. A problem with using questionnaire approaches to study imagery, especially when surveying what athletes "usually do," is that they are retrospective, and consequently there could be problems with accuracy of memory.

PERFORMANCE STUDIES

Internal and external imagery studies have generally compared the effects of internal and external perspective groups or internal and external imagery-training programs on performance of motor skills or sport skills. In this section we review studies investigating the effects of internal and external imagery, first on performance of a single motor or sport skill, then on different types of skills.

PERFORMANCE STUDIES OF ONE SKILL

Several studies have compared internal and external imagery groups on learning or performing a skill. For instance, Epstein (1980) investigated the effects of imagery perspective on dart-throwing performance. Undergraduate students were randomly assigned to one of three groups: internal imagery, external imagery, or control. The two imagery groups threw 30 darts in an assessment of baseline ability, then undertook imagery training and practice (2 min), performed 30 trials of mental-rehearsal-aided throwing, underwent another 1 min of rehearsal training, and threw 30 more rehearsal-aided darts. Epstein found no significant effect on dart-throwing performance based on perspective. Responses to the imagery perspective questions suggested that instructed perspective was not always adhered to, with extensive switching of perspectives.

Neisser (1976) described a study by Nigro and Neisser that also investigated mental practice (MP) and dart-throwing with college students. The researchers assigned participants to a control group and four experimental MP groups: positive field, negative field, positive observer, and negative observer. Thus, instructions for the MP groups varied across two dimensions: positive or negative and point of view (field or observer). In the positive and negative condition, Nigro and Neisser instructed participants to imagine successful or unsuccessful throws. In the field condition, they instructed them to imagine using a first-person perspective or a third-person perspective. There was a significant increase in performance for the MP groups. The positive and negative dimension made no difference in performance enhancement, but the field (internal) condition produced greater performance improvements than the observer (external) condition did.

A study by Mumford and Hall (1985) investigated imagery and figure-skating performance. The skaters performed a figure as a pretest measure and then were randomly assigned to one of four imagery groups: internal kinesthetic, internal visual, external visual, and control. No differences in performance were noted between the three types of imagery training, and imagery-training participants did not perform better than control participants. This could have been due in part to a ceiling effect, because although the participants had not skated the figure before, only the sequence of elements was unfamiliar since they were skilled skaters.

Gordon et al. (1994) investigated the effectiveness of internal versus external imagery training on cricket bowling performance with high school students. Participants were randomly assigned to an internal imagery, external imagery, or control group after being matched on general bowling ability and vividness of imagery. The imagery groups improved performance over time, but there were no significant differences between the two imagery perspective groups. The postexperiment questionnaire indicated that approximately 50% of participants reported switching between internal and external imagery.

The performance studies reviewed here do not support the concept that an internal imagery perspective is superior to an external perspective for performance enhancement. Most of the studies that compared internal and external imagery groups (e.g., Epstein 1980; Mumford and Hall

1985; Gordon et al. 1994) found no difference between the perspectives but suggested that both improve performance. Many of these studies, in which participants were either trained or given instruction in internal or external imagery (e.g., Mumford and Hall 1985; Gordon et al. 1994), assigned participants to a group randomly. None of these studies have investigated whether imagery perspective is trainable because they have not compared pretraining perspective use with posttraining perspective patterns, which would determine whether training actually increased use of the trained perspective. What they have investigated is whether training in a perspective leads to increased performance. Some studies have used retrospective reports to test whether participants actually used the experimental condition. This is preferable to no test but is subject to problems with memory accuracy. One finding that emerged from these studies is the extensive amount of switching between perspectives when participants were assigned to internal or external imagery groups (e.g., Epstein 1980; Gordon et al. 1994). This could suggest that preferences for a particular perspective might be important (Hall 1997), or that switching is a necessary or perhaps desirable method for experiencing imagery (Collins et al. 1998). Alternatively, perhaps it indicates that in complex tasks certain parts are best imaged internally and others externally, or in combinations thereof.

PERFORMANCE STUDIES OF MULTIPLE SKILLS

The nature of a task may govern the best perspective for the athlete to use. Annett (1995) stated that introspective reports suggested that "different kinds of imagery may be more or less effective when used with different tasks" (p. 162). Other researchers have also suggested that task type, such as open versus closed skills, might influence the effectiveness of imagery perspectives (Harris 1986; Kearns and Crossman 1992; McLean and Richardson 1994). "... It seems plausible that closed skills would benefit more from an internal focus, while open skills may gain most benefit from an external orientation . . . but, no systematic research has yet been published to provide any convincing evidence on the relevance of this orientation variable" (McLean and Richardson 1994, 66). This kind of prediction of the influence of task type is displayed in figure 6.1*b*. Open and closed skills essentially lie on a continuum from extreme closed skills, which are performed in a totally stable environment, to extreme open skills, in which factors are constantly changing. In Gentile's (2000) taxonomy of skill classification, an essentially closed skill might include stationary environmental conditions, no intertrial variability, body stability, and no object manipulation. An essentially open skill might include changing environmental conditions, intertrial variability, body transport, and object manipulation (Magill 2004). Most of the research on imagery perspectives has focused on closed skills (e.g., gymnastics, skating).

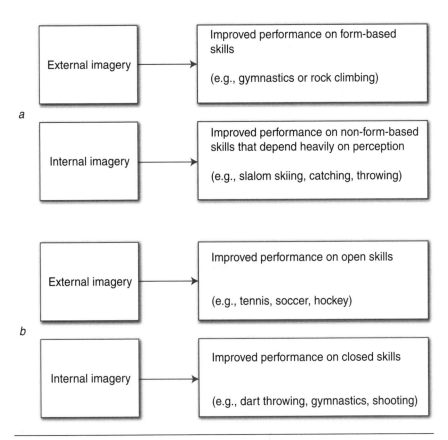

Figure 6.1 Predictions for imagery perspective and task type. (*a*) Form-based predictions; (*b*) open and closed skill predictions.

Based on Hardy and Callow 1999.

Hardy (1997) and Hardy and Callow (1999) suggested that the failure to consider different demands of different tasks has contributed to the confusion and myths revealed in the imagery-perspective literature. Hardy proposed that imagery's beneficial effect on the acquisition and performance of a motor skill depends on the extent that the images add to the available useful information. For instance, Hardy and Callow proposed that external imagery might assist the imager to see precise positions and movements required for successful performance in tasks that depend on form. For example, little additional beneficial information is provided about performance in imaging a handstand or cartwheel from an internal perspective. In tasks such as gymnastics or rock climbing, in which body shape and positioning are important, an external perspective allows rehearsal of the movements and positions. Hardy and Callow argued that the converse might also apply: that internal imagery allows the performer to rehearse the precise spatial locations, environmental conditions, and timings in skills that depend heavily on perception for successful execution. For example, in a slalom-type task, an internal perspective allows rehearsal of precise locations for initiations of maneuvers. This prediction of the relationship between task type and the imager's perspective is diagrammed in figure 6.1*a*.

TASK-TYPE STUDIES

Based on the hypotheses regarding the influence of task type, several recent studies have compared various tasks. For instance, Glisky et al. (1996) compared performance on a cognitive-visual task (angles estimation) with performance on a motor-kinesthetic task (stabilometer) for "natural" internal or "natural" external imagers as classified on the Imagery Assessment Questionnaire (IAQ; Vigus and Williams 1985). Participants were split into internal or external imagery groups and a control group based on the classification. Compared to the control group, the external imagers improved performance more on the stabilometer task and the internal imagers improved more on the angles task.

White and Hardy (1995) conducted two studies to examine the efficacy of internal and external imagery on a slalom-type task, using wheelchairs (open skill) and a gymnastics-type task utilizing clubs (closed skill) with university students. Participants were randomly assigned to internal visual imagery or external visual imagery groups. In the slalom task, internal imagers completed the transfer trials with significantly fewer errors than did the external imagers, but the external imagers completed them significantly faster than the internal imagers. White and Hardy claimed that this finding indicated that the two imagery groups had different speed–accuracy tradeoffs, with the external imagers focusing on the speed of performance and the internal imagers focusing on accuracy. On the gymnastics task, internal visual imagery was more effective than internal visual imagery for both learning and retention.

To investigate the suggestions by White and Hardy (1995) and Hardy (1997), Collins et al. (1998) compared internal and external imagery groups' performance on a karate *kata* task. On the basis of imagery ability and previous *kata* performance, Collins et al. assigned participants to four groups: internal imagery, external imagery aided by a coping model, external imagery aided by a mastery model, and a control group who performed stretching exercises. Collins et al. found that during the learning phase, many participants in the internal group reported switching between internal and external imagery; that is, they used both perspectives. Collins et al. compared these participants with the other groups and found that the "switching" internals performed significantly better than the "per instruction" internals and the external mastery group. In the practice phase, several participants in each group reported switching between internal and external imagery. Analysis revealed that the "switching" groups and the "internal-only group" performed significantly better than the other groups.

Spittle and Morris (1999a, b, 2000) conducted a series of studies investigating imagery-perspective use and training, and the influence of task type. The initial study (Spittle and Morris, 1999b) investigated the use of imagery perspective in open and closed skills. Participants experienced more internal imagery than external imagery across imagination of eight generic sport skills, but reported more external imagery with the closed skills than the open ones. In two follow-up studies (Spittle and Morris, 1999a, 2000), participants reported more internal than external imagery in imagining both an open skill (table tennis) and a closed skill (darts) before imagery training. However, they experienced more external imagery with the open skill than the closed skill.

Spittle and Morris (1999a) investigated whether participants could be trained to use internal or external imagery when imaging an open skill (table tennis) or a closed skill (darts). Based on pretest scores on imagery-perspective use, participants were assigned to mismatched training groups, with those who ranked lower on internal imagery use assigned to internal training and those lower on external imagery use assigned to external training. The internal training group increased its use of internal imagery significantly for both skills, and the external training group showed a trend toward increased use of external imagery.

Spittle and Morris (2000) went a step further and explored the influence of imagery-perspective training on the performance of an open skill (table tennis), and a closed skill (darts). Participants were assigned to a control group or mismatched imagery-perspective training groups. The design for this study is detailed in figure 6.2. Participants were assigned to groups, completed a performance pretest on each skill before engaging in imagery-perspective training, then completed posttests on performance of both skills. The perspective-training groups showed no difference in performance gains; however, both improved performance on both skills significantly more than the control group. In addition, an analysis of actual reported use of imagery perspective, irrespective of training group, revealed that internals improved performance significantly more in darts than externals, and externals improved performance in table tennis significantly more than internals.

In a study that replicated much of the one by Spittle and Morris (1999a) on perspective use during imagery, Fogarty and Morris (2003) examined perspective use during imagery of open (return of serve, ground strokes) and closed (different types of serves) tennis skills. As in all three studies by Spittle and Morris (1999a, b, 2000), participants tended to use more internal than external imagery. There was no difference between

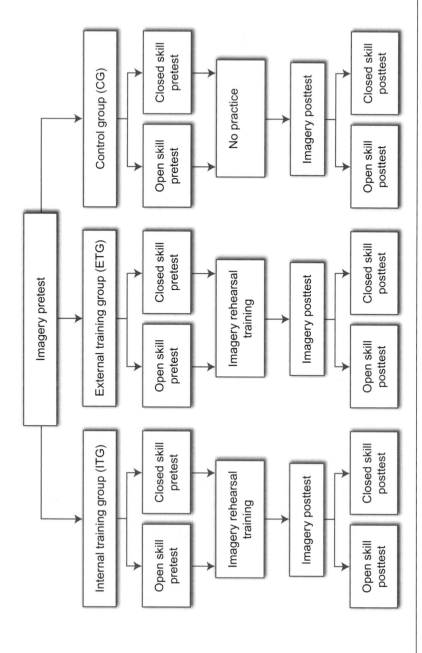

Figure 6.2 Design of a study of the effect of perspective training on performance of open and closed skills.

imagery-perspective use for open and closed tennis skills. The higher use of internal imagery by participants might suggest a preference for this perspective. It has been suggested that individual preference for one perspective or another may influence perspective use (Hall 1997), but no studies have examined this. In fact, researchers have found that categorizing participants as internal or external imagers is very difficult because many report extensive switching between the two perspectives, both between and within imagery trials (Epstein 1980; Gordon, Weinberg, and Jackson 1994; Harris and Robinson 1986; Mumford and Hall 1985; Spittle and Morris 1999b; Wang and Morgan 1992).

A tentative theoretical paper by Morris and Spittle (2001) has proposed a default theory hypothesis to explain imagery-perspective use or preference. It is based on the idea that internal imagery may be the default perspective, and the extent to which external imagery is used depends on experience, particularly during childhood. Thus, internal imagery may be more natural to us, but external imagery might add something new and different to our experience, which might make it more beneficial in some cases. The basic premise of default theory is that when variables can exist in two or more states, one condition is the default unless other factors are active to establish the alternative state(s). The obvious example of default theory is the determination of gender (Crews 1994). In mammals, embryonic sexual tissue is initially undifferentiated. Gender depends on genetic triggers that determine the presence or absence of androgens, or male hormones. If androgens are absent, the embryo will feminize. If androgens are present it will become masculine. Thus, female gender is the default, which develops unless the conditions for the male gender are triggered by the genes (Crews 1994). In fact, gender is not a simple dichotomy; depending on variations in the basic default mechanism, different levels of "maleness" and "femaleness" are possible.

Default theory can be applied to many other biological and psychological phenomena. Researchers have discussed a perspective preference (e.g., Glisky 1996; Hall 1997); for instance, Glisky et al. (1996) referred to their participants as "natural internal or external imagers" (p. 3). This appears to beg the question of how this "natural" perspective develops. Morris and Spittle proposed that the limited evidence so far suggests that the development of imagery perspective might be a case of default theory. For instance, in the three studies conducted by Spittle and Morris (1999a, b, 2000), more athletes reported a preference for internal than external imagery, athletes reported using more internal than external imagery during imagery trials, and an internal-imagery perspective was more difficult to alter than an external one in perspective training. These observations are all consistent with the proposition that imagery perspective is initially internal and the extent to which it becomes external or mixed depends on experience, particularly during childhood.

Certain predictions flow from the default hypothesis, and these could be tested in future research. An obvious prediction is that younger people will more strongly favor the internal perspective. Another prediction is that experience will influence perspective use; studies could explore the sport experience of adolescents and adults and compare those results with imagery-perspective use. External imagery is described as similar to watching oneself on TV or video, and video has been used extensively in many sports, especially body-movement sports like gymnastics and diving. It seems reasonable to suggest that athletes who are trained with extensive use of demonstration and video are more likely to become experienced in taking an external perspective. Researchers could investigate the relationship between training methods and imagery-perspective use or the influence of video training on imagery-perspective use in learning a motor skill.

Although the research on task type suggests that different tasks influence the efficacy of perspective use, it is still not clear exactly what this relationship is. More research is needed on the influence of imagery perspectives on performance of sport skills, including studies that address issues of task type, imagery-perspective preference, the interaction of external and kinesthetic imagery, and imagery-training effects on perspective use. In addition, an examination of the default hypothesis of imagery-perspective use would add much to the understanding of perspective preference in sport and exercise.

Visual/Kinesthetic and Internal/External Imagery Research

The research on task type suggests that task and perspective preference may be important in using imagery perspectives effectively in sport. As mentioned earlier, visual and kinesthetic imagery appear to be important to the effective use of imagery in sport. Some studies have now investigated the impact of task type with imagery modality (visual and kinesthetic) on the effectiveness of imagery-perspective use.

In the perspective literature, Hardy (1997) and Hardy and Callow (1999) suggested that imagery's beneficial effect on the acquisition and performance of a motor skill depends on the extent that the images add to the available useful information. A similar notion could apply to visual and kinesthetic imagery, according to the belief that visual and motor (kinesthetic) imagery activate different neural networks in a functionally equivalent way, like in actual movement (Jeannerod 1994). The combination of visual and kinesthetic imagery would be more effective than either type alone because it activates both neural pathways and adds to the information from imagery (Hardy and Callow 1999). Thus the most effective imagery might be that which utilizes internal and external imagery with visual and kinesthetic imagery.

Hardy and Callow (1999) conducted three studies to investigate the effect of different imagery perspectives with visual and kinesthetic imagery on task performance of largely form-based movements. These movements consisted of a karate *kata* task, a gymnastics floor routine, and a rock-climbing task. In study 1, Hardy and Callow had karateists learn a new *kata,* called *Jion,* which consists of 52 separate movements. Hardy and Callow assigned participants to external visual imagery, internal visual imagery, or control conditions and found that the external visual group performed significantly better than the internal visual group, which performed significantly better than the control group.

Study 2 extended the initial study by manipulating both the visual perspective (internal and external) and kinesthetic imagery using a gymnastic sequence as a performance task. Sport science students were randomly assigned to one of four treatment groups: external visual imagery with kinesthetic imagery, external visual imagery only, internal visual imagery with kinesthetic imagery, or internal visual imagery only. Hardy and Callow concluded that the external visual imagery groups performed significantly better than the internal visual groups. The external visual imagery with kinesthetic imagery group performed better than the internal visual imagery with kinesthetic imagery group.

Study 3 replicated study 2 but with a rock-climbing (bouldering) task and experienced rock climbers. The results suggested that external visual imagery was superior to internal visual imagery and that kinesthetic imagery was superior to no kinesthetic imagery on all performance measures. Overall, Hardy and Callow (1999) concluded that external visual imagery was superior to internal visual imagery for the acquisition and performance of tasks that depend on form for successful performance. Interestingly, a later study on form-based movement by Cumming and Ste-Marie (2001) failed to support this; they found no difference between imagery perspective on synchronized figure skating that emphasized form and body position. Hardy and Callow further suggested that the results offered some support for the claim that kinesthetic imagery provides an additional beneficial effect regardless of perspective adopted.

Until the recent studies by White and Hardy (1995), Hardy and Callow (1999), Glisky et al. (1996), and Spittle and Morris (1999a, b, 2000) researchers have failed to recognize that the tasks being imaged and performed might mediate the relationship between imagery perspective and performance enhancement, so that one perspective is not superior in all situations. These studies have also begun to investigate the impact of imagery modality on perspective use. They tentatively concur with Hardy and Callow that kinesthetic imagery provides a beneficial effect regardless of the perspective adopted.

CONCLUSIONS

Imagery perspectives and modality appear to be important considerations in using imagery effectively in sport. Imagery modality (visual and kinesthetic) can be differentiated and may provide discrete information. Research on visual and kinesthetic imagery suggests that both are important in sport and their effectiveness may be related to the purpose of imagery (e.g., motivation or confidence) or the type of sport skill being learned or performed. Similarly, the research on imagery perspectives suggests that the purpose of imagery (e.g., motivation or confidence) or task being imagined (e.g., open or closed, form based or nonform based) is important in the efficacious use of perspectives. A general conclusion about imagery modality and imagery perspective is that imagery is beneficial to the extent that it adds useful information to the movement experience (Hardy 1997). Since it is likely that visual and kinesthetic imagery and internal and external imagery provide different information about a movement experience, practitioners are advised that an effective approach to imagery might be to combine modalities and perspectives. In other words, using both modalities and both perspectives is often better than using only one perspective or modality. Using a combination of perspectives and modalities allows athletes to gain as much information as they can about a movement experience and makes imagery maximally effective.

CHAPTER 7

PSYCHOPHYSIOLOGICAL RESEARCH ON IMAGERY

Engaging in imagery of an action can have physiological effects that are very similar to those that occur during actual performance of that action. Jeannerod (1997) cited an example that may seem familiar to those of you who have coached or taught sport skills. As an instructor demonstrates a skill, the learner does not move but imagines the actions needed in order to replicate the skill. Then, while watching the learner's practice attempts, the instructor probably has strong feelings about which actions should be done and how the learner is doing them. Or perhaps you have watched a sports match and experienced extremely strong feelings during the game, such as frustration when a player misses an opportunity, or perhaps you mentally performed the appropriate actions to kick or catch the ball. The vividness of this imagery can be enough to produce physiological changes.

Chapter 2 explains that imagery in sport is the creation or re-creation of an experience involving quasi-sensorial, quasi-perceptual, and quasi-affective characteristics and that is under the volitional control of the imager. The imager undergoes sensations and experiences similar to actual perception and action. Because imagery appears to be integrally linked to perception and action, it has powerful potential to produce change (Simons 2000). That close relationship between imagery and perception and action is one of the reasons why imagery in sport can be so fascinating. The feelings experienced during imagery and imagery's close link to perception and action suggest that psychophysiology is important to the imagery experience. Understanding the psychophysiology of imagery may lead to a better understanding of imagery use in sport.

Psychophysiology involves understanding the relationships between the physiological structures of the body, such as the sensory and nervous systems, and mental processes (Hayward 1997). It is the study of the relationship between brain and behavior in the framework of peripheral and central physiological responses (Hugdahl 1995). A basic assumption is that behavioral, cognitive, and emotional events are mirrored in physiological processes; therefore, mental activities such as thoughts and feelings have effects on bodily processes (Hugdahl 1995). In terms of imagery this involves understanding how, as a mental process, it may affect physiological processes. The study of the psychophysiology of imagery is quite extensive; this chapter focuses on the psychophysiological research on imagery related to movement tasks.

The psychophysiological approach to the study of movement imagery is not new; in fact, some of the earliest studies of such imagery addressed physiological aspects (e.g., Allers and Scheminsky 1926; Clark 1916; Jacobson 1930a, b, c, d; Meakin 1903; Shaw 1938; Slaughter 1902). Since then, researchers have continued to investigate the psychophysiology of movement imagery. Their explorations have largely been driven by theoretical interest in the psychoneuromuscular theory, the functional equivalence between imagery and movement, and Lang's bioinformational theory. (These concepts are reviewed in detail in chapter 3.)

The psychoneuromuscular explanations of imagery propose that imaging a task activates central nervous processes that prime the peripheral nervous system to produce minute muscle innervations that are identical in pattern and location to those that occur in the muscles used in performance. The efficacy of imagery rehearsal (IR) of a motor task results from providing feedback or inflow resulting from the muscle activation.

The psychoneuromuscular theory is essentially a peripheral explanation of the effects of imagery. A more central explanation is functional equivalence, which purports that imagery and perception or imagery and movement recruit common structures and processes (Finke 1980, 1985; Finke and Shephard 1986). The peripheral and functional-equivalence explanations are called "inflow" and "outflow" theories, respectively (Decety and Ingvar 1990; Kohl and Roenker 1983; Slade, Landers, and Martin 2002). They differ in that inflow explanations propose that feedback is important to learning and performance due to mental practice (MP) or IR, whereas outflow explanations propose that changes in central representations are important to the learning and performance effects of MP or IR. Like IR or MP, imagery is used for much more than skill practice; for example, for motivation and self-confidence enhancement. As such, psychophysiological measures could give clues regarding affective responses in imagery. For instance, autonomic indices during imagery might indicate affective states. Lang's bioinformational theory places importance on linking stimulus and response propositions; when imagery involves response propositions, it is more effective and should produce more affective and emotional reactions.

We begin our discussion of the psychophysiology of movement imagery by examining the measurement of psychophysiological processes. We then look at research that has used such measurement to investigate the imagery of movement.

PSYCHOPHYSIOLOGICAL MEASURES

The measurement of psychophysiological responses can be regarded as a "window" into the brain and mind during imagery (Hugdahl 1995). To try to understand the relationship between mental and physiological processes, psychologists have developed measures of psychophysiological aspects of human behavior. Technological advances have made research on these aspects of movement imagery more sophisticated and have stimulated recent interest in the psychophysiology of imagery. Various psychophysiological measures are available to psychologists, which can be divided into peripheral and central measures.

PERIPHERAL MEASURES

Peripheral measures generally relate to the peripheral nervous system (PNS) and include a variety of responses from skeletal muscles and the organs under control of the autonomic nervous system (ANS). They include measures of the electrodermal system, such as skin conductance (SC) and skin resistance (SR); cardiovascular system, such as heart rate (HR), electrocardiogram (ECG), oxygen consumption ($\dot{V}O_2$), ventilatory minute volume ($\dot{V}_E$), respiratory exchange ratio (RER), blood pressure (BP), and respiration rate (RR); and muscular system, such as electromyography (EMG) and electrooculography (EOG). Table 7.1 provides descriptions of these peripheral measures.

The activity of the electrodermal system tends to vary in relation to a person's emotional state; thus we may be able to study these states by measuring electrodermal activity. For instance, because people tend to sweat more during periods of stress, an increase in electrodermal activity during imagery of a stressful situation may indicate that it is producing a stress response. Cardiovascular responses are common effects of changes in psychological state and also are influenced by movement. Consequently, changes in these indices during imagery indicate changes in psychological state or the similarity between movement and movement imagery. Muscular responses to imagery have been studied extensively in the sport psychology literature. Researchers have used muscular activity in a variety of ways; the most common is to compare the amount of

Table 7.1 Peripheral Psychophysiological Measures Used in Imagery Research

Measure	Description
Skin conductance (SC)	The ability of the skin to conduct electricity (the reciprocal of skin resistance [SR]). It is a measure of general arousal, based on the activity of sweat glands in the skin. As the activity of these glands changes, so does the electrical conductance of the skin.
Skin resistance (SR)	The resistance offered by the skin to an externally applied current.
Heart rate (HR)	Average number of beats of the heart per minute.
Electrocardiogram (ECG)	A more sophisticated form of heart rate measurement that presents information graphically as a waveform.
Oxygen consumption ($\dot{V}O_2$)	The volume of oxygen consumed by the body each minute (determined by calculating the difference between the amount of oxygen inhaled and exhaled).
Ventilatory minute volume ($\dot{V}_E$)	Ventilation is the movement of gas in and out of the lungs. Minute ventilation is the total amount of air inhaled ($\dot{V}_I$) or exhaled ($\dot{V}_E$) each minute.
Respiratory exchange ratio (RER)	The ratio of the volume of carbon dioxide expired per minute ($\dot{V}CO_2$) to the volume of oxygen ($\dot{V}O_2$) consumed during the same time interval.
Blood pressure (BP)	The pressure, or force, exerted by the blood on the walls of the body's main arteries resulting from the pumping action of the heart. BP measurements are made when the heart's ventricles are contracting (systolic pressure), and when they are at rest (diastolic pressure).
Respiration rate (RR)	The number of breaths per minute.
Electromyography (EMG)	Measures electrical activity in the muscles (action potentials).
Electrooculography (EOG)	Records electrical activity in eye muscles, indicating eye movements.

muscular activity generated by different types of imagery (e.g., internal versus external imagery, stimulus versus response propositions) or to prove "mirroring" between imagery and movement. Movement involves electrical activity in the muscles (action potentials) that can be measured by electromyography (EMG). Researchers measure EMG by attaching surface electrodes to the skin over muscles of interest or inserting fine wire electrodes into a specific muscle. Electrooculography (EOG) refers to a technique for recording eye movements.

CENTRAL MEASURES

Central measures relate to central nervous system (CNS) responses, including the brain. Much progress has been made in developing measures of brain activity, so determining where and when certain processes occur in the brain is now possible. Central measures are based on the principle of brain organization known as functional differentiation, which states that certain brain areas seem to be responsible for specific functions (Eysenck 2002). For instance, occipital areas seem important in visual actions, and specific sensory and motor areas are involved in movement-related actions. The central measures differ in terms of how precisely they identify which areas of the CNS are active and when the activity starts and finishes; that is, they differ in their spatial (where) and temporal resolutions (when). In general, recordings from electrodes on the outside of the skin have poor spatial but good temporal resolution, and imaging or scanning techniques have good spatial but poor temporal resolution. Central measures include electroencephalography (EEG) and event-related potential (ERP), which use surface electrodes on the scalp; brain-imaging techniques such as computerized axial tomography (CAT scan), positron emission tomography (PET scan), and magnetic resonance imaging (MRI); and transcranial magnetic stimulation (TMS), which involves magnetic stimulation of the neurons in the brain. Table 7.2 provides brief descriptions of some of the central measures used in imagery research.

An EEG is a recording of the difference in electrical activity between various points of the cortex using electrodes placed at specific points on the scalp. EEG patterns tend to be wavelike, and analysis centers on the frequency and amplitude of the waves, with differences indicating different types of activation. For instance, alpha waves (frequencies of 8 to 12 Hz) represent relaxation. They are typically attenuated or blocked during cognitive activity. Beta waves (14 to 25 Hz) represent alertness and are generally associated with increased activation. Event-related potentials (ERP), sometimes called evoked potentials (EP), refer to changes in the EEG recording in response to an internal or external stimulus. EEG and ERPs are useful because they provide good temporal information about brain activity, but they do not provide much spatial resolution.

Table 7.2 Central Psychophysiological Measures Used in Imagery Research

Measure	Description
Electroencephalography (EEG)	A recording of the difference in electrical activity between various points of the cortex using electrodes placed at specific points on the scalp. EEG patterns tend to be wavelike.
Event-related potential (ERP) or evoked potentials (EP)	Changes in the EEG recording in response to an internal or external stimulus.
Computerized axial tomography (CAT) scan	A beam of X rays moves in a horizontal cross-section, detecting differences in tissue density and generating a 2-dimensional image of the brain and its structures.
Positron emission tomography (PET) scan	A detectable radioactive isotope is injected into the blood and tagged to a substance that indicates brain activity, such as glucose or oxygen. The PET scan is displayed as a picture with different levels of brain activity indicated by different colors.
Regional cerebral blood flow (rCBF)	Uses a tracer so that changes in radiation are detected in various regions of the brain to measure brain function.
Magnetic resonance imaging (MRI)	Radio waves excite atoms in the brain, which are detected by a large magnet that surrounds the individual. Changes are displayed in a 3-dimensional picture of the brain structures.
Functional MRI (fMRI)	Uses the different magnetic properties of oxygenated (arterial) and deoxygenated (venous) blood to identify blood flow.
Transcranial magnetic stimulation (TMS)	A magnetic field stimulates specific cortical neurons during imagery to determine the stimulated area's contribution to imagery. A measurement of the consequences of stimulation in terms of motor excitability, such as motor-evoked potentials (MEPs) and motor threshold.

Brain-imaging techniques cover a range of approaches that measure changes in blood flow, glucose metabolism, and X-ray images. They also provide different structural and functional information. A CAT scan provides structural information on the brain by moving a beam of X rays in a horizontal cross-section, detecting differences in tissue density. This allows the computer to generate a 2-dimensional image of the brain and its structures. PET detects positrons, which are atomic particles emitted by some radioactive substances (Eysenck 2002). A radioactive isotope is injected into the blood and tagged to a substance used by the brain, such as glucose or oxygen. The radioactive molecules emit positrons that are detected and analyzed. When a brain area is more active, more blood is supplied to that area, which is picked up in the PET scan. The results are converted to a picture of brain functioning in which different colors indicate different levels of activity. PET has reasonable spatial resolution but poor temporal resolution (Eysenck 2002). Two approaches that are very similar to PET are single photon emission computed tomography (SPECT) and regional cerebral blood flow (rCBF). SPECT involves ingestion of a technetium isotope (HMPAO), a biologically active radio-labeled (meaning it emits gamma rays that can be detected by the scanner) drug, and produces good functional imaging but with a static image (Hugdahl 1995). In rCBF, a tracer detects changes in radiation in various regions of the brain to measure function.

In an MRI, radio waves excite atoms in the brain, which are detected by a large magnet that surrounds the individual. The changes are displayed in a 3-dimensional picture. MRI is a structural technique that maps the structures of the brain rather than its functions. However, brain function can be assessed using an approach called functional MRI (fMRI), which uses the different magnetic properties of oxygenated (arterial) and deoxygenated (venous) blood to identify blood flow. Active areas of the brain show an increase in oxygenated blood supply that can be detected by the fMRI. The test provides good spatial and temporal resolution and may be more useful than PET because it provides better temporal information. Because they detect blood flow, PET and fMRI are indirect measures of neural activity.

TMS has become popular recently as an approach to studying motor neurophysiology (Sack and Linden 2003). In TMS a magnetic field passes directly through the scalp and stimulates specific cortical neurons (Maeda and Pascual-Leone 2003). Early TMS equipment allowed stimulation only every 3 sec, but new machines allow for repetitive TMS (rTMS), which can send as many as 50 stimuli per sec. In investigating higher cognitive functioning such as in imagery, studies typically use this stimulation to interfere with neuronal function in order to determine the contribution of the stimulated area, such as the primary motor cortex (M1), to performance of a particular task, such as motor imagery of moving the fingers (Sack and Linden 2003). TMS approaches measure the consequences of stimulation in terms of motor excitability, such as motor evoked potentials (MEPs) and motor threshold. An MEP is the electrical potential recorded from a muscle, peripheral nerve, or the spinal cord in response to CNS stimulation (Maeda and Pascual-Leone 2003). Motor threshold is the minimum intensity that will evoke a small motor response of a criterion level (Maeda and Pascual-Leone 2003). The advantage of TMS over neuroimaging techniques such as PET and MRI (which can provide only correlational data because they demonstrate only that a specific brain area is active during task performance) is that it can establish causal roles for specific areas of the CNS because it has an impact on performance (Kosslyn, Ganis, and Thompson 2001).

PSYCHOPHYSIOLOGICAL RESEARCH

Research that has investigated imagery of movement using psychophysiological approaches may provide clues for understanding the relationships between the physiological structures of the body and the mental process of imagery. Hopefully this brief review will stimulate the reader to consider some of the issues concerning the psychophysiology of imagery in sport. Although there is substantially more research on sport and motor skills using peripheral measures, the amount of literature on motor imagery using central measures is growing.

PERIPHERAL ACTIVATION DURING IMAGERY

The research using peripheral measures is separated into sections measuring muscular activity, spinal activity, and autonomic responses. The research on muscular response in imagery has been a productive area in sport psychology, and there are also quite a few studies on autonomic effects of imagery in sport.

MUSCULAR ACTIVITY

Psychophysiological research on the muscular activity that occurs during imagery has a long history in sport psychology, and many studies have investigated it during imagery of motor tasks. Much of this research can be traced to interest in the psychoneuromuscular theory and the distinction between internal and external imagery. Lang's bioinformational theory has also generated some research interest, with researchers comparing the muscular activity generated by scripts weighted with stimulus and response propositions. The majority of these studies have found that muscular activity increased during imagination, although it was considerably less than during actual movement. One issue for researchers is determining whether muscular activity is localized and mirrors movement rather than being a general activation of the body.

Several studies provide support for mirrored and localized muscular activity during imagery. In the early 1930s Jacobson (1930a, b, c, d; 1931a, b, c) conducted several studies comparing muscular activity during various imagined and executed activities, such as bending the arm, sweeping, climbing a rope, rowing, boxing, scratching the chin, plucking a flower, combing hair, playing the piano, and performing a biceps curl. He concluded that movement imagery produces increased activation of the muscles specific to the movement being imagined, but noted that the level of activity was considerably less than during actual movement. Visual imagery produced more eye activity, and kinesthetic imagery produced more muscular activity.

Hale (1982) attempted to replicate Jacobson's (1930a, b, c, d and 1931a, b, c) modality-specific findings comparing internal and external imagery. Hale hypothesized that internal images are more likely than external images to result in muscle activity due to the external perspective's greater kinesthetic element and its reliance on visual imagery. As discussed in chapter 6, this may represent a confounding of imagery perspectives with sensory modality. Hale measured EMG activity in the biceps brachii muscle and dominant-eye EOG activity during imagery of performing a biceps curl with a 25 lb weight. Internal imagery produced more biceps activity than external imagery. There was no significant effect for EOG activity.

In another study comparing imagery types, Bakker, Boschker, and Chung (1996) investigated Lang's model of stimulus and response propositions using imagery of lifting 4.5 and 9 kg weights. Bakker et al. recorded EMG of both biceps brachii muscles during imagery. Response propositions resulted in greater muscular activity than stimulus propositions. EMG activity in the active arm was greater than in the passive arm, and a significant difference in EMG activity between 9 kg and 4.5 kg weights was noted. Participants who had more EMG activity did not have higher scores for imagery ability.

Harris and Robinson (1986) investigated whether muscular innervation during imagery was specific to muscles used in actual performance and if skill level or internal and external imagery produced differing levels of muscular activity with karate athletes. Muscle innervations were specific to the muscle group necessary for task execution. In addition, advanced students produced more EMG activity during imagery than did lower-level students, and internal imagery produced more EMG activity than external imagery.

To investigate whether EMG activity during imagery (mental training) is task specific, Wehner, Vogt, and Stadler (1984) measured EMG of the biceps synchronously to a paced contour-tracking task. They assigned participants to paced contour-tracking (active), mental-training, or control groups. They found a similar frequency characteristic in the mental-training and active-training EMGs. In another study of adult participants, Livesay and Samaras (1998) found that HR and EMG activity of the dominant forearm increased during imagery of squeezing a rubber ball. Nondominant forearm EMG did not increase during imagery. Tremblay, Tremblay, and Colcer (2001) found increased EMG motor-evoked potential (MEP) activity in the quadriceps (agonist) but not biceps femoris (antagonist) during imagery of a leg extension, indicating that imagery is specific to the agonist muscle.

Reports of increased muscular activity during imagery of sport and motor skills often claim that it mirrors actual performance. For instance, Suinn (1976a), in an anecdotal report with an alpine skier, found that the skier's leg-muscle EMG during imagery mirrored the downhill course being imagined. Bird (1984) reported similar results in a series of case studies investigating imagery by five athletes from equestrian, rowing, breaststroke swimming, water skiing, and basketball.

Several studies have failed to show localized or mirrored muscular activity during imagery, suggesting that the activity is more general and may represent overall activation of the body. Shaw (1938, 1940) also conducted early research into the psychophysiological aspects of movement imagery. In a series of studies, Shaw (1938) measured muscular activity during imagery of various activities, such as squeezing a hand dynamometer in the right hand and typing the alphabet. Shaw concluded that there appeared to be a concomitant increase in muscular activity from most muscle groups during imagery of the various tasks, but it was not localized to the muscles involved. The same researcher (1940) measured muscular activity during imaginal and actual lifting of weights ranging from 100 to 500 g in 100 g increments. There was a tendency for a corresponding increase in muscular activity with increases in weight for both imagery and actual lifts.

In a replication of Hale (1982), Vigus and Williams (1985) compared EMG activity of dominant biceps, triceps, and nondominant triceps during IR of a biceps curl in both perspectives but found no significant differences for perspective. Similarly, Shick (1970) investigated muscular and ocular responses as part of her paper on MP of volleyball skills. She measured anterior deltoid and anterior tibialis EMG activity in addition to EOG activity. Unlike Jacobson, Shick was not able to identify any EMG or EOG patterns. In a recent study, Slade, Landers, and Martin (2002) compared biceps and triceps EMG activity patterns in both the active and passive arms during actual and imagined dumbbell curls. EMG activity increased during imagery in the active arm compared to rest and the passive arm, but this activity pattern did not mirror that of actual performance. During the IR of 8- to 11-year-old table-tennis players, Li-Wei (1991) found no significant increase in EMG activity.

In supporting psychoneuromuscular explanations or feedback theories, one limitation of many EMG studies that have found increased activity is that they have not linked EMG activity to physical-performance improvement. Some researchers have begun to investigate this relationship. Lutz and Lindner (2001) measured EMG activity during real and imagined dart throwing using four conditions: control imagery, stimulus propositions imagery, stimulus plus response propositions imagery, or physical practice. EMG activity during response propositions imagery was greater than during imagery control. The imagery groups showed a trend for increased performance, but it was not significant. EMG activity in the biceps during imagery was a significant predictor of performance. Lutz (2003) examined the impact of EMG activity during imagery on the learning of dart throwing. Imagery practice significantly improved dart-throwing performance at retention, but EMG activity was not a mediator of the relationship, suggesting that it may be a by-product of IR or MP rather than the cause of performance increases.

Most studies have suggested that increased muscular activation occurs in imagery, but some, as the review of central studies that follows shows, have not found a significant increase in EMG activity (Decety, Jeannerod, Durozard, and Baverel 1993; Roland, Larsen, Lassen, and Shinhoj 1980). The issue from a theoretical perspective is whether this increase in muscular activity is important to performance enhancement due to IR or MP or is a by-product of central changes. Overall, research is not conclusive that muscle activity during actual and imaginary practice is localized to the specific muscles involved in the activity being imagined. Even if we accept that it is localized, in order to provide strong evidence for the inflow explanations, researchers must show that localized muscular activity and feedback from IR or MP are the cause of performance improvements. Researchers have only begun to test this. In inflow or functional-equivalence views, peripheral activity is due to motor processes that have leaked to the spinal level and muscles. Research that has investigated activity at the spinal level is discussed next.

SPINAL ACTIVITY

At the spinal level the research is very inconsistent (Slade et al. 2002). Studies have shown imagery to increase spinal excitability (Bonnett, Decety, Jeannerod, and Requin 1997), decrease it (Oishi, Kimura, Yasukawa, Yoneda, and Maeshima 1994), or have no significant effect on it (Hashimoto and Rothwell 1999; Kasai, Kawai, Kawanishi, and Yahagi 1997; Yahagi, Shimura, and Kasai 1996). For instance, Oishi et al. (1994), as reported in more detail later in this chapter, investigated motor neuron excitability and autonomic reactions during mental imagery of speed-skating sprints. To measure motoneuron excitability Oishi et al. also measured Hoffman reflex (H-reflex) from the right soleus. The H-reflex decreased significantly during imagery. Bonnet et al. (1997) measured spinal reflex (H-reflex and tendon reflex [T-reflex]) and EMG activity during imagery and performance of putting pressure on a pedal with the foot. Imagery resulted in a greater increase in spinal reflex and EMG activity in the movement leg than in the contralateral leg. Hale, Raglin, and Koceja (2003) found that during imagery of plantar flexion of the right leg, changes in H-reflex and EMG did not reflect the percent of maximal contraction being imaged, and therefore did not support a mirroring of imagery and movement. Jeannerod (1995) and Decety et al. (1993) suggested that some descending neural mechanism that blocks motoneuron excitability could be activated during imagery.

AUTONOMIC ACTIVITY

In addition to peripheral muscle and spinal activity, autonomic effects have been reported during movement imagery. These effects are important in theories that emphasize the meaning or experience of imagery to the imager, such as Lang's bioinformational theory and Ahsen's triple-code theory. They also indicate a similarity between imagery and action and perception. For instance, early studies by Pickenhain (1976) and Pickenhain and Beyer (1979) found that increases in RR in imaging and actually swimming a given distance matched: RR increased rapidly, then leveled to a steady state for the duration of the swim. Beyer, Weiss, Hansen, Wolf, and Seidel (1990) also had participants imagine swimming a distance of 100 m in their preferred style. Beyer et al. recorded EEG, HR, SC, and RR during imagery; the latter three increased during imagery.

Wang and Morgan (1992) recorded $\dot{V}O_2$, $\dot{V}_E$, RR, RER, HR, systolic blood pressure (SBP), and diastolic blood pressure (DBP) during imagery of exercise. Immediately after imagery participants rated the perceived exertion (RPE). The psychophysiological responses (HR, RPE, and the metabolic responses) tended to be less during imagery than during actual exercise. Decety, Jeannerod, Germain, and Pastene (1991) measured cardiac and respiratory activity (HR, $\dot{V}_E$, $\dot{V}O_2$, oxygen uptake [true O_2], and CO_2 elimination) during imagery of and actual walking and running on a treadmill. Decety et al. concluded that the amount of activity during imagery of running was similar to that of actually walking. Decety et al. (1993) measured muscle metabolism (nuclear magnetic resonance [NMR] spectroscopy), and cardiorespiratory changes (HR and RR) during actual and imagined leg exercise. During imagery HR and RR rate increased immediately. RR increased more than in actual exercise, but NMR spectra did not change from resting levels. Cardiorespiratory response (HR, RR, $\dot{V}_E$, partial pressure of carbon dioxide [PCO_2]) to imagery of treadmill running versus control imagery (imaging letters) in male athletes versus male nonathletes was investigated by Wuyam, Moosavi, Decety, Adams, Lansig, and Guz (1995). Cardiorespiratory response tended to increase for athletes but not for nonathletes during imagery of treadmill running versus control imagery. This suggests that the psychophysiological response is specific to the image content.

Oishi et al. (1994) investigated motor neuron excitability and autonomic reactions during mental imagery of speedskating sprints with elite speedskaters. The sound of a signal gun initiated the imagery trial, skaters turned on a stopwatch at the signal, and the trial continued until the skaters turned off the stopwatch once they had finished their imagery. Imagery trials lasted 36 to 38 sec, which were very close to the actual personal bests of each skater. The autonomic effectors recorded were SC, HR, and RR. To measure motoneuron excitability Oishi et al. also measured H-reflex from the right soleus. Results indicated that the autonomic effectors were very active during imagery, with SC average increased by 51%, HR increased by 57%, and RR increased by 76% when compared with rest. The H-reflex decreased significantly during imagery. In another study with speed-skaters, Oishi, Kasai, and Maeshima (2000) measured autonomic responses (SR, HR, and RR) during a mental arithmetic task and imagery of a 500 m speedskating sprint. Duration of imagery closely matched actual performance. Both mental arithmetic and imagery showed significant decreases in SR and increases in HR and RR compared to rest. The only significant difference between mental arithmetic and imagery was on HR. RR was generally regular during mental arithmetic but irregular during imagery, which the authors suggested was similar to RR during actual performance.

Deschaumes-Molinaro, Dittmar, and Vernet-Maury (1991) found a decrease in skin blood flow, skin temperature, SR, and an increase in skin potential, HR, and RR during actual and imaged rifle and archery shooting. Roure et al. (1999) measured autonomic responses during volleyball-skill performance (receiving a serve) at pre- and posttest with IR between actual performance tests. The autonomic responses measured were skin potential and SR, skin temperature and heat clearance, HR, and RR. A strong correlation between the autonomic responses in performance and imagery indicated that similar autonomic responses occurred in imagery and performance. Interestingly, the imagery group, but not a nonimagery control group, showed a decrease in autonomic response in the posttest performance. The imagery group also performed better on the posttest.

A recent study with professional and amateur violinists that measured fMRI and EMG during actual and imagined performance of Mozart's Violin Concerto in G Major by Lotze, Scheler, Tan, Braun, and Birbaumer (2003) found that professional musicians generated higher EMG amplitudes and greater activity in the primary sensorimotor cortex, parietal lobes, cerebellum, and right primary auditory cortex during actual movement. The authors suggested that this indicated increased audio-motor connectivity, or an "auditory-motor loop," in professionals. In imagery, professionals also had greater activation in motor areas; however, the auditory-motor loop was not involved. So during actual performance auditory and motor systems were coactivated, but in imagery only the motor system was.

The autonomic studies suggest that the autonomic nervous system can be activated during imagery of movement. This again reinforces the similarity between imagery and perception or action and may indicate why imagery is such a powerful tool in helping athletes deal with sport situations. This increased autonomic activity may be a by-product of central processes when being used as a form of MP, but it may also represent important cognitive activity, such as changes in motivation and anxiety associated with performance.

CENTRAL ACTIVITY DURING IMAGERY

The functional equivalence of motor imagery and movement has recently attracted attention in the sport psychology literature (Holmes and Collins 2002) and encouraged much research in psychophysiology using central measures. The hypothesis of functional equivalence is that imagery and perception or movement recruit common structures or processes (Finke 1980, 1985; Finke and Shephard 1986). Researchers have addressed two forms of functional equivalence in the literature: of visual imagery and visual perception, and of motor imagery and motor preparation. The two forms of functional equivalence and their predictions for activation of central areas are shown in figure 7.1. It indicates that motor imagery should activate areas similar to actual movement or movement preparation, and visual imagery should activate areas similar to visual perception.

In this section we briefly discuss the research on visual imagery and visual perception, and then turn our attention to the research on motor imagery and motor preparation. Too much research on motor imagery

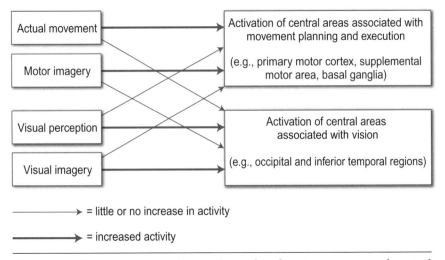

Figure 7.1 Functional equivalence of visual and motor imagery and central nervous system activity.

using central measures exists to review it all in detail, so we emphasize studies that have utilized more complex motor skills and the few that have considered sport skills.

VISUAL IMAGERY

Support for the functional equivalence of visual imagery and perception from a psychophysiological standpoint is strong (Farah 1989; Jeannerod 1994). Many studies have found similar activation of occipital and inferior temporal regions during performance of visual perception and visual imagery tasks (e.g., Kosslyn et al. 1993; Farah, Peronnet, Gonon, and Giard 1988; Peronnet and Farah 1989; Roland and Friberg 1985; Goldenberg et al. 1989; Rosler, Heil, and Glowalla 1993; Stuss, Sarazin, Leech, and Picton 1983; Wijers, Otten, Feenstra, Mulder, and Mulder 1989). Tasks requiring motor imagery or nonimaginal thinking did not activate the same areas. Reviews of the research on the equivalence of visual imagery and visual perception have generally concluded that it suggests a functional equivalence and that electrophysiological and blood-flow measures demonstrate activity in visual areas during the formation of visual mental images (e.g., Farah 1989; Jeannerod 1994).

MOTOR IMAGERY

Jeannerod (1994), in a substantial review of neurophysiological research on imagery, proposed that the similar neural substrate for visual imagery and visual perception could be translated to motor physiology. That is, the relationship between motor imagery and motor physiology is similar to the relationship between visual imagery and visual physiology. The benefits of motor imagery to motor execution through this central explanation would be due to increased traffic in neural circuits that are responsible for improving synaptic efficacy in critical parts of the motor system. According to this hypothesis, the peripheral EMG activity observed during imagery would be an effect rather than a cause of the learning process. This central explanation, therefore, suggests that because the neural substrate would be the same for both, learning by performing would not be substantially different from learning through motor imagery. Motor imagery is seen as a force generating representation of the self in action. During motor imagery the imagers feel themselves executing the action. Visual imagery is experienced in the same way as a spectator who watches a scene (Jeannerod 1997). The sidebar "Central Areas Important in Motor Control" on page 168 summarizes the central areas of the nervous system that appear to be important in human motor control and have been investigated in studies of motor imagery.

EEG studies   A substantial number of studies have utilized EEG to investigate movement imagery, and they date back further than the more advanced blood-flow and scanning studies. Adrian and Matthews

CENTRAL AREAS IMPORTANT IN MOTOR CONTROL

Several central structures that appear to be important in human motor control have been studied in relation to motor imagery. Areas of the brain that play important roles in motor control include the cortical areas of the primary motor cortex (M1), posterior parietal cortex, premotor cortex (PMC), and supplemental motor area (SMA), and subcortical areas of the cerebellum, and basal ganglia. A very brief review of the functions of these areas is included here to help in understanding the research on motor imagery.

The primary motor cortex (M1) is directly involved in producing muscle contraction. It generates neural impulses that control execution of movement in terms of direction and force (Rosenbaum 1991). M1 transforms the desired movement pattern into muscle-activity patterns and sends these commands to the spinal cord for execution. The posterior parietal cortex is important for transforming visual information into motor commands, including spatial localization of the body and external objects (Rosenbaum 1991). It sends this information to the PMC and SMA. The PMC and SMA appear to be primarily involved in the preparation of movement (Leonard 1998). The PMC is important in orienting the body and preparing postural muscles, and the SMA is important in the planning and production of complex movement sequences (Rosenbaum 1991). They appear to have different movement-preparation functions related to whether the movement is externally or internally cued. The PMC is important in controlling movements in relation to external cues, and the SMA is involved in sequencing movements from internal memory (Latash 1998). The SMA and premotor regions send information to the M1 and brain stem motor regions. M1, SMA, and PMC neurons lead to fibers of the corticospinal tract, the main pathway for the control of voluntary movement (Rose 1997).

The subcortical structures of the cerebellum and basal ganglia are also heavily involved in motor control. The cerebellum receives feedback on movement from the spinal cord and information on movement plans from the cerebral cortex (Shumway-Cook and Woollacott 2001). This allows it to compare intended movement with actual movement commands, so that it can modulate movement (Rose 1997). This also means that it is involved with skill learning (Shumway-Cook and Woollacott, 2001). The basal ganglia appear to play a role in initiating movement and scaling movement parameters, such as velocity, direction, and amplitude (Rose 1997).

(1934) were among the first to report a link between EEG changes and imagery. Golla, Hutton, and Walter (1943) and Short (1953) suggested that suppression of occipital EEG alpha rhythm indicated visual imagery. Additionally, Costello and McGregor (1957) concluded that the amount of alpha rhythm suppression was a result of vividness of imagery and the degree of involvement of higher-order thought processes.

In an EEG study that tested functional equivalence, Romero, Lacourse, Lawrence, Schandler, and Cohen (2000) measured EEG activity over the SMA and premotor area, and the primary motor area, during imagery and execution of a discrete isometric contraction. Activation patterns were similar during imagery and execution at SMA and premotor areas but not at the motor area. Other EEG and neuromagnetic studies also support the involvement of the primary motor cortex in motor imagery (Cochin, Barthelemy, Roux, and Martineau 1999; Lang, Cheyne, Hollinger, Gerschlager, and Lindinger 1998; Schnitzler, Salenius, Salmelin, Jousmaki, and Hari 1997).

In one study, Marks and Isaac (1995) collected EEG during performance and imagery of two motor tasks, finger touching and fist clenching. They instructed participants to imagine themselves touching the thumb with the four fingers of their preferred hand sequentially, and then to actually perform this task. They then instructed participants to imagine creating a fist with their preferred hand, then to actually create a fist. Visual imagery was associated with alpha attenuation in the left posterior cortex, while motor imagery had the opposite effect, alpha enhancement. The greatest difference occurred in the left posterior region. Another EEG study by Williams, Rippon, Stone, and Annett (1995) considered performance of the Vandenberg and Kuse Mental Rotations Test (MRT). They found that better performance on the MRT was associated with higher alpha amplitude at a number of frontal, parietal, and occipital sites, but during actual rotation parietal and frontal alpha amplitude was reduced.

Davidson and Schwartz (1977) assessed the patterning of occipital and sensorimotor EEG activation during visual and kinesthetic imagery. Participants imagined, in separate trials, a flashing light (visual imagery), a tapping sensation on the right arm (kinesthetic imagery), and both the light and tapping together. Visual imagery elicited greater relative occipital activation than kinesthetic imagery. The activity associated with imagining both conditions fell between the visual and kinesthetic conditions. The difference between the visual and kinesthetic imagery conditions was primarily a result of greater occipital activation during visual imagery. The researchers found no difference in overall alpha activity. Davidson and Schwartz (1977) concluded that imagery in different modalities elicits specific changes in the sensory regions of the brain responsible for processing information in the relevant modalities.

Martinez (2000) compared EEG activity during rest, visual imagery, and kinesthetic imagery of items of the Movement Imagery Questionnaire (MIQ). Martinez reported that kinesthetic imagery seemed to elicit more cortical activation than visual imagery, but it was not clear if they were distinct processes. Tokumaru, Mizumoto, Takada, and Ashida (2003) investigated imagery of in-flight training (IFT) with experienced and novice fighter pilots using EEG. IFT is a common technique used in training of fighter pilots. Results suggested that visual and motor cortical areas were active during IFT.

The EEG studies suggest that similar central structures are involved in imagery and movement (Decety and Ingvar 1990). They also suggest different activation patterns for different types of imagery, such as motor, kinesthetic, or visual. As expected, motor imagery appears to activate areas involved in motor preparation, and visual imagery activates visual perception areas, suggesting a functional equivalence or at least specificity of imagery type to cerebral activation.

Brain-scanning studies   Reviews of studies on motor imagery and motor planning and execution have supported Jeannerod (1994, 1995) by suggesting a common neural substrate for motor imagery and motor preparation (Annett 1986; Berthoz 1996; Decety 1996a, b). Cerebral blood-flow studies demonstrate that execution of a movement skill is accompanied by activation of the M1, SMA, and basal ganglia (Toates 2001). Movement imagery also seems to activate these same areas, although there is debate over the involvement of the M1 (Jeannerod 1997).

Most of the research involves imagery of relatively simple movement skills of a short duration, such as pressing a button, simple hand movements, clenching a fist, or moving the fingers. But the research on motor imagery suggests that cortical activation during motor imagery occurs in areas related to motor control and that it follows a specific pattern that closely resembles action execution (e.g., Besteiner, Hollinger, Lindinger, Lang, and Berthoz 1995; Decety et al. 1994; Deecke 1996; Deiber, Passingham, Colebatch, Friston, Nixon, and Frackowiak 1991; Fox, Pardo, Peterson, and Raichle 1987; Hallett, Fieldman, Cohen, Sadato, and Pascual-Leone 1995; Ingvar and Philipsson 1977; Naito and Matsumura 1994; Roland, Shinhoj, Lassen, and Larsen 1980; Stephan, Fink, Frith, and Frackowiak 1993). These structures include the PMC, lateral cerebellum, basal ganglia, dorsolateral prefrontal cortex, inferior frontal cortex, and posterior parietal cortex (Parsons and Fox 1998; Grafton, Arbib, Fadiga, and Rizzolatti 1996; Mellet, Petit, Mazoyer, Denis, Tzourio 1998; Deiber, Ibanez, Honda, Sadato, Raman, and Hallett 1998).

The pioneering studies in this area were conducted by Ingvar and Philipson (1977), who measured rCBF while participants either imagined or actually clenched a hand; they found that blood flow increased in premotor and frontal regions. Another early study by Roland, Larsen,

Lassen, and Shinhoj (1980) found a localized increase in rCBF, mainly in the SMA, while participants imagined a sequence of finger movements. Decety, Philipson, and Ingvar (1988) compared imagery of and actual execution of a writing movement. During imagery, activity in the prefrontal cortex, SMA, and cerebellum increased. In execution, the same areas were active, as well as the primary motor and somatosensory cortices. Decety, Sjoholm, Ryding, Stenberg, and Ingvar (1990) used the SPECT technique to compare rCBF during rest, silent counting, and imagery of tennis movements. In both silent counting and mental imagery, rCBF to the cerebellum increased, suggesting that the increased activity was nonspecific and that the cerebellum is important in mental activity. They also measured EMG activity but found no increase in any of the conditions.

As research in the area of motor imagery progressed, increasing evidence showed that areas utilized in the planning of movement (for instance, the SMA) were involved. This evidence strongly supports the functional equivalence of motor imagery and motor preparation. Studies suggest that the SMA is involved in assembling an established motor pattern (e.g., Roland, Larsen, Lassen, and Shinhoj 1980), and others have found that the SMA is also activated in the imagination of movement (e.g., Decety, Sjoholm, Ryding, Stenberg, and Ingvar 1990; Cunnington, Iansek, Bradshaw, and Phillips 1996; Roland, Shinhoj, Lassen, and Larsen 1980; Ryding, Decety, Sjoholm, Stenberg, and Ingvar 1993; Stephan et al. 1995).

Several studies suggest that even the M1 may be active in imagery (Hallett, Fieldman, Cohen, Sadato, and Pascual-Leone 1995; Lang, Cheyne, Hollinger, Gerschlager, and Lindinger 1996). For example, Lotze et al. (1999) found that with both imagery and performance of hand movements the fMRI blood flow indicated significant activation in the SMA, PMC, and M1. The somatosensory cortex was significantly active only during performance, whereas the cerebellum's activity was decreased during imagery, suggesting that the posterior cerebellum is involved in the inhibition of movement during imagery.

In addition to activation in the M1, evidence suggests that imagery activates motor areas specific to the type of movement being performed. For instance, Ehrsson, Geyer, and Naito (2003) investigated imagery of finger, toe, and tongue movements using fMRI. Imagery resulted in increased activity in the M1, PMC, caudal cingulated motor area, and the SMA. In addition, they found that the activity in these areas was specifically related to the somatotopically organized sections in a systematic manner. That is, hand movements specifically activated the hand sections of the M1, and foot movements activated foot zones of the SMA and M1.

One of the limitations of most of these studies in comparing them to imagery of sport skills is that they have utilized simple movement skills. Some studies, however, have measured central indices during imagery of more complex skills. For instance, Ross, Tkach, Ruggieri, Lieber, and Lapresto (2003) used fMRI to measure blood flow during imagery of a golf swing by golfers of various handicap levels. Increases in activation were seen in areas involved in motor control (motor cortex), image generation (parietal cortex), execution (frontal lobe, cerebellum, vermis), action planning (frontal and parietal cortex and SMA), and error detection (cerebellum). Brain activation in the SMA and cerebellum decreased with higher skill levels, which would reflect the increased automatization of the skill.

Malouin, Richards, Jackson, Dumas, and Doyon (2003) used PET to study imagery of locomotion, including standing, initiating gait, walking, and walking with obstacles. Imagery of the locomotor activities resulted in increased activity in areas including the prefrontal cortex and parietal lobe. As the complexity of locomotor activity increased, activity increased in the pre-SMA and precentral gyrus, suggesting that higher brain centers become engaged when the task difficulty increases.

Thus, the central blood-flow studies suggest the existence of a similar neural substrate for motor imagery and motor performance, with motor areas involved in movement planning becoming activated during both imagery and performance of movement. It seems that in imagery, movement execution is inhibited. The debate about the central aspects of motor imagery now seems to focus on the degree of involvement of the motor pathways and the M1 (Jeannerod 1997), specifically, whether there is subliminal activation of the motor system during imagery. Findings seem to vary based on the measures used; PET studies do not suggest activation of the M1 (Deiber et al. 1998), but fMRI studies do suggest involvement of the M1 in motor imagery (Ehrsson, Geyer, and Naito 2003; Lotze et al. 1999; Porro et al. 1996; Roth et al. 1996). A logical consequence of increased motor cortex activation is that it should cause increased activity at the motoneuron level, but controversy still surrounds this (Jeannerod 1997) because, as mentioned previously, research at the spinal level is inconsistent.

More recent research with TMS, however, has demonstrated increases in M1 excitability during imagery of voluntary-muscle contraction (e.g., Facchini, Muellbacher, Battaglia, Boroojerdi, and Hallett 2002; Hashimoto and Rothwell 1999; Kasai, Kawai, Kawanishi, and Yahagi 1997; Kuhtz-Buschbeck, Mankopf, Holznecht, Siebner, Umer, and Jansen 2003; Li, Latash, and Zatsiorsky 2004; Stinear and Byblow 2004; Yahagi and Kasai 1998). These studies suggest that in actual movement and motor imagery, M1 excitability is muscle and task specific (Stinear and Byblow 2004). For instance, Stinear and Byblow (2004) investigated motor excitability during actual and imagined movements of the index finger pressing a mouse button and of the thumb during abduction in time with a

1 Hz auditory metronome. The results suggested that motor imagery leads to an increase in corticospinal excitability. Temporal and spatial modulation of the increased excitability was found for the thumb movement but not for the finger movement, which provides some support for the idea that actual movement and motor imagery modulate excitability in similar ways (Stinear and Byblow 2004). As with most of the brain-scanning studies, these TMS studies have all used simple movements, usually of the finger or thumb; further research using TMS with imagery of more complex skills would help clarify the neurophysiology of sport-skills imagery.

PSYCHOPHYSIOLOGICAL EFFECTS

Based on a functional-equivalence view of imagery, motor-skill learning and performance improvements from imagery of a skill would be due to changes in the motor system resulting from imagery, but this concept has not yet been adequately addressed by the research literature (Jeannerod 1997). At least one study has investigated cerebral changes with IR or MP. Jackson, LaFleur, Malouin, Richards, and Doyon (2003) used PET to examine the functional changes associated with IR (MP) for a movement skill. The skill was a sequence of foot movements, and participants performed MP over several days (300 MP trials in all). IR (MP) led to increases in performance and in blood flow in the orbitofrontal cortex (OFC) and to a decrease in the cerebellum. A positive correlation between performance improvement and blood flow in the OFC was noted. Jackson et al. concluded that IR (MP) led to cerebral functional changes similar to those observed in physical practice (PP) in a previous study (LaFleur et al. 2002).

CONCLUSIONS

The psychophysiology of imagery refers to the study of the relationships between the physiological and mental processes involved in imagery. Peripheral studies have measured muscular and autonomic activity during movement imagery. The autonomic literature suggests that imagery can produce changes in indices such as HR, RR, VE, SC, and SR. The literature on muscular responses during imagery clearly shows that imagery can produce changes in muscular activity. This activity is of a lower level than during actual movement, and debate exists as to whether it is localized and mirrors actual movement.

Research on motor imagery using central measures such as rCBF, fMRI, and PET has become a hot topic for neuroscience (Jeannerod 1999). It has suggested that motor areas involved in movement planning, such as the PMC, basal ganglia, and SMA, are activated during imagery. The debate at present focuses on the level of involvement of motor pathways and the M1 (Jeannerod 1997), although recent research with TMS supports the involvement of the M1 in motor imagery (Stinear and Byblow 2004). Although the research clearly indicates that imagery can elicit psychophysiological responses, the relationship of these to the learning and performance effects that result from IR and MP remains hypothetical.

Most of the psychophysiological studies have used simple movements such as biceps curls, clenching a fist, or moving the fingers. Hopefully, as technology advances we will see studies that measure central psychophysiological responses during more advanced movements, as in sport skills, or that use advanced or elite performers as participants. One aspect that has not yet been adequately addressed by the psychophysiological research literature is the training effects of IR or MP. Studies utilizing central measures have suggested that areas involved in motor preparation show increased activation during imagery, but a logical consequence would be that IR or MP causes changes in these areas that are responsible for performance enhancement or effects on learning. Similarly, in the peripheral studies, research linking peripheral activity to performance is lacking, as are training studies suggesting that feedback from muscular activity during IR or MP is responsible for learning effects or performance enhancement.

We hope that this brief review of psychophysiological research on imagery in sport and exercise has stimulated an interest in the topic, and we encourage more research on imagery that utilizes psychophysiological approaches, especially in the area of sport skills.

PART III

APPLYING IMAGERY IN SPORT

In part III of *Imagery in Sport* we move away from the theoretical to focus on the practical application of imagery in sport. We have intentionally split the practice of imagery into two components. First, chapter 8 describes how imagery is applied in sport, looking at principles and guidelines developed by many applied sport psychologists whose experiences with imagery have been supported, in some cases, by research. Second, in chapter 9, we consider the kinds of applications for imagery that exist in sport contexts, proposing that the potential applications for it are as wide ranging as the imaginations of the athletes, coaches, and sport psychologists who use them. In chapter 10 we introduce new technologies that have provided adjuncts to imagery that enhance its effectiveness; Scott Fletcher helps us discuss video modeling, biofeedback, and flotation. And in chapter 11, Michelle Walsh adds her expertise to our discussion of the application of imagery to the increasingly important area of sport-related injuries.

CHAPTER 8

STRATEGIES FOR APPLYING IMAGERY

Imagery is an important performance-enhancement technique regularly used by sport psychologists and athletes. At this time, although many different imagery-training paradigms have been developed, no one set of strategies or procedures has achieved universal approbation among practitioners and coaches. Due to this lack of consensus, a substantial range of material exists regarding the application of imagery-training strategies in sport.

Many recent sport psychology texts provide summaries of generalized principles for applying imagery in the contexts of training and performance (Cox 2002; Gould, Damarjian, and Greenleaf 2002; Moran 2004; Morris, Spittle, and Perry 2004; Vealey and Greenleaf 2001; Weinberg and Gould 2003). In addition, several authors, including Martens (1987), Orlick (1990, 2000), Rushall (1991, 1995), and Suinn (1984, 1993), have presented detailed descriptions of their specific techniques for developing imagery skills in sport. The general principles and the descriptions of specific techniques provide important information on the elements of an imagery training program. This chapter provides a synthesis of the essential components that sport psychology researchers and practitioners recommend for inclusion in programs intended to enhance athletes' imagery skills, and thus their physical performances.

This chapter begins with brief descriptions of several specialized imagery-rehearsal techniques that have been used successfully with athletes. Next, we concentrate on the presentation of an organized framework of the key components typically incorporated in an imagery training program (ITP). Highlighting the broader collection of skills and procedures required in imagery training will aid practitioners in understanding specific programs and in creating and implementing personalized plans. We also integrate an examination of the typical problems and hindrances that participants or practitioners may experience, explore possible solutions and alternative approaches, and present a sport-based example of an imagery training program.

OVERVIEW OF IMAGERY-BASED INTERVENTIONS

A number of texts in sport psychology provide valuable, detailed overviews of existing imagery-based interventions (e.g., Cox 2002; Korn 1994; LeUnes and Nation 2002; Morris 1997). Our purpose in discussing alternative regimens is to briefly describe some of the more popular procedures, highlight the importance of imagery to them, and indicate the frequency of their use in sport. Psychologists, coaches, and athletes may benefit from understanding current procedures prior to preparing an individualized ITP involving the purposeful selection of elements from the sample model presented later in this chapter. The interventions covered in this section and summarized in table 8.1 are visuomotor behavior rehearsal (Suinn 1984), AIM strategy (Korn 1994), sport imagery training (Martens 1987), guided imagery (Ungerleider 1996), stress inoculation training (Meichenbaum 1977, 1985), and the five-step strategy (Singer 1988).

Table 8.1 Summary of Existing Interventions Involving Imagery Training

Intervention strategy	Author	Involvement of imagery	Extent of use in sport
VMBR	Suinn (1984, 1993)	High	Substantial
AIM strategy	Korn (1994)	Moderate	Rare
Sport imagery training	Martens (1987)	Very high	Decreasing
Guided imagery	Ungerleider (1996)	Very high	Occasional
Stress inoculation training	Meichenbaum (1977, 1985)	Low	Occasional
Five-step strategy	Singer (1988)	High	Increasing

VISUOMOTOR BEHAVIORAL REHEARSAL

Suinn (1984, 1993) developed an intervention technique known as visuomotor (or visual motor) behavior rehearsal (see chapter 2), which he described as "a covert activity whereby a person experiences sensory-motor sensations that reintegrate reality experiences, and which include neuromuscular, physiological, and emotional involvement" (1993, 499). VMBR is characterized by the use of progressive muscular relaxation to induce a relaxed state that will facilitate a rich, multimodal imagery experience. Imagery activity occurs during the second phase of VMBR and typically targets the demands of the athlete's sport. The third phase also involves imaginal rehearsal but focuses on specific skills and elements of a sport performance in lifelike situations, which attempt to mimic the stresses associated with actual performance. This phase is then followed by relaxation activity. Morris (1997) emphasized that VMBR provides only a framework for imagery because it does not prescribe the content, since the process of content development is always context specific. VMBR provides a procedure for effective rehearsal of the imagery protocol determined by the practitioner and athlete, using a controlled blend of imaginal activity and relaxation. It has received extensive research evaluation and remains in consistent use in practice (e.g., Gough 1989; Hall and Erffmeyer 1983; Seabourne, Weinburg, Jackson, and Suinn 1985).

AIM STRATEGY

The AIM strategy is an intervention procedure proposed by Korn (1994) as part of a broader analysis of mental imagery use in performance enhancement. It is an attempt to blend "the steps, sequences, and strategies needed to use relaxation and imagery" (p. 203) into a single paradigm. The *A* stands for active relaxation, which Korn perceived as the most important component. He suggested that this procedure decreases oxygen use, respiration, heart rate, blood pressure, and muscle tension, increases blood flow to the brain, and produces alpha, or quiet, rhythm on the EEG. These physiological effects protect the individual from excessive stress, which can have a negative impact on physical performance. The *I* refers to imagery of the end result, which consists of a targeted, realistic image of the desired outcome as having already occurred (a form of goal-oriented imagery). The final component, *M*, is mental rehearsal. Korn described this activity as the generation of images of an actual or fantasized scenario from which an effect can be attained. The fantasized aspect is directed toward increasing performance efficiency by having athletes imagine a perfect performance of an action they are still mastering or have yet to attempt, such as a difficult gymnastics movement or a dive from the 10 m board. In addition, imagery of actual physical actions may involve the mental rehearsal of specific steps; for example, in a high jump, the steps include prepreparation, the run to the bar, the glide over it, and the landing. Overall, Korn's description of the intervention is thorough but is not supported by empirical reports of its use in applied settings.

SPORT IMAGERY TRAINING PROGRAM

One of the early authors in the field of sport imagery, Rainer Martens, presented his representation of a sport imagery training (SIT) program. It was developed as an outcome of his own review of research evidence and his practical experience in using imagery with athletes. SIT includes four key phases (Martens 1987). The first is sensory awareness, which involves athletes determining and understanding what they see, feel, and hear, and how their emotions operate in the context of sport performances. This facilitates development of the skills associated with creating and manipulating imagery. Second is vividness development, which involves the use of a series of practice exercises to enhance the athletes' vividness skills for all senses that are important in their sport. As with vividness development in general, Martens proposed that exercises should match the athlete's imagery abilities, so that those with less developed skills commence with simple exercises and progress to more advanced activities as they improve. Third is controllability development, which has a structure similar to the vividness development phase. Athletes are evaluated in terms of their skills in this area and then prescribed exercises to develop their abilities to manipulate and control images. Fourth is the practice phase, which requires the practitioner to monitor and facilitate certain attributes and activities that are most likely to produce optimal conditions for the earlier three phases. It involves preparing an appropriate setting or environment, establishing relaxed attention, fostering the correct attitude for using imagery or expectancy about involvement in SIT, motivating the athlete to undertake the practice exercises, and organizing the systematic rehearsal of skills. Unfortunately, no specific evaluations of the efficacy of SIT were reported by Martens or are available in the sport psychology literature.

GUIDED IMAGERY

Ungerleider (1996) presented details of a framework for using imagery for performance enhancement in conjunction with principles and activities associated with mental training for peak performance. The program uses a self-help approach that is applicable to both practitioner and athlete. The process of guided imagery, as described by Ungerleider, focuses on the primary attributes of sport imagery. The first step in the process addresses how imagers see what they see. It involves evaluating an athlete's imagery skills to determine the main areas to address in the intervention. Ungerleider framed this step around three questions: "How do you experience images?" "Do you perceive an image by sight, hearing, touch, or feel?" "Which sensory modes allow you to experience an image?" Ungerleider promoted the use of the Sport Imagery Questionnaire (Martens 1982), described in chapter 4.

The second step in guided imagery, labeled "Details make visions vivid," relates to its practice and has three components: The athlete is to develop vivid images, control those images, and understand his perspective of imagery. The third step relates to imagery's application to specific sport activities; the athlete rewinds and reviews the important images of the sport, varies his vantage point in order to use both imagery perspectives, and accesses his image bank to target images that suit his style and preference in representing his physical performances. Guided imagery is a general set of strategies that can be applied with a limited degree of expertise as part of a broader psychological-skills-enhancement program. Recent review of the sport psychology literature indicates that guided imagery partnered with relaxation is used consistently (e.g., Mastrich 2002; Reid et al. 2001).

STRESS INOCULATION TRAINING

Recent overviews of sport imagery by Cox (2002) and LeUnes and Nation (2002) provide detailed descriptions of the cognitive-behavioral intervention known as Stress Inoculation Training (SIT: Note, acronym should not be confused with Sport Imagery Training). The intervention, developed by Meichenbaum (1977, 1985), primarily involves the progressive exposure of athletes to increasingly stressful situations so that they learn a coping strategy that will serve as a form of inoculation for the effects of anxiety (Cox 2002; LeUnes and Nation 2002). Similar to the AIM strategy, SIT incorporates relaxation training, imagery, and coping behaviors into a single plan.

Three key stages constitute SIT, which Cox (2002) and LeUnes and Nation (2002) summarized. The first is conceptualization, when the practitioner and athlete establish a collaborative relationship. The experiential conditions that lead to stress and anxiety are clarified and their effects on mood, emotions, and performance are identified. The phase can involve procedures such as interviews, questionnaires, or review of sport and personal goals. Next is the skills-acquisition phase, which involves educating and training athletes to understand the determinants of the stress response and develop coping skills such as progressive relaxation, imaging, cognitive restructuring, or self-regulation. The third phase is application and follow-through, when athletes practice and apply the strategies they have learned. Stressful situations are the stimuli for the execution of coping behaviors. Initially, athletes are exposed to minor, manageable, stressful situations, then to progressively more stressful scenes, while in a relaxed state. They then practice the behaviors they have learned in order to manage these events. Finally, they rehearse this procedure in real-life settings, where once again their exposure to stress is progressive, allowing them to rehearse coping behaviors. Theoretically, the graded management of the stress leads to a greater level of inoculation to the anxiety produced by the situation. SIT is grounded in a large amount of research in the field of general psychology, in addition to studies involving athletes in performance-oriented settings (e.g., Kerr and Leith 1993; Kress, Schroeder, Potteiger, and Haub 1999).

FIVE-STEP STRATEGY

The five-step strategy is an intervention framework developed by Singer (1988) that involves phases called "readying," "imaging," "focusing," "executing," and "evaluating." The program is specifically directed toward establishing a preperformance routine for motor skills in general. The readying stage includes physical preparation, in conjunction with relaxation activities. Imaging comes next, making these first two stages similar to those of other interventions, such as VMBR and AIM. Critical focusing is the next stage, and its importance is related to its role in performance readiness. It includes the use of preperformance routines to facilitate on-task behaviors such as concentration and attention. Execution of the skill is next, after the athlete completes the requirements of readying, imaging, and focusing. The final step involves evaluating the intervention in relation to performance enhancement and establishing a set of indicators regarding how the other steps might be modified and improved. Morris (1997) stated that the evaluation stage should be used only in training, on both expediency and motivational grounds. "Expediency because, in matches, play continues on in many sports, and motivation because a critical evaluation in the middle of a match could result in diminished effort or reduced confidence" (p. 39). An overview of evidence suggests that use of the five-step approach in research or applied settings is increasing (e.g., Bar-Eli 2002; Lidor 1997).

The intervention programs reviewed here may be best suited to specific, predetermined uses of imagery, in which practitioners can capitalize on their knowledge of the program and the athlete to target the behaviors they perceive will benefit from that type of intervention (e.g., stress reduction, preperformance routine). These programs typically involve many of the key strategies we will discuss in our ITP model; in the majority of circumstances they would prove beneficial as a base framework for imagery training. At this stage, we propose that Ungerleider's guided imagery is the best of the interventions examined. Although each of these six programs lacks certain aspects of our ITP model, particularly in relation to the extension and manipulation of content, expanding any of them to include the missing strategies or procedures might be useful in constructing a thorough intervention.

KEY COMPONENTS OF AN IMAGERY TRAINING PROGRAM

Figure 8.1 outlines a detailed list of the primary components and procedural sequences that sport psychology practitioners could include in an ITP. Imagery is a very personalized experience, so training programs should incorporate only those components that meet the specific needs of each athlete. The framework is divided into six categories that detail the key components typically suggested for generalized approaches in

Prerequisites for ITP

- Performer's characteristics
- Athlete's knowledge and understanding of the athletic task
- Athlete's knowledge and understanding of the imagery process
- Athlete's goals
- Athlete's psychological state
- Athlete's physiological state

Environment for ITP

- Quiet and free of distractions
- Athlete should feel comfortable
- Incorporate imagery in both training and competition
- Athletes can use imagery of the skill in almost any environment

Content of ITP

- Stimulates the development of vividness and control of imagery
- Progresses gradually from simple to complex competitive situations
- Involves all of the senses
- Uses images that emphasize kinesthetic sensations
- Uses images that are as realistic and dynamic as possible
- Uses both the internal and external perspectives
- Imagery should be performed in real time
- Operates from a positive performance or outcome focus
- Involves memory for re-creation and creation
- Imaging includes both the complete skill and the outcome of performance
- Scripts should contain stimulus, response, and meaning elements
- Extend content detail for performers with advanced imagery skills
- Content should reflect the performance needs of athletes

(continued)

Figure 8.1 Primary components and procedural sequences of an ITP.

Rehearsal routine for ITP

- Requires scheduled practice sessions
- Practice should be systematic and fully integrated within the total training package
- Timing of sessions should account for the athlete's competition schedule
- Practice sessions could occur
  - before or after training
  - before or after competition
  - during breaks in action
  - during personal time
  - when recovering from injury
- Regular, quality sessions of short duration in the initial program phases, e.g., 15 min per day
- Sessions can occur as required when athlete is more proficient at using imagery
- Individual preferences and skills should be considered in determining rehearsal routines (e.g., superior athletes tend to use imagery with greater frequency)
- Encourage athletes to practice on their own
- Team sports may involve group practice sessions

Enhancements to ITP

- Incorporate triggers or cues to facilitate the imagery process
- Cues may be visual, auditory, imagery, or language based
- Determine skill-related movement labels or cues
- Devise mnemonic devices based on cues to aid retention
- Audio- and videotapes may facilitate imagery
- Video modeling of expert performers can be used to aid imagery
- Covert modeling through the observation of actual performance
- Relaxation techniques as an aid to imagery
- Flotation as an aid to imagery
- Biofeedback of arousal level via physiological monitoring

Evaluation of ITP

- Regular verbal reports on the effectiveness of the ITP are required
- Athletes should keep a log of their involvement in the ITP
- Athletes should self-evaluate performance after each imagery activity
- Feedback should be immediate when possible in early phases
- Monitor associated changes in physical and competition performances
- Program coordinator should undertake a major evaluation of relevant aspects of the previous five categories

---

Figure 8.1 *(continued)*

the application of imagery techniques in sport. A model of this framework is shown in figure 8.2. Additionally, the framework summarizes the strategic elements needed for successful implementation of an ITP. In certain instances, other chapters of this text provide supplementary analysis of the underlying theoretical or research basis of particular framework components.

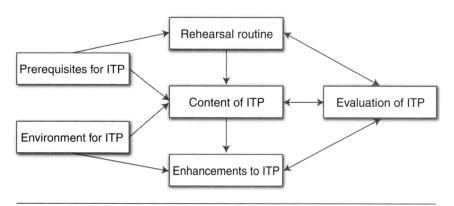

Figure 8.2   Model of key elements of an imagery training program.

PREREQUISITES FOR ITP

The prerequisites that are important in developing an ITP include assessment of performer characteristics, an understanding of the imagery process and the cognitive and physical demands of the athletic task, and the identification of the athlete's goals and psychological and physiological states.

PERFORMER CHARACTERISTICS

Athletes are most successful in imagery training when practitioners understand which individual characteristics might influence their performance. Age needs to be taken into account due to the belief that, irrespective of skill level, older athletes are better able to use imagery (LeUnes and Nation 2002). Several studies, however, have demonstrated that athletes as young as 7 can benefit from imagery training (Li-Wei, Qi-Wei, Orlick, and Zitzelsberger 1992; Partington 1990). The key consideration concerning age is that the concepts presented in the ITP are within the athletes' cognitive capabilities to comprehend and understand.

Determining athletes' levels of physical ability is an important component of the ITP. If athletes have difficulty performing a task physically, the effectiveness of imagery of that task will be limited (Perry and Morris 1995). Research evidence has shown that although both novice and experienced performers may be helped by imagery, the greater the physical skill level, the greater the performance gains from imagery training (Feltz and Landers 1983; Howe 1991; Janssen and Sheikh 1994). Perry and Morris (1995) suggested that the complexity of the ITP should increase as the physical skills of the athlete develop.

Practitioners should include the quantification of an athlete's imagery abilities in any ITP (Weinberg and Gould 2003). Research has indicated that imagery training is more effective with athletes of higher imagery ability (Hall 1985; Isaac 1992), and imagery-ability variations can be a distinguishing factor between elite and non-elite athletes (Goss, Hall, Buckolz, and Fishburne 1986; Watt and Morris 1999a). Information regarding the dimensional and sensory characteristics of athletes' imagery can be of substantial benefit in the development of an ITP. Imagery ability is normally assessed by using a self-report imagery questionnaire. Of the various measures available (see chapter 4), we recommend the Sport Imagery Ability Measure (Watt and Morris 1998b) for the thorough evaluation of (a) image generation, quality, and control, (b) the involvement of the six major senses, and (c) the experience of emotion in relation to typical sport situations. Discussing and explaining the results of any assessment procedure with the athletes is vital to ensuring that they understand that they can improve their imagery ability through training (Rodgers, Hall, and Buckolz 1991).

KNOWLEDGE AND UNDERSTANDING OF THE ATHLETIC TASK

Both the athlete and the practitioner must clearly understand the specific task or activity performed in the ITP (Bird and Cripe 1986). Feltz and Landers (1983) reported that tasks with a greater cognitive component benefited more from imagery rehearsal than motor or strength activities. Cognitive tasks, such as specific play development, require imagery programs that emphasize rehearsal of the symbolic components of the task. Motor and strength activities might benefit more from imagery training that emphasizes arousal control or attending to specific task cues (Bird and Cripe 1986; Weinberg and Gould 2003).

KNOWLEDGE AND UNDERSTANDING OF THE IMAGERY PROCESS

Many of the recent sport imagery reviews that outline general imagery principles emphasize the need to educate athletes about the imagery process (Gould et al. 2002; Perry and Morris 1995; Sargent 1996). Sargent (1996) has provided an excellent summary of the important steps in this process: (a) presenting relevant anecdotal material describing imagery use by successful athletes; (b) outlining specific theoretical material and scientific evidence that demonstrates imagery's usefulness in enhancing performance; (c) ensuring that significant role models reinforce the positive outcomes of an ITP; and (d) presenting simple imagery exercises as a way to convince athletes of the technique's efficacy. Athletes should understand that imagery is a legitimate skill that they can develop, which is limited only by their capacities as learners (LeUnes and Nation 2002).

PROGRAM GOALS

Athletes must have clear expectations of what they can achieve from involvement in an ITP. Specific goals should be set by the practitioner, athlete, and those directing the overall training plan. Program outcomes must be realistic and meet the athlete's specific needs (Nideffer 1985; Sargent 1997). Woods (1998) suggested six characteristics of goal setting related to psychological-skills training in sport that can be applied to an ITP: Goals should be specific, controllable, challenging, attainable, measurable, and personal.

PHYSIOLOGICAL STATE

Much of the literature that examines sport imagery presents the view that athletes benefit from being in a relaxed state before beginning imagery activities (Janssen and Sheikh 1994; Kolonay 1977; Martens 1987; Perry and Morris 1995; Smith 1987; Weinberg and Gould 2003; Weinberg, Seabourne, and Jackson 1981). Relaxation enhances imagery by reducing somatic tensions, calming and centering the mind, and inhibiting the influence of cognitive distractions (Janssen and Sheikh 1994).

Several authors disagree that relaxation is essential to imagery-training strategies (Murphy and Jowdy 1992; Rushall 1995). Specific studies have found that including relaxation activities in imagery programs produces no greater benefits than using imagery alone (Gray, Haring, and Banks 1984; Hamberger and Lohr 1980). Rushall (1995) was emphatic that relaxation has no use in imagery programs that target competition preparation, stating that "relaxation is not what is needed prior to a contest, nor is it part of performance-enhancement imagery" (p. 55). Although this may be true for many team and power-type sports, athletes in sports such as pistol shooting or archery may benefit from relaxation just prior to performance. Rushall and Lippman (1998) later conceded that for less experienced athletes, relaxation may limit distractions and improve focusing during imagery.

Janssen and Sheikh (1994) highlighted an interesting point about the role of relaxation by suggesting that it can serve as a starting point for the generation of vivid and controlled imagery and need not be maintained during an entire rehearsal session. Nideffer (1985) suggested that to develop good imagery skills athletes should determine their "optimal level of arousal and attend to those physiological cues (indicators of muscle tension) that are directly related to performance" (p. 53). Until researchers achieve greater clarification of the relationship between relaxation and imagery, the consensus opinion supports including relaxation in an ITP. However, consideration of the timing of the imagery activity and the nature of the athletic task in program development is necessary.

Psychological State

The psychological states that appear to be important in imagery training are motivation and attention. Athletes require a level of motivation that ensures that they fully apply themselves to the practice regimen of the ITP (Martens 1987; Weinberg and Gould 2003), and they must direct attention to the ITP's specific task requirements rather than to other potentially distracting cognitive activity (Martens 1987; Smith 1987; Weinberg and Gould 2003). Program coordinators should ensure that athletes have no doubts about their involvement in the program and understand that their full participation will lead to goal achievement (Martens 1987; Wann 1997).

Environment for ITP

The necessary environmental considerations for implementation of the ITP are a quiet and distraction-free setting, athletes' comfort level, incorporation of imagery within both training and competition environments, and encouragement of imagery-proficient athletes to use the skill in any environment.

Quiet and Distraction Free

For athletes unskilled in the use of imagery, successful participation in program activities typically requires a quiet environment that is free from distractions, particularly in the initial stages of the imagery training (Cox 2002; Sargent 1996). Skilled athletes are more adept at undertaking imagery activities in less controlled settings, such as a noisy arena or stadium; however, engaging in precompetition imagery rehearsal in a quieter setting should still prove beneficial.

Comfortable Setting

Practitioners who use imagery techniques agree that athletes need to feel comfortable before attempting any imagery activity (Orlick 1990; Ungerleider 1996). What constitutes a comfortable environment will vary from athlete to athlete depending on their experience and the task requirements. Novice athletes may need to be lying down or sitting in a relaxing chair, whereas experienced performers may be comfortable using imagery while standing and waiting for an event to commence. A task such as imagining the positive outcome of a future event is better suited to an imagery session in which the athlete can fully relax and feel comfortable. Alternatively, taking a deep breath and closing their eyes can provide comfort to athletes who imagine a movement sequence just before performing it.

TRAINING OR COMPETITION SITUATION

As athletes become more experienced in an ITP they can rehearse their skills in increasingly distracting environments (Sargent 1996). Practitioners can use training environments to simulate game conditions and assess an athlete's ability to generate images amid various distractions (Perry and Morris 1995). An important goal of the ITP is to prepare the athlete to use imagery successfully in the competition environment. Imagery use is regularly observed in high jumpers and downhill skiers immediately before participation in important competitions (Sargent 1996).

ANY TIME, ANY PLACE APPROACH

Athletes who are highly proficient at imagery can rehearse their imagery skills in many different environments (Harris and Harris 1984). For example, athletes with substantial background in the ITP should be as comfortable using imagery to rehearse specific skills in an event situation as they are imagining competition successes prior to going to sleep.

CONTENT OF ITP

The selection and presentation of ITP content are strategy areas of particular importance. Consideration must be given to specific image characteristics relating to content, including development of vividness and control, image progression, involvement of senses, image realism, image perspective, timing of image execution, imagery of performance outcomes, utilization of a positive focus, involvement of memory in image creation or re-creation, imagery of complete skills, use of stimulus, response, and meaning propositions, and use of extended detail for performers with advanced imagery skills.

SIMPLE ACTIVITIES TO FACILITATE VIVIDNESS AND CONTROL

Vividness and control are important imagery characteristics that are influenced by the content of images used in the ITP (see chapter 4). Vividness refers to an image's quality, clarity, or realism (Bird and Cripe 1986). Controllability is the manipulation of the content and action of images to produce intentional variations (Bird and Cripe 1986). These characteristics should be developed in the early phases of the ITP by using highly familiar images, such as the family home or pet, or manipulating a wooden cube as a start point for imagery activities. Practitioners recommend using several other specific imagery exercises during the introductory phase of an ITP that highlight mind–body links (Martens

1987; Perry and Morris 1995), including imagining one's home venue or imagining execution of a simple sport skill (Vealey and Greenleaf 2001; Martens 1987). The goal at this stage should be to ensure the selection of simple imagery activities that allow athletes to familiarize themselves with the imagery characteristics of vividness and control, which they will need later in the ITP.

GRADUAL PROGRESSION

Sport psychologists from the U.S. Olympic Committee have made useful recommendations regarding content progression in imagery training (USOC 1998). They suggested that initial exercises should focus on nonthreatening, nonstressful, nonsport-based images. Content material that includes familiar sport skills should be used in the next phase of the ITP. Finally, the program should progress toward including images of more complex competitive situations.

INVOLVE ALL THE SENSES

Substantial agreement exists regarding the inclusion of content material that involves using all the senses (Lavallee et al. 2004; Moran 2004; Perry and Morris 1995; Vealey and Greenleaf 2001; Weinberg and Gould 2003; Woods 1998). Suinn (1983) suggested that imagery is a "total retrieval of experience that is holistic and fully dimensional in sensations" (p. 512). Content should focus on images that include the visual, auditory, olfactory, gustatory, tactile, and kinesthetic senses. Including as many senses as possible enhances the image's vividness, which in turn may increase the effectiveness of the ITP (Moran 2004; Vealey and Greenleaf 2001; Woods 1998). Sport psychologists have emphasized the specific benefit that athletes will gain by feeling the imagined movements. Focusing on the kinesthetic sensations of their sport is particularly relevant for athletes involved in sport-imagery training (Morris 1997; Sargent 1996; Smith 1998; Weinberg and Gould 2003).

INVOLVE THE KINESTHETIC SENSE

The traditional acknowledgement of the visual modality as the primary sense still remains in both general discussion and research pertaining to sport imagery (Moran 2004). Several researchers have chosen to target the kinesthetic sense to determine its role in imagery use by athletes. Moran and MacIntyre (1998) reported that 75% of an athlete sample incorporated the kinesthetic sense. An extension of this is the convincing finding reported by Munroe et al. (2000): Detailed interview content showed that kinesthetic imagery was used most frequently, slightly more than visual imagery. This type of qualitative data serves as a strong argument for practitioners to ensure that the kinesthetic modality is promoted appropriately in the content of an effective ITP.

ENSURE IMAGE REALISM AND DYNAMISM

A key element in the creation of effective images is to encourage the imager to reflect on actual performance recollections and environmental representations (LeUnes and Nation 2002). Existing research indicates that images that are representative of an athlete's typical sport-oriented activities may be more likely to contribute to improved performance (e.g., Hecker and Kaczor 1988; Lee 1990); therefore, they should represent life as accurately as possible (Perry and Morris 1995). Suinn (1997), in discussing the practical applications of sport imagery, suggested that practitioners maintain an awareness and understanding of the bioinformational theory and incorporate its emphasis on constructing detailed, relevant scene descriptions that attempt to replicate the dynamic nature of many sports and their environments.

USE IMAGERY PERSPECTIVES

Research efforts associated with determining the superiority of either the internal or external perspective have led to an emphasis on outcome, within which athletes may utilize one or both perspectives depending on their performance or practice needs (e.g., Holmes and Collins 2002; Moran 2004; Suinn 1997). Early studies by Mahoney and colleagues (e.g., Mahoney and Avener 1977; Mahoney, Gabriel, and Perkins 1987) indicated that more successful athletes tended to use the internal orientation. Hinshaw (1991) further promoted the emphasis on the internal perspective, following the results of a meta-analysis that indicated a larger effect size for imagery interventions using the internal perspective compared with the external perspective. It should be noted, however, that both the effect sizes were large and above .8, suggesting that using either frame of reference could result in improved performance. In contrast, the work of Hardy and associates indicated that differences in task requirements may affect the use or involvement of each perspective (Hardy 1997; Hardy and Callow 1999; White and Hardy 1995). For example, Hardy and Callow (1999) found that an external visual perspective was superior to an internal perspective for athletes learning new movements in which the need to visualize position and movements were critical elements (e.g., gymnastics, karate). Hall (2001) summarized the general patterns of Hardy's studies:

> The internal perspective has superior effects on the acquisition and performance of skills that depend heavily on form for their successful execution, whereas the external perspective is superior for the acquisition and performance of open skills that depend heavily on perception and anticipation for their successful execution. (p. 536)

Moran (2004) recently highlighted the need for additional research to resolve issues pertaining to perspective use, such as efficacy and modality involvement (visual versus kinesthetic). For the present time, several authors have suggested that decisions surrounding perspective choice may well depend on the goals of the ITP and the specific requirements and activities associated with the task (Holmes and Collins 2002; Suinn 1997; Weinberg and Gould 2003).

PERFORM IMAGERY IN REAL TIME

The speed of the rehearsal of imagery scenes in an ITP represents another important area (e.g., perspective, sensory involvement) for which the strategies proposed in earlier texts (e.g., Martens 1987) have been shown to be less effective than alternative approaches (e.g., Holmes and Collins 2002; Rushall 1995). The two key patterns discussed in the context of practice speed are slow-motion and real-time rehearsal. Slow-motion rehearsal was originally promoted by several authors (e.g., Martens 1987; Hale 1986), based on the idea that it allowed athletes time to isolate weak elements of their performance and eventually correct faulty components, which should then result in improved execution. Martens (1987) did note, however, that the slow-motion practice should be sped up over time to eventually mimic actual performance.

In contrast, several authors (Harris and Harris 1984; Holmes and Collins 2002; Rushall 1995) suggested that rehearsing actions or movements in slow motion may elicit inappropriate neural patterns that are different from those created during physical performance or real-time imagery and consequently lead to errors in actual execution (Harris and Harris 1984; Rushall 1995). Interestingly, some texts (e.g., Lavellee et al. 2004; Harris and Harris 1984) do detail the possible benefit of slowing down movements within imagery during the early stages of skill acquisition. However, the issue has not generated sufficient research to resolve the question.

Evidence supporting the use of real-time rehearsal of imagery within an ITP centers on two key areas. First, Moran and MacIntyre (1998) demonstrated athletes' capacity to mimic the imagination of an athletic performance in the actual physical experience. They reported that the amount of time taken by slalom canoeists to imagine a recent race performance showed a strong, significant correlation with their actual time to complete the event. This finding highlights that athletes are capable of accurately re-creating performance in real time without using slow motion to increase the lifelikeness or accuracy of their constructed images. Second, Holmes and Collins (2002) promoted the theory of functional equivalence as a framework supporting real-time imagery practice. The link between theory and practice is based on the principle of athletes capitalizing on the similarity between the neural activity of imagery and performance in developing their sport skills. Holmes and

Collins proposed that matching "movement tempo and consistency of relative timing for both physical and mental practice conditions" (p. 131) should eventually lead to improved preparation and execution of both imagery and the equivalent motor performance. They also highlighted the importance of incorporating realistic timing (which matches the temporal characteristics of an activity or event) in developing an ITP's imagery scripts. Overall, the current consensus within sport psychology is that athletes should rehearse imagery of performance using a real-time rhythm and tempo wherever possible (e.g., Gould et al. 2002; Moran 2004).

Use Imagery With Positive Performance and Outcome Focuses

Sport psychology practitioners have regularly stressed the importance of incorporating, within the ITP, imagery that focuses on both positive performance and outcome (e.g., Rushall 1995; Suinn 1996; Weinberg and Gould 2003). The content of the images should emphasize winning or involve the repetition of scenes in which the athlete performs both confidently and successfully (Suinn 1996). Guidance should be directed toward generating images that attempt to simulate feelings and sensations that exist during the favorable execution of the skill (Bird and Cripe 1986). Practitioners should encourage athletes to try to image the skill or event in the exact manner in which they hope they will perform (Hall, Schmidt, Durand, and Buckolz 1994).

The basis for the focus on positive and successful outcomes within the ITP derives from research associated with the contrasting of positive and negative imagery. Powell (1973) found that positive imagery of dart-throwing outcomes led to improved performance, whereas negative imagery resulted in performance deterioration. Similarly, Woolfolk, Parrish, and Murphy (1985) compared performances of a golf-putting task by positive-imagery, negative-imagery, and control groups. Again, the group given a positive performance scene improved its execution significantly compared to the negative-imagery group (which showed a performance decline) and the control group (which showed an insignificant increase). These types of findings reinforce the concept of encouraging sport-oriented imagery that focuses on accuracy and success and avoiding negative images, which may affect proper skill acquisition and lead to incorrect execution or performance failure (Hall et al. 1994). Recently, Hall (2001) noted that research investigating the imagery content of experienced athletes (e.g., Barr and Hall 1992; Hall et al. 1990) highlighted the trend that such athletes rarely imagine themselves performing poorly or losing; consequently negative imagery should not be a major concern in the context of the ITP for elite performers with advanced imagery skills.

Applied representation of this strategy appears frequently in the details of existing imagery-training frameworks (e.g., Korn 1994; Rushall 1995;

Weinberg and Gould 2003). Rushall (1995) was adamant that positive, successful imagery is a critical factor in the development of an effective program. Rushall suggested that athletes should focus on and rehearse only the positive, desirable aspects of their performances. This approach should lead to the creation of efficient physiological bases for successful performance, stimulation of effective forms of skill functioning, and enhancement of an athlete's overall self-efficacy for performing. Weinberg and Gould (2003) presented a less rigid format in which imagery rehearsal of poor performance may be used as a foundation from which to recognize and analyze mistakes. In subsequent repetition of imagery rehearsals, the focus must shift to an ongoing emphasis on positive outcomes.

In addition to these straightforward outlines of practice, Korn (1994) used case-study-style scripts that incorporate specific positive language and images (e.g., removal of heavy weights, the positive propulsion of a lever) to serve as a basis for the formulation of an ITP in which positive imagery is a key strategy. Overall, the evidence that positive imagery is superior to negative imagery, in conjunction with the obvious preference of practitioners to work with athletes using a positive imagery focus, indicates that ITP content should include images associated with successful outcomes (except for specific, short-term imagery tasks such as problem solving).

BASE IMAGES ON MEMORIES

Memory is possibly the most powerful mechanism involved in the imaginal re-creation of past events and the formation of new images. In many cases, both sport and general psychology literature make specific reference to memory as a critical element in the imagery process (e.g., Lavallee et al. 2004; Richardson 1999; Simons 2000; Vealey and Greenleaf 2001). Although memory is normally acknowledged as integral to the imagery process, its actual role, at both the physiological and phenomenological levels, is yet to be fully understood; as a consequence existing ITPs describe it as serving a wide range of content-oriented functions. For example, Vealey and Greenleaf (2001) suggested that because imagery is based on memory, memory is the basis of all reconstructions in an ITP.

Ungerleider (1996) presented a useful outline of memory's role in generating images with the specific purpose of performance enhancement in athletes. Ungerleider adopted a nonscientific jargon approach as a strategy to facilitate understanding of how memories serve as a foundation for sport-oriented imagery. Briefly, the outline uses a computer analogy to describe the physiological bases of imagery in which memories, drawn from structures such as the parietal and temporal lobes, represent "what" and "where" databases of athletes' previous experiences. Ungerleider went on to detail how the brain searches these databases and directs required information to a visual holding station in the brain, where the memories can be re-created into images on their own or combined with new sensory input to create new images. Ungerleider also noted that actual and imaginal information flows in both directions within the memory systems, so that databases are continually updated in order to facilitate improved future images. Overall, Ungerleider's description of sport-imagery use reinforces its dependence on memory at all stages of the generation and manipulation of images.

Many recent sport psychology texts that provide details of the application of imagery for performance enhancement incorporate elements that infer the use of memories in the ITP (e.g., Cox 2002; Vealey and Greenleaf 2001; Weinberg and Gould 2003). Vealey and Greenleaf (2001) expanded on their premise of imagery as a product of memories by describing how athletes can build an image from whichever pieces of memory they care to use. The involvement of memories beyond re-creation and in the creation of new images is also important to the definition of sport imagery that Vealey and Greenleaf have promoted. For example, it can involve reflections of previous performances, images of sport environments well in advance of actual competition, varying representations of the implementation of game plans and tactical strategies, and imaginal rehearsal of critical physical actions that athletes have performed many times in developing skills. Memory constitutes an invaluable component of any ITP, not simply in the re-creation of existing performance but as a framework for the creation of new images that represent successful execution or familiarization with new environments or experiences.

INCLUDE STIMULUS AND RESPONSE PROPOSITIONS

As an outcome of imagery conceptualizations such as the bioinformational theory (Lang 1977) and the triple-code model (Ahsen 1984), ITP scripts should endeavor to include both stimulus and response propositions (see chapter 2). Current sport psychology texts that include ITP guidelines maintain that specific text segments that are weighted with stimulus and response propositions (functionally organized and finite sets of statements representative of the image details stored in the brain) are likely to be more effective than scripts without them (e.g., Moran 2004; Murphy and Martin 2002; Vealey and Greenleaf 2001; Weinberg and Gould 2003).

According to Lang's (1977) bioinformational theory, stimulus propositions are statements that detail the content characteristics of the scenario to be imagined. For example, a stimulus-oriented script prepared for a middle-distance athlete would include references to the environment (e.g., weather, track surface), equipment (e.g., shoes, tracksuit), performance actions (e.g., leg tempo, stride length), and performance setting (e.g., crowd, other athletes). Response propositions, according to Lang, describe the individual's responses to the scenario stimuli with the goal of promoting and facilitating physiological reactions. Examples of response characteristics content in relation to the middle-distance runner include body-organ execution (e.g., heart rate, breathing rate), skeletal and muscular activity (e.g., muscle fatigue, sore feet), environmental feedback (e.g., sensation of cold air on the skin), and metabolic maintenance (e.g., sweating, dry mouth).

Ahsen's (1984) triple-code model is similar to Lang's theory; however, it is extended by the recognition of the importance of an image's meaning to an individual and the subsequent inclusion of this characteristic within the model's structure. In preparing imagery scripts, incorporating statements that acknowledge the specific significance an image may impart is important, because "the same set of imagery instructions will never produce the same imagery experience for any two people" (Weinberg and Gould 2003, 293). In the example of the middle-distance runner, appropriate script content would include statements that refer to meaning characteristics, such as desired performance outcome (e.g., winning a medal), prior event history (e.g., previous victories or positive performances), long-term goal achievement (e.g., progression from sub-elite to professional), feedback from others (e.g., family validation, crowd response), and personal emotions (e.g., achievement satisfaction, performance elation).

Previous examinations of script quality have provided examples of best practices in developing the types of scripts that should be used with an ITP. Hale (1994) presented a useful overview describing how to include response propositions in an imagery script, outlining suitable physiological responses to incorporate in the application of Lang's model. The detail in Hale's applied principles of sport imagery, however, would have benefited from additional acknowledgement of stimulus and meaning statements as critical elements in ITP content. Suinn (1997) used the comparison of an inadequate scene (one lacking in sufficient stimulus detail and containing no response information) with an ideal scene that included content full of setting, performer, physiological, and meaning details. Suinn stressed the importance of practitioners' reviewing the scripts they create to ensure that they provide sufficient opportunity for athletes to utilize their images for the most efficacious outcome of the ITP. Content must reflect theory where possible, and incorporating elements of both the bioinformational and triple-code models in imagery scripts will contribute to best practice in applying imagery in sport psychology.

Extend Content Detail for Advanced Imagers

Results of major meta-analysis studies by Feltz et al. (1988) and Hinshaw (1991) indicated a trend in the outcome of imagery-based training programs: Athletes who were experienced in their sport demonstrated greater improvements in performance than novice athletes. These findings support the proposition that athletes with prior imagery experience may benefit from extending the ITP content to include more detail and an increased range of use orientations. Holmes and Collins (2002) suggested that because the neural representation of athletic skills changes over the duration of an activity, as a consequence, the content of imagery scripts "must change to accommodate learning and to maintain functional equivalence" (p. 132).

Rushall (1995, 1998) provided a useful outline of performance-oriented imagery content that would be suitable for athletes at a more advanced stage of development in an ITP. The key components are (a) an emotional arousal component that serves to "psych-up," or excite, an athlete toward optimal preperformance levels; (b) a neuromuscular facilitation component to prepare athletes for highly skilled events (e.g., high jump, gymnastics), within which the imagery stresses skill-oriented cues and movement routines; and (c) an organizational component that focuses on enhancing the appropriate resources and actions utilized in performance, such as positional play and tactics in ball-based team events or timing and focus in individual sports such as diving or figure skating. Similar to this breakdown of content are the two key functions in the Sport Imagery Use Model (Martin et al. 1999): the cognitive and the motivational. These two areas of the taxonomy (see chapters 2 and 3) serve as valuable guidelines for the extension of the general uses of sport imagery to match the content needs of higher-performing athletes.

Many practitioners have also detailed clinically related content goals from involvement in an ITP for the advanced athlete. Unestahl (1986) suggested using elements of emotional therapy as a framework to help athletes deal with the intensities of elite competition. Suinn (1997) proposed that highly skilled performers require less cognitive orientation in an ITP and a greater emphasis on elements related to arousal, self-efficacy, and self-instruction. Anxiety reduction is another a key psychological procedure that several practitioners have described as essential in constructing an ITP for a superior player in their sport (e.g., Hale 1994; Perry and Morris 1995; Unestahl 1986). This procedure is necessary because of the possibility of elite performers experiencing severe cognitive and physiological manifestations from involvement in anxiety-provoking situations. Finally, imagery to develop coping skills is a recent theme in the prescriptive repertoires of sport psychologists (e.g., Orlick 2000; Weinberg and Gould 2003). Appropriate content for athletes who may experience pressure scenarios needs to cater to both the re-creation of the images associated with the areas of concern and to the creation of new images that represent strategies that typify successful coping. Practitioners who aim to develop comprehensive ITPs must ascertain the imagery backgrounds and track the progression of higher-level performers to ensure that the content of their individualized programs matches their needs and pertains to the nature of their involvement in elite sport.

REFLECT ATHLETES' PERFORMANCE-IMAGERY NEEDS

The final aspect of ITP content to be examined is one of the most important: the reason why the practitioner, coach, or athlete has decided to use imagery. Once again, existing literature includes a valuable overview of the many uses for imagery in the performance-enhancement field (e.g., Korn 1994; Perry and Morris 1995; Vealey and Greenleaf 2001; Weinberg and Gould 2003). This section briefly outlines those uses so that future ITP developers can benefit from the knowledge that others have found imagery to be a useful strategy to service their performance requirements. Weinberg and Gould (2003) proposed that imagery training benefits athletes by helping them (a) improve concentration, (b) establish confidence, (c) control emotional responses, (d) acquire and practice sport skills, (e) acquire and develop game and event strategies, (f) facilitate injury rehabilitation, (g) develop coping strategies, and (h) solve problems associated with performance.

REHEARSAL ROUTINES FOR ITP

As with physical practice, an ITP requires that attention be paid to the schedules for its various tasks and activities. Appropriate liaison and communication between the sport psychology practitioner, coaching personnel, and athletes is essential. This section provides guidelines for various approaches that have been used and promoted within the field. Again, as with physical preparation, the information presented here must be tailored to the individual athlete's unique goals for imagery training.

SCHEDULING PRACTICE SESSIONS

ITP development must take into account both the short- and long-term availability of the athlete. Practice sessions need to be carefully planned within the context of performers' overall training and competition timetables. All those involved in an athlete's preparation need to monitor imagery practice schedules in a systematic manner to foster the integration of imagery into the greater physical- and psychological-performance plan (Vealey and Greenleaf 2001).

Most practitioners agree that the ITP should be maintained throughout practice and competition (e.g., Gould et al. 2002; Janssen and Sheikh 1994; Nideffer 1985). In the early part of a season, or with athletes new to involvement in an ITP, sessions should occur primarily during practice activities (Perry and Morris 1995). As athletes move closer to the more intense phase of the ITP and gain confidence in their participation in it, imagery activities should extend to include the competition environment (Gould et al. 2002; Harris and Harris 1984; Nideffer 1985). Hall, Schmidt, Durand, and Buckolz (1994) presented useful advice about how the athlete and practitioner can both allow ITP scheduling to be spread across the performance timetable, suggesting that as athletes develop their imagery skills during the practice phase, they can become more creative in their use of imagery. This increase in imagery skills should coincide with a greater motivational orientation for the use of imagery, which is especially suited to competition through functions such as imagining being in control and successful. Harris and Harris (1984) suggested that most imagery rehearsal should take place during training and practice, but that wherever possible, imaging a performance immediately before participating in the event (e.g., diving, golf swing) is extremely beneficial. They did note that this activity is impractical in many sports (e.g., team events, tennis forehand). Specifically in regard to competition, Morris (1997) made the important distinction between scheduling preperformance and performance routines in an ITP. Preperformance imagery is undertaken in the lead-up to participation in an event (to establish an ideal performing state), while performance routines occur during sport events in which imagery can be practiced between physical actions (e.g., golf, archery).

Several authors have created similar sets of scheduling guidelines that overview times when imagery use would be most effective (Janssen and Sheikh 1994; Vealey and Greenleaf 2001; Weinberg and Gould 2003). We have summarized their suggestions:

a. During the entire practice phase of the season

b. Before and after individual training sessions

c. Prior to competition at both the season and individual-event levels

d. During competition at points when a break in the physical performance of the event occurs

e. During athletes' personal time

f. When recovering from injury, as a component of rehabilitation

Understanding that each of the scheduled uses is not independent from the others is important; they should be undertaken in conjunction with each other in the manner that is best suited to the prescribed ITP. Scheduling is a critical aspect in the implementation of the ITP, and each phase requires attention in the context of the athletes' overall timetable, to ensure the highest level of efficacy for the intervention.

PATTERNING AND DURATION OF PRACTICE SESSIONS

In addition to scheduling, practitioners must consider the framework of each individual session in terms of pattern and duration of practice within the entire ITP. The pattern of a routine in an individual session of the ITP represents structural elements, such as number of repetitions of the imagery experience, when the imagery rehearsal could occur, and whether the completion of the imagery rehearsal is in association with other psychological-skills training activities. "Duration of practice" refers to the time that athletes engage in imagery rehearsal during a scheduled practice session.

Most experts make the point that once an ITP has begun, imagery practice should occur regularly (Morris 1997; Suinn 1997; Vealey and Greenleaf 2001). Review of the literature produced no definitive estimate of the number of sessions required for maximum efficacy. Recommendations varied only minimally, from daily, the most commonly reported rate (e.g., Vealey and Greenleaf 2001), to twice a day (Nideffer 1985), to the maximum an athlete feels comfortable undertaking (Rushall 1995). Rushall (1995) suggested that the number of repetitions is likely to increase for athletes performing at a higher level, particularly as they move closer to a contest or event, and as a consequence more repetitions are appropriate. The recommendations by practitioners that athletes should practice imagery on their own also affects monitoring and controlling of the exact number of repetitions in which they engage (e.g., Bird and Cripe 1986; Harris and Harris 1984; Sargent 1996). Advanced athletes, however, can usually rely on their own judgment to effectively regulate the number of sessions that they undertake (Rushall 1995).

Athletes who are involved in an ITP must perceive imagery rehearsal as integral to their daily routine and not as an unnecessary additional activity (Sargent 1997). For this reason, they should be encouraged to practice routinely, at similar times during the day, at times that suit their performance timetable, and during free time when they feel comfortable completing some imagery exercises. As discussed earlier, the pattern of sessions or activities can vary from specific set training times regulated by the coach or practitioner to regular but brief preperformance sessions before every competition engagement. Harris and Harris (1984) noted that some players reported that immediately prior to falling asleep was a very effective time to use imagery rehearsal. Suinn (1997) and Weinberg and Gould (2003) reinforced the need to align imagery practices with physical practices to ensure that the structure of rehearsals has an integral and committed pattern.

Once the ITP has taken shape, imagery-rehearsal routines will vary according to their association with other psychological-skills activities (e.g., relaxation, video modeling, flotation). The key point in relation to patterning is that routines in which imagery is partnered with procedures such as relaxation will vary greatly from those involving only imagery. Morris (1997) detailed that in many ITPs relaxation precedes imagery activities or follows a session as a form of debriefing. Other nonimagery activities can be interspersed within imagery-practice schedules if the practitioner perceives that they will lead to a more effective overall ITP.

In general, consistency exists within the sport psychology literature about duration of imagery sessions (e.g., LeUnes and Nation 2002; Nideffer 1985; Sargent 1997; Suinn 1997); the typical recommendation is that sessions last approximately 10 min. No empirical basis was given for this particular interval other than the general guideline that short sessions accompanied by long rest periods appear to suit the majority of athletes (LeUnes and Nation 2002). Variations of this recommendation proposed that individual sessions should last a minimum of 1 min but never exceed 5 min in duration (Weinberg 1982). Wichman and Lizotte (1983) found that 15 min of imagery rehearsal was too long in target-shooting-related sports; participants found it to be an overly intense experience. Suinn (1984) suggested that in the VMBR procedure, an imagery scene should be rehearsed for 30 to 45 sec, followed by a relaxation period prior to the next repetition.

The shortest repetition lengths for imaging were reported between activity sessions in bursts of 3 to 10 sec, as a component of normal coaching and training behaviors (Gould et al. 2002). In contrast, Perry and Morris (1995) proposed that at later stages of the training day (such as prior to sleeping) athletes are capable of committing 20 to 30 min to imagery-rehearsal activities. Suinn (1997) presented a less restricted guideline in which the primary consideration is to avoid mental fatigue within the repetitions, irrespective of the length or number of repetitions undertaken. This type of monitoring approach seems appropriate in conjunction with the 10 min recommendation, with the number of repetitions set at a minimum greater than 1 and a maximum dependent on the characteristics of the imagery experience. For example, simple skill-rehearsal scenes (e.g., free-throw shooting) may utilize a high number of repetitions, while performance-anxiety reduction scenes (e.g., mastering complex gymnastic routines in elite competition) may benefit from limited daily practice only.

MATCHING ROUTINES TO ATHLETE REQUIREMENTS

The practitioner, coach, and athlete should overview the goals of the ITP and match them with the scheduling of rehearsal routines. Specific areas that require consideration in developing routines are status of the athlete in relation to competition and psychological-skills training, nature of the sport, and the individual needs of each performer (e.g., Janssen and Sheikh 1994; Vealey and Greenleaf 2001).

Morris (1997) suggested a sound basic rule: Practitioners must ensure that the routines they develop fit in with the athlete's personal style and sport. As a component of his imagery program, Rushall (1995) paid specific attention to acknowledging the capacities of advanced athletes to capitalize on their maturity in relation to performance preparation, allowing them to set and maintain their own imagery-rehearsal routines. In consultation with the coach or sport psychologist, they are capable of varying their routines to suit both training and competition phases. Prescriptions developed for the less elite competitor may require more input and an increased level of monitoring from overseers of the ITP.

The type of sport that an athlete is involved in substantially influences the patterns of imagery rehearsal. Janssen and Sheikh (1994) stated that specific characteristics of the sport, such as its open or closed nature, affect the patterning of routines. For example, a gymnast is likely to require a significantly different schedule than a middle-distance swimmer. And several authors have presented case-study materials that highlight the necessity for differences between team and individual routines. Korn (1994) outlined imagery training programs suitable for team sports that included information related to establishing routines at group and individual levels. Similarly, Simons (2000) used information from a set of case studies pertaining to individual sports to facilitate a clearer understanding of the imagery schedules used by athletes in events such as discus, high jump, and javelin. The formulation of routines requires close attention by the practitioner in an effort to facilitate schedules and patterns that lead to enhanced performance.

ENHANCEMENTS TO ITP

In constructing ITPs, practitioners should incorporate various enhancements to improve their effectiveness. The possibilities include cues and triggers, audio and video aids, exposure to modeling, and relaxation, flotation, and biofeedback. Several of these are discussed in detail in chapters 9 and 10, so here we limit ourselves to exploring the process of integrating these elements within the broader ITP. Many of these enhancements cannot actually be included in an ITP for practical reasons, such as a lack of availability of equipment (e.g., a flotation tank) or limited practitioner experience (e.g., familiarity with biofeedback devices). Sport psychologists who want to extend the base ITP must consider the realities of enhancing the program before making suggestions to athletes.

TRIGGERS, CUES, AND LABELS

Perhaps the simplest way to enhance imagery-rehearsal strategies is to incorporate triggers, cues, and labels. Several texts provide valuable outlines of these procedures in relation to constructing an ITP (e.g., Bird and

Cripe 1986; Gould et al. 2002; Sargent 1997). Triggers are the techniques used by athletes to help them attend to critical elements of the program (Sargent 1997). Gould et al. (2002) noted that triggers can involve any of the five senses. The most common form appears to be cues or labels, such as words, phrases, objects, or physical gestures, that serve as signals to engage in a predetermined action or behavior that facilitates concentration and focus on a sport. Bird and Cripe (1986) suggested that this type of instructional strategy often involves "the labeling of movement components and instructions to code movement information symbolically" (p. 204). Examples of movement labels include words such as "varoom," representing an explosive sprinting start, or the phrase "rock of Gibraltar" as a cue for a water-polo team to maintain concentration under pressure (Sargent 1997). Bird and Cripe (1986) proposed two important factors that have an impact on the effectiveness of labeling: the ease with which the label evokes imagery and the concreteness of the cue. They recommended that practitioners ensure that labels are clear, precise, and meaningful to the athlete. Finally, Bird and Cripe briefly discussed the use of cues as mnemonic devices; that is, the phrase or keyword is used to facilitate retention during the imagery rehearsal. Overall, an effective trigger leads to the creation of the desired image (Gould et al. 2002; Sargent 1997).

AUDIO AND VIDEO AIDS

Audio and video materials are practical resources for enhancing the ITP. Vealey and Greenleaf (2001) outlined several procedures for using audio devices to facilitate and strengthen imagery rehearsal. First, the practitioner or athlete can use commercially available audio-based imagery materials that address skills such as relaxation and concentration. Second, those involved in the ITP can construct their own audio materials, incorporating strategies such as scripting and triggering into the verbal components and adding music or sound effects that stimulate appropriate images for the athlete. Finally, the psychologist, in consultation with the client, can record the imagery sessions so that the athlete can replay and review the strategies and skills covered.

The use of video materials and procedures is slightly more complex. Recent technological advances in equipment (e.g., cameras, computers) and an increase in knowledge about materials preparation have facilitated the integration of these techniques within the ITP. (In this book we use the term "video" to include all available recording media, including DVD or VCD.) Specific video-related activities that can be paired with imagery rehearsal include film loops, slow-motion playback, helmet camera (to simulate the internal visual perspective), video modeling, and the creation of success tapes (Gill 2000; Gould et al. 2002; Unestahl 1986; Vealey and Greenleaf 2001). Vealey and Greenleaf (2001) provided an excellent example of how to prepare a success tape that focuses on the presentation of performance highlights and motivational triggers. The task involves editing existing footage of the athlete's peak performances and representations of success (e.g., receiving a medal) and adding special effects and motivational music chosen by the athlete. Practitioners must be open to using audio and video aids in the ITP because of their performance-enhancement capacity (e.g., Gray 1990). These aids represent a novel approach to the construction of a varied, stimulating program.

INCORPORATING MODELING ACTIVITIES

Improvements in technology have minimized the skills required of sport psychologists, coaches, and athletes in developing the materials used in modeling. The two primary areas of modeling are direct observation and video. Perry and Morris (1995) reinforced the rationale underlying modeling, which is Bandura's (1977b) social learning theory. This theory, when considered in the context of imagery, is based on the principle that "vicarious experience (observation of a model performing a task successfully) enhances performance" (Perry and Morris 1995, 372).

In direct observation, athletes view an actual performance of an activity (in either a training or competition setting) by someone who can complete it at a high-quality level of execution. Later they try to re-create an image of that "perfect" performance and use the imagery to assist their own development in performing the skill.

In video modeling, a video recording of the athlete's best execution of the skill or footage of an elite performer completing it forms the basis from which to generate future imagery. Martens (1987) provided a practical summary of the procedure that specifies that all members of the ITP team should have input into the video footage. Only perfect or near-perfect movements or performances should be included, which are recorded repeatedly on the video. The athletes then watch these activities over and over. They watch the material again in a relaxed state as a part of their imagery-rehearsal sessions, then practice imaging the skill.

Modeling is a powerful procedure that is well suited to imagery training. The ITP team needs to include it in training activities in an effort to extend the athletes' access to all available means of maximizing performance. (Chapter 10 includes a more detailed discussion of video modeling.)

RELAXATION, FLOTATION REST, AND BIOFEEDBACK

This final category of ITP enhancements extends from one of the most likely activities to be implemented (relaxation) to one that is rarely incorporated in the applied setting (biofeedback). The three areas represented in our ITP model occur in a pattern similar to their usage in the field (from common to rare): relaxation, flotation REST, and biofeedback (e.g., Gould et al. 2002; Perry and Morris 1995; Suinn 1997).

Relaxation is highly valued by practitioners of imagery training in sport as an adjunct to general imagery-based strategies (e.g., Gould et al. 2002; Suinn 1997). Perry and Morris (1995) inferred that this was an outcome of tradition rather than confirmation of the efficacy of relaxation partnered with imagery. However, some researchers have demonstrated that relaxation used in conjunction with an ITP is more effective than imagery used without relaxation (Kolonay 1977; Weinberg, Seabourne, and Jackson 1981). Gould et al. (2002) proposed that the use of relaxation exercises (e.g., passive progressive relaxation, deep breathing) prior to imagery rehearsal reduces interference from distractions and focuses the athlete's attention on the imagery activities. Another advantage of relaxation strategies is that they foster the scheduling of rest breaks between imagery repetitions and thus limit the likelihood of fatigue (Suinn 1997). Also, they may help athletes who are in the early stages of imagery training concentrate on the novel requirements of the imagery tasks (Gould et al. 2002). Perry and Morris (1995) suggested that relaxation be included in the ITP, irrespective of whether it enhances imagery effectiveness or not, because it can ensure that the athlete's muscles are relaxed prior to execution of the physical activity.

Flotation REST and biofeedback are covered in detail in chapter 10. Briefly, in flotation Restricted Environmental Stimulation Therapy (REST), the athlete is immersed in an enclosed tank that minimizes and controls sensorial input and contains a salt solution dense enough to support the body (Perry and Morris 1995). Perry and Morris proposed that utilizing the flotation REST procedure with athletes, in the context of an ITP, enhances their sport-oriented imagery because they are able to attend purposefully to this task due to the minimal presence of external stimulation and distractions. They suggested "in these quieted circumstances for the central nervous system, it is argued, images can be produced more vividly and with greater control, so they are more effective" (p. 375).

Biofeedback also requires access to specialized equipment, and therefore, its applicability is limited to the most advanced-level ITPs. The exercise is typically used to manage arousal levels and to emphasize the close connection between mind and body (Perry and Morris 1995). Physiological characteristics, such as heart rate, breathing rate, or galvanic skin response, are monitored by an exercise-physiology expert. Responses are measured while the athlete engages in a predetermined set of imagery tasks. The athlete receives feedback regarding the associated changes in physiological response rates that occur both during and between imagery sessions. Overall, the activities demonstrate that athletes can control their arousal levels through the use of imagery, and that they can transfer this skill across the stages of the ITP that involve the generation and manipulation of images.

Relaxation, flotation REST, and biofeedback are enhancements that highlight the powerful nature of the imagery experience to the athlete. Whenever possible, or when deemed appropriate by the ITP team, athletes should participate in these activities, which should prove beneficial to their progression and engagement in the program.

EVALUATION OF ITP

As athletes progress through the ITP, practitioners must evaluate its effectiveness. This should occur in the context of periodic feedback from the athlete and as an end-of-program appraisal of the ITP outcomes in terms of psychological, physical, and competition developments. Imagery training is typically undertaken with the goal of facilitating improvements in performance. Thus all those involved in the creation and maintenance of the ITP must recognize that performance improvements should serve as the primary indicator of efficacy. Other assessments that can be undertaken over the course of the ITP include athlete logs or diaries, verbal and written reports, independent measures of the status and progression of imagery skills, and comparative information related to improvements in both skill levels and competition results.

VERBAL AND WRITTEN REPORTING

The initial phase of evaluation should rely on an immediate form of feedback, such as verbal reports from the ITP participants. Practitioners should instruct the athletes to describe what is taking place during each practice activity. As their confidence develops, their responses should become increasingly detailed and precise (Bird and Cripe 1986). Appropriate management of this early stage of the ITP will also help to establish rapport with the athlete, which in turn should improve communication about the qualities of the imagery experience.

Written reporting is a more formal evaluation technique. The most common format suggested in the literature is the use of an imagery journal or log (e.g., Gould et al. 2002; Harris and Harris 1984; Janssen and Sheikh 1994; Sargent 1997; Vealey and Greenleaf 2001). Gould et al. (2002) described advantages of this format that represent the written frameworks proposed by others in the field. First, imagery diaries assist athletes with the daily monitoring of imagery progress and practice of areas such as vividness, clarity, control, and imagery outcomes. Second, they can include details of the exercises undertaken and the extent to which the athletes perceive them to be helpful. Third, they can include information related to best performance in both competition and training, which can be used in the ITP at a later date. Fourth, they can be used to document the nature of triggers or cues that athletes use in their imagery rehearsals. Finally, the logs facilitate the "athletes' awareness with regard to the practice they devote to imagery as well as the effectiveness of this practice" (Gould et al. 2002, 66).

Another form of written report is a task-analysis document, in the form of a worksheet (Rushall 1995; Smith 1998). These documents require athletes to review the completion of the imagery activity and report on outcomes in relation to the set items detailed by the practitioner. Rushall (1995), for example, requested that the participants provide information in relation to image-generation abilities and an evaluation of their overall performance on the task. A second example is the worksheets developed by Smith (1998), on which athletes document chronological information and details of the imagery rehearsal. Once the task is completed (a detailed copy of the task requirements is also provided), the athletes note their perceived improvements in relation to the goals they set prior to undertaking the task. Written reporting provides a useful format that allows athletes to track their progression through the ITP.

SELF-EVALUATION AND OBSERVATIONAL FEEDBACK

Self-evaluation activities should be seen as an extension of the verbal and written reporting procedures. The key difference is that this form of reporting may reflect learning and progress of a more personal nature. Self-evaluation allows the athletes to express emotions and feelings (both positive and negative) regarding their participation in the ITP. Information pertaining to features of the imagery activities that are relevant only to the participant (commitment, enjoyment) but are crucial to performance could also be detailed in the context of self-evaluation (Rushall 1995). The athletes should keep these documents and decide whether they want to incorporate these assessments into the broader evaluation of the program.

Like much of the involvement in elite sport, feedback from observation may also prove beneficial when reviewing the ITP. In its simplest form, practitioners or coaches document their accounts of the athletes' involvement in the ITP for the purposes of evaluation. Feedback from observation, in consideration of the goals and exercises established in the ITP, includes improvements associated with skills, movements, and physical abilities and the tracking of competition results. Communications constructed on the basis of practitioners' intimate understanding of the entire ITP and observations of the athlete's performances can play an important role in periodic evaluation.

COMPARISON WITH PHYSICAL AND COMPETITIVE PROGRESS

As mentioned previously, evaluation should reflect athletes' progress in relation to their physical development and competition performances. A direct comparison of athletes' performance goals with the nature of the imagery rehearsal undertaken should be made (Rushall 1995). Pre-performance and performance imagery activities should be analyzed in terms of their contribution to competitive outcomes. Rushall (1995) suggested that this type of evaluation contributes valuable information in determining the actual bounds of performance imagery. Similarly, step-by-step evaluation of imagery tasks undertaken in conjunction with physical-development phases of training should also occur. Orlick (2000) proposed that imagery of each physical action and subsequent assessment helps athletes know what to focus on to feel good, perform well, and push their limits.

END OF ITP REVIEW

The final phase of the ITP should entail a full review of the outcomes and effectiveness of the interventions. It should constitute a written report of all aspects of the ITP derived from reviewing documents prepared during each phase. Gould et al. (2002) proposed that the end-of-program evaluation provides guidance for the practitioner as to whether they can continue the program with confidence. Critical examination of the program identifies problems or obstacles and allows solutions to be formulated. For example, athletes may feel that they have poor imaging skills, but rigorous evaluation could reveal that the problem is the imagery strategies being used. Broad feedback related to the efficacy of the ITP allows all those involved to ascertain those strategies and activities that interest the participants and lead to effective outcomes. The chance to alter and refine the ITP should arise as an outcome of this end-of-program review.

Monitoring and evaluation of the ITP by psychologists, coaches, and performers are the bases of highlighting successes and celebrating them as well as acknowledging and resolving problems. Orlick (2000) adopted the perspective of the performer and promoted how essential a thorough evaluation of the ITP is to the athletes' overall progress. The evaluation phases must lead to athletes becoming "more attuned to the thoughts, feelings, and emotions which lead to successful performance" (Sargent 1997, 33).

APPLIED EXAMPLE

This section presents an example of how the main elements of an ITP may be operationalized in relation to an elite junior gymnast, William, who is developing his imagery skills as a component of a broader performance-advancement program. Space does not permit detailed description of the development and practice of such a program, so we illustrate the process by describing some key elements of the ITP that are relevant to our example.

Initially, William and his coach discuss the goals of the ITP with Sarah, the elite gymnastics program's sport psychologist. Sarah uses her expert training in gathering information to encourage coach and athlete to communicate appropriate details regarding William's background and history of elite gymnastics performance, physiological and psychological attributes, and experience in psychological-skills training. This provides information for the "prerequisites" and "environment" elements of the ITP model. In addition to using informal interview techniques, the sport psychologist also employs reliable sport-specific measures to glean critical information. The Sport Imagery Questionnaire (SIQ; Hall et al. 1998) is administered to permit William to describe his current, largely unsystematic use of imagery in relation to his gymnastics activity. William also completes the Sports Imagery Ability Measure (SIAM; Watt et al., 2004) to assess the effectiveness of his current imagery skill, in terms of dimensions and sense modalities.

The interview indicates that William is highly skilled in gymnastics and confident about performing in local events, which he has done for several years now. However, higher-level events are a new experience for him, and he has not performed up to his capabilities in recent major competitions. The SIQ results show that William typically uses imagery for motivational-general purposes, usually imagining himself on the podium after winning. He rarely does cognitive-specific imagery. His scores on the SIAM are generally sound, although appropriate training could enhance William's imagery on most dimensions and sense modalities. The one surprise on the SIAM is that William reports low ability in the kinesthetic sense modality. This is unusual for a skilled athlete in a body-movement sport like gymnastics, where visual input is limited and the richly varied sequences of movements, especially on the high bar and the pommel horse, should produce a high level of kinesthetic information. This information is added to the "prerequisites" for imagery.

After reflecting on this information, the sport psychologist arranges a meeting with William to discuss imagery training and how she expects his program to function. Based on William's performances at major events, Sarah suggests that it sounds like William gets uptight before important competitions. She proposes that he practice the pleasant-scene imagery technique at home at night to help him relax. Once he can relax well there, William will try the technique at the noisy gymnastics hall where he trains, then take it to minor competitions. Finally, once he is truly comfortable with the technique, he will use it at major competitions well before he competes to provide a foundation of relaxation.

The sport psychologist also introduces William to an imagery-training device to enhance his kinesthetic imagery ability: William is to physically perform well-rehearsed routines while focusing on the sensations he experiences in his muscles and joints. Immediately after the physical practice, he must image the same routine, again focusing on the feelings in his muscles and joints that he just experienced. Once William reports the transfer of an enhanced kinesthetic sense to his imagery in general, Sarah plans to introduce more kinesthetic material into his main imagery-rehearsal program.

Sarah believes that William will benefit greatly from using imagery to practice his competition routines for the high bar and the pommel horse. In particular, she wants him to use cognitive-specific imagery, for two reasons. First, he can benefit from imagining the sequence of moves in each routine, so that he learns them very well. Second, by imagining himself performing the routine well in front of a big audience at a major event, he will enhance his confidence that he can perform at his best in such circumstances. This should be much more effective than William's daydreams of receiving the gold medal without any context of performance or environment.

To ensure that the cognitive-specific imagery rehearsal involves William's best possible performance of his routines, his coach videotapes an outstanding performance in a local competition. The sport psychologist then employs this in the video-modeling technique immediately before William does his imaging in a quiet area at the training venue. Again, the plan is for William to move the imagery program, excluding the video-modeling element, to a busy training hall, minor competitions, and finally to major events. This procedure demonstrates and reinforces the "content," "routines," and "enhancements" aspects of the ITP model for the performer.

The goal for William and his coach is to use the imagery programs in the buildup to the state and national competitions, which are several months away. The coach and sport psychologist review the scripts to ensure that they are clear and meaningful for William, and that they contain sufficiently detailed content that relates to the targeted gymnastics activities. Sarah then discusses a schedule with William for use at home and at the gymnastics facility, which includes the amount of imagery practice he is expected to undertake. After five weeks of two sessions per week, Sarah talks with William about his progress and perceptions of the ITP. William is happy with his involvement, so the sport psychologist decides to extend the imagery practice into the progressively more stressful environments of the open gym and minor competitions. The coach then arranges a competitive training session involving all male members of the elite squad. The sport psychologist attends this session and communicates regularly with William during the competition phase, looking for feedback from him about the effectiveness of the imagery routines in a more stressful competitive situation. Sarah and the coach also discuss the performance indicators that suggest that the ITP is contributing to improved competition outcomes. This process involves an element of evaluation that can be considered formative. That is, the ITP is being assessed as it develops, so that it can be fine-tuned.

As a result of the reports received from both the training activities and the simulated competition, the ITP team agrees that William will use the ITP routines in the state championships. William is now feeling very comfortable with the activities that he regularly engages in to enhance his imagery abilities and physical performance. The national championships ITP is modified to take into account William's lowered arousal levels in major competitions, which have resulted from the pleasant-scene imagery. This involves an added emphasis on concentration during the imagery associated with the performance of his high-bar and pommel-horse routines. They expect the concentration during imagery to transfer to actual performance. In addition to the benefits for performance, this strategy distracts William from any lingering worries that could induce anxiety.

William performs well in the competition and has now established a framework for the future incorporation of imagery training into his overall training package. The team sets a date immediately after this competition to review the ITP (summative evaluation) and develop a new program. Because William aspires to compete at senior national and international levels, the new ITP will target his capacity to apply imagery directly in attempting to master the difficult routines his coach will introduce over the next 6-month training period.

CONCLUSIONS

This chapter reflects the broad range of literature and research regarding imagery training in sport and discusses the strategies and procedures for constructing programs proposed within that literature. The principles proposed in this chapter may benefit from the addition of new perspectives that result from both research and application of ITPs.

The inclusion of a model and summary of strategic components should allow practitioners, coaches, and athletes to apply a systematic framework to the development of personalized imagery programs. We have endeavored to cover the key aspects of imagery training as proposed by researchers and psychologists who prepare and implement these types of programs.

In addition, this chapter presents a brief summary of the major imagery packages used in sport psychology, which allows interested readers to compare the generalized strategic components framework with formulated interventions and may help them decide which program will best suit their needs.

The development of ITPs requires substantial additional review and analysis. Only limited research examines how the various components of the ITP have an impact on its effectiveness as a performance-enhance-ment tool. We propose that new studies be undertaken to logically evalu-ate the contributions of the program elements to the physical, psychologi-cal, and competition changes that athletes experience by participating in a high-quality imagery training program.

CHAPTER 9

USES FOR IMAGERY

One of the most appealing aspects of imagery is that it is an extremely versatile technique that can be applied to a wide range of situations in sport and exercise. Its application is limited only by the imaginations of athletes, coaches, and sport psychologists. Perhaps this is one of the reasons why imagery is reported to be one of the most commonly used psychological tools in sport and exercise. In fact, elite athletes report extensive use of imagery. For instance, 99% of 1984 Canadian Olympic athletes who were surveyed by Orlick and Partington (1988) reported using imagery and tended to do so on a regular, systematic basis. Elite-level coaches and sport psychology consultants also report using imagery extensively (DeFrancesco and Burke 1997; Gould, Tammen, Murphy, and May 1989; Hall and Rodgers 1989). We know that elite athletes use imagery, and research on *how* and *why* athletes use imagery in sport and exercise is growing.

Another reason why imagery is so popular may be that it is such a natural way of thinking. Most of us use it, and we tend to find it easy to understand. Imagery is one way that we process information. Just as we can process information verbally, we can also process it through images (Paivio 1971, 1975, 1986). Developmentally, imagery is a basic memory system that humans probably used before they could use language to remember things (Simons 2000). In fact, for many centuries people have recognized imagery as an effective way of remembering information (Reed 1996). For instance, if you try to recall your best sport performance, you probably create an image of it. As we said in chapter 2, imagery is a multisensory experience; as such, we can recall images in a variety of forms, such as sights, sounds, tastes, smells, feelings, and emotions. Because of imagery's close link with perception and action, it is a powerful tool for learning and changing thoughts and behavior. It is most effective, however, when it is used for a specific purpose rather than in a random or nondirected fashion (Simons 2000; Vealey and Greenleaf 2001). Research suggests that imagery is most effective when its use and the athlete's need are matched (Martin, Moritz, and Hall 1999; Munroe, Hall, Simms, and Weinberg 1998). That is, if the athlete is experiencing difficulties with concentration at certain points in a game, it is probably more effective to use imagery to rehearse these situations than to use it for mental practice of the sport's basic skills. Athletes, coaches, and sport psychologists should think about the athlete's needs so that imagery can be used effectively in a systematic fashion. The specificity principle probably applies here, because systematic, well-structured, and specific imagery use is the most effective application of imagery in sport.

Much of the research on imagery in sport has focused on its use as a form of mental practice (MP); however, athletes and exercisers use imagery for much more than merely learning and practicing skills (Murphy and Martin 2002). Recent models of imagery use in sport and exercise (see chapter 2) indicate that aside from its role in learning and developing skills, athletes use it to develop a range of cognitive, behavioral, and affective outcomes. Research on imagery use in sport has suggested that athletes do use imagery for both cognitive and motivational functions (Hall 2001). Exercisers also use imagery for appearance reasons, as well as technique development and energy management (Gammage, Hall, and Rodgers 2000; Hausenblas, Hall, Rodgers, and Munroe 1999).

In this chapter, we explore the potential uses of imagery in sport. We discover how it can be used to enhance performance and how other uses of it may influence performance. We pay special attention to the use of imagery with different populations, such as children, adolescents, and athletes with disabilities, and how their needs can be best met. This chapter introduces some of the potential applications of imagery in sport that are listed in table 9.1. That list is by no means comprehensive; readers will probably think of other uses of imagery from their experiences in sport and exercise.

USES OF IMAGERY IN THE GENERAL ATHLETIC POPULATION

Since imagery can be used in a variety of ways and for a range of functions in sport and exercise, this section describes some of its potential uses in sport. Those uses are categorized as (a) skill learning and practice, (b) tactical and game skills, (c) competition and performance, (d) psychological skills, and (e) recovery from injury or heavy training. Each is briefly explained, and then an example of how imagery might be used in

Table 9.1 Imagery Uses in Sport and Exercise

Skill learning and practice	Skill learning or acquisition Skill practice Error detection and correction
Tactical and game skills	Strategy development Strategy learning Strategy practice Problem solving
Competition and performance	Familiarization of competition sites Mental warm-up Pre-performance routine Preview Review
Psychological skills	Managing arousal/anxiety control and stress Improving concentration and attention Increasing self-awareness Building confidence and self-efficacy Increasing motivation Controlling psychophysiological response Developing interpersonal skills
Coping with injury and heavy training	Coping with pain and injury Dealing with long-term injury Recovering from injury or heavy training

this way is given. (To learn how to develop imagery programs or imagery scripts for specific uses, see chapter 8.)

This chapter provides some examples of situations in which imagery might be used in sport. As chapter 8 indicates, imagery scripts should be developed in conjunction with the athletes to ensure that they are clear and meaningful for them. Consequently imagery scripts will vary for each individual and according to the imagery's purpose and the sport skill being imagined. The scripts in this chapter are merely examples of how imagery *might* be used; practitioners should work closely with their athletes to develop individualized scripts.

SKILL LEARNING AND PRACTICE

One of the most common uses of imagery is MP for skill learning and practice. Sometimes imagery used in this fashion is referred to as imagery rehearsal (IR) or cognitive-specific (CS) imagery. Using imagery in this way allows athletes to learn and maintain technical skills for their sport.

SKILL LEARNING OR ACQUISITION

In models of skill acquisition, the initial stage of learning is often characterized as a cognitive phase in which the learner tries to grasp the concept of the movement skill (e.g., Fitts and Posner 1967; Gentile 1972, 1987, 2000). MP can help learners acquire this mental blueprint or cognitive plan. For instance, golfers practicing putting, soccer players practicing shooting a penalty, or high jumpers practicing their jump all can learn aspects of their skill without actually performing it.

Imagery can be used on its own to mentally practice a skill, or it can be combined with physical practice. A beginner learning a gymnastics routine might practice it several times in her head to get an idea of the movement sequence before physically practicing it. Physical practice might reveal problems that require changes to the movement originally imaged. In such cases, further imagery rehearsal of the skill is advisable as soon as it has been modified. A physical education teacher could get his students to mentally practice the skill of hitting while waiting for their turn at bat. This would partially alleviate the common problem in physical education classes of students spending a lot of their time doing nothing constructive.

Scripts for skill learning and practice should incorporate the activity's main elements along with details to make the imagery more realistic (such as the sensory stimuli and movement qualities). For example, in a script for learning to hit a baseball, the main skill elements to emphasize would be to watch the ball, take a relaxed stance at the base, use a powerful but controlled bat swing through the ball, and follow through on contact. Details added to make the imagery more realistic could include the feel of the bat in the hand, the color of the ball, and the smell of the grass. The sidebar offers an example of such a script.

SKILL PRACTICE

Just as we repeatedly practice skills to retain them, so can we reinforce well-developed ones through practice. At the elite level, learning new skills is not needed often, but practicing already acquired skills is valuable in keeping them well tuned. Although MP can never replace physical practice, it is very effective when combined with physical practice. MP might also be used to fine-tune or alter techniques (for instance, by a hurdler who wants to change her stride pattern). Imagery can also be used in situations where athletes cannot practice physically, such as during travel or when they are injured.

ERROR DETECTION AND CORRECTION

Imagery can also be used to examine a skill to detect and correct a problem before the next physical practice session or competitive performance. This recall of performance can be used to help athletes determine how

Imagery Script for Skill Learning in Baseball Batting

"As you step up to bat, you detect the unmistakable smell of fresh-cut grass. Glancing down, you see the light-colored, wooden bat in your hands and feel the pressure of your hands gripping the bat. You see the bright-white ball with red stitching in the pitcher's glove as you step into the batter's box and ready yourself in your stance. With your feet shoulder-width apart facing the pitcher, you feel your relaxed shoulders and hands as you hold the bat in preparation for the swing. Now you focus on the ball and see the pitcher begin his windup. You see the ball as it is released from the pitcher's hand and the red stitching rotating on it as the ball approaches the base. You feel your foot step forward and plant and feel the rotation of your hips and shoulders as power develops and is transferred up through your arms and hands to the bat, developing into a fast swing. You hear and feel contact of the ball on the bat and see the ball explode off the bat, then feel your arms and hands follow through as the bat swings over your shoulder."

errors occurred and what caused them to make certain decisions. The athlete can mentally correct the errors and practice the correct response.

For example, a gymnast who is an experienced imager can use internal and external perspectives to help identify problems in a beam routine. She could use several external orientations, such as viewing from the side, front, back, and even from above to help detect any errors in the routine. Running through the skill at a normal pace in imagery to locate where the problem occurs could be followed by a slow-motion rerun for detailed examination. Once she identifies the error, the gymnast could imagine correct execution of the skill several times until it is clear, then proceed to actual physical execution of the routine.

TACTICAL AND GAME SKILLS

In looking at how imagery can be used for skill acquisition and maintenance, we have given examples involving technical skills, in which correct movement technique is important. However, in most sports, tactical and game skills are equal to, if not more important than, technical skills. Tactical skills involve tactics, strategies, and game plans (Martens 2004). Tactics are plans or methods to win a game or achieve a goal, such as using a fake in basketball. A strategy is a more elaborate plan of action, often for a series of contests. For instance, in soccer a team may pass the ball into the forwards in the air rather than along the ground because they have tall attackers who have a height advantage when the ball is in the air; in an endurance event, such as a triathlon or a 10,000 m race, an athlete might plan to sit on the shoulders of the leaders and then kick near the finish. A game plan refers to an individual or team's strategy for a particular opponent or contest. For example, a field hockey team might decide to concentrate on attacking its opponent down the left side of the field, where it has a weaker defender.

STRATEGY DEVELOPMENT

Players and coaches can use imagery as a means to develop or create new strategies to get the best out of themselves or their teams, or to develop game plans to combat specific opponents before getting to the competition. Skilled athletes, especially in open-skill sports, need to be able to develop a variety of strategies. They need to be able to think through or imagine the best strategies for their own and their teams' performances. Creating images of what needs to be done and possible alternatives can help athletes make correct decisions in planning for their performance. Imagery can be used in this way as a form of preperformance planning.

For example, an American football quarterback or a soccer player might imagine the different defenses that they will confront and the plays that might be used to break them. An Australian Football League (AFL) team may sit down together for a meeting during the week leading up to a game and use imagery to help create game plans. Coaches can often also use imagery to develop new plays before trying them out at training or in a game. The sidebar provides an example of how to use video with imagery to help develop tactical skills.

DEVELOPING TACTICAL SKILLS USING VIDEO

One approach to developing tactical skills such as strategy development is to show players game footage and scenarios and stop the footage at certain points (a technique called "temporal occlusion") and ask the players to decide what to do next. The players could imagine the action they would take and its possible consequences. For example, footage of three attackers approaching two defenders in a field hockey game could be stopped as the attackers approached the first defender. The two defenders watching the video could be asked to use imagery to decide on possible strategies for defending the attack.

Strategy Learning

Once new strategies have been created, athletes can use imagery to rehearse them in an attempt to learn them before a competition. To familiarize themselves with the roles of their teammates and see how to fit their own part in with the others, both temporally and spatially, each team member might use imagery to enhance his performance of a new offensive strategy. For example, after developing new strategies, an American football quarterback practices the strategies in training and uses imagery to keep rehearsing the plays to reinforce them in memory, so that they are automatic by game time.

Strategy Practice

A common situation in team games is that alternative strategies must be adopted against each opposing team, because they all play with different styles. Often, in football codes such as soccer or Australian Football for instance, the B team is drafted to play like the upcoming opposition, but its speed and competence may not match the real thing. Imagining strategy implementation against the actual players who will confront the team, playing up to form and at full speed, can help players sharpen that strategy during the week before the match. For example, a cricket or baseball batter might mentally prepare to bat by imagining the various pitches used by a particular pitcher whom he has played against before. The batter would then use imagery to practice the strategies that he will use to counteract each pitch.

Problem Solving

Just as imagery can be used to review performance or detect and correct errors, it might be used to solve problems in performance. Players who are in a slump or having problems with technique, strategy, or psychological skills might use imagery to imagine when they were performing at their best and compare this to their current performance to find the factor(s) causing the slump. Coaches might also use imagery to make decisions about strategies to combat problems arising during a game. Imagery could allow them to think ahead and consider all the possible options of using a particular tactic or strategy. For example, if a springboard diver is having trouble with a particular part of her dive, she can imagine what she is doing and compare it to what she did in the past, thus identifying any problems in her technique. Or a tennis player who has difficulty against a particular opponent may use imagery to come up with ways of coping with his opponent's style.

Competition and Performance

So far we have looked at uses for imagery in terms of technical and tactical aspects of performance. Athletes can also use imagery to get themselves ready for a particular competition or to reflect on a competition when it is over. That is, imagery can be applied to performance and competition, not just practice.

FAMILIARIZATION OF COMPETITION SITES PRE-EVENT

To help themselves feel more comfortable and reduce distractions on the day of competition, athletes can imagine competing at that day's venue. For example, cricket players might go onto the field the night before or the morning of the match and imagine themselves performing there later. Or, if they have played there previously, they might use this memory to recreate the scene in the days or even weeks leading up to the game. They could imagine all aspects of their performance and successfully executing their technical and tactical skills on game day. Players may find that imagery performed in the venue is more realistic and reduces the potential distractions of being in a new environment on the day of the event.

MENTAL WARM-UP

All top-level athletes know that being physically warmed up when the match starts is important, not only to avoid soft-tissue injuries (which are more likely to affect cold, tight muscles) but also to ensure that they are physically ready to give maximum effort in the vital first few minutes of the match. Athletes are less aware that the same sort of early game disaster can occur if they are mentally cold. Imagery can be used shortly before a game to focus on performance. For example, in table tennis, players hit to each other in the pregame knock, going through a range of shots for 1 or 2 min each. The skills involved use automatic rather than controlled processing, which means a player could be thinking of a film he saw the night before instead of attending to his actions. Athletes who, shortly before going to the table, image the end of the knock, the toss-up, the start of play, and the first 10 rallies against an opponent who is playing well and stretching them will go into competition much more mentally alert and in the right mood state when the game starts.

PREPERFORMANCE ROUTINE

Imagery might be utilized as part of a preperformance routine to help athletes focus on performance. Preperformance routines take place immediately before execution of a sport skill, before or during a game or performance. They are designed to focus the athletes' concentration on the task and away from task-irrelevant cues and thoughts (such as the crowd or what will happen if they make a mistake) so that they will not become distracted. This is especially useful for closed-skill performances that occur in a stable, predictable fashion (e.g., golf, weightlifting, swimming, and batting in baseball or softball) and for sports that have breaks in play that provide opportunities to use the routine (e.g., between points in tennis, before kicking for goal in Australian Rules football, and between plays in American football). Research supports the use of routines that include imagery to enhance performance (Cohn 1990; Lidor and Singer 2000; Spittle and Morris 1997).

A general principle of preperformance routines is that they should be practiced (at training and also in competition) and temporally consistent. A routine can incorporate behavioral activities (e.g., standing behind the ball and reading the green in golf, throwing grass in the air to read the direction of the wind prior to kicking for goal in Australian Rules football, and deep breathing) and mental ones (e.g., cue words, affirmations, and imagery). For example, a high jumper might develop a prejump routine that is carried out prior to every jump in training and competition to help focus attention on correct movement execution. It might involve standing at the beginning of the run-up, taking two deep breaths, focusing on the bar, imagining the execution of the jump from the run-up to landing (not only clearing the bar but also the kinesthetic feeling associated with the correct execution), repeating the cue word "spring," again imagining the perfect execution of the skill while thinking "spring," and then executing the imagined movement.

SAMPLE PREPERFORMANCE ROUTINE FOR SOCCER

A preperformance routine incorporating imagery could be useful for a soccer player who is about to take a penalty shot at the end of an important game. Such a routine might consist of placing the ball on the penalty spot; marking out a consistent run-up (e.g., five steps); standing at the end of the run-up, looking toward the goal, and making a confident decision about where the kick will go (e.g., a powerful kick, low to the right); taking a deep breath; focusing on the ball and then the target; imagining the perfect kick to that target (feel the run-up, sweet contact with the foot, and see and hear the ball hitting the back of the net); then taking a deep breath and doing it.

PREVIEW

Although preperformance routines are used immediately before skill execution, a preview can be used as preparation during the lead-up to an event. For example, a performer can use imagery in the week leading up to or even on the morning of a competition to prepare for the event.

Preview is a technique that is more applicable than a preperformance routine to open-skill sports due to the lack of time available during them or their reactive nature. For example, in soccer, players are constantly involved in the game, constantly reacting to the game situation, which allows little time for preperformance routines prior to skill execution. When using imagery as a preview, the athletes imagine the upcoming performance and go through it in their minds, perhaps on the night before or the morning of the game or competition. This allows them to practice strategies and responses to situations in the performance. Because open-skill sports, such as various football codes and field hockey, are often unpredictable, the players must react to things going on around them. Running through various situations as a preview to performance helps them plan and prepare mentally for these unpredictable events. For example, a field hockey defender can use imagery as a preview before the game or the night before the game to focus herself on defending against a particular opponent and practice reacting to her and the attacking setup of the opposition team. She could create various scenarios and imagine how she would react.

REVIEW

After performance, imagery can be used to "replay" the whole performance or a part of it. The imager can "fast forward" through uninteresting phases of the performance and examine the critical parts in "slow motion," as if watching a video. Review using imagery should emphasize positive aspects of performance without neglecting the negative. Detecting weaknesses and errors, and replacing them with the correct response, should help future performance. Because positive and negative emotions are often aroused by performance and outcome, review should be postponed for a few hours or until the day after the event, when the imager can be more objective. However, in long events with substantial breaks, such as cricket batting, tennis, or golf, players often review each shot and immediately image corrections to it. This can also involve physical correction. This use of imagery is recommended only for skilled performers who know and will image the correct version of the stroke or shot.

An example of the review technique is a field hockey coach who encourages his players to use imagery to review performance before a practice session on the Monday following a weekend game. This could lead to consideration of what went well and not so well, or discussion about how to improve performance the next time that opponent is confronted. The coach could give the athletes a review sheet on which they comment about technical, tactical, or psychological skills or areas that need improvement. Following the imagery session and discussion, the team could use the practice session to run through individual or team drills designed to work on those areas identified in the imagery.

Psychological Skills

The focus on imagery uses so far has been on performance-related aspects of sport, but imagery can also influence an athlete's psychological state. It can enhance psychological skills such as concentration, confidence, motivation, and anxiety control.

Arousal or Anxiety Control and Stress Management

Imagery can be used to increase or decrease arousal. For instance, scenes that "pump up" a player, such as playing aggressively in front of a crowd, might be used prior to a game to increase arousal. Alternatively, imagining a successful performance, relaxing scenes (such as a peaceful place), or muscular tension floating out of the body reduces feelings of anxiety. Imagery can also help athletes cope successfully with problems or situations that might provoke anxiety by allowing them to create plans for dealing with these situations and imagine using those plans successfully. Imagery might also be used in this way to help athletes deal with stress that occurs due to the demands of sport, work, or school.

For example, a pistol-shooter who suffers somatic anxiety prior to and during competition will not perform well with trembling arms. The shooter can decide on a scene that he finds pleasant and relaxing, such as lying in soft, white sand on a beach, with the waves gently rolling in and the sun making him feel warm and comfortable (but not drowsy). A script of a relaxing scene is provided in the sidebar. When the anxiety is cognitive, raising self-doubts about performance and not producing bodily reactions, using a scenario in which the imager copes with the performance situation effectively might reduce the anxiety. For instance, the pistol-shooter might get anxious about shooting on cold, wet days and could use imagery to imagine coping effectively with this performance situation.

Concentration and Attention

Imagery can help athletes focus attention and regain focus when they become distracted. To help focus attention, athletes can imagine relevant aspects of the upcoming performance. This narrows focus to those relevant aspects and limits the impact of irrelevant cues. To learn to remain focused during performance, athletes could imagine the upcoming performance and all the potential distracters that might be present and develop coping strategies to deal with them before they become a problem. Athletes also need to be able to refocus their attention if they are distracted or if something goes wrong. They can imagine themselves in situations in which they often lose concentration, and then imagine being composed and focused on the game. By imagining what they want to do and how to do it, they may remain more focused on their performance.

SAMPLE RELAXATION IMAGERY SCRIPT

"Take a few moments to image a beautiful beach scene. Imagine that you are alone on this beach. It is one of the most beautiful and peaceful places you have ever seen. Notice the white sand as it meets the crystal-clear waters. Overhead the sky is blue with a couple of white, fluffy clouds. Walk toward the water and feel the grit of the sand beneath your feet and between your toes as you walk. You can hear the waves breaking on the shore as you approach the water and the cooling effect and salty taste of the sea spray hitting you in the face. Step into the water and feel the cool sensation on your feet and legs. Immerse yourself in the water. Everything is completely perfect here. There are no sounds except for the water. Everything is peaceful. Enjoy this feeling for a few moments. Take in the warmth of the sun on your back and shoulders. You are completely relaxed, at peace, warm, and calm."

For example, a high jumper could use imagery as part of a prejump routine to help her focus on the relevant performance aspects. Imagery of what she wants to do and how to do it prior to actual execution would help her prepare for the jump. According to functional-equivalence views, in which imagery is considered to be functionally equivalent to motor preparation, this imagery would help prepare the motor system for the jump. Or, a soccer player who often loses concentration after making a mistake during a game could use imagery to help him overcome the negative thinking that plagues him after he "messes up." He tends to keep thinking about the error rather than about what is going on in the game at the moment. Before the game, the player could imagine himself dealing with situations in which he has made an error; during a game, after making a mistake he could imagine correct execution of the skill and then move on with the game rather than dwelling on the mistake.

SELF-AWARENESS

By using imagery, athletes can become more aware of themselves and their performance. One of the first steps for athletes in most psychological-skills training (PST) programs is to develop an awareness of themselves and the situations in which they perform best. Imagery can be used to create or re-create performance situations so that athletes can develop a stronger understanding of themselves. For example, a swimming coach might help a swimmer develop an awareness of her ideal psychological state for performance by re-creating past performances to recall her psychological states when she swam well and when she did not.

CONFIDENCE AND SELF-EFFICACY

Imagery has been widely suggested as a means of enhancing self-confidence. Images that create feelings of competence and success, such as performing well or executing skills correctly, increase an athlete's confidence. Self-efficacy is a situation-specific form of self-confidence (Weinberg and Gould 1999). According to Bandura's (1977a, 1986) theory of self-efficacy, an individual's feelings of self-efficacy are based on six sources of information: performance accomplishments, vicarious experiences, verbal persuasion, imaginal experiences, physiological states, and emotional states. Athletes can influence self-efficacy beliefs by imagining themselves (performance accomplishments) or others (modeling) effectively performing specific tasks in their sport.

For example, a softball batter who is in a slump could imagine himself hitting well or think back to when he was in good form and remind himself that he is capable of playing well in the match. Care should be taken that imagery for confidence building is realistic. This batter might not believe an imagery script in which he hits every pitch out of the park, but making some base hits might seem realistic and thus be more effective. A squash player who lacks confidence when competing against higher-ranked opponents, even though he has the ability to do so, might imagine successfully competing with these opponents to enhance confidence.

MOTIVATION

Imagery can also be used to increase motivation. Athletes can use images of successful performance or doing well in major competitions to keep them going when training gets tough. For example, during his long hours of training a boxer might imagine the sense of accomplishment and feeling of joy that would come with winning the upcoming bout. Or a distance runner who is having trouble getting out of bed to go for a run on winter mornings might imagine the satisfaction she will feel when she completes the marathon in a few months. Or she could imagine the positive aspects of training, such as the feeling of running fast and how much better she feels during the day if she has been for a run. A distance runner might develop a script that describes getting ready for a race, the feeling of running fast and confidently in the early stages, the feeling of strength that comes later, and the joy of crossing the finish line and completing the race in a good time. The sidebar presents an example of a script for a distance runner.

Imagery for Motivation

"Imagine that it is the day of the marathon. You arrive at the venue for the race start and you see hundreds of other athletes in their running gear. They all look like they have trained hard for the event. You go to the officials' area to collect your number and attach it to your shirt. You find a space to prepare for the race and spend some time stretching and going over the race plan in your head. You are well prepared and feeling confident. The official is calling all starters. Imagine yourself at the start line—you have put in all the preparation you could, so you are ready for this race. The starter begins the race and you set off aiming for a personal best. You focus on maintaining a steady rhythm and check your time at each 5K interval. You are able to maintain this level comfortably because of all the hard work you have put in during training. As you begin your run home you still feel very strong and are passing other runners—you've trained hard for this race and it feels great. As you get close to the finish you feel your speed increasing. With each step you dig deeper into your training base and push yourself beyond your expectations. The line approaches, and as you cross it you feel exhausted and completely spent, but you glance at the time and see that it is a personal best. The feelings of accomplishment and satisfaction at achieving this make all those early-morning starts and the time spent training worthwhile."

Psychophysiological Response

As chapter 7 points out, imagery can influence psychophysiological responses, including heart rate, blood pressure, respiration rate, and skin conductance. This influence can be important in sport because performance is often influenced by the ability to control or limit the effects of psychophysiological responses. This is especially true in many closed or fine-motor-skill sports and those that require precision of movement. For example, in shooting, archery, darts, and snooker athletes must have a steady hand; in martial arts the athletes' movements must be very precise; in underwater free diving the divers must relax autonomic body systems in order to deal with the water pressure and hold their breath for extended periods.

How can athletes control their responses by using imagery? A biathlete skis cross-country, but then must steady her physiological responses in order to effectively shoot at the target. To do this she creates an image of her heart and imagines it gradually slowing to resting levels. An Australian rugby player is lining up for a penalty kick to win an important test match against England and feels his heart racing and his fast, shallow breathing. He must steady his psychophysiological responses if he is to be successful in his kick. To do so, he imagines himself kicking as he used to do as a child at home in his backyard with no one present.

INJURY AND HEAVY TRAINING

Because imagery is a mental activity and is not associated with physical movement, it has uses associated with injury and heavy training. Aside from allowing athletes to work on technical, tactical, and psychological skills when they can't or shouldn't physically practice, it may also help them cope with and recover from injury.

MINOR INJURIES

Athletes often experience pain or discomfort from minor injuries, such as bruising, or from pushing their bodies during performance. They can use imagery to help them cope in such situations. For example, a runner who is struggling during training may use imagery as a dissociation technique to distract him from the run and help him cope with performance pain.

LONG-TERM INJURIES

Long-term injuries can be very difficult for athletes to handle, but using imagery can help them cope with some of the problems associated with a lengthy absence from sport. A concern for many athletes is that they will fall behind other athletes who are able to train and compete. During extended layoffs due to injury, athletes can use imagery to work on the technical, tactical, and psychological skills related to performance mentioned previously in this chapter. For instance, they can use imagery as MP to learn new skills; practice and maintain existing skills when they cannot do so physically; or develop, learn, and practice strategies to keep them fresh for their return to sport. However, this imagery use's prime importance is that it helps people deal with injuries and decreases their feelings that they are losing ground. So in effect, it offers athletes a double benefit.

When athletes return to sport after an injury, they often have less confidence in their ability to perform due to the time away, the feeling that they have lost ground, and concerns about the injured body part. Imagery can help overcome these concerns. Athletes can also think positively about improving their performance by using imagery for aspects of their game that they may not normally have time for during regular practice, such as developing new skills or strategies or refining technique. Again, this focus helps athletes avoid dwelling on negative aspects of the injury and the rehabilitation process. During rehabilitation, adherence to the programs may be difficult due to fluctuating motivation levels and confidence. Imagery of a successful return to sport may keep an athlete motivated during a lengthy recovery. For example, an attacking soccer player who has a long-term ankle injury may use imagery to keep her shooting skills fresh and to work on previously ignored defensive skills. She may also use imagery of her successful return to the game to keep her motivated during difficult rehabilitation sessions.

RECOVERING FROM INJURY OR HEAVY TRAINING

Imagery can be employed to facilitate physical recovery from injury, especially to soft tissue. The same process can be applied to the soreness associated with heavy training. Greater blood flow to an injured area, as well as applying warmth to damaged tissue can be therapeutic. Applying heat to an injured area increases blood flow to the tissues, which promotes recovery. Studies have shown that imagery of increased blood flow and warmth can lead to measurable increases in an area as specific as a finger (Blakeslee 1980).

For example, a long jumper with a pulled hamstring could image the flow of warm, rich, bright-red blood flooding the muscles of the back of the thigh two or three times a day. After heavy training with weights or on the track, a sprinter might use the same imagery but apply it to every major muscle group for 1 min or focus on the sorest muscles. Also, many athletes now use hyperbaric chambers to assist in recovery, and they can use the time in the chamber to apply imagery to relax and recover from training or to mentally practice aspects of performance.

INTERPERSONAL SKILLS

Imagery is valuable not only for enhancing performance but for personal development and coping with off-the-field aspects of sport, work, school, and social life. It can help athletes prepare for difficult situations, such as work or university presentations or job interviews. For example, a soccer player who is concerned about the amount of playing time he is getting and his position on the team may be reluctant to confront the coach on the issue. To help himself devise a plan for how to approach the coach and what to say, the player might use imagery to determine and practice the best approach.

USES OF IMAGERY IN SPECIAL ATHLETIC POPULATIONS

Our discussion of imagery use has largely focused on performance enhancement in the general athletic population, but imagery can be applied to specific groups involved in sport and exercise. Although the uses reviewed so far apply to everyone, some special considerations or applications are particularly relevant to certain groups. This section considers the application of imagery in special populations such as elite athletes, children and adolescents, and athletes with disabilities.

CHILDREN AND ADOLESCENTS

Imagery has many potential applications with children, including most of those described previously. In some areas, imagery is particularly useful with children and can be applied and introduced to them in different ways, such as teaching them sport and motor skills, especially in physical education settings.

In using imagery with children, especially as a complement to instructions and demonstrations, two types are particularly useful: direct and indirect (Short, Afremow, and Overby 2001). Direct imagery is intended to be an exact replica of the skill. That is, athletes image the skill as if they were actually performing it. For example, in MP a learner re-creates a skill as realistically as possible and practices it as if actually performing it. Indirect (or metaphorical) imagery involves using images that can be related to the motor skill. The imagery is not a direct copy of the skill; instead the person uses familiar images that can be related to the movement skill. The aim is to develop the quality of movement by relating it to something similar, such as pouncing like a tiger, streamlining like a dolphin, or swinging an arm like a windmill. These images can help complement instructions and help children learn and remember skills (Short et al. 2001).

Imagery can be a very effective tool with children because they are often open to using their imagination. Imagery is a part of mental processing and is used extensively by children in memory, planning, learning, creating, and performing activities (Simons 2000). In fact, younger children can have very good imagery skills because it is a natural way to remember and create things, perhaps even easier than using a symbolic form of information processing such as words. We can all remember how much time we spent as children in play activities that involved creativity and imagination. As children grow up they seem to use imagery less (Simons 2000). Instructors can utilize children's imaginations for learning and performing motor skills. Imagery can complement the other cognitive skills and learning strategies that instructors employ and help children increase their enjoyment and creativity in movement and exercise (Short et al. 2001). The use of imagery with children is limited only by the imagination of the coach, teacher, or exercise leader. It is a natural strategy that children often use to rehearse skill sequences, learn practice strategies, and develop skills (Weiss 1991). Our focus here is on these uses as well as the psychological skills of motivation and confidence, but children can use imagery for many of the purposes outlined previously, such as managing stress, improving attention and concentration, preparing for competition and performance, previewing and reviewing performance, and detecting and correcting errors.

SKILL LEARNING AND PRACTICE

As stated previously, imagery has been used extensively as MP, which is a practical application of it for children who are learning new skills. The first stage of learning is primarily cognitive (e.g., Fitts and Posner 1967; Gentile 1972, 1987, 2000), and using imagery in this way can help children develop an idea of what they have to do in order to perform a skill. Imagery can complement instructions and demonstrations and help children learn and remember the skills. In learning a new skill, direct imagery can be used to mentally practice the skill and indirect imagery can be used as a complement to instructions and demonstrations to enhance understanding of the quality of movement. For example, in bowling a cricket ball, children must learn to keep their elbow straight rather than bend it as they would in throwing. To get an idea of this action, an image of a windmill's blades turning may be used to complement instructions and demonstrations. When learning the skill, the children could use imagery as a form of MP to reinforce the movement pattern, especially when waiting in line for their turn to perform it. The application of imagery also extends beyond sport; young children are capable of using imagery in many settings, such as in play, games, school, music, and dance.

TACTICAL AND GAME SKILLS

In addition to technical skills, part of development in a sport is learning and understanding the game and strategies of play. Although technique is important, it has often been taught in isolation, without requiring players to apply the techniques to given situations. In approaches to teaching children, emphasis is growing on learning to apply skills rather than merely acquiring and developing them. For example, the game-sense approach to teaching and coaching uses games as the focus of the practice session. By focusing on the game rather than individual skills in isolation, children are challenged to think about what they are doing and why. Just as learning by playing can help children learn the strategies of games, imagery can help children develop these skills by allowing them to create and experience different scenarios. For example, in soccer children could be encouraged to imagine specific game situations and decide what to do next, such as pass or shoot.

People process information and make decisions naturally through imagery. For instance, immediately before you perform a skill in your sport, do you "picture" how you will do it? For instance, if you are asked to throw a ball at a target, just before throwing it do you "see" the movement and the ball going to the target? This kind of processing is akin to the functional-equivalence view that imagery is involved in motor preparation and planning; that is, imagery is closely linked to perception and action (Simons 2000). So children might be taught to use imagery to help them plan their next move by "picturing" what they will do next before actually doing it. Experts are faster and more accurate than beginners at using sport-specific cues, so they can adapt to novel environments more easily (Starkes, Helsen, and Jack 2001; Wrisberg 2001) and may appear to have all the time in the world (Magill 2004). For example, an expert soccer player dribbling the ball down the field can look at one or two players and make a quick decision about whether to pass, dribble, or shoot. To help children progress to higher skill levels, they need to be able to quickly process information and make decisions in game situations.

Another advantage of using imagery to process information and think about a skill is that it can help children and beginners avoid the kind of "paralysis by analysis" that seems more likely to occur in the verbal learning of movement. For instance, if you were trying to kick a soccer ball to the bottom-right corner of the goal, which do you think would be the most effective approach: forming an image of the shot and then kicking the ball, or trying to remember a long list of static instructions, such as "locate the target, watch the ball, place the left foot next to the ball, keep the head down, swing through with the right foot and make contact with the instep, follow through in the direction of the ball"? Or let's say you are teaching a young swimmer the butterfly stroke. It is probably easier for the swimmer to process an image of the arm movement being like a butterfly or the leg movement being like a dolphin than to run through the skill step by step. In other words, developing an image of a movement is generally quicker, easier, and more fluid than learning the skill step by step from verbal instructions. Images can contain much information that would be difficult to describe in words.

PSYCHOLOGICAL SKILLS

Research with adults suggests that athletes often use imagery to influence their motivation and confidence (Abma, Fry, Li, and Relyea 2002; Callow and Hardy 1997; Moritz, Hall, Martin, and Vadocz 1996), in line with the applied model of imagery use in sport (AMIUS; Martin, Moritz, and Hall 1999) reviewed in chapter 2. Although research on the use of imagery in sport by children in relation to motivation and confidence is limited, it seems likely that they could and do use it for these purposes. Studies with elite and sub-elite youth athletes suggest that they use imagery extensively for motivational and confidence purposes. For example, Cumming, Hall, Harwood, and Gammage (2002) compared sub-elite young swimmers on their use of imagery. No differences were found between younger (mean age = 12 years) and older (mean age = 16.5 years) swimmers, suggesting similar use for both groups. The youth swimmers used significantly more MG-M imagery than CS, MG-A, MS, or CG imagery. Similarly, Harwood, Cumming, and Hall (2003) found that elite youth athletes with an average age of 16.6 years from a broad range of sports (track and field, badminton, basketball, field hockey, American football, goalball, lacrosse, netball, rugby, and volleyball) used MG-M imagery the most, followed by MS and CS imagery.

When using imagery with children, the approach is important. Orlick and McCaffrey (1991) provided some guidelines to consider when using psychological intervention approaches such as imagery with young children in sport.

- Use simple strategies. Young children must be able to form a clear image of what you want to imagine.

- Keep it fun. Young children are probably not going to respond as well to a serious delivery of imagery as would an elite adult performer. Make use of children's creativity in imagery.

- Include a concrete, physical component. Strategies that allow the child to physically act out the image seem to work well. For example, if in teaching the golf swing you use an indirect image of an elephant swinging its trunk, allow the child to physically act it out.

- Individualize your approach. Knowing the child well will help you select appropriate imagery.

- Use multiple approaches. If something doesn't work, try another approach. If one type of image does not work, a different one might.

- Be positive and hopeful. Project a positive belief in the children and their ability to learn and use imagery.

- Use role models. Children generally respond well to positive examples to emulate, especially when learning a motor skill. For example, videos of high-level athletes in a sport might provide clear images of the skill to emulate.

- Involve parents. Draw on all available support systems to reinforce the concepts and approaches you are trying to teach.

ATHLETES WITH DISABILITIES

Today, people with disabilities participate in most sports and exercise activities and their reasons for doing so are similar to those of able-bodied participants, including the physical benefits as well as the excitement of competition (Humara and Willard 2002). Participation provides athletes with enjoyment and social contact, feelings of mastery and competence in developing sport skills, and the challenges of competing. The term "people with disabilities" encompasses too broad a range of issues to cover in this brief section. However, we will discuss a few features of imagery and its application with these athletes.

An individualized approach is as important when working with athletes with disabilities as it is with able-bodied athletes. Coaches, teachers, and sport psychologists should treat all athletes as individuals, not as types of people. They vary in gender, race, religion, geographical region, and goals in sport and life. Stereotyping people as disabled does not acknowledge them as individuals (Travis and Sachs 1991). Great differences exist between individuals at the same level of disability as well as between levels and types of disability (Travis and Sachs 1991), which include mental disabilities, hearing or vision impairments, amputation, cerebral palsy, paraplegia and quadriplegia, and motor-control difficulties. Within these categories are great variations in levels of disability.

Psychological skills, especially imagery, can be utilized by athletes with disabilities. Research about the psychology of athletes with disabilities is limited, but it does indicate that able-bodied and disabled athletes are psychologically very similar, with high levels of commitment to their sport involvement (Hanrahan 1998; Humara and Willard 2002). Some have argued that athletes with disabilities show even more commitment due to the additional obstacles they face (Humara and Willard 2002).

At the elite level in sport, often only small differences in performance separate individuals; therefore the mental components of performance are as important for elite athletes with disabilities as they are for able-bodied athletes. Psychological skills training (PST) is crucial for these athletes. In addition, for many athletes with disabilities the psychological aspects of performance may be even more important in the initial stages of participation, because of the obstacles that they need to tackle to begin competing (Humara and Willard 2002). It takes much confidence to confront issues related to disabilities, such as feeling "incomplete" or inferior to other athletes.

Although athletes with disabilities can benefit from the use of PST, including imagery, these approaches may need to be modified. Hanrahan (1998) recommended that those who work with athletes with disabilities should remember that they are using imagery in sport because they are athletes, not because they are disabled. An athlete with a disability can use imagery without the disability affecting the imagery in any way. If a disability does affect imagery use, the imagery can be modified to suit the individual athlete. In such cases, discussing this with the athletes is often best, because they are more familiar with their disability than anyone else (Hanrahan 1998). For example, an athlete who is blind may not benefit from traditional, vision-dominated imagery techniques and may need to rely more on other senses involved in the sport skill.

Imagery can be particularly useful when teaching new skills to some athletes with disabilities, especially those with mental or learning difficulties. As mentioned earlier, imagery is one way to process large amounts of information quickly; for some athletes processing imagery may be easier than following complicated instructions. For athletes with hearing impairments, using demonstration and imagery may be a more efficient means of communication than trying to describe the skill. Indirect or metaphorical imagery could also be useful in describing the skill to athletes who have a lower information-processing threshold, to avoid overloading them with information. For instance, coaches and teachers should minimize explanations and maximize guided demonstrations for clients with an intellectual disability.

In general, Humara and Willard (2002) suggested that in using PST with athletes with disabilities, coaches, teachers, and sport psychologists should consider the physical and psychological trauma that the athletes may have experienced, their motivations for competing, and performance problems (like anxiety) due to limitations imposed by the disability.

Although the term "visualization" has been used to describe imagery, athletes with visual impairments can use imagery effectively. Imagery is a multisensory experience that includes kinesthetic, spatial, tactile, auditory, olfactory, gustatory, and emotional experiences (see the SIAM in chapter 4). The fact that imagery is multisensory means that there is no reason why athletes with visual impairments can't use it (Eddy and Mallalieu 2003). Apparently, visual pathways can be activated during imagery even in individuals with visual impairments (Cornoldi, Bertuccelli, Rocchi, and Sbrana 1993; Eddy and Mallalieu 2003; Tinti, Galati, Vecchio, De Beni, and Cornoldi 1999; Vecchi, Monticelli, and Cornoldi 1995), which means visual imagery might operate in similar ways for athletes with and without visual impairments.

Although studies of imagery use by athletes with disabilities are limited (Screws and Surburg 1997), they suggest that imagery can be effective in teaching motor skills to children and adolescents with mental disabilities (Poretta, Surburg, and Gillespie 1999; Screws and Surberg 1997; Surburg 1991; Surburg, Poretta, and Sutlive 1995). Research also suggests that athletes with disabilities use imagery for similar functions as the general population in sport. For instance, Eddy and Mallalieu (2003) found that elite goalball players with disabilities used imagery for cognitive and motivational functions. Players reported that they experienced imagery largely from an internal perspective with a range of sense modalities.

In summary, few differences exist between athletes with disabilities and able-bodied athletes in their participation and psychological approach to sport; therefore there should be few differences in their use of imagery. Practitioners may need to address some considerations in the application of imagery with athletes with disabilities, including the need to individualize imagery programs to the athlete and the disability.

Conclusions

Imagery is a powerful and useful psychological tool that can be applied for various purposes in sport and exercise. Although we have described some of those potential applications, many more uses than we can imagine probably exist. The applications we discussed include skill learning and practice, development and practice of tactical skills, competition preparation and performance, improvement of psychological skills, and coping with injury and heavy training.

Imagery is a useful technique for children, due to their creativity and imagination. Recommendations for tailoring imagery to children and adolescents include keeping it simple, making it fun, and using role models in the imagery. Athletes with disabilities can also use imagery in sport and exercise; they compete in sport for the same reasons as able-bodied athletes, and as such, can and do use imagery for much the same reasons. It is important, as it is for all athletes, to tailor imagery to the individual.

Imagery is a fascinating device for influencing thoughts, affective states, and behaviors in sport and exercise, and its application is limited only by our imagination and creativity.

CHAPTER 10

TECHNICAL AIDS TO IMAGERY

WITH SCOTT FLETCHER, VICTORIA UNIVERSITY, MELBOURNE, AUSTRALIA

In this chapter, we discuss three technologies that have been used in practice with imagery and have been subject to research as adjuncts to imagery, which suggests that they are worthy of consideration in the application of imagery in sport. First is the use of video technology as an aid to effective imagery. Observational learning has long been a subject of study in sport psychology and motor learning. Developments in video technology have made access to observation processes (especially self-observation) easier, more affordable, and nearly immediate. We explain the rationale for using video technology as an adjunct to imagery, considering both research and applications.

In biofeedback, people use technology to gather information about one or more of their basic biological processes (which are otherwise inaccessible to them) with the intention to use the feedback to manage those biological processes. Biofeedback informs a person about the status of a physiological process; that person then uses imagery to modify the process. In addition, biofeedback can provide information about the impact of imagery, especially when it is being used to influence those biological processes. Again, we review the rationale for using biofeedback with imagery and look at research on biofeedback and its application related to imagery.

Flotation is a technique in which a person is suspended in a dense salt-water solution in an opaque, dark tank, so that the stimulation to their senses is drastically reduced. This typically triggers deep relaxation and can also facilitate imagery. In the final section of this chapter, we discuss propositions about why flotation might facilitate imagery, and research on flotation and imagery. We also describe use of the flotation technology, in conjunction with imagery, by elite sport performers. Table 10.1 illustrates the propositions underlying the use of these technical aids as an adjunct to imagery, along with the research methods used to examine their efficacy. The table also includes the main ways that they are applied in practice to support imagery.

VIDEO MODELING AND IMAGERY

The ability to learn or modify skills is an important part of performance enhancement. One of the techniques used in sport psychology to enhance imagery rehearsal and athletic performance is video modeling, which involves the observation of a model or expert performer executing a specific skill successfully (Perry and Morris 1995). The premise of video modeling as a performance-enhancement technique is supported by Bandura's (1977a, b) social learning theory, in which Bandura proposed that the vast majority of habits formed by human beings are acquired through observing and imitating others. Observational learning is said to enhance performance in the same manner as performance accomplishment (Bandura 1977a, b; Perry and Morris 1995). Bandura identified four processes that mediate observational learning: (a) attention to modeled events, (b) retention of what is observed, (c) reproduction of modeled behaviors, and (d) motivation to reproduce those behaviors. Essentially, observers learn by watching others perform a task very well; the observers are then (theoretically) able to model the skill or task without the errors that occur in attempts to perform the tasks without modeling (Shaffer 2000).

HOW VIDEO MODELING WORKS

Video modeling involves replaying a videotape of an expert performer, which allows athletes to view a skill being performed correctly and creates a mental representation of the correct skill in their minds, so that they can physically model or image it. Research has shown that observational learning is enhanced when the model being viewed is similar to the observer in age, gender, and competence in the activity, because similar models may enhance self-efficacy and performance (McCullagh and Weiss 2001; Ram and McCullagh 2003; Schunk, Hanson, and Cox 1987). The underlying principle is that the cognitive representation of the model is more effectively imaged if the model is similar to the observer. For effective observational learning to occur, athletes must translate the cognitive representation of the images being viewed to their

Table 10.1 Technical Aids to Imagery

Technical aid	Proposition	Typical research	Typical practice
Video modeling	Watching ideal or correct movement being modeled increases accuracy of imagery.	Comparison of effect on skill performance of imagery alone vs. watching video of the skill and then imagining it	*Skilled performers:* record video of their own best performance of skill *Less skilled performers:* select video of skill being performed very well, preferably by person similar to them *Both:* watch video and immediately imagine performing the skill several times
Biofeedback	Providing information about biological processes during imagery increases control over those processes.	Comparison of effects of imagery alone vs. imagery with biofeedback on muscle activity during skill performance or on level of a psychophysiological function	*For a skill:* imagery of skill accompanied by biofeedback of muscle activity associated with correct performance of the skill *For a psychophysiological function:* imagery of function adjusting in desired way, accompanied by biofeedback of psychophysiological function *For both:* meaning of biofeedback signal must be clear to performer
Flotation REST	Performing imagery in a dark, quiet, relaxing environment enhances the efficacy of imagery.	Comparison of effect on skill performance of imagery alone vs. imagining it while lying in a flotation environment or tank	Imagining performance of a skill during a flotation session, after 15-20 min of resting quietly in the tank to attain a relaxed state. Script can be played from a tape, memorized by performer, or live instructions can be given via intercom. Video modeling can be integrated immediately prior to start of imagery.

own motor performance. If the model is similar to the athlete, then the translation from the mental image to motor performance is likely to be more effective.

Viewing an image of themselves performing a skill effectively in a video not only provides athletes with a representation of how to perform the skill correctly, it also reinforces their belief (self-efficacy) that they have mastered the skill. Thus, video modeling of his own excellent performance enables the athlete to relate exactly to the image, because model–performer similarity is 100%. It also enhances self-efficacy, because the athlete exhibits excellent performance.

In video modeling associated with imagery, the performer watches an expert performer execute the skill successfully, then attempts to image himself performing the same skill. With elite athletes, videotapes of their own successful performances (or of only the highlights) are used. They view edited examples of themselves executing the skill in near-perfect fashion. The idea of video modeling is to ensure that the ideal or near-ideal performance becomes the image that the athlete uses in the mental rehearsal. When the performer views and images herself performing the skill successfully, this can act as an example of performance accomplishment, which, according to Bandura, is the strongest antecedent of self-efficacy that leads to successful performance.

RESEARCH ON VIDEO MODELING AS AN ADJUNCT TO IMAGERY

The limited research that uses video modeling to aid imagery has not been entirely consistent. In early research, Hall and Erffmeyer (1983) used video modeling in a study on relaxation and imagery in female college basketball players. The 10 participants were split into two groups: One received video modeling and relaxation and imagery training, while the other received only imagery and relaxation training. The video group watched a player perform 10 consecutive foul shots and then imaged themselves performing the "perfect 10." Hall and Erffmeyer found that the video-modeling group improved significantly more than the group that received no video modeling. Gray (1990) and Gray and Fernandez (1990) supported these findings in a sample of 24 beginner racquetball players. Gray found significantly greater improvement in participants who received relaxation, imagery, and video modeling than those with relaxation, imagery and no video modeling; Gray and Fernandez also replicated Hall and Erffmeyer's results. A study by Onestak (1997), however, did not support the conclusions of Hall and Erffmeyer. Onestak found that participants experiencing Visuomotor Behavior Rehearsal (VMBR) and video modeling did not increase their basketball-shooting performance significantly more than the nonvideo-modeling group.

Onestak concluded that none of the conditions was more or less effective in enhancing free-throw-shooting performance.

Atienza, Balaguer, and Garcia-Merita (1998) examined the effects of video modeling and imagery training on tennis-serve performance over 24 weeks. The results showed that tennis performance improved for groups that received mental training. Atienza et al. concluded that the combination of physical training with mental training (using video modeling), as well as a combination of video-model observation and imagery, could improve tennis-serve performance. In particular, Atienza et al. stated that the systematic viewing of similar video-modeling productions might facilitate the ability to create internal representations that allow for the integration of complex movements, such as those involved in a tennis serve. They concluded that the best result seems to be to combine video modeling and physical practice with imagery.

Research has shown that imagery of successful skill demonstration, including the correct process or outcome, can be beneficial to athletes. Woolfolk, Parrish, and Murphy (1985) found that participants who used negative imagery in a golf-putting task experienced a significant decrease in performance compared to those who used neutral, as well as positive, imagery. As a result, performance enhancement is more likely to occur if the athlete first views the correct technique required in the skill before imagery rehearsal occurs. Furthermore, imagery is more beneficial if the images are of the athletes' own performance. Ram and McCullagh (2003) stated that the research on self-modeling or video modeling in the physical domain has shown inconsistent results. Research that reports positive effects of video modeling on physical and psychological responses in sport and exercise settings has not been replicated sufficiently at this time. Researchers who have studied imagery and video modeling have mainly reported results that indicate performance outcomes for video modeling and imagery that are superior to imagery alone. More studies are needed to clarify why video modeling is sometimes ineffective.

APPLICATIONS OF VIDEO MODELING TO SPORT

Video modeling as an applied technique that is often used by coaches in the training environment has yet to be thoroughly investigated by sport psychology researchers. Researchers using video in coaching have found that, by showing athletes a tape of their own performance, they see themselves from a different perspective (i.e., first person versus third person), therefore gleaning new information regarding their actions. This relates to the imagery-perspective research reported in chapter 6. Video modeling enables athletes to create a mental representation of the correct technique required for a skill. Videotapes are used to develop and reinforce constructive imagery. Vealey and Greenleaf proposed that highlight tapes be used in conjunction with imagery to enhance confidence in returning from injury or when form slumps. McCullagh and Weiss (2002) cited the example of the San Francisco Giants baseball team, whose players employed a video coach to watch and edit replays using a high-tech digital-video system behind the dugout, so that they could view their own performances.

The Giants' approach could represent an example of a little bit of knowledge being a dangerous thing because the imagery and video-modeling literature shows that imagery of incorrect performance increases the likelihood of a subsequent performance being incorrect. Showing players what they did wrong on video in the dugout could lead to imagery of the incorrect skill being the last thing the batter does before going to the plate again. Corrective video can be an effective technique, but applied sport psychologists recommend its use away from competition, when there is time to follow demonstration of what was done wrong with ample video and imagery of correct performance. Of course, the Giants could be using the video in the dugout in different ways, such as showing what the pitcher is doing to help players pick the pitch. In itself that should be helpful, but care should be taken not to show a player's wayward hit.

Success or highlight tapes made from clips of athletes' actual practices can be used to reinforce specific techniques from the training environment (Gould and Darmarjian 1996). The videotape can act as a trigger, or cue, for experiences associated with an athlete's successful performance, which improve the quality of the imagery rehearsal. Triggers can include a specific sensory experience, such as a given technique or the kinesthetic feel of a movement (Gould and Darmarjian 1996). The advent of small, portable digital cameras with instant playback provides an innovative way to take video modeling into the field. These cameras could be used as part of a preperformance imagery routine immediately before a competition or performance. For example, an athlete could view a specific highlight tape during the warm-up for competition as a performance enhancement aid.

Perry and Morris (1995) cited the example of video modeling and imagery use in the sport psychology department of the Australian Institute of Sport. The elite athletes at the Institute have access to a comprehensive video-editing suite, where they are taught to edit videos to be used with imagery rehearsal. These are often combined with flotation sessions. After about 20 minutes in a flotation tank, the athletes enter a very relaxed state; video modeling is then introduced via a monitor mounted in the top of the tank, allowing the athletes to view the screen while lying down in a relaxed state with minimal distraction (Perry and Morris 1995). Blank spaces can be left on the videotape, allowing the athletes to re-create or model, through mental imaging, the example they have just viewed.

CONCLUSIONS ON VIDEO MODELING

The application of video modeling to aid imagery has been widely practiced in elite sport in institutions like the Australian Institute of Sport and the United States Olympic Training Center. Research on video modeling and imagery rehearsal has been sparse and the results are not clear, which might be related to the quality of the studies. Video modeling might not be informative or helpful for many reasons, but when it provides appropriate information, it does appear to help imagery facilitate performance. Further research is warranted, using the new, portable video technology, to investigate the effects of video modeling on imagery rehearsal and performance. From a theoretical perspective, Bandura's social-learning theory dictates that athletes will emulate role models from elite sport, and imagery of correct skill production does enhance performance; thus, the combination of video modeling of experts and imagery could be adapted to enhance developing athletes' learning skills and enable them to perfect them more quickly. Video self-evaluation is a technique that has been used in applied coaching settings for years, but further research is required to investigate the merits of the technique in regard to imagery and performance enhancement. Clearly, effective self-modeling depends on selection of appropriate examples from previous performance.

An interesting line of research that has not been examined concerns how athletes and their coaches select video examples. Can we assume that the best examples are always chosen? Maybe athletes select performances in which the outcome is incorrect, regardless of the process. It is also possible that athletes select examples in which the outcome is correct but results from luck or opponent error, while the process in the video example is incorrect. Imagery of such video clips could detract from correct skill development. The best time to show a video and perform imagery is also not clear. Immediately before performance might not be a good time for some athletes, or it might be effective under specific conditions. A basic question that should also be considered is whether athletes automatically use imagery when they are shown a video, especially of themselves. Imagery that occurs in such circumstances, whether an athlete intends it to or not, is like incidental learning in the more general sense and would have major implications for video use. For example, much greater caution would need to be employed in the wide range of applications of video in sport, including use of video modeling as an adjunct to imagery.

Another question that appears likely to benefit from further research is whether use of video modeling to facilitate imagery depends on the skill level of the athlete with reference to the specific task. Perhaps athletes who are more skilled can effectively integrate the information

provided by video modeling, especially self-modeling of best performances, whereas less skilled performers run a greater risk of using
unhelpful information from the video or simply not converting it into
effective imagery. More research is needed to guide the widely used
practices in more effective directions.

BIOFEEDBACK AND IMAGERY IN SPORT

For centuries, biomedical practitioners and researchers have monitored biological signals, such as heart rate, respiration, and temperature. Over time, the technologies used to measure and monitor such
vital signs have developed in sophistication and precision. Although
physicians still listen to the heart using a stethoscope and even take
the pulse with their fingers and a watch, electrocardiograph (ECG)
systems now show the frequency and amplitude of the heartbeat more
accurately. Various parts of the heart can be monitored independently.
More complex indicators, such as the interbeat interval, can be easily
monitored too.

In the last 25 years, the development of telemetry (the transmission
and reception of electrical signals in wave form, without the need for
wires) means that people can monitor their own heart rate easily (see
page 247). The measurements of biological processes taken by biomedical
personnel represent physiological monitoring, and communication of
information about such processes *to the person who is generating the signals*
is called *biofeedback*.

In this section we define biofeedback and show how it can be used
for training purposes. Then we link it to imagery and focus on the
sport context. Next, we consider research on the efficacy of biofeedback as an adjunct to imagery and discuss its applications as an aid
to imagery.

DEFINITIONS OF BIOFEEDBACK
AND BIOFEEDBACK TRAINING

The definitions of biofeedback are numerous. Blumenstein, Bar-Eli, and
Tenenbaum (1995, 344) described it as "a technological interface among
external senses, the voluntary and automatic branches of the central
nervous system, to provide typically inaccessible information about
biological states to the individual." Zaichkowsky and Fuchs (1988)
stated that biofeedback is the use of instrumentation to detect and
amplify internal physiological processes to the individual in a meaningful, rapid, precise, and consistent manner. Others have focused on
the augmentation aspect of biofeedback. For example, Magill defined

it as a "type of augmented feedback that provides information about physiological processes through the use of instrumentation" (2004, 287). Coker adopted a similar approach, stating that biofeedback is a "form of augmented feedback that measures physiological information that is concurrently available to a learner through some form of instrumentation" (2004, 222). The key elements of these definitions are that physiological information is provided to the person who is generating the biological signals, that the information is not normally accessible to that person, and that some form of external instrument is used to monitor the signals.

Typically, biofeedback uses two instruments that are connected. A device measures the biological signal, such as electrodes that measure heart activity based on the electrical signals associated with the stimulation of the heart muscle. Another device presents the information, such as the watch, which displays the heart rate as a number of beats per sec or as a heart-shaped graphic that pulses at the rate recorded. Coker's definition adds two more aspects of biofeedback: The information is provided concurrently (i.e., at the time that it is being produced), and the person is involved in a learning process. These are not essential elements; however, biofeedback is often used in the context of learning or training.

When biofeedback is employed as a training device, we may refer to "biofeedback training." Biofeedback can be used to help an athlete gain control over a physiological process. For example, someone who is experiencing anxiety attacks accompanied by large increases in heart rate may not find relaxation techniques, such as imagery of a pleasant place, effective. Providing biofeedback in the form of a visual display of a numerical heart rate or as an auditory tone (which might interfere less with the imagery) can help people in two ways. First, as the tone slows down, indicating that the heart rate is decreasing, they know they are doing the right thing. Second, discovering that they are achieving their goals can motivate them and give them confidence. Small changes in the desired direction can help them focus more effort on the relaxation technique, leading to larger, more meaningful decreases in heart rate.

Technological advances in the measurement of physiological indices in recent years have facilitated the application of biofeedback training. Figure 10.1 illustrates the process of biofeedback as well as how people can use it to train their physiological processes. If the biofeedback training box in the figure (the one in bold) is omitted, the process is simply biofeedback.

Recently, athletes have become more interested in the potential of biofeedback training as a technique that can enhance performance directly or that can help them indirectly, by enabling them to manage physiological processes so they support rather than interfere with performance. An

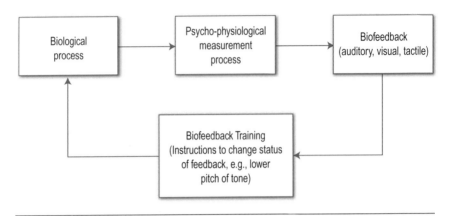

Figure 10.1   The biofeedback process and biofeedback training.

example of using biofeedback to directly support performance would be a pistol shooter monitoring muscle activity in his forearms to ensure the smoothest trigger squeeze. If he wanted to learn to control physiological processes, he could use heartbeat biofeedback to learn at which point in the heart's cycle is the best time to fire. In this way, biofeedback modalities can provide psychophysiological signals to athletes in visual (e.g., on a screen) or auditory (e.g., continuous or intermittent tones) form, which train them to gain voluntary control of the involuntary psychophysiological processes (Zaichkowsky and Fuchs 1988). The psychological and physiological demands placed on elite athletes during training and competition led Tenenbaum, Corbett, and Kitsantas (2002) to suggest that biofeedback training is highly appropriate for them.

BIOFEEDBACK MODALITIES

The term "biofeedback modalities" describes the various instruments used for recording or detecting physiological signals for feedback (Blumenstein 2002). Biofeedback modalities that have been used in exercise and sport settings include HR, ECG, electrodermal feedback (EDA), electromyogram (EMG), and electroencephalogram (EEG).

ELECTROCARDIOGRAPHIC FEEDBACK

ECG feedback is a sophisticated form of heart rate measurement. ECG equipment produces information that can be presented graphically as a waveform. Statistics, such as the mean (average) heart rate, the mean power (strength), and the mean interbeat interval, can also be presented. For training purposes, a simple auditory signal that lets athletes know how fast the heart is beating, can be an effective biofeedback-training mechanism.

HEART RATE TELEMETRY

The advent of more sophisticated technology (see "Using Personal Heart Rate Monitors in Exercise") has allowed HR measurement to become portable. Today, HR can be measured during exercise anywhere via electrodes in a chest strap linked by telemetry (no wires) to a wristwatch. The chest-strap transmitter sends the exerciser's HR to the watch, where targeted HR levels are programmed to monitor exerciser intensity. A tone is emitted when the HR goes above or below the targeted level.

USING PERSONAL HEART RATE MONITORS IN EXERCISE

The advent of telemetry has made a big difference to the application of HR biofeedback in sport. Athletes can now check on their heart rate at any moment during a training session. Personal HR monitors can be used for athletic training, fitness, weight management, or even cardiac rehabilitation. Their portability also allows coaches to monitor their athletes' progress throughout a training session.

These personal HR monitors are designed for all levels of involvement in sport, from the recreational jogger to the elite athlete. Different models target different athletes or sports. A company called Polar (www.polar.fi), for example, manufactures portable HR models designed for skiers, cyclists, and runners, and water-resistant models for swimmers and divers. Polar has developed HR telemetry aimed at targeting weight management, personal training, and increasing general fitness. Whereas earlier models required a cable to download information to a computer, the latest models incorporate infrared technology to send data straight from the exerciser to a computer for instant analysis. The computer software can show heart rate graphs, training improvements, cadence, and power outputs, and can be set to limit overtraining, plan training sessions, record training sessions, or monitor energy intake, energy expenditure, calorie expenditure, and much more. HR telemetry has provided sport with its most accessible, meaningful, and increasingly sophisticated form of self-managed biofeedback that can be applied in real-world settings.

ELECTRODERMAL FEEDBACK

The measurement of sweat-gland activity at various skin sites is termed "electrodermal feedback." For training purposes, a simple auditory tone sounds when the electrical activity reaches a targeted point. The athlete must then lower or increase activity to stay within the targeted range.

ELECTROMYOGRAM FEEDBACK

An EMG measures the electrical activity (microvolts) associated with muscle contractions (Blumenstein 2002; Jeannerod 1994). EMG values also reflect the amount of tension in a muscle, because muscles produce ongoing electrical activity unless they are completely relaxed. Electrodes are attached to the muscle at specific points, and the electrical activity produced is shown in graphical form.

ELECTROENCEPHALOGRAPHIC FEEDBACK

The EEG measures the electrical activity produced by the brain (Blumenstein 2002). The magnitude of brain activity is so small that very sensitive equipment is needed to accurately detect and record EEG signals. The signals from electrodes on the participant's head are filtered and amplified many thousands of times to produce a discernible EEG, which is usually presented in graphical form.

COMBINING BIOFEEDBACK AND IMAGERY

Imagery is the performance-enhancement technique that is most widely used by athletes (e.g., DeFrancesco and Burke 1997). Chapters 3 through 7 illustrate the substantial amount of research that has been conducted on various aspects of imagery in sport. Biofeedback has also gained popularity among athletes and stimulated much research (e.g., Blumenstein 2002). It can act as an adjunct to imagery in various contexts in sport, both for learning and refining skills and for managing physiological reactions to competitive environments. At this time, however, the research that has directly examined whether particular kinds of biofeedback do enhance the impact of imagery interventions is limited and piecemeal.

Focusing first on HR and ECG biofeedback, Blumenstein et al. (1995) found that when imagery formed part of a larger intervention with relaxation and music, and participants were given heart rate biofeedback, there was an augmenting effect on HR. The three treatment groups (autogenic and imagery training, imagery training and music, or autogenic and imagery training and music) showed a decrease in HR compared to the placebo and control groups. This result is not definitive because the participants were given packages, making it difficult to identify the effects of each element of the training.

Galvanic Skin Response (GSR) has primarily been employed in athletic anxiety studies or as one modality in a larger biofeedback application. Blumenstein et al. (1995) found that biofeedback increased the effects of imagery training on relaxation. This study appears to suffer from the same difficulty as the previous one. In this case, not only was imagery combined with relaxation, but GSR was a component of a multimodal biofeedback package.

A little more research has been done on biofeedback regarding muscle activity. De Witt (1980) investigated cognitive and biofeedback training to reduce stress in university athletes. During a comprehensive biofeedback and cognitive-skills training program, participants completed mental rehearsal (imagery) with emphasis on maintaining positive and success-ful images of excellent and poor games. The participants completed 11 sessions involving the mental rehearsal of free throws, guarding, field goals (depending on the sport being played), and images specific to a player's position. Athletes participated under different arousal condi-tions. De Witt found that biofeedback training and mental rehearsal decreased EMG activity levels during feedback sessions.

Blumenstein (2002), Blumenstein et al. (1995), and Blumenstein et al. (1997) used EMG biofeedback training in conjunction with relaxation and imagery. The training consisted of a 20 min session during which athletes were connected to the EMG feedback system. They were instructed to relax their limbs, stomach, chest, and face, while soft music was played. They then completed 10 min of relaxation before completing 10 min of imagery training, in which they were asked to imagine a competitive situ-ation, with many spectators, that required them to run 100 m. They were to imagine that their leg muscles were relaxed, working smoothly and fast, and that the run was being performed very efficiently (Blumenstein et al. 1995). The electrical activity was displayed on a computer monitor. The participants then tried to modify the EMG signal in the appropriate direction by relaxing tense muscles in one study and by activating injured muscles in another study. Blumenstein et al. found that EMG biofeedback training increased the effects of autogenic training and imagery on HR, GSR, and breathing patterns. In these studies, EMG appears to act as a measure of general arousal, because the effect of providing participants with information about muscle tension was to reduce several other physi-ologic indicators of arousal rather than to change muscle tension itself.

EEG biofeedback has rarely been examined as an adjunct to imagery, although the EEG has been employed as an outcome measure in several imagery studies (e.g., Cremades 2002; Hung et al. 2002). Collins (1995) stated that most research has focused on measuring the alpha bandwidth because alpha brainwave activity has been linked to enhanced perfor-mance, learning, and better concentration and decision-making skills. Alpha activity also reflects relaxed awareness.

The limited research on biofeedback as an adjunct to imagery is dis-appointing. It seems clear that an alpha brainwave state is likely to be more conducive to effective imagery rehearsal in general. Attaining such a state can also aid relaxation, which is often an aim of psychological-skills training. It has also been suggested that theta brainwave activity is associated with hypnagogic imagery, which could be even more potent than alpha. An exciting area to explore could be the facilitation of certain types of imagery by targeted training of brain activity. For example, when the aim is to enhance perceptual skills, the focus of EEG biofeedback training could be the occipital cortex, where visual perception occurs. A small number of studies show some promise, primarily for the role of arousal-related biofeedback as an adjunct to imagery that is intended to alter (typically reduce) arousal level.

APPLICATIONS OF BIOFEEDBACK AND IMAGERY

As mentioned earlier, biofeedback can be used in a variety of ways to provide information that promotes the efficacy of imagery in sport contexts. As biofeedback training, biological information can be used to enhance imagery for learning skills or affecting psychological variables that tend to influence performance. A popular framework for considering the uses of imagery is Paivio's (1985) cognitive–motivational dimension, which he combined with a specific–general dimension to derive four uses of imagery: cognitive specific (CS), cognitive general (CG), motivational specific (MS), and motivational general (MG). Hall et al. (1998) identified independent mastery and arousal uses of MG imagery. This is a helpful framework for looking at the potential applications of biofeedback as an adjunct to imagery.

CS imagery use involves applications of imagery in the context of learning specific skills. EMG biofeedback can be used as an aid to imagery of a specific skill, whether during the learning or performance stage of skill development. Although this approach could be applied to any skill, in practice it is easier to envisage for a skill that is produced by a specific part of the body, while the rest of the body is relatively stationary. Archery might be a suitable sport to exemplify the application of EMG biofeedback. Archers must hit a specific target, so they must develop precise aim and release skills. Imagery can be used to practice the sequence of aim and release, as well as its timing, to produce the smooth process that is likely to yield the best outcome. We know from the classic work of Jacobson (1930a, b, c, d, 1931a, b, c) that electrical signals are observed in the muscles responsible for actions during imagery. Thus monitoring the activity being produced by the key muscles involved in the aim or release parts of the action is possible, using EMG biofeedback. Trying to work on both together is not advisable, because the archer would have to concurrently focus on different signals, presumably mainly from the left arm for the aim task and from the right arm for the release task in a right-handed archer. Skills like this have an added element. Although we know what the EMG signals mean and, more important, what needs to be done with them in an arousal-reduction task, we would need to monitor them during performance of both accurate and less effective shots to demonstrate to the archer which muscle activity works and which does not. Once the archer understands the goal of biofeedback, imagery with biofeedback can be used to enhance performance.

Practicing a team move in basketball is an example of CG imagery use. During such imagery, the players would need to use images of their teammates and opponents moving around the court, as well as their own movement in catching, passing, or shooting. EEG biofeedback training could be employed to support imagery by providing information about the levels of activity in the visual cortex and the motor cortex at appropriate times during the perception–action sequence. The aim would be to focus attention on the appropriate aspect of the skill at the right time in the sequence. This kind of use for biofeedback training is probably the most speculative proposed in this discussion.

MS imagery is associated with the achievement of specific goals. An important specific goal for shooters is to squeeze the trigger at the right moment in the breathing cycle, between inhaling and exhaling, because this is when disruption caused by body movement is at a minimum. Biofeedback of the respiration cycle during imagery of shooting in competition could assist shooters in perfecting their timing. MS biofeedback training might not readily apply to some activities. However, the applications of biofeedback as an aid to imagery, like the use of imagery itself, are likely to depend on the creativity of athletes, coaches, and sport psychologists in specific contexts.

Motivational general mastery (MG-M) imagery use relates to the feeling of mastering skills and achieving goals. It is largely linked to the motivation-enhancing aspect of mastery rather than actual skill production. Thus, emotion is central to this kind of imagery, and the feelings involved include pride, elation, happiness, and satisfaction. Many biofeedback modalities reflect these emotions and feelings, but they are commonly registered as increased levels of arousal that are not distinguishable from the arousal associated with anxiety. Nonetheless, when the imagery rehearsal is clearly related to scenes of mastery (in which anxiety, stress, fear, or other negative feelings do not play a part), HR, ECG, GSR, or other biofeedback monitoring of increases in physiological activity should be associated with those positive emotions. Theory and research suggest that imagery of the sights, sounds, feel, smell, and other sensations associated with a particular scene tend to be more effective when the appropriate emotion is included. Biofeedback that increases the positive emotion associated with imagery of mastery should enhance the impact of the experience.

MG-A imagery involves applying imagery specifically to manage arousal and emotion. Increased arousal is desirable in contexts that require extreme effort, whether this is associated with strength, power, or endurance. Imagery of performing a challenging weightlifting task would benefit from the generation of a high level of arousal for a short period of time. Biofeedback that helps a lifter increase the level of arousal during imagery of such lifts should help generate such arousal during actual lifts. By far the most common use of biofeedback discussed in the literature and examined in research to date relates to the opposite kind of MG-A imagery use: reducing arousal, which has been exemplified previously. Suffice it to say that imagery of relaxing in stressful competition (or pre- or postcompetition) situations can be facilitated by biofeedback of physiological responses related to arousal, such as GSR, HR, or EMG.

Some of the applications of biofeedback as an adjunct to imagery in sport that we have presented here are less common than others in current practice. It would be interesting to see research on some of these more speculative uses before they are put into practice in elite sport or in the skill-learning process. The examples presented do illustrate the potential for biofeedback training to be used in a variety of sport contexts. Its application as an aid to imagery is most highly developed in the context of arousal management; an example cited by Blumenstein, Bar-Eli, and Collins (2002) illustrates a more fully developed imagery and biofeedback program.

Blumenstein, Bar-Eli, and Collins (2002) and Blumenstein, Bar-Eli, and Tenenbaum (1997) constructed a biofeedback training program called the Wingate five-step approach. The program involves the use of several biofeedback modalities aimed at providing positive performance effects in elite athletes. The five-step approach for mental training involves individualized biofeedback sessions with a VCR or DVD player. The steps are as follows:

1. *Introduction:* Here the aim is learning self-regulation techniques. This stage involves 10 to 15 sessions that teach athletes to regulate their mental state through observation of their psychophysiological response on a screen. After recording the baseline measures, athletes are asked to imagine themselves in different settings, including competition, for around 2 min.

2. *Identification:* The purpose of this stage is to identify and strengthen the most efficient biofeedback response modality through auditory and visual feedback.

3. *Simulation:* The aim of this stage is to experience biofeedback training with simulated competitive stress. It involves 15 sessions of mental practice, including video scenes of the athlete competing. While watching the video, athletes rehearse a relaxation and imagery program that they learned in stage 1. Blumenstein et al. (1997) stated that this stage targets the specific needs of each sport and allows the athletes to practice the techniques they learned.

4. *Transformation:* The goal of this stage is moving what's been learned from the laboratory to the field. The material learned in steps 1 through 3 is transferred to actual training settings.

5. *Realization:* In this stage, the athlete applies the techniques during competition. (Blumenstein, Bar-Eli, and Collins 2002)

Blumenstein, Bar-Eli, and Collins (2002) stated that the Wingate approach has been successfully applied to elite athletes in sailing, windsurfing, judo, swimming, canoeing, and kayaking. The Wingate approach shows how a biofeedback training system can be applied to improve athletic performance. According to Blumenstein, Bar-Eli, and Collins (2002), however, biofeedback training is expensive, time consuming, and detached from real life, which makes it difficult to access for most athletes and coaches. Still, the potential benefits mean that biofeedback training should not be discounted as a mental-training aid.

Conclusions on Biofeedback

Biofeedback is widely used in training people, including athletes, to control their movements and manage physiological functions. These kinds of applications have great potential to be employed in sport contexts. At this stage little research has examined specific applications of biofeedback in combination with imagery interventions; however, the studies that have been reported are promising. Research on biofeedback's role as an adjunct to imagery appears to depend on access to relatively sophisticated equipment. The development of less elaborate or expensive technology, such as GSR devices smaller than a computer mouse and telemetric heart rate monitors that can be worn as watches, does show the potential for wider application of biofeedback as an adjunct to imagery. Opportunities abound for research to guide future application.

Flotation and Imagery

Following World War II, American psychologists began to study the effects of sensory deprivation, which had been used as a technique to brainwash prisoners during the war. These researchers identified powerful negative effects of long periods of time (e.g., 24 hours) spent lying on a soft bed in a dark room, wearing a blindfold, with headphones playing white noise, and cotton wool pads covering the hands and feet, thus reducing most sensation to a minimum (e.g., Bexton, Heron, and Scott 1954; Heron 1957). Curiously, participants in these studies reported feeling very relaxed, even euphoric, during the first one to two hours of sensory deprivation (Bexton et al. 1954; Zubek 1969). Some researchers began to focus on the positive reactions experienced by people who had their senses restricted for limited durations (e.g., Lilly 1977). To distinguish the positive process from the negative effects of sensory deprivation, it was termed "restricted environmental stimulation," and its use as a relaxation technique was called Restricted Environmental Stimulation Therapy, usually abbreviated to REST, and the rooms in which it was conducted were called REST chambers (Suedfeld 1980). Researchers, including Lilly (1956), began to use alternative environments. A popular one was a tank of water in which the person was immersed vertically. Floating in water minimized the sensation imposed on the back, buttocks, legs, and heels by gravity when the person lay on a couch or bed. These large tanks were expensive and unwieldy, so Lilly (1977) developed the kind of flotation tank used today.

The modern, fiberglass flotation tank looks somewhat like an Egyptian sarcophagus. Figure 10.2 illustrates a common style of tank. It is approximately 230 cm long, 130 cm wide, and 90 cm deep, with a sliding door in the top that is kept closed during the flotation session. In the tank is approximately 35 cm of water, containing Epsom salts to make the solution dense enough for a person to float in it. The water is maintained at body temperature (34.4° C) to minimize the sensation

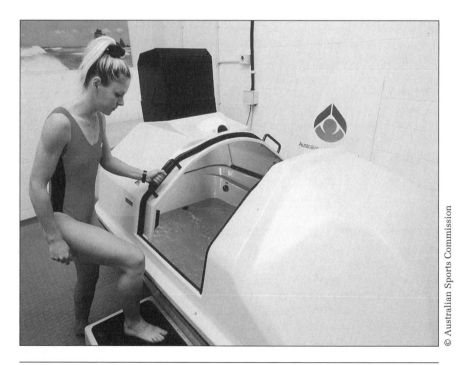

Figure 10.2 A flotation tank in action.

of a temperature gradient between skin and water. The person floats supine, with most of the body (except the face, chest, and abdomen) under water. The tank usually contains an emergency-alarm button, a light, and a two-way communication system, so that the floater and the session supervisor can talk and relaxing music or instructions, such as an imagery script, can be piped in. Flotation sessions usually last for around an hour.

HOW FLOTATION FACILITATES IMAGERY

Psychologists have proposed various theories to explain why flotation is effective (Hutchison 1984; Suedfeld 1980). Most are speculative and only a few, which we describe here, seem to bear any relation to imagery. An obvious proposition is that flotation is deeply relaxing, and it is the very relaxed state that facilitates imagery (Hutchison 1984). The powerful relaxation effect reported during flotation has been related to quieting of the central nervous system due to sensory reduction. In particular, the apparent lack of gravitational effects experienced during flotation have been proposed as a reason why flotation is more relaxing than other arousal-reduction techniques, such as progressive muscle relaxation and autogenic training (Hutchinson 1984). Many imagery researchers have linked imagery to relaxation, the most notable being Suinn (1976a) in his VMBR, an imagery technique that was particularly popular in the 1970s and 1980s. Murphy and Jowdy (1992) argued that there was little research evidence to support this claim; nonetheless, relaxation is still widely employed as a foundation for imagery rehearsal.

Alternatives to the relaxation proposition focus on ways in which stimulus reduction lowers the nervous system's activity level. One hypothesis is that REST, including flotation, reduces brain stem activity (Suedfeld 1980). Another is that during REST theta waves are more easily produced in the brain. Theta activity is associated with creativity and insight, which could enhance the impact of imagery (Hutchison 1984). A cognitive explanation, as opposed to the more neuropsychological hypotheses just reviewed, is that the restricted environmental stimulation permits people to focus on their thoughts, thus enhancing the effect of imagery (Suedfeld 1980). Little research has directly tested these speculations. Most of the research on REST has focused on its effects. Research specifically on flotation REST has found that flotation does induce a deep state of relaxation (Lilly 1977; Suedfeld, Turner, and Fine 1990), reduce stress (Turner and Fine 1983), improve concentration (Norlander, Bergman, and Archer 1999), and relieve pain (Barabasz and Barabasz 1989). Several studies have investigated the effect of flotation REST on imagery rehearsal in sport.

RESEARCH ON FLOTATION AS AN ADJUNCT TO IMAGERY REHEARSAL

Several studies have addressed the issue of whether flotation facilitates the effectiveness of imagery in sport. Table 10.2 summarizes these studies. Lee and Hewitt (1987) examined the performance and anxiety of 36 novice- to intermediate-level female gymnasts. Lee and Hewitt employed three conditions: imagery in a flotation tank, imagery on a mat, and a no-imagery control. The gymnasts had six sessions on a weekly basis, each lasting 40 min. Imagery in flotation was associated with higher levels of performance and more "facilitative" anxiety than the other two conditions, which did not differ. The finding that the imagery condition did not differ from the control condition raises some concern because imagery does usually show an effect. This anomaly may have been caused by unconscious signals from the experimenters indicating that they did not expect imagery alone to be effective. Nonetheless, there is no doubt about the positive result for the imagery with flotation condition in this study.

Suedfeld and Bruno (1990) examined the effect of imagery during flotation on basketball free-throw shooting in 30 university students who were all novices at the task. Suedfeld and Bruno compared four conditions: imagery during flotation, imagery in an alpha chair (a kind of dry sensory-reduction environment), imagery in an armchair, and a control group. Once again, only the participants in the imagery and flotation condition showed a significant improvement in performance following the intervention. Participants who performed imagery in an armchair showed worse performance after the imagery than before it. Again, this result casts some doubt on the study, because in the history of research on imagery and performance, rarely has an imagery-rehearsal script that was designed to facilitate performance had a negative effect. Aldridge (2002) noted that the imagery program in this study was presented only once and the participants were given no imagery training, nor were they tested to determine their level of imagery ability (a weakness in the imagery literature in general; see, for example, the section in chapter 4 on the measurement of imagery ability). Bearing in mind that the participants were novices at free-throw shooting, these design limitations are noteworthy. Once again, imagery in flotation produced positive results.

Two studies conducted by Barabasz and his colleagues examined the effect of imagery during flotation on performance during competition in high-level performers. McAleney, Barabasz, and Barabasz (1990) investigated aspects of tennis performance in 20 male and female varsity players. They compared the imagery and flotation condition to an imagery-only condition. Examining the effects of these conditions on three aspects of

Table 10.2 Studies of Imagery and Flotation in Sport

Authors	Date	Design	Results	Conclusion
Lee and Hewitt	1987	Flotation + imagery vs. relaxation on a mat + imagery vs. control; female gymnasts; 6 40-min sessions; postintervention competition scores	Higher competition scores for flotation + imagery condition	Flotation enhances imagery effectiveness.
Suedfeld and Bruno	1990	Flotation + imagery vs. imagery in alpha chair vs. imagery in armchair vs. control; university students; task, basketball shooting; 1 session; no imagery training	Flotation + imagery scores higher than other conditions	Flotation enhances imagery effectiveness.
McAleney, Barabasz, and Barabasz	1990	Flotation + imagery vs. imagery; male and female varsity tennis players; tennis serve; 6 50-min sessions	Flotation + imagery associated with higher service percentages	Flotation enhances imagery effectiveness.
Wagaman, Barabasz, and Barabasz	1991	Flotation + imagery vs. imagery "control"; college basketball players; 6 40-min sessions; coaches' ratings of game performance	Flotation + imagery condition had higher coaches' ratings, but no difference in players' expectancy between conditions	Flotation enhances imagery effectiveness.

(continued)

Table 10.2 *(continued)*

Authors	Date	Design	Results	Conclusion
Suedfeld, Collier, and Hartnett	1993	Flotation + imagery vs. flotation alone vs. imagery alone vs. control; dart-throwing among novice university students; one session	Flotation + imagery and flotation alone improved; imagery and control conditions did not.	No difference between flotation + imagery and flotation conditions.
Aldridge, Morris, and Andersen	2003	Flotation + imagery vs. autogenic training + imagery; free-throw shooting; skilled performers; 3 55-min sessions	Flotation and autogenics increased relaxed state; flotation associated with deeper relaxation.	Both conditions enhanced free-throw shooting. Flotation condition improved free-throw shooting more.
Larner and Morris	1997	Flotation + video modeling + imagery vs. flotation + imagery; pike dive; skilled performers; 3 35-min sessions	Both groups improved; no difference between groups.	Video modeling did not enhance imagery in flotation.

performance (percentage of first serves in, key shots, and points won), McAleney et al. found a significant effect for first serves only, with the imagery-in-flotation participants producing a higher percentage of first serves in than the imagery-alone participants. Claiming that key shots and points won depended more on the opponent's influence than service, McAleney et al. argued that the results provided support for the benefit of imagery in flotation on a skill that is within the performer's control.

Wagaman, Barabasz, and Barabasz (1991) observed the performance of 22 elite college basketball players, who were assigned to either an imagery-and-flotation condition or an imagery-alone condition. Wagaman et al. followed the imagery protocol of Lee and Hewitt (1987), so participants carried out several imagery sessions. In an interesting innovation, Wagaman et al. asked participants to rate the effectiveness of the condition in which they practiced. Based on these ratings, they found no differences in expectancy between the two conditions. But the performance scores used, which were ratings of passing and shooting during the game by coaches who were blind to the players' imagery-condition assignment, significantly favored the participants who practiced imagery in flotation.

An alternate explanation for the pattern of results reported here is that the imagery programs had variable or no effect on performance and it was the flotation that enhanced performance. To test this, it would be necessary to include a flotation-only condition. Suedfeld, Collier, and Hartnett (1993) did this in a study of dart-throwing performance. They employed four conditions: imagery and flotation, flotation alone, imagery alone, and a no-practice control. Participants in both flotation conditions showed significant improvement, whereas those in the other two conditions did not improve. Further, there was no significant difference between performance in the flotation-alone and flotation-plus-imagery condition. Suedfeld et al. concluded that flotation, rather than imagery, produced the performance effects. They argued that participants improved their concentration skills during flotation. Again, the participants' skill levels in relation to the imagery program could explain the absence of an imagery effect. Nonetheless, flotation does appear to be beneficial.

A recent study by Aldridge, Morris, and Andersen (2003) throws more light on the role of flotation as an aid to imagery. Aldridge et al. examined free-throw shooting in 18 (9 male, 9 female) 15- to 19-year-old, A-grade basketball players. Players were screened to ensure that they were skilled shooters. They were pretested on the Vividness of Visual Imagery Questionnaire (VVIQ; Marks 1973) and the Vividness of Movement Imagery Questionnaire (VMIQ; Isaac, Marks, and Russell 1986) to ensure that they had sound imagery ability. Each participant was then pretested on 50 free-throw shots in a field study setting. Participants were matched on gender, age, and shooting ability (based on the pretest) and assigned to either an imagery-plus-flotation condition or an imagery-plus-autogenic training condition. Sessions in each condition lasted for 55 min, including 25 min of relaxation, 15 min of imagery (based on the same script in both conditions), 5 min of consolidation, and 10 min of wake-up activities. Each participant had three sessions. Before each session, in each condition, the participant was fitted with a waterproof Polar HR telemetry system, which recorded HR every 60 sec during the session.

Participants in the flotation condition had significantly lower HRs at the end of the third session, when HRs at the start of the session were used as covariate. The effect size was very large. Visual analysis of HR graphs showed that participants in both conditions showed a reduction in HR during the sessions, but that the reduction was larger and occurred more quickly for participants in the imagery-plus-flotation condition. Basketball free-throw-shooting performance after the three imagery sessions was significantly higher for participants in the flotation condition, using preintervention scores as covariate. The effect size was extremely large. Performance for the imagery and autogenics participants did not improve at all from preintervention to the postintervention shooting test. In addition, self-efficacy for free-throw-shooting increased significantly more for participants in the imagery-plus-flotation condition than those in the imagery-plus-autogenics condition, with a large effect size.

These findings support previous studies that showed that imagery and flotation enhanced performance more than imagery in other contexts. The results also suggest that relaxation is not an adequate explanation for the effect of flotation and imagery combined, because there was a substantial relaxation effect in the imagery-plus-autogenic training condition but no improvement in performance. This study addressed a number of the concerns with previous research. Nonetheless, the absence of a flotation-only condition and the lack of any performance improvement in the imagery-plus-autogenics condition, despite evidence that it was relaxing, means that the proposition that flotation alone enhanced performance cannot be refuted in favor of the interpretation that the combination of imagery and flotation is needed to achieve the desired effects. Still more sophisticated studies are needed to resolve this issue.

An exploratory study by Larner and Morris (1997) examined the impact of combining video modeling with flotation. Larner and Morris assigned 12 state- to national-level divers (4 males, 8 females), aged 11 to 20 years, to one of two conditions: imagery plus flotation or imagery plus video modeling plus flotation. Divers in both conditions experienced a 40-min flotation session in which a brief relaxation period was followed by verbal instructions for imagery of the performance of a forward dive pike. A number of imagery trials were worked through, viewing the dive from different positions. A 10-min consolidation period followed the imagery, before the divers were taken through a wake-up protocol. Verbal instructions were given on videotape. The only difference was that the visual channel of the tape was blank in the imagery-plus-flotation condition, while in the condition that included video modeling, the video showed examples of the dive that matched the audio description. The VMIQ was completed before and after the interventions, which consisted of three sessions of flotation and imagery, with and without video modeling.

The degree of improvement in real performance of the dive, which was significant, was the same for the two conditions. For performance, there were two measures: judges' ratings of the dive and peak height jumped above the diving board. Ratings showed no difference between the two intervention conditions and there was little meaningful change from pre- to postintervention, despite the difference being statistically significant. For the peak-height variable, participants in the video condition started at a much higher level than those in the imagery-plus-flotation condition. Again, although statistical analysis was significant, neither group showed a meaningful level of change from pre- to posttest. This study showed no support for the value of video modeling as an adjunct to imagery and flotation. Its limitations included the small sample size and the possibility that the divers had reached a plateau for that dive prior to the study, as well as the possibility that the combination of flotation and imagery has a large enough effect that any video modeling effect was swamped. This is not likely, given that neither condition showed noteworthy improvement. Further research is needed to examine the effects of imagery combined with video modeling in flotation.

APPLICATION OF FLOTATION FOR IMAGERY REHEARSAL

Although how flotation facilitates the imagery process is still unclear, elite athletes have employed flotation techniques for some time. In Australia, for example, sport psychologists at the Australian Institute of Sport have supervised flotation sessions involving imagery rehearsal for well over a decade (Bond 1987). Flotation is a voluntary activity for AIS athletes, yet demand has been sufficient that the AIS Sport Psychology Unit has long supported two flotation tanks with accompanying technology. Bond and Sargent, AIS staff at the time, stated that "flotation provides an ideal environment for the enhancement of visualization/imagery" (1995, 410). The South Australian Sports Institute (SASI) has operated a similar facility for more than 10 years.

For a typical flotation session, athletes need to allow at least an hour. They shower before entering the tank to minimize the risk of bringing infection into it. They are not permitted to float if they have open wounds. Before their first flotation session, athletes are screened to minimize the risk that they will have an adverse reaction to the experience. Although looking at a tank from the outside leads one to assume that those at greatest risk of psychological abreaction would be people with a tendency to claustrophobic responses (fear of small, enclosed spaces), people who tend to have agoraphobic reactions (fear of wide-open spaces) might also respond negatively to the environment. In fact, people with claustrophobic tendencies are more likely to react negatively to the impression of the tank from the outside, so they would be unlikely to enter it. Once a person is inside, with the light out, the tank gives more of an impression of having no boundaries. People feel like they are floating in a limitless environment; hence the risk to those with agoraphobic tendencies.

Once all physical and psychological precautions have been addressed, sessions that include imagery typically involve flotation for 45 min to 1 hour. For athletes new to flotation, the first few minutes are used to familiarize the person with the tank, including the alarm button and other communication facilities. Then the light is dimmed and there is a period of 20 to 30 min of relaxation. This can be done in silence or with relaxing music to suit the individual. It is also possible for the sport psychologist supervising the session to give verbal instructions to the athlete, again with the goal of inducing relaxation, as in other relaxation techniques such as progressive muscle relaxation, autogenic training, or the relaxation response. Again, an experienced sport psychologist discusses these issues with athletes in advance. Alternatives, such as calming music or a reassuring voice might be tried if floating in silence does not lead to rapid relaxation for a particular person.

Once the relaxation phase is satisfactorily completed, imagery can commence. Because many athletes do experience deep relaxation in the initial phase, especially if there has been no verbal communication, the sport psychologist should gain their attention with live (as opposed to recorded) verbal communication. This needs to be sufficient to ensure that the athletes are concentrating on the information being presented but should not jolt them out of the relaxed state. Nonetheless, they should be required to give a verbal response to ensure that they are aware of the communication.

The imagery script should follow the principles discussed in previous chapters. A recorded script has advantages over live instructions, such as the use of carefully prepared language, the opportunity to edit out verbal errors and unwanted background sounds, and the capacity for checking the pace of the session. At the same time, taped imagery scripts lack the ability to make changes in response to specific circumstances, such as speeding up or slowing down, or repeating a section to which the floater does not respond. For example, in the early stages of imagery scripts, a common strategy is to include material like detailed description of the imagery environment. Such imagery can assist the novice imager to create vivid images of familiar scenes, as a foundation for the critical-skills-imagery component of the script. With some experience, athletes are often able to quickly generate vivid images of frequently experienced scenes, such as the practice or performance environment. If the script is on tape these performers cannot move on quickly to the skills imagery but must still listen to the description of the scene that they are already vividly imaging. The imagery phase usually lasts for 15 to 20 min.

To end the session, a consolidation phase of approximately 5 to 10 min is recommended, before the final wake-up phase of 5 to 10 min. This is based on the proposition from memory research that a period of quiet time for consolidation following a learning or practice activity can enhance the effectiveness of information storage in memory. Bearing in mind that the level of relaxation can be deep, a 5- to 10-min wake-up procedure is essential at the end of the session. Like the process that is used at the end of a hypnosis session, this phase involves activities that gradually arouse the floater to ensure that they are fully alert before they exit the flotation tank. Physical activities include shaking and bending limbs, as well as increasing breathing rate and opening eyes, if they were closed, or blinking a few times. To examine mental alertness, sport psychologists should ask the floaters questions to which they must make responses. These can constitute a debriefing, focusing on issues like the depth of relaxation attained, the vividness and control of their imagery, and their overall reactions to the session. Still, the session supervisors should help the athletes out of the tank since this is when accidents are most likely, partly because there is usually salt solution on the steps and floor, and partly because the person might not yet be fully alert. The athletes should then shower to ensure that all the residual salt solution has been removed from their skin. Then a final, short debriefing should take place, in which the sport psychologist reviews the session, explains the next stage or session, and again asks how the session went. This is advisable for future reference and to ensure that the athlete is fully alert.

The content of the imagery script that is included in a flotation session can address any one or a combination of the applications of imagery discussed in previous chapters. Thought must be given to the script content to ensure that it does not contain instructions that contradict the psychophysiological and psychological relaxation process. However, the inclusion of imagery of peak performance need not prove problematic in this respect. Research on flow in sport, an experience that is closely related to peak experience, has indicated that athletes who are in flow often report feeling energized yet relaxed. It is possible that repeated imagery of peak performance while in a deeply relaxed state could facilitate the prized combination of energy and relaxation during actual performance.

Recently, some practitioners have combined the technologies of flotation and video modeling. Once again, the AIS was a prime mover in this innovation. Athletes there had access to a state-of-the-art video editing and playback unit, where they could create highlight tapes of their own performances for use in imagery rehearsal. Many also used the flotation facilities described earlier. By mounting a video monitor in the top of the flotation tank and linking it to a VCR in the control room, AIS sport psychologists provided athletes with the opportunity to use both technologies together to support their imagery work. Such sessions are similar to the flotation session described previously, except that when imagery is introduced, the audio script (which has been recorded onto the videotape) accompanies visual images that cue imagery. The videotape has blank periods recorded to alternate with visual examples of the skills to be imaged. The blank periods are of appropriate length for the athlete to perform the preplanned imagery rehearsal. Alternatively, the tape can be manually stopped during the period when the athlete images. An advantage of using tapes with blank periods is that the process is fully automated. The obvious disadvantage is that there is no flexibility for the athlete to image for longer or shorter periods than the blanked-out sections of the tape. Also, video controls can be put in the flotation tank so that athletes can work at their own pace. AIS athletes who are experienced in imagery use often perform imagery in flotation without guidance, focusing on self-modeling videotapes of their own best performances, which they edit themselves.

In the previously discussed study of imagery and flotation in basketball free-throw shooting, Aldridge et al. (2003) employed a video-modeling component during flotation. They came close to combining all three technical aids to imagery that we have discussed in this chapter. To monitor and record HR during flotation, they used a telemetry system. Sometimes researchers hold the receiver so that they can monitor HR without the research participants receiving feedback that might affect their behavior in ways that are not appropriate to that study. In this study the flotation tank was dark, as is typically the case, and the HR monitor display was not luminous, so the participants could not read it. Thus, participants were not provided with any source of feedback that could have affected their behavior or the outcome of the study.

In applied sessions, however, biofeedback to the imager might facilitate imagery by enhancing relaxation (HR, GSR, EMG) or providing information about the presence of patterns of brain activity (EEG) that are conducive to the hypnagogic state thought to promote imagery. Auditory biofeedback is preferable in most cases, because then the imager does not have to monitor two visual sources, a videotape of the skills to be imaged and a graphic representation of the biological system involved. (It might be interesting to compare the use of split-screen video, where parts of the same screen display each of these signals, with a video and audio combination.) In the practical application of auditory biofeedback with video modeling during flotation, we suggest that an audible tone should sound only when the desired biological state is not present, so that no signal disturbs the imager once the appropriate level of relaxation is attained.

We propose that different approaches and combinations of imagery aids should be examined empirically. The only study we know of that compared imagery in flotation with and without video modeling is the one conducted by Larner and Morris (1997) in diving, which found no benefit from video modeling beyond that gained from flotation. However, since the participants were experts in the skill being monitored, a ceiling effect might have been present. Also, the imagery training was of relatively short duration, which might have limited the opportunity for differential outcomes from the video-modeling group to emerge. Further research is needed on this issue. Meanwhile, anecdotal evidence indicates that elite athletes find the combination of imagery and video modeling in flotation to be helpful to their preparation.

CONCLUSIONS ON FLOTATION AS A TECHNICAL AID TO IMAGERY

Research on the application of imagery has consistently shown sport performance to be enhanced more by imagery rehearsal during flotation than by the same imagery rehearsal done under quiet conditions or even with other forms of relaxation. Many elite athletes appear to find the flotation environment subjectively conducive to the conduct of imagery sessions. Although elite performers often practice flotation, frequently in combination with video modeling, the need exists for further research that examines how flotation facilitates imagery. Research that distinguishes between the independent effect of flotation on performance and its effect on imagery that leads to enhanced performance would also be desirable. Careful study of expectancy effects might be a fruitful direction here. In chapter 8, we stressed the importance of belief (or expectancy) in the effective application of imagery. The impressive technical look of a flotation laboratory could have a powerful expectancy effect that might overshadow imagery, especially if research designs in flotation studies do not make an effort to emphasize the efficacy of imagery.

Study of the relative effectiveness, as a technical aid to imagery, of flotation alone and flotation in combination with video modeling or biofeedback would also be of value. The cost effectiveness of flotation is hard to assess; flotation facilities are relatively expensive and difficult to maintain. At the same time, research and anecdotal evidence support the benefits of flotation as an aid to imagery, above and beyond other relaxation or sensory-restriction techniques. Research comparing flotation as the sole adjunct to imagery to flotation combined with video modeling or biofeedback (or both video modeling and biofeedback) would be of great interest. Each technical aid may have a benefit, but combining them may not simply add those benefits together. For example, if different technical aids use the same mechanism to facilitate imagery, when they are used simultaneously only one of them would be able to access the mechanism. Another potential research issue is the level of sport expertise in relation to the benefit of technical aids. Finally, the athlete's familiarity and competence with the technical aid might influence the outcome of its use with imagery rehearsal.

Conclusions

The limited research evidence available to date, along with a substantial body of anecdotal reports, suggests that in some circumstances the use of video modeling, biofeedback, and flotation can increase the potential of imagery in sport. Clearly, we do not understand the mechanisms by which these technical aids facilitate imagery. Thus, there is great scope for further research to clarify how and under what conditions video modeling, biofeedback, and flotation have their optimal impact on the imagery-performance and imagery-psychological-process relationships.

One issue that needs to be examined is the extent to which the effects of the technical aids described in this chapter transfer to competition conditions. Much of the research and training has been conducted in sports institutes and laboratories, and since most of the equipment is not easily transportable, athletes must manage without the technical aids at the competition site. So do the effects transfer or could they lead to dependence, so that the athlete founders when they are removed?

We maintain that the quest for greater understanding of the role that technical aids play in imagery processes will lead to greater insight into those processes. At the same time, the practice of sport psychology benefits from a greater understanding of the most effective ways to employ video modeling, biofeedback, and flotation. Practitioners aim to employ technical aids as effectively as they can, and little doubt exists that many athletes are attracted to approaches that involve new technology. Practitioners must use video modeling, biofeedback, and flotation cautiously. We trust that this chapter has increased applied sport psychologists' understanding of the technical aids to imagery so that they can employ them appropriately.

CHAPTER 11

Injury Rehabilitation and Imagery

with Michelle Walsh, Victoria University, Melbourne, Australia

Injury in sport is one of the most significant obstacles to achieving peak athletic potential. For recreational and elite athletes alike, the risk of sustaining an injury can be a real and ongoing threat. As a result of rigorous training and competitions, immense physical effort, and intense emotional feelings invested in success, many athletes experience injuries that keep them away from their sport for periods of time.

Fortunately, with the aid of continually advancing surgical and rehabilitative technology, the majority of athletes may reasonably assume to make a full physical recovery and, in most cases, return to their sport. Some athletes, however, despite the potential to return to their peak physical ability in fitness, strength, stability, and flexibility, do not regain preinjury performance levels (Taylor and Taylor 1997). In recent years the sports medicine community has become increasingly aware of the key psychological and social factors involved in the rehabilitation of sport injuries, as evidenced by the increasing number of studies relating to this topic. (For a comprehensive review of the literature, see Brewer [2001] and Petrie and Perna [2004].)

For many athletes (recreational and elite), the injury and the accompanying rehabilitation process can be stressful, painful, and worrisome (e.g., Kolt 2000). The extent to which physical injury affects athletes' lives depends on a number of factors, including the nature and severity of the injury, the importance of sport to the athlete, and the reaction of the athlete's support network to the injury (Petipas and Danish 1995). For athletes who derive significant amounts of self-worth and personal competence from their sport and their ability to perform, an injury and the subsequent rehabilitation process could prove to be emotionally devastating (Petipas and Danish 1995).

According to Heil (1993), injury can exert a direct influence on an athlete's psychological well-being, which can, in turn, affect the athlete's health and future athletic performance, as well as increasing the risk of further injury. Therefore, athletes, sport psychologists, coaches, and other personal and medical staff who work with sports performers must address psychological issues that may arise due to the injury or rehabilitation process, in addition to attending to the physical care of the athlete (Heil 1993; Kolt 2000; Russell 2000). For further discussion of the integration of the physical and psychological care of athletes in sports-medicine settings, refer to Shaffer and Wiese-Bjornstal (1999) and Wiese-Bjornstal, Gardetto, and Shaffer (1999).

ROLE OF IMAGERY IN REHABILITATION

Imagery is one of a number of psychological interventions aimed at enhancing the psychological well-being of injured athletes and facilitating their physical rehabilitation. Rehabilitation imagery has the potential to address the diverse concerns and challenges that injured athletes experience during rehabilitation (Green 1999; Taylor and Taylor 1997). Table 11.1 illustrates the primary uses of imagery for rehabilitation in sport. Research has supported the effectiveness of those uses, including reinjury anxiety reduction (Cupal and Brewer 2001), pain management (Sthalekar 1993), and preparation of athletes for their return to sport (Johnson 2000). Imagery can aid the recovery of the injured body part and enhance the rehabilitation process (Jones and Stuth 1997). Imagery uses in rehabilitation can be categorized into four groups: healing, pain-management, rehabilitation-process, and performance imagery. This chapter discusses each type of imagery.

Despite the potential benefits of rehabilitation imagery, it is generally underused in the sports community, primarily due to a lack of understanding of its uses and applications by athletes and rehabilitation professionals. This notion is evidenced in two studies. In a study of athletic trainers, Wiese, Weiss, and Yukelson (1991) found that although imagery was considered a useful psychological intervention in the rehabilitation process, its use as a healing technique was not as highly regarded as other psychological techniques. Wiese et al. concluded that the apprehension about using imagery as a healing technique in rehabilitation was associated with a lack of knowledge about how imagery can aid physical recovery, as well as uncertainty regarding its correct use. Due to the

Table 11.1 Uses of Imagery for Injury Rehabilitation in Sport

Imagery use	Imagery process	Other outcomes
Healing process	Imagery of physical healing process speeds up that process (e.g., flow of fresh, warm blood to injured tissue)	Confidence in rehabilitation process Stress reduction Attention distraction–pain management
Pain management • pleasant imaginings • pain acknowledgement • dramatized coping	Imagery helps person to cope with pain of injury • imagery of pleasant scene distracts • imagery of pain reducing (e.g., color, size) • imagery of self handling pain—provides motivation	Confidence in imagery for rehabilitation Stress reduction Attention distraction–pain management
Process of rehabilitation	Imagery of activities in rehabilitation helps person to anticipate them so they can cope with them as required	Confidence in rehabilitation Stress reduction Attention distraction–pain management
Performance imagery • practice while injured • confidence in injured area on return	Imagery of self performing skills of sport • maintains skills, routines, components • imagery of maximum performance with injured part functioning perfectly	Stress reduction Confidence in outcome of rehabilitation Attention distraction–pain management

Based on Cupal and Brewer 2001, Sthalekar 1993, Johnson 2000, and Jones and Smith 1997.

lack of recent research on this topic (a relevant and important area for further study), whether or not these perceptions are still held by athletic trainers today is unknown.

Brewer, Jeffers, Petipas, and Van Raalte (1994) assessed perceptions of three types of psychological interventions: goal setting, imagery, and counseling. In one study, undergraduate students rated their perceptions of the psychological interventions as applied to a hypothetical athlete; in a second study, injured athletes rated their perceptions of brief introductory sessions of goal setting, imagery, and counseling. Both studies revealed that athletes preferred goal setting, although positive perceptions were obtained for imagery as an intervention. Brewer et al. attributed the lesser support for imagery compared to other psychological interventions to the lack of rapport between the psychologist who delivered the intervention and the participants, an aspect considered essential to the delivery of effective imagery services (Simons 2000). The findings of Brewer et al. and Wiese et al. (1991) indicate that educating athletes and health professionals involved in the rehabilitation process about the "how" and "why" of imagery techniques is important (Green 1999).

USE OF IMAGERY IN REHABILITATION

As mentioned previously, rehabilitation imagery can be divided into four types: healing, pain management, rehabilitation process, and performance. Healing imagery involves visualizing and feeling the injured body part healing. Pain-management imagery helps the athlete cope with pain associated with the injury, by focusing attention either on or away from the pain. Rehabilitation-process imagery can help athletes deal with challenges, such as adhering to treatment programs, staying positive and focused, and dealing with setbacks. And finally, performance imagery involves athletes in mentally practicing physical skills and visualizing themselves performing successfully and injury free. In the following section, we discuss these types of imagery and the relevant research that investigates their uses and effects.

HEALING IMAGERY

Athletes can use healing imagery to envision the internal processes and anatomical healing that occur during rehabilitation. Numerous researchers and practitioners (e.g., Price and Andersen 2000; Taylor and Taylor 1997) have suggested that in order for healing imagery to be effective, injured athletes must form a clear, accurate mental image of the injured area. It has also been proposed that athletes need to have a sound understanding of the injured anatomical structures, the healing process, the treatment modalities used during rehabilitation, and the eventual appearance of the healed injury (Taylor and Taylor 1997; Williams, Rotella, and Scherzer 2001). Colored illustrations, X rays, and descriptions of the healing process in language that athletes will understand can assist them in developing a clear mental image (Heil 1993).

As an addition to the imagery process, Heil (1993) suggested using "personalized or fantasy-based" images to aid healing. For example, he recommended that each treatment technique and the rehabilitation process as a whole be given a vivid, positive image, such as ultrasound creating a healing glow, ice shutting down pain receptors, and resistance training causing blood to surge to the muscles and aid in the rebuilding process. Heil also proposed that athletes should develop images of the healed area that are positive and meaningful, such as a back injury being represented as the tendons, ligaments, and muscles supporting the spinal column, like the rigging of a sailing ship. Importance is placed on the athletes forming images that are positive, strong, and meaningful to them (Heil 1993) and that symbolize their bodily resources as effective and powerful (Ievleva and Orlick 1991).

In order for these detailed images to be effective, some form of relaxation response is essential. This enhances the receptivity of the mind and reduces any unnecessary muscular contractions that might hinder the healing imagery process (Ievleva and Orlick 1999; Russell 2000). Progressive muscle relaxation or autogenics can achieve the desired relaxation level needed for healing imagery to be most effective. (See Price and Andersen [2000] for a detailed script of healing imagery that includes eliciting the relaxation response.)

In an attempt to evaluate athletes' use of healing imagery in rehabilitation, Sordoni, Hall, and Forwell (2002) conducted a study using their revised questionnaire, the Athletic Injury Imagery Questionnaire-2 (AIIQ-2). Preliminary evidence from Sordoni, Hall, and Forwell (2000) suggested that athletes use both motivational imagery (i.e., imagining a specific goal and the general feeling of arousal and affect associated with performing) and cognitive imagery (i.e., imagining specific skills and general strategies of play) during rehabilitation from injury. However, even after this initial study, little was known about the use of healing imagery in rehabilitation. Based on their previous study and other research, Sordoni et al. (2002) predicted that athletes would use more motivational and cognitive imagery than healing imagery in rehabilitation. They believed that athletes would be less familiar with the use of healing imagery as a rehabilitation technique. Contrary to their hypothesis, Sordoni et al. found that injured athletes reported using healing imagery as much as motivational and cognitive imagery. This was a positive finding, indicating that athletes may be more aware and have a greater understanding of the potential benefits of healing imagery than was previously assumed.

Although no firm evidence shows that imagery has a definable physiological effect on healing, extensive support for its effectiveness in the rehabilitation process comes from research, reviews, and anecdotal evidence (Taylor and Taylor 1997). For example, Green (1999) cited numerous studies that support the use of imagery in producing physiological responses, such as increasing heart rate (HR), producing changes in skin temperature and muscle activity, and even enhancing immune systems in cancer patients. In addition, Surgent (1991) offered support for the mind–body connection that facilitates the healing process:

> Your immune system doesn't work alone . . . your mind also has a voice in what goes on. Feelings, attitudes, and beliefs are organized in your brain and communicated to your immune system by chemical messages. These can have an effect on the healing process, which can be either positive or negative. (p. 4-5)

Very few studies have investigated the specific effects of using healing imagery in the rehabilitation of athletic injuries. Ievleva and Orlick (1991), however, were among the first researchers to conduct a controlled investigation into the relationships between psychological factors (including attitude and outlook, belief, stress control, social support, goal setting, positive self-talk, and mental imagery) and physical recovery rates among injured athletes. Thirty-two former sports-medicine clinic patients with previous knee or ankle injuries participated in this retrospective study by completing the Sports Injury Survey (SIS; designed by Ievleva and Orlick, 1991). In examining the results relating to imagery, it was found that athletes used three types: healing imagery (in which athletes saw and felt the body parts healing), treatment imagery (in which athletes imagined the treatment promoting recovery), and total-recovery imagery (in which athletes imagined themselves being fully recovered). The participants reported that all three types of imagery were helpful, but the healing imagery demonstrated the strongest relationship to recovery time. Although retrospective studies have inherent problems, Ievleva and Orlick (1991) provided the most convincing evidence to date for the link between healing imagery and improved recovery for injured athletes.

Perhaps more important than whether imagery facilitates physical healing is its effect on the athlete's psychological well-being (e.g., motivation, confidence, anxiety reduction, pain management, and adherence to the rehabilitation process). If an injured athlete who practices imagery feels more relaxed, confident in the injured body part, and motivated to adhere to the rehabilitation plan, then the technique must be considered appropriate and useful (Heil 1993). In support of this claim, Sordoni et al. (2002) found that the use of healing imagery was significantly related to self-efficacy. They concluded that the more healing imagery injured athletes use, the higher their self-efficacy and belief in their capabilities with respect to rehabilitation.

PAIN-MANAGEMENT IMAGERY

Pain is the most common and compelling aspect of rehabilitation, and therefore, according to Heil (1993), should be addressed on the "psychological agenda" of rehabilitation. Pain-management imagery is effective in reducing pain. Fernandez and Turk (1986, cited in Heil 1993) identified six pain-management techniques involving imagery that have been demonstrated to be effective: external focus, neutral imagining, rhythmic cognitive activity, pleasant imagining, pain acknowledgement, and dramatized coping. The latter three are most relevant to this chapter.

Pleasant imaginings involve individuals picturing and feeling themselves in a relaxing and comfortable setting, such as lying on a beach or spending time with a loved one (Fernandez and Turk 1986, cited in Heil 1993). This type of dissociative imagery reduces sympathetic nervous system activity and muscle tension, which can decrease the delivery of pain impulses and have a calming effect (Heil 1993). This strategy is beneficial early in the rehabilitation process. Taylor and Taylor (1997) proposed that athletes identify a couple of relaxing scenes that allow them to develop multisensory images (including sounds, smells, and feelings) with pleasant associations.

With pain acknowledgement, the individual assigns the pain physical properties, such as size, shape, color, and movement (Fernandez and Turk 1986, cited in Heil 1993). Defining what the pain looks, sounds, and feels like creates an image that can be changed to bring relief. For example, a sharp stabbing pain in the knee may be imagined as being caused by a sharp knife. Imagining that the knife becomes duller with each cut may decrease the intensity of stabbing pain. The metal of the knife may be imaged as changing to a soft plastic until the pain is perceived as a slow, dull throb (O'Connor 2003). Imagining the pain physically leaving the body (for example, seeing the pain being washed away by a rush of water or cool colors soothing and reducing inflammation) can also reduce the discomfort caused by the injury (Ievleva and Orlick 1999).

Dramatized coping involves viewing the pain as part of the challenge of achieving goals and aspiring to personal excellence, which changes the context of the pain (Fernandez and Turk 1986, cited in Heil 1993). It can reframe the pain of rehabilitation as a motivational tool that can help athletes overcome difficulties and setbacks involved in the rehabilitation process (Taylor and Taylor 1997).

Pain-management techniques can be categorized as associative (focused on pain) or dissociative (focused away from pain). Pleasant imaging is a dissociative strategy, and pain acknowledging and dramatized coping are associative strategies. Dissociative strategies tend to be used more often because of their diversity and because they are easier to learn (Heil 1993) and tend to be more effective than associative strategies (Fernandez and Turk 1986; cited in Heil 1993). They are not always, however, the safest strategy to use. Pain can be a useful gauge of the limits of rehabilitation exercises, and if athletes move past these limitations by using dissociative strategies, additional damage may be caused (Taylor and Taylor 1997). These types of strategies, therefore, need to be carefully monitored by an expert. Associative strategies are very useful in rehabilitation. They can reduce pain but also use it to provide information about physical limits. These strategies can also be employed to give injured athletes a sense of control over their pain and rehabilitation, which is an important aspect of the rehabilitation process (Heil 1993).

Research on the effectiveness of pain-management imagery is scarce. The research reported in this chapter refers to studies that have used imagery with the primary intent of reducing pain. Not all of them, therefore, have specifically used pain-management imagery as described here.

In one study that attempted to reduce pain, Sthalekar (1993) provided imagery and hypnotic relaxation to a partially paralyzed water skier who was injured during a waterskiing accident. The athlete was experiencing severe, chronic phantom pain in the limb that had complete loss of function and sensation. After an 8-week hypnotherapy program, including mental imagery, relaxation, and positive suggestions, the athlete reported experiencing less pain and was able to resume some of his preaccident activities. Another researcher, Nicol (1993), also used a case study design, investigating the effects of hypnotic relaxation, mental imagery, and counseling on a person with repetitive strain injury. Following the psychological intervention, the participant reported reduced pain and inflammation, returned to work, and said she felt happier and more in control of her life.

In these two studies (and others reported in this chapter), ascertaining whether the psychological intervention's outcome (e.g., pain reduction) was a direct result of the imagery is difficult due to the absence of a control group. Stating that athletes who received a psychological intervention experienced less pain than they would have without the intervention is not definitive. In addition, because imagery is usually coupled with relaxation, positive self-talk, or other psychological interventions, differentiating the effects of imagery itself is difficult. Further investigations, using control groups, need to determine the effects of mental imagery (as a primary intervention) on psychological well-being and rehabilitation. Such studies, in which researchers believe that an intervention can prevent or reduce pain but withhold it from some participants, would have ethical implications. Nonetheless, studies that include control groups provide the strongest evidence for treatment efficacy.

Cupal and Brewer (2001) conducted a study that was strengthened by the inclusion of placebo and traditional control conditions, to control for the nonspecific effects of the treatment, such as attention and support. They examined the effects of relaxation and guided imagery on the rehabilitation process of 30 athletes (ranging from recreational to competitive levels), following an anterior cruciate ligament (ACL) reconstruction. Ten relaxation and guided-imagery sessions were administered to each participant in the treatment condition, with the content of sessions varying over the course of the intervention according to the physical-recovery goal. Support, encouragement, and attention were provided to the placebo-condition participants, and the control group received no intervention. Cupal and Brewer found that the treatment-condition participants, at 24 weeks postsurgery, experienced significantly less pain (measured by a subjective pain-experience rating by the participants) than those in both the placebo and control conditions. The imagery was, therefore, considered effective in facilitating recovery following ACL reconstruction. Further research of this type, conducted on a wider group of athletes and injuries, is warranted, because this study's results can be generalized only to the population of patients from a predominantly white, middle-class background who undergo ACL reconstruction.

In summary, although research on pain-management imagery in rehabilitation from a sport injury is limited, the findings of reduced pain following such treatments in studies such as those by Cupal and Brewer (2001), Nicol (1993), and Sthalekar (1993) support the effectiveness of this type of imagery. The wide variety of imagery strategies that can be used to reduce pain should encourage athletes, coaches, and sport and medical personnel to incorporate some form of pain-management imagery into the rehabilitation process.

REHABILITATION-PROCESS IMAGERY

Imagery can help athletes anticipate and deal with the challenges of the rehabilitation process and increase their belief in their ability to succeed in rehabilitation (self-efficacy). It can be used early in the rehabilitation process if psychological-adjustment problems surface or in anticipation of a particularly challenging aspect of rehabilitation. Likewise, this type of imagery can be used later in the process in response to specific problems (Heil 1993). Athletes can image many aspects of the rehabilitation process, such as completing set exercises, adhering to the program, overcoming obstacles and setbacks, and staying positive and focused, in order to potentially speed up the recovery time (Heil 1993; Ievleva and Orlick 1991; Jones and Stuth 1997; Ross and Berger 1996; Wiese et al. 1991).

Heil (1993) described two approaches to coping: mastery and coping imagery. In the mastery approach, rehabilitative events are rehearsed with favorable outcomes and without setbacks, demonstrating high levels of self-efficacy for rehabilitation. For example, an athlete recovering from a major knee operation may construct a mastery-rehearsal scenario that focuses on key transitions that will occur during rehabilitation: leaving the hospital, beginning the rehabilitation program, removing immobilization devices, becoming involved in team training sessions, returning to limited and full training, experiencing a high-risk reinjury situation, and returning to competition (Heil 1993). Athletes typically image these scenarios while feeling relaxed and confident. The mastery approach builds the athlete's motivation and confidence in the rehabilitation process and fosters a sense of control (Heil 1993; Russell 2000).

A coping style of imagery can be used to address any problem that occurs during rehabilitation. Anticipated or actual problems are introduced into the rehearsal scenario, and the athlete uses coping skills such as positive self-talk or refocusing of attention to create a positive outcome (Heil 1993). Heil cited the example of an athlete who had been involved in a rehabilitation regimen for several weeks and was experiencing recurring stressful events: feelings of weakness and inadequacy due to a lack of independence; anger, boredom, and impatience with the rehabilitation process; and frustration with the frequent setbacks. The coping rehearsal should be preceded and followed by a relaxation procedure, such as autogenics or progressive muscle relaxation (PMR), and may include rehearsal of the coping mechanisms being implemented in the stressful situations. Heil suggested that coping-style imagery enables the athlete to practice specific coping skills as well as build confidence.

Research on the effectiveness of rehabilitation-process imagery is extremely limited and has primarily focused on using imagery to aid adherence to the rehabilitation process. In a study of athletic trainers, Wiese et al. (1991) found that the athletes' willingness to listen to their trainers' advice, their ability to maintain a positive attitude, and intrinsic motivation were key factors in successful rehabilitation. Green (1999) proposed that rehabilitation programs should initially include imaging the behaviors associated with these factors. Once this has been done, athletes are encouraged to apply the behaviors to their rehabilitation program. Imaging the behaviors that are important to a successful rehabilitation may, therefore, enhance athletes' adherence to a rehabilitation program.

Scherzer et al. (2001) examined the relationship between psychological skills and adherence to a rehabilitation program in 54 patients undergoing rehabilitation after an ACL reconstruction. An abbreviated version of the Sports Injury Survey (SIS; Ievleva and Orlick 1991) was administered approximately five weeks after surgery to assess the participants' use of goal setting, imagery, and positive self-talk. Four adherence measures were also obtained during the remainder of the rehabilitation program. Self-reported use of healing imagery was not associated with any of the adherence measures. Scherzer et al. suggested that the favorable impact of imagery on sport-injury rehabilitation outcomes occurred independent of adherence to the rehabilitation program. They also noted the study's limitations, including the problems associated with using a survey that included a single-item scale for imagery. Reliance on one item to determine athletes' use of imagery is less than optimal and places the internal consistency and reliability of research measures at risk. Further studies, therefore, need to use a standardized instrument that includes multiple-item scales. Due to the limitations of this study and the lack of other related research, firm conclusions about the effects of imagery on rehabilitation adherence cannot be drawn.

Ievleva and Orlick (1991) investigated the importance of focusing on positive images during the rehabilitation process. In their retrospective study of previously injured athletes, they found that healing and performance imagery were related to a faster recovery time only when the athlete did not report extensive injury-replay imagery. Injury-replay imagery is the continual reenvisioning of the injury experience and the pain and negative feelings associated with it. Likewise, Foster and Porter (1987, cited in Ievleva and Orlick 1999) reported case studies with athletes in which negative images (i.e., of the injury, tearing, breaking) interfered with positive imagery of healing and recovery and, therefore, impeded recovery. Green (1999) also proposed that focusing on positive images that promote an optimistic and relaxed attitude is crucial to the recovery process.

Although the research literature is inconclusive, athletes do appear to benefit from some form of rehabilitation imagery (e.g., focusing on adherence, experiencing a positive outcome, staying motivated during the rehabilitation process). Adopting such techniques could potentially speed up the recovery process. In addition, athletes are advised to include positive images of recovery from their injury and to avoid engaging in negative injury-replay imagery.

Performance Imagery

Many athletes consider rehabilitation from injury as forced downtime from their sport, a time in which all of their energy is directed toward healing the physical injury (Taylor and Taylor 1997). The rehabilitation process can, however, allow athletes to further develop their sport-related skills. Performance imagery can enable them to work on aspects of their sport performance, such as technique, tactics, and mental preparation (Heil 1993). Based on the literature to date, imagery can focus on various aspects of performance and serve two main purposes: creating confidence in athletes about returning to sport (by seeing themselves performing successfully and injury free) and reducing stress and facilitating rehabilitation (by engaging in tasks that take their minds off the injury, e.g., mentally practicing physical skills).

Taylor and Taylor (1997) suggested that for injured athletes to gain the most benefit from performance imagery, they must develop training and competition scenarios, including technical, tactical, psychological, and competitive situations, to follow during the imagery sessions. They also proposed developing a hierarchy of the training and competition scenarios so that the least demanding situations are imaged early in the rehabilitation program and imagery of the more demanding and high-level competition situations are included toward the end of rehabilitation. Ievleva and Orlick (1999) suggested that performance imagery should include positive, successful images of rehabilitation, competition, and training. Injured athletes could identify critical areas that might affect their return to sport and address them in imagery sessions, such as developing confidence in the injured body part and minimizing anxiety about reinjury (Ievleva and Orlick 1999; Taylor and Taylor 1997). By using successful performance imagery at different stages of the rehabilitation process, athletes can strengthen confidence in their ability to perform at their desired level, increase their motivation, and reduce the anxiety often associated with returning to sport (Taylor and Taylor 1997).

Performance imagery can be a powerful tool that helps athletes maintain skill level. Because injured athletes are unable to practice physically, mental rehearsal of skills and tactics becomes even more important (Ievleva and Orlick 1999). With the aid of imagery, injured athletes can maintain a performance-oriented mind-set and focus attention on rehabilitation and the process of returning to sport (Heil 1993). Green (1999) and Korn (1994) proposed that performance imagery can also facilitate closure of the rehabilitation process and injury experience once the athlete has returned to sport.

A wealth of knowledge demonstrates the value of performance imagery in enhancing numerous aspects of sports performance. Research has indicated that performance imagery improves technique, tactics, mental preparation, skill development, and competitive performance in the absence of actual physical practice. For reviews of the uses of performance-enhancement imagery, refer to Hall (2001), Jones and Stuth (1997), Murphy and Martin (2002), Morris, Spittle, and Perry (2004), and other chapters in this book, particularly in part 2.

In injury rehabilitation, imagery research tends to focus on varying aspects of returning to sport and performance, such as reducing anxiety (Cupal and Brewer 2001; Ross and Berger 1996), increasing confidence and readiness for competition (Evans, Hardy, and Fleming 2000; Johnson 2000) and increasing mood and self-esteem (Johnson 2000; Nicol 1993; Sthalekar 1993). At times, the research does not indicate the specific type of imagery used (e.g., performance or rehabilitation imagery); however, for our purposes we will assume that the primary outcome of the imagery was based on the sport performance (or return to performance) of the athlete.

As mentioned previously, the psychological effects of injury for some athletes can be emotionally devastating, particularly for those who derive significant amounts of self-worth and personal competence from their sport and their ability to perform (Heil 1993; Petipas and Danish 1995). Mood, self-esteem, and confidence can often be negatively altered by an injury and a problematic rehabilitation process (Petipas and Danish 1995).

Johnson (2000) explored the effectiveness of psychological interventions, using an outcome measure of mood, for a sample of competitive athletes with long-term injuries. Every 4th athlete in the sample of 58 participants was assigned to the treatment condition ($n = 14$) and the other participants formed the control condition ($n = 44$). Participants in the treatment condition received traditional sports-medicine physiotherapy, in addition to one session of each of the following interventions: stress management, goal setting, and relaxation and guided imagery. The guided imagery included aspects of healing and performance-based imagery (focusing on performing desired activities well and imagining their bodies functioning perfectly). Participants in the control condition received only physiotherapy. Johnson (2000) reported that the athletes in the treatment condition (according to ratings by the athletes themselves and the treating physiotherapists) had a higher overall mood level at the midpoint and end of rehabilitation and felt more ready for competition than those in the control condition. The only strategy to show any statistical significance, however, was guided imagery.

Two case studies involving an intervention of hypnotherapy and imagery support these findings. Nicol (1993) and Sthalekar (1993) found that these interventions improved mood, self-esteem, and general outlook on life, in addition to decreasing pain. A limitation of the Nicol and Sthalekar studies, however, is the fact that a standardized tool was not used to determine mood level; instead, the researcher assessed that mood and self-esteem had moved in a positive direction following the intervention.

Athletes' confidence in the injured body part and their ability to return to full sport participation are vital components of psychological rehabilitation. Successes during the rehabilitation process can improve confidence, yet setbacks and difficulties can hurt confidence and impede progress toward the goal of returning to sport (Taylor and Taylor 1997). Johnson (2000) reported that those athletes who received the intervention program rated themselves (and were rated by their physiotherapists) as being more ready to compete than those in the control condition. Evans et al. (2000) conducted an action research intervention study with three injured athletes. The participants reported that confidence in the injured body part and an ability to meet game demands were important to successful return to competition. Imagery designed to increase confidence was, therefore, introduced into the intervention program, with successful results. The research examined indicates a likelihood that confidence is important to a successful return to sport and that performance imagery used to promote and enhance confidence is beneficial.

In addition to decreasing mood, self-esteem, and confidence, physical injuries can lead to an increase in anxiety levels (Heil 1993; Taylor and Taylor 1997). Fear of reinjury can be the most significant form of distress that injured athletes experience, and it can be a real threat to their confidence and focus after their return to sport (Heil 1993). Cupal and Brewer (2001), in their imagery intervention study with athletes undergoing ACL reconstruction rehabilitation, found that reinjury anxiety was significantly reduced in those athletes who received the guided imagery sessions. Cupal and Brewer (2001) suggested that the reductions in pain and reinjury anxiety may have enabled the athletes to relax, be more motivated, and engage more fully in the rehabilitation program. Although further research is required to substantiate these findings, it appears that one benefit of imagery in rehabilitation (such as reducing reinjury anxiety) may be causally related to another benefit (such as increasing motivation for the rehabilitation process).

In a similar type of study, Ross and Berger (1996) implemented a cognitive–behavioral intervention of stress inoculation training (SIT), including relaxation, positive coping and self-reinforcement statements, and imagery, to 60 male athletes who had undergone arthroscopic knee surgery. The State-Trait Anxiety Inventory (STAI; Spielberger, Gorsuch, and Lushene 1970) was used to assess anxiety, and athletes indicated their current level of pain intensity on a visual analogue scale. Participants were randomly assigned to either the treatment condition (consisting of the SIT and physical therapy) or the control condition (physical therapy only). Compared to the control group, the SIT group reported significantly reduced anxiety and postsurgical pain and required less time to return to physical functioning. Ross and Berger also proposed that the relationship between psychological intervention and cooperation with (and adherence to) a rehabilitation program warrants further research.

In summary, a great deal more research has been done on performance imagery than on the other types of rehabilitation imagery. Performance imagery has been shown to reduce rehabilitation and reinjury anxiety, increase confidence about performance, positively affect mood and self-esteem, and potentially decrease recovery time. Although no firm conclusions can be drawn, current evidence from research and practitioners suggests likely benefits from implementing performance imagery in athletes' rehabilitation programs. The associated benefits of imagery indicate, at the least, the usefulness of this psychological intervention in rehabilitation from injury, and more likely, its potential strength in improving the psychological well-being of injured athletes, enabling them to return to their sport and achieve athletic and personal success.

IMPLICATIONS FOR PRACTICE

By providing information on the uses and applications of imagery in injury rehabilitation and highlighting its potential benefits, we hope to encourage practitioners, coaches, and athletes to include imagery in rehabilitation programs and discover how it can improve psychological and physical well-being and possibly contribute to a quicker rehabilitation process and return to sport.

Although research and anecdotal evidence has supported imagery use in rehabilitation, athletes still tend to use it less frequently when injured than when they are competing and training (Sordoni, Hall, and Forwell 2000; Sordoni et al. 2002). A possible explanation for this could be the limited research and information on this type of imagery (compared to competition imagery), and the uncertainty associated with using it in rehabilitation. Sordoni and colleagues (2000) proposed that athletes' use of rehabilitation imagery (specifically, imaging rehabilitation skills) could be limited for a number of reasons. It might be that the prescribed exercises are not difficult enough to warrant the use of such imagery, or that athletes might not perceive the rehabilitation exercises as "skills" in the same way they perceive athletic skills. Further research is needed to investigate why athletes do not use imagery more extensively in rehabilitation. The roles of practitioners, support and medical staff, and coaches are therefore crucial in supporting the use of rehabilitation imagery and encouraging athletes to play an active role in the rehabilitation process.

Although imagery in rehabilitation can have specific uses and benefits, athletes are encouraged to incorporate imagery according to their individual needs, abilities, goals, and personal styles. Each person should determine exactly what should be imaged in order for it to be meaningful and most effective. An important feature of rehabilitation imagery is that the athletes imagine their own bodies as resourceful, powerful, and successful in achieving their desired goals (Ievleva and Orlick 1999). Practitioners, coaches, and sport and medical personnel can help athletes develop an individualized imagery program that addresses their rehabilitation and performance goals. (See chapter 8 for strategies for developing imagery programs.)

One important consideration in using imagery in rehabilitation from sport injuries is timing. Figure 11.1 illustrates how certain types of imagery may be more appropriate than others at times during the rehabilitation process (Ievleva and Orlick 1999). For example, immediately following a sport injury, focusing on stress-management techniques, such as relaxation and pain-management imagery, may be advisable before commencing with healing imagery (Taylor and Taylor 1997). Dissociative pain-management techniques (i.e., those that focus attention away from pain) can be effective early in the rehabilitation process, when the athlete is coping with pain. Dissociative techniques are also believed to be easier to learn for people who have no previous experience with using psychological techniques (Heil 1993). Associative pain-management techniques (i.e., those that focus on the pain) may be more appropriate in the active stages of rehabilitation (such as during physiotherapy) to ensure that the injury is not exacerbated and to enable the athletes to read their bodies and be aware of changes in pain. Once athletes have sufficient knowledge about the injury and rehabilitation process, using healing and rehabilitation imagery can be an effective way to improve their psychological well-being and speed up the recovery process. Per-

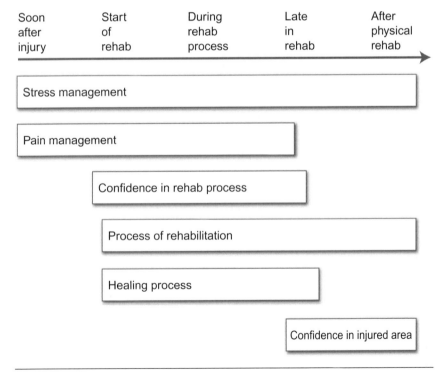

Figure 11.1 Use of imagery at different stages in the rehabilitation process.

formance imagery is most appropriate once enough healing has taken place that the athletes feel comfortable imaging a successful return to performance (Ievleva and Orlick 1999).

Cupal and Brewer (2001) implemented an imagery intervention over a 6-month recovery period with athletes who had injured their ACL. Every two weeks, the imagery content was adjusted to follow the rehabilitation process of the athletes. For example, the first few sessions focused on pain management, acceptance of the injury, and healing imagery. The last couple of sessions involved imagery that emphasized the athletes acquiring strength and endurance in the injured body part, increasing confidence in the replaced ligament, and imaging themselves performing successfully and at their peak. The timing and organization of an imagery intervention in rehabilitation, therefore, requires consideration and planning to optimize the program's effectiveness.

CONCLUSIONS

Due to the limited number of studies conducted on the uses and effectiveness of imagery in rehabilitation, the scope for further research is substantial. This chapter makes suggestions about areas that require further development and highlights the need for replication of certain studies in order to generalize findings to other sports injuries and athletes. In general terms, future research needs to include larger sample sizes to address the issues of validity and generalizability. Studies should also include control or placebo groups, or both (similar to Cupal and Brewer 2001), homogenous populations, and randomization to control for extraneous variables that can affect treatment (Cupal 1998).

Specifically, more intervention studies are needed to determine the effectiveness of the different uses of imagery. The majority of research does not separate the outcomes and benefits of specific types of imagery (e.g., healing or rehabilitation imagery), and, therefore, determining the effects of one particular type is difficult. In fact, a large proportion of the current research does not separate imagery interventions from other types of psychological interventions, such as self-talk and goal setting. Ross and Berger (1996) stated that further research is needed to investigate the relative contributions of the various components of SIT in achieving positive outcomes. Although imagery-intervention studies are often coupled with relaxation or positive self-talk, researchers should aim to focus on imagery as the primary intervention.

More research is also required to expand on the applications of imagery in rehabilitation. Many researchers and practitioners claim that imagery "should" be done in a certain manner, yet no research evidence supports the proposed ideas. For example, the literature often suggests that in order for healing imagery to be effective, the imager needs to have an accurate vision of the physiological and anatomical structures involved in the healing process. Current research, however, has not proven this contention to be true. It may be that rather than the physiological and anatomical accuracy of the image, the person's belief that the image is accurate is the important factor in successful healing imagery. These ideas and others surrounding imagery's applications and uses in rehabilitation require further development in order to expand our current knowledge and understanding of a potentially powerful, effective psychological intervention.

Rehabilitation from sport injury is an area with great potential for imagery interventions. As mentioned, imagery has numerous uses immediately following an injury, during the rehabilitation process, and in preparation for a return to sport. Practitioners need to make their own judgments about which imagery techniques are ethical and appropriate to use with particular athletes during the rehabilitation process. The limited research conducted to date shows that the effects of imagery in rehabilitation are largely positive. Future research opportunities in this area are plentiful, due to the many aspects of imagery in rehabilitation that are not well understood, particularly concerning the benefits and applications of its specific uses. Based on appropriate future research, the practical benefits could prove substantial and ensure that athletes give themselves the best chance at a successful rehabilitation process and a quick return to sport.

PART IV

ADVANCING IMAGERY IN SPORT

Part IV addresses the future. In chapter 12 we describe some exciting new research that applies our knowledge of imagery in sport to the related area of exercise. Michelle Walsh again offers her skills to this chapter. In chapter 13 we draw conclusions about the status of imagery in sport and exercise and its potential for development, and we consider future directions for imagery research in sport and exercise and how to apply those results. We make some bold statements about issues, related to weaknesses in previous research, priorities for research in the future, assumptions currently held in practice, and possible new directions for the application of imagery in sport. We end by revisiting the achievements of this field and recognizing the many challenges still to come.

CHAPTER 12

EXERCISE AND IMAGERY

WITH MICHELLE WALSH (VICTORIA UNIVERSITY)

The first 11 chapters of this book cover the major aspects of sport-related imagery and its theory, research, and application. Imagery can facilitate many processes related to behavior in sport, including setting goals, increasing motivation, building confidence, learning skills, managing anxiety, physically and mentally preparing for performance, learning and practicing strategies, detecting errors, solving problems, and rehabilitating from injury. However, only recently have experts in the study and practice of sport-related imagery proposed that imagery could have similar benefits in the context of exercise. This is surprising, because physical activity does not consist of two separate categories of sport and exercise. Whether one is involved in sport or exercise is essentially in the eye of the participant; for example, many people play golf or tennis, even football or basketball, as exercise. Perhaps friends play a round of golf together, scoring each hole and maybe even wagering on the outcome, but their motivation for participating is the physical activity. Conversely, aerobics is a popular, noncompetitive exercise activity, but some participants inevitably try to outdo others by moving up to more advanced or higher-intensity groups or by looking better than the rest of the class while performing the exercises. There are even world aerobics championships in which the physical intensity, movements, sequences, and team synchronization would be beyond the physical capacities of many top athletes!

Researchers have examined peoples' motives for participating in sport and physical activity (see Frederick-Racascino and Morris [2004], for a recent review). Morris, Clayton, Power, and Jin-song (1995) conducted a large study of participation motives that included 2,601 participants of both genders ranging in age from under 10 to more than 70 years old. They examined participants with a wide range of skill levels, up to national competition, in 14 activities, including individual, racket, and team sports, as well as exercise activities and martial arts. Using a 50-item version of the Participation Motivation Questionnaire, which they developed, Morris et al. reported various motives for participation, with health emerging as the most important one for both sport and exercise participants. The goal of health, in the context of that study, included more specific motives such as getting fit, staying in shape, being in good health, improving appearance, and treating existing medical conditions. Other major motives included fun, learning new skills, challenge, affiliation, status, and energy control (both releasing and increasing energy).

Rogers and Morris (2003) recently developed a measure of motives for participation in recreational exercise, the Recreational Exercise Motivation Measure (REMM). The REMM measures a similar range of motives that resolved to eight factors, which Rogers and Morris defined as mastery, physical condition (including health, fitness, and energy), affiliation, psychological condition (stress reduction, relaxation, distraction), appearance, others' expectations, enjoyment, and competition or ego. REMM has been used effectively with recreational exercise and recreational sport competition samples. The research on motives for participation supports the intuition that the same spectrum of reasons covers people's motives for participation in sport and exercise and reinforces the argument that imagery should have applications in the exercise context, given that it is has proved so effective in sport.

Hall (2001) claimed that Hall (1995) was the first to make this argument proposing that the theoretical framework put forward by Paivio (1985) could be applied to exercise. Paivio maintained that imagery has motivational and cognitive uses, which can be either specific or general. Hall argued that imagery should have motivational and cognitive uses in exercise, as has been shown in sport (Hall 2001; Martin, Moritz, and Hall 1999). Based on this proposition, Hall and his colleagues, especially Rodgers (e.g., Rodgers, Hall, Blanchard, and Munroe 2001; Rodgers, Munroe, and Hall 2002) and Hausenblas (e.g., Giacobbi, Hausenblas, Fallon, and Hall 2003; Hausenblas, Hall, Rodgers, and Munroe 1999), have begun to explore the use of imagery in exercise and physical activity.

This chapter's discussion of imagery as applied to exercise is largely based on the work of Hall and his colleagues. First, we briefly discuss the theoretical basis for imagery use in exercise. Next, we examine the existing research, including the development and implementation of an exercise-related measure of imagery use. We then look at the application of imagery within exercise settings, addressing a variety of uses and some strategies for applying imagery effectively in the context of exercise. Finally, we consider future directions for research on imagery applied to exercise and draw some conclusions about this new focus for imagery.

THEORETICAL BASIS FOR IMAGERY USE IN EXERCISE SETTINGS

Hall (1995) made the case for imagery being useful in exercise in a contribution to a book on exercise addiction (Annett, Cripps, and Steinberg 1995). His focus was on the motivational function of imagery in exercise participation, and he based his argument on the motivational aspect of imagery proposed by Paivio (1985). Paivio presented a model of imagery use that distinguished between a cognitive function (e.g., when a basketball player imagines the coordination of movements involved in the task of shooting free throws) and a motivational function (e.g., when that player imagines shooting 10 consecutive clean baskets from the free-throw line). Paivio proposed that these two functions of imagery could be classified as specific, as in the two examples just given, or general. An example of a motivational general use of imagery is when an athlete imagines being cool, calm, and in control during a high-pressure phase of a match. A cognitive general use could be when a football player imagines the team performing a set move that is part of its strategy for an upcoming match. (Paivio's model is discussed in chapters 2 and 3.)

Along with Paivio, Hall and his colleagues operationalized Paivio's imagery-use model in the Sport Imagery Questionnaire (SIQ; Hall, Mack, Paivio, and Hausenblas 1998). The four types of imagery use proposed by Paivio emerged in factor analyses, except that motivational general imagery produced two factors, one identified as motivational general arousal (MG-A) imagery and the other called motivational general mastery (MG-M) imagery by Hall et al. (See chapter 4 for a detailed discussion of the development and validation of the SIQ.)

In his theoretical speculations, Hall (1995) focused on the motivational specific (MS), MG-A, and MG-M aspects of imagery use, based on an oral presentation of earlier results from the work on development of the SIQ (Hall, Mack, and Paivio 1995). Hall cited a study by Salmon, Hall, and Haslam (1994), who examined motivational and cognitive functions of imagery in 362 soccer players. They found that the players used imagery more for motivation than for cognitive purposes. Further, Hall, Toews, and Rodgers (1990) found that participants who were instructed to practice a laboratory-based motor task using imagery practiced more often and for longer periods of time under voluntary practice conditions than control participants did. Hall's link was predicated on the statement

"Given that imagery is a powerful motivator in sport, it is very possible that imagery operates in a similar fashion in exercise" (p. 18).

Hall proposed a model of participation motivation for exercise in which the direct influences on exercise are self-confidence and outcome expectancy. Hall acknowledged that this model was based on Bandura's (1986) social cognitive theory, in which self-confidence is represented by self-efficacy, or the belief people have in their ability to perform a specific task. Hall argued that the three forms of motivational imagery can influence self-efficacy or self-confidence. In support of this, he cited results from a study by Hall, Rodgers, and Barr (1990) in which MG-A was the best predictor of state sport confidence, measured by the State Sport Confidence Inventory (SSCI; Vealey 1986) and state sport competition self-confidence, measured by the self-confidence subscale of the Competitive State Anxiety Inventory–2 (CSAI-2; Martens, Burton, Vealey, Bump, and Smith 1990). Hall clarified the distinction between sport confidence, which measures general confidence in the ability to perform well, and self-efficacy, which is a belief that is specific to each particular task. Hall did not cite the already existing evidence that imagery enhances self-efficacy (Callery and Morris 1993; Feltz and Reissinger 1990; Lee 1990), perhaps because none of this research adopted the imagery-use model.

Because the studies by Feltz and Reissinger (1990), and Lee (1990) used performance on two effort-based tasks, the skier's squat and sit-ups, the improvements in performance could have been due to increases in motivation related to the increased self-efficacy recorded by those researchers. Callery and Morris (1993) focused their imagery script for kick passing in elite footballers on high-quality production of the skill. Although cognitive-specific imagery of the kick-pass process dominated the script, substantial imagery of successful performance outcomes (that is, motivation-specific imagery use) was included. More recent studies in Australian Rules football (e.g., Callery and Morris 1997a, b) and baseball hitting (She and Morris 1997) have verified that imagery of successful task performance enhances self-efficacy. She and Morris also found that imagery of baseball hitting enhanced state sport confidence, as measured by the SSCI.

Hall (1995) proposed that imagery enhances self-confidence and self-efficacy, which then directly affects exercise participation. Callery and Morris (1997c) made a similar prediction about the imagery–self-efficacy–performance links. A causal modeling analysis of Australian Rules football goal kicking did not support their proposition that self-efficacy mediated between imagery and performance. This structural equation modeling analysis indicated that imagery directly influenced both self-efficacy and performance but that self-efficacy had no direct influence on performance. Of course, elite sport performance is different from recreational exercise participation, so it will be interesting to see how such causal modeling analyses test this aspect of Hall's model.

The other direct antecedent of exercise participation in Hall's (1995) model was outcome expectancy. Bandura (1986) proposed that behavior is a function of people's confidence that they can perform a task and their expectations about the outcome(s) that will follow it. People must value the outcome they expect or performing the task is not attractive. Even if they have confidence that they can perform the task and value the outcome, they will be unlikely to perform if they believe that the outcome has low probability. For example, if someone is told that he will lose weight and tone his physique by doing 30 minutes of intensive exercise four times a week (self-efficacy), he might believe he is capable of doing it and value the outcomes of losing weight and toning his body (outcome value). But if he does not believe that he will actually lose the weight and have a better physique, perhaps because he has exercised before without those outcomes (outcome likelihood), then he probably will not do the exercise. Hall argued that imagery is more likely to affect a person's perception of the likelihood of an outcome than to influence outcome value. Thus, by imagining that he is doing the exercise well (to augment self-efficacy) and imagining the outcome of a leaner, more muscular body (to increase outcome likelihood), his motivation to participate in exercise should be enhanced, provided that outcome value is also high. Hall pointed out that specific predictions about the effects of imagery in the exercise context can be derived from this model.

Hall stated that some of the relationships that can be generated from the model have already been confirmed in sport settings. This is true for imagery's effect on self-efficacy and for self-efficacy's effect on performance, but studies that have attempted to examine the influence of outcome expectancy on performance in sport have been unsuccessful (Feltz and Lirgg 2001). This may be because the majority of people who play sport, especially elite performers, have high levels of outcome expectancy; that is, everyone values the outcomes they seek from participating and believes those outcomes are likely to result from doing the activity (Morris and Koehn 2004). When a variable does not actually vary within a population, whether it is uniformly high, low, or moderate, it has little value as a predictor. Outcome expectancy would be anticipated to vary much more in exercise contexts, especially with people who have low involvement in physical activity and whose increased participation is particularly important in our increasingly sedentary world.

RESEARCH ON IMAGERY AND EXERCISE

Hall and his colleagues have examined aspects of the relationship of imagery and exercise in various studies, which are summarized in table

12.1. In this section we consider each of these studies in detail to draw out issues for further development in this new and potentially fruitful area of research.

DEVELOPMENT OF AN EXERCISE-IMAGERY MEASURE

Hausenblas, Hall, Rodgers, and Munroe (1999) developed a measure of exercise imagery. In the first phase of the development, they asked 144 volunteer aerobic exercisers (92.3% female) from a university community whether they ever used exercise imagery and, if so, what they imagined and why and when they used it. Responses were open ended. Hausenblas et al. found that 75.7% of their participants reported using exercise imagery, and the frequency of use was relatively high. The most frequent use was before going to bed or to sleep. Other commonly reported times when imagery was used were during class or while studying, while daydreaming, before or after exercising, while walking or driving, and while exercising. Hausenblas et al. classified what they imagined into nine categories (from most to least frequent): body image, technique and strategies, feeling good about oneself, motivation, general exercise, fitness and health, music, goals, and maintaining focus. The researchers grouped their reasons for using imagery into 11 categories (from most to least frequent): motivation, feeling good about oneself, body image, strategies and techniques, stress relief, fitness health, goals, habit or routine, music, getting energized, and maintaining focus.

In phase 2 of the measure's development, Hausenblas et al. (1999) devised a 23-item scale based on the categories that emerged in response to the reasons-for-use question. They omitted "habit or routine," leaving 10 categories. Items were based on the participants' statements made during phase 1. Ratings were made on a 9-point Likert scale, with 1 meaning "never engaging in this type of imagery" and 9 meaning "always engaging in this type of imagery." The participants came from two distinct samples. Sample 1 included 307 volunteer aerobic-exercise participants (97.4% female) from a university community. Sample 2 comprised 171 volunteer aerobic-exercise participants (97.7% female) from another university community. A three-factor solution emerged from an exploratory factor analysis (EFA). The factors were labeled "energy," "appearance," and "technique." Internal consistency was sound, with Cronbach's ranging from .81 to .90. Hausenblas et al. examined concurrent validity by dividing the participants in sample 2 into extreme groups: low-frequency exercisers (those who reported exercising 3 hours per week or less) and high-frequency exercisers (those who reported exercising 8 hours per week or more). Comparisons of subscale means for these two extreme groups showed that the self-reported high-frequency exercisers also reported imaging about exercise significantly more often for all

Table 12.1 Research on Imagery and Exercise

Authors	Date	Aims	Design	Results	Conclusions
Hausenblas, Hall, Rodgers, and Munroe	1999	Develop exercise imagery measure	Three studies: 1: Open-ended uses of imagery in exercise 2: Exploratory factor analysis of items generated in study 1 3: Confirmatory factor analysis of model generated in study 2	Generated range of uses; produced 23 items. Three factors identified: appearance, energy, technique. The 23-item scale did not fit model; 9-item version fit model.	Developed 9-item Exercise Imagery Questionnaire, with three subscales: appearance, energy, technique.
Gammage, Hall, and Rodgers	2000	Examine variations in exercise imagery by gender, exercise frequency, and activity type	Large sample from range of activities; administered EIQ 9-item version	Appearance imagery used most, energy least. Females used appearance more than males; males used technique more than females. Higher-frequency participants used all three types more. Runners used less appearance imagery; weight trainers used more technique imagery.	Differences found for gender, frequency and type of activity, largely as predicted. No prediction made about gender and technique.

(continued)

Table 12.1 *(continued)*

Authors	Date	Aims	Design	Results	Conclusions
Rodgers, Hall, Blanchard, and Munroe	2001	Determine whether obligatory exercisers use more exercise imagery, especially appearance	Participants from range of activities; administered EIQ and Obligatory Exercise Questionnaire; regression analysis	Appearance imagery used most; energy imagery least. Time 1: Only energy predicted obligatory exercise. Time 2: Energy and appearance predicted obligatory exercise.	Didn't support hypotheses: Appearance not used most, obligatory exercise not maladaptive.
Rodgers, Munroe, and Hall	2002	Determine whether exercise imagery can predict intentions and behavior	Mainly female aerobics; administered EIQ and self-reported exercise intentions and behavior; regression analysis	Moderate scores on EIQ subscales; appearance predicted intention; no subscales predicted behavior.	Appearance related to intention but not behavior. Suggested appearance imagery might affect intention; energy and technique help sustain it.
Giacobbi, Hausenblas, Fallon, and Hall	2003	Provide blueprint for future research through in-depth study	16 female participants; in-depth interviews, based on grounded theory	Eight uses: technique, routines, context, appearance, competitive outcomes, fitness/health, emotions, self-efficacy.	Broadens range of imagery uses well beyond EIQ subscales.

three subscales. Hausenblas et al. pointed out that this "result parallels those found for athletes; elite athletes use imagery more than novice and recreational-level athletes (Barr and Hall 1992; Hall, Rodgers, and Barr 1990)" (p. 176). It should be noted that amount of time spent in an activity is not the same as skill level, although most elite athletes would be expected to spend more time practicing than most novices.

To further examine the psychometric properties of what Hausenblas et al. (1999) now called the Exercise Imagery Questionnaire–Aerobic Version (EIQ–AV), a confirmatory factor analysis (CFA) was conducted in two distinct samples. Sample 1 comprised 144 volunteer exercisers (89.0% female) from a university community; sample 2 comprised 267 volunteer exercisers (97.6% female) from another university community. A range of commonly used CFA fit indices was applied to the data. Five out of nine indices failed to meet the fit criteria, so Hausenblas et al. concluded that there was a poor model fit. Based on modification indices, items were removed from all three factors, leaving a 9-item measure that yielded good fit indices. This version of the EIQ–AV had three items on each subscale. Test–retest reliability was conducted over a 5-day period with 18 participants with the result of $r = .88$, which is satisfactory.

Hausenblas et al. (1999) noted a number of limitations of their study. First, they pointed out that the EIQ–AV had been developed and validated within the context of one form of exercise only; participants were almost exclusively from aerobic-exercise classes. Another aspect of the research that limits its generalizability is that almost all the participants in its three phases and five samples were female. Furthermore, they were all from two universities and were predominantly students, which impose limitations related to age and educational background. Hausenblas et al. also noted that the study was limited because it was correlational; they proposed the need for longitudinal and experimental studies to examine exercise imagery thoroughly. They also recognized that their samples were self-selecting and appeared to be highly motivated. Perhaps more important, they noted that all the measures were self-reported, which is a particular concern because correlations among self-reported measures might reflect personal dispositions rather than actual patterns. For example, some people tend to overestimate and others to underestimate, especially with respect to socially desirable traits or behaviors. This can artificially inflate a correlation, such as that between imagery use and self-efficacy. Hausenblas et al. acknowledged the need for random sampling and for the use of measures that are not self-reported, such as behavioral observation.

Hausenblas et al. (1999) did not report the specific bases on which they reduced a 23-item scale to a 9-item scale; they simply referred to the modification indices. Nor did they present the original 23 items, so examining the ones that were discarded is impossible. The reduction from 23 to 9 items seems large; more than 60% of them were removed. It should be observed that the original rationale for the construction of the scale was the categories of reasons for imagining exercise that emerged in phase 1 and the specific statements made by exercisers. The remaining 9 items do not appear to reflect even 9 out of the 10 categories generated in phase 1. Thus, the 9-item EIQ–AV cannot be considered a genuine reflection of the open-ended approach adopted in phase 1. Further, the interpretation of the "appearance" subscale deserves comment. In the original 10 categories that formed the basis of the 23-item version of the EIQ–AV, there were two health-related reasons for using exercise imagery: body image and fitness or health. Although feeling good about oneself could be interpreted as a health-related reason for imagery, it is more commonly identified with self-concept than physical condition.

Most of the participation-motivation literature has identified specific, health-related reasons for participating in physical activity, such as to stay in shape, get fit, be healthy, treat a medical condition, and improve appearance. In that literature, the superordinate category is typically "health" or "health and fitness," within which appearance is one aspect (Frederick-Racascino and Morris, 2004). In their Motivation for Physical Activity Measure–Revised (MPAM–R; Ryan, Frederick, Lepes, Rubio, and Sheldon 1997), Ryan et al. did distinguish between fitness and appearance motives, which formed one factor in their original scale. Similarly, in the REMM, Rogers and Morris (2003) identified an 8-item physical-condition (health) factor separately from a 9-item appearance factor. In a second-order analysis of the REMM first-order factors, three factors emerged, one of which included physical condition, psychological condition, and appearance. Rogers and Morris called this factor "body–mind motives."

Although appearance might seem more consistent with the visual nature of imagery, images arise in all sense modalities and people can just as well "feel" out of condition or overweight. Of the 3 appearance items in the 9-item version of the EIQ–AV (toning up, becoming healthy, and losing weight), none is specifically about appearance. Although losing weight can be done to improve appearance, it can also be done to improve health, and although toning up can enhance shape, it has a strong connotation of feeling in good shape. Interpretation of the EIQ–AV subscales deserves further scrutiny. In particular, to support interpretation in the future, the name of the appearance subscale might be amended to "health" or "health and appearance." The test–retest reliability of the EIQ–AV reported by Hausenblas et al. should be considered cautiously because the sample is very small and the delay between testing is very short.

FACTORS THAT INFLUENCE EXERCISE IMAGERY

Following up on their initial research on exercise imagery, Gammage, Hall, and Rodgers (2000) examined how exercise imagery varies with gender, frequency of exercise, and activity type. They predicted that females would use more appearance imagery to enhance their motivation for exercise, given that females have been found to exercise more for appearance reasons than males (e.g., Markland and Hardy 1993). They also hypothesized that high-frequency exercisers would use more exercise imagery than low-frequency exercisers based on research by Rodgers and Gauvin (1998), who reported that high-frequency and low-frequency exercising women differed in terms of their motives for participation. Finally, Gammage et al. anticipated that exercise imagery would vary with activity type, but because of the absence of previous research to guide any hypothesis, they made no prediction.

The study's participants were 577 (264 male, 312 female) exercisers who engaged in a wide range of activities, including weightlifting, running, aerobic-exercise classes, swimming, team and individual recreational sports, and cardiovascular equipment use. Of these, 287 reported that they exercised one or two times per week and 290 participants indicated that they participated three or more times each week. Participants completed the EIQ immediately before or after exercising. The EIQ used in this study was a 9-item version that had been generalized from the EIQ–AV for use with a wider range of exercise activities. Participants rated the frequency of their imagery use from 1 ("never") to 9 ("always") on a 9-point Likert scale.

Gammage et al. found that participants reported using appearance imagery most often and energy imagery least frequently. In terms of the three variables on which the study focused, patterns were largely consistent with predictions. For gender, women used more appearance imagery than men, and men employed technique imagery to a greater extent than women. Gammage et al. did not predict the latter finding. High-frequency exercisers used all three kinds of imagery as measured by the EIQ subscales (i.e., appearance, energy, and technique) more than low-frequency exercisers. Gammage et al. noted a concern that almost all the aerobic exercisers were female, whereas most of the weight trainers were male, which could result in a confounding effect of exercise activity and gender. The analysis of activity type involved only 405 of the participants because some activities produced cell sizes too small to meet the recommended criteria for analysis of variance. Because no significant gender-by-activity-type interaction was present, both genders were included in the same analysis. This showed that runners used less appearance imagery than the participants in the other three activities included in this analysis (aerobics, weight training, and cardiovascular equipment use), whereas weight trainers used more technique imagery than participants in the other activities. Gammage et al. noted the importance of the finding that all three variables examined in this study significantly influenced exercise imagery, although effect sizes for gender and activity type were very small.

Gammage et al. identified two limitations of the study. First, some of the results were based on small sample sizes. Second, activity type was based on self-reported primary activity, but many participants listed more than one activity. Gammage et al. suggested that participants' determination of primary activity might have depended on their most recent exercise sessions. A concern not reported is that Gammage et al. did not disclose the process of conversion of the EIQ. They referred to an oral conference presentation (Rodgers, Hall, Blanchard, and Munroe 1999) in noting that the EIQ had been modified for more general use. Rodgers, Hall, Blanchard, and Munroe (2001) did publish a paper on the study reported in the conference presentation. (The Rodgers et al. [2001] study is reported next in this chapter.) In that paper, they referred to Gammage et al. (2000) and Hausenblas et al. (1999) for the origin of the EIQ. Due to this oversight, no written documentation of the process by which the EIQ–AV was modified to produce the generalized EIQ exists. Gammage et al. ended by stating that the results of their study indicate that gender, frequency of participation, and activity type are all variables that should be considered in tailoring exercise-imagery programs to individuals. They also noted that research that moves from the present descriptive approach to experimental methods is warranted, including intervention research.

Rodgers et al. (2001) based their study of exercise imagery and obligatory exercise on the propositions made by Hall (1995). As noted previously, Hall's paper was part of an edited text on exercise addiction. He argued that imagery is likely to be used by exercisers, especially for motivational purposes, based on its widely demonstrated use in sport. Hall linked the proposition about exercise imagery to the theme of that book by arguing that people who exercise more often are likely to use imagery more frequently, an idea that the aforementioned studies by Hausenblas et al. and Gammage et al. supported. Thus, according to Hall, people who are addicted to exercise are likely to use imagery of themselves exercising a lot, frequently to motivate themselves by imagining the positive aspects of exercise. Rodgers et al. examined this proposition, but they employed the term "obligatory exercise" rather than "exercise addiction," mainly because they operationalized the dependency on exercise in the form of the Obligatory Exercise Questionnaire (OEQ; Thompson and Pasman 1991). The OEQ is a 20-item measure in which items like "When I don't exercise, I feel guilty" are rated on a 4-point scale from 1 ("never") to 4 ("always").

The 243 participants (144 males, 97 females [numbers taken directly from the paper actually add up to 241]) from a number of exercise activities, including weight training, running, and aerobics, completed the generalized version of the EIQ and the OEQ on two occasions 10 weeks apart. Test–retest reliability of the three subscales of the EIQ was $r = .70$

for appearance, $r = .74$ for energy, and $r = .66$ for technique; for the OEQ, $r = .85$. The authors stated that these values were acceptable, although in his standard psychometrics text Kline (1993) advised that such values should not fall below .8.

As in previous studies, appearance imagery was used the most and energy imagery the least. Obligatory exercise means were 50.52 at time 1 and 50.55 at time 2, indicating relatively high levels of addiction. Rodgers et al. conducted regression analyses at each time. At time 1, they found that only energy imagery predicted obligatory exercise. At time 2, energy imagery was again a significant predictor, but technique imagery also predicted obligatory imagery. Rodgers et al. acknowledged that the results did not support their hypothesis that obligatory exercise would be most strongly associated with appearance imagery; instead, energy and technique imagery were linked to obligatory exercise. Rodgers et al. concluded that the underlying motives for obligatory exercise might not be maladaptive in the same way that those for some pathological addictions, such as anorexia nervosa and bulimia nervosa, are. Rodgers et al. stressed that the issue of health risk associated with obligatory exercise was not addressed in this study, which focused specifically on motivation for obligatory exercise. Nonetheless, Rodgers et al. did point out that it is surprising that appearance imagery did not predict obligatory exercise, given that such exercisers are frequently concerned with health, fitness, weight, and body shape and that the EIQ items relating to appearance "clearly relate to weight concerns" (p. 154).

EXERCISE IMAGERY, EXERCISE INTENTIONS, AND EXERCISE BEHAVIOR

Rodgers, Munroe, and Hall (2002) examined whether exercise imagery contributed to the prediction of exercise intentions and exercise behavior beyond the variance explained by self-efficacy. Rodgers et al. studied two samples. Sample 1 consisted of 388 male and female aerobic-exercise participants (96% female) from two universities, who took part in step, low-impact, and hi/lo aerobics classes. Sample 2 included 223 participants (91% female) from university- and community-based exercise classes involving aerobics, weight training, and running activities.

Participants completed the EIQ–AV (sample 1) or the EIQ–General (sample 2), a measure of self-efficacy developed for exercise settings by Rodgers and Sullivan (2001), and a self-report measure of intention and behavior developed by Godin, Jobin, and Bouillon (1986). The self-efficacy measure comprised 10 items, 3 measuring coping efficacy, 4 assessing task efficacy, and 3 evaluating scheduling efficacy. Task efficacy, which refers to someone's belief in their ability to perform the task at various levels, is the type that is commonly measured. Coping efficacy refers to belief in one's ability to cope in challenging and difficult situations. Scheduling efficacy concerns belief in one's capability to organize exercise sessions and adhere to the schedule.

Each item on the measure was rated on a 100% scale with reference to the participant's confidence in performing the task stated in the item, from 0 ("no confidence") to 100 ("completely confident"). The score on each subscale was represented by the mean for the items on that subscale. Rodgers et al. assessed behavioral intention by asking participants how often per week they intended to undertake physical activity during the next four weeks and offering six response options, ranging from none to three or more times per week. They assessed behavior by asking participants how often per week they had engaged in physical activity during the past four weeks. Response options ranged from none to three or more times per week.

Rodgers et al. found that participants reported relatively high self-efficacy, with task efficacy highest, followed by scheduling and then coping efficacy. Participants also reported using a moderate amount of each type of exercise imagery, with appearance imagery being used most often. In regression analysis, self-efficacy was found to predict intention to exercise and exercise behavior. Scheduling efficacy was the strongest predictor of intention in both samples. In sample 1, coping efficacy also predicted intention, whereas task efficacy did in sample 2. Both scheduling and coping efficacy predicted behavior in both samples. Also, appearance imagery predicted intention but not behavior. Rodgers et al. concluded that scheduling and coping efficacy are important component behaviors of initiating and maintaining regular exercise. Rodgers et al. also noted that they found appearance imagery to be the only imagery type that significantly predicted intention to exercise, but it was not related to obligatory exercise (Rodgers et al. 2001). They suggested that perhaps appearance motives are important in the intent to exercise, but energy and technique imagery play roles in sustaining exercise activity.

Rodgers et al. (2002) acknowledged the limitation of the cross-sectional design that they employed in this study: It identifies associations between variables but cannot determine causal relationships. They also noted that the participants' high activity levels limited the generalizability of the study's findings. They recognized the need to apply exercise-imagery interventions to low-frequency exercisers and nonexercisers. The researchers claimed that most important, in terms of the study's aims, was the finding that "self-efficacy and imagery are not isomorphic to each other, and each makes an independent contribution to the prediction of exercise behavior" (p. 63). This statement's wording could be clearer, but it appears to contradict the results: Rodgers et al. reported that appearance imagery was significantly related to intention but not to exercise behavior.

As the researchers stressed, the study's results do not indicate that either self-efficacy or imagery bears a causal relationship to intention or behavior. Another limitation not stated by Rodgers et al. is the use of different imagery measures in the two samples. This makes comparison of findings relating to imagery for the two samples problematic. Finally, using a self-report measure of exercise behavior is a weakness; problems are associated with inferences drawn from studies in which all the measures are self-reports, particularly when they are collected from all of the participants at the same time. Exercise behavior is more accurately measured in ways other than self-report, especially retrospective self-report. Exercise logs kept by participants about their exercise sessions are usually more reliable, but independent observations have greater trustworthiness. If logistics prevent the researchers' performing the observations themselves, they can enlist the help of staff at exercise venues.

Qualitative Research on Exercise Imagery

Giacobbi, Hausenblas, Fallon, and Hall (2003) pointed out that most of the research on exercise imagery had employed survey methods. They argued that because the study of imagery related to exercise is new, a grounded theory approach could "provide a theoretical and conceptual blueprint for future investigations" (p. 161). Giacobbi et al. conducted a qualitative study, using in-depth interviews and based on grounded theory principles and methods (Strauss and Corbin 1990). Participants were 16 females, aged 18 to 39 years, from two universities, who engaged in activities including aerobics, running, softball, swimming, weightlifting, cardiovascular exercise using machines, golf, tennis, and kickboxing. The interviewers asked participants open-ended questions, followed by specific probes. First, they asked them to talk about their use of imagery, if any, with regard to exercise participation. The interviews covered the time of day, location, content, and function of exercise imagery. Giacobbi et al. reported that the questions about participants' uses of imagery "were in accordance with Paivio's (1985) model of imagery that includes both motivational and cognitive functions" (p. 162).

Giacobbi et al. described the elaborate grounded theory analytic procedures they employed to maximize the quality of the theory that emerged from the data. By using NU*DIST, a computer software package that organizes qualitative data, as well as multiple independent readings of transcripts and discussions of data, the researchers became very familiar with the content of the interviews and developed data themes. Giacobbi et al. also employed sensitizing concepts (ideas from the discipline that help researchers look at data in meaningful ways), the constant comparative method, which is a standard part of grounded theory analysis, and various coding methods. External experts in qualitative data analysis were also asked to play "devil's advocate." The involvement of these experts, who were external to the research team, helped to ensure trustworthiness in discussions as the group developed higher-order themes and constructed a hierarchy of knowledge, leading to a more complex conceptualization. Triangulation of evidence, through the involvement of multiple observers whose independent constructions were then compared and contrasted, as well as the analysis of negative cases, also supported the trustworthiness of the analysis that lead to this conceptualization.

Giacobbi et al. (2003) reported that in terms of location and timing of exercise-imagery use, participants' comments indicated that half of them used imagery away from exercise settings only, some employed it in exercise contexts only, and a few used it both in and outside of those environments. Giacobbi et al. did not observe any differences in the content of imagery conducted within and outside of exercise settings.

With reference to the functions of exercise imagery, Giacobbi et al. identified eight higher-order themes that reflected types of imagery use: exercise technique, aerobics routines, exercise context, appearance images, competitive outcomes, fitness and health outcomes, emotions associated with imagery, and exercise self-efficacy. The exercise technique and appearance imagery themes are consistent with studies reported previously in this chapter, and that of emotions associated with imagery is similar to the energy imagery concept. The other themes broaden the range of imagery uses. The aerobics-routines theme referred to participants mentally rehearsing specific step-aerobics routines using imagery, and the exercise-contexts theme reflected participants' reports about imagining aspects such as the equipment, locations, and other people.

Giacobbi et al. noted that these categories extended previous research, reflecting unique characteristics of exercise-imagery use. They also commented on the emergence of fitness and health outcomes and exercise self-efficacy. Giacobbi et al., in observing that participants recognized imagery's role in confidence enhancement in sport, drew attention to the research that supports this function. They also acknowledged the motivational value of fitness, health, and appearance outcomes. The theme of competitive outcomes, they said, was predominantly reflected in the exercise imagery of runners in the study, who reported using imagery related to run times, winning in competition, and improving performance. The researchers did not include any substantive consideration of this theme in their discussion.

In discussing these findings, Giacobbi et al. emphasized the three themes that matched the subscales of the EIQ—appearance, technique, and energy—mostly focusing on appearance and technique. They also discussed the uniqueness of their findings regarding routines and context and participants' recognition of the confidence-building function of imagery. They introduced the PETTLEP model of Holmes and Collins (2001), which is discussed in previous chapters. Based on a neuroscience approach to imagery, Holmes and Collins proposed that scripts should incorporate seven elements: the physical, environmental, task, timing, learning, emotional, and perspective aspects of imagery tasks. Giacobbi et al. suggested that much of this model fits with the functions of imagery identified in the qualitative analysis in their study. Giacobbi acknowledged several limitations of their study. First, the participants were all female university students, representing a narrow range with respect to gender, age, and educational level. Second, the interview design focused on the verbal reports of participants, so it did not examine nonconscious imagery processes. Giacobbi et al. suggested that future neuroscience research on exercise imagery might be of value.

In their study, Giacobbi et al. (2003) adopted a different approach to examining exercise imagery than those reported earlier in this chapter. The conduct and analysis of in-depth interviews identified some functions of imagery that had not emerged out of the questionnaire studies (what Giacobbi et al. somewhat imprecisely call "survey" studies). As noted earlier, those questionnaire-based studies originated in an open-ended study, phase 1 of the Hausenblas et al. (1999) development of the EIQ. Hausenblas et al. might have made a premature assumption in phase 3 of that developmental process, where they argued that because the 23-item version of the EIQ did not provide a good fit for the 3-factor model that emerged in the exploratory factor analysis in phase 2, this meant that some of the items were at fault. In modifying the EIQ, Hausenblas et al. discarded 14 of the 23 items that had been developed on the basis of the open-ended phase. Another way of looking at the CFA result would have been to consider whether the 3-factor model was incorrect.

Hall, Hausenblas, Rodgers, and their colleagues have consistently argued that one major purpose of exercise imagery is motivational. As we pointed out earlier in this chapter, more than the three motives for participation in physical activity that Hall and colleagues included in their model have been identified. Recognising the tremendous flexibility of the imagery process, motivational imagery can be used in association with all motives for participation in physical activity. Interestingly, the 8-factor structure of the Recreational Exercise Motivation Measure (REMM; Rogers and Morris 2003) bears a substantial degree of similarity to the eight functions of imagery related to exercise that were derived as higher-order themes in the Giacobbi et al. study. We suggest that researchers go back to the original studies of Hausenblas et al. and examine the approach of refining the 23-item EIQ, based on the results of the study by Giacobbi et al., to see if it leads to a different factor structure than the 3-factor EIQ, which has since been used in several studies by Hall,

Hausenblas, Rodgers, and colleagues. For example, we propose that separate health-and-fitness and appearance factors are consistent with the participation-motivation research and with the themes that have emerged from Giacobbi et al.'s analysis.

The competitive-outcomes theme of Giacobbi et al. could also be linked with the competition or ego factor in the REMM. Imagining the outcome of competition with others or with one's own past performance might depend somewhat on the type of activity and the context, but the participation-motivation literature indicates that it is likely to be a more common use of exercise imagery than Giacobbi et al. suggested. Researchers who adhere to the original perspective and procedures espoused in the grounded theory approach would question the statement quoted earlier by Giacobbi et al., in which they indicated that the imagery-use questions employed in the data-collection phase were based on Paivio's (1985) model. As Giacobbi et al. stated in their paper, Strauss and Corbin (1990) argued that existing theories or models should not be used in the grounded theory examination of an issue. Further, Giacobbi et al. indicated that the previous literature was used as a source for deriving labels for themes that emerged. These practices mean that the existing framework for exercise imagery provided by the EIQ could have biased the data collection and the data analysis and interpretation stages of their study, which otherwise involved some of the most rigorous analytic procedures used in research on grounded theory to ensure credibility, dependability, and trustworthiness. Nonetheless, Giacobbi et al. found a wider range of themes than previous work on exercise imagery had, which seems a promising basis for further research, including reconsideration of the measurement of exercise-imagery use.

The original paper by Hall (1995) and the research that has emanated from it represent an exciting step into a new field with the potential for important applications as well as theoretical insights. Although the idea that people use imagery in exercise contexts is widely acknowledged, the key innovation in Hall's paper was the generation of a conceptualization that allows imagery in exercise to be systematically examined. The research questions that the published articles stimulated by Hall's chapter have addressed are based on sound rationales and provide useful information about the role of imagery in exercise motivation and performance. Suggestions about the application of imagery to facilitate exercise or physical activity are made in the next section.

Reflection on several aspects of the work is useful, however. One is the development of the EIQ, which we propose should be reconsidered. Another is the selection of samples. The vast majority of the participants across several studies conducted by Hall, Hausenblas, Rodgers, and colleagues were female university students. More puzzling than this is the fact that the researchers stated this to be a limitation of every study, but they continued to use such samples in subsequent studies. Imagery is used by people across a wide range of ages, both genders, and varying educational levels. People in all of those categories participate in exercise, so broadening the characteristics of samples early in the study of exercise imagery seems important. Also noteworthy is the fact that although most of the researchers mentioned in this chapter recommend that research should be conducted on the effect of imagery interventions in exercise contexts, they have not, to date, done such a study. Hall and colleagues have laid a foundation for others to build on. We look forward to research that involves a much wider range of people and activities and examines exercise imagery interventions in meaningful contexts.

Applications of Imagery in Exercise Settings

In discussing the underlying theoretical ideas and possible uses and benefits of applying imagery in the exercise setting, we have shown that research does suggest that exercise-imagery interventions may help sustain participants' motivation and self-efficacy, which may then lead to increases in physical activity and exercise adherence. In this section, we discuss the significance of these outcomes, address issues involved in applying imagery to the exercise setting, and offer practical advice to practitioners and exercisers for designing exercise-imagery interventions.

One of the key findings of the current exercise-imagery research is the potential link between exercise imagery and exercise adherence. Physical activity has numerous physical, social, psychological, and financial benefits for individuals. Conversely, physical inactivity represents a major and increasing public health concern and contributes to approximately 6,400 premature deaths per annum in Australia, resulting from coronary heart disease, type 2 diabetes, and colon cancer (Driscoll and Wood 2001), and 200,000 deaths from the same diseases in the United States (Buckworth and Dishman 2002). In addition to affecting people's physical and psychological well-being, the economic burden of physical inactivity in Australia is estimated to be around $380 million per year (Driscoll and Wood 2001), and the comparable figure in the United States would run into many billions of dollars.

Australia's Victorian Government Department of Human Services conducted the Victorian Population Health Survey (2002) and found that 46% of Victorians are insufficiently active for health gain (i.e., exercising below the level recommended by the National Physical Activity Guidelines). In particular, 50% of middle-aged Australians and 65% of older Australians are insufficiently active. Similarly, Buckworth and Dishman

(2002) reported that 30 to 40% of U.S. residents over 18 years of age do not participate in leisure-time physical activity. They also noted that approximately 75% of American adults do not do enough physical activity to reduce premature mortality or maintain cardiorespiratory fitness. These figures indicate that an extremely large number of Americans and Australians are not exercising enough to experience the health benefits associated with physical activity, and that many of them may encounter problems associated with physical inactivity. Such patterns are repeated in many so-called developed countries.

In addition, Buckworth and Dishman (2002) reported that the pattern in which 50% of sedentary adults who began an exercise program dropped out within 6 months has been shown to be relatively stable. These findings indicate the need to develop effective interventions designed to increase exercise self-efficacy and exercise adherence, and the importance of continued research into the links between exercise imagery and exercise adherence, including motivation. Exercise practitioners, health-care professionals, and exercisers need to be educated about the "hows" and "whys" of exercise imagery. Through further research, these questions should be addressed more thoroughly.

According to the current research, exercise-imagery interventions appear to be useful and effective for a wide variety of exercisers. The findings of Gammage et al. (2000) have led to the suggestion that in order to increase an imagery intervention's effectiveness, the participant's gender, frequency of exercise, and type of exercise activity should be considered separately. For example, a program designed for a woman who participates in two aerobics sessions per week will most likely contain substantially different images compared to one designed for a man who performs five weight-training sessions per week.

Gammage et al. (2000) also encouraged exercisers to focus their imagery programs on what motivates them, while attempting to incorporate all three aspects of imagery (i.e., appearance, technique, and energy). Accordingly, the most effective imagery program for a female aerobic participant who is motivated to exercise primarily for appearance reasons would likely include predominantly appearance-based images, in addition to some technique and energy images. An important message for practitioners and exercisers alike is that exercise-imagery programs must be tailored to the individual, specifically taking into account personal beliefs about exercise that influence motivation (Gammage et al. 2000).

Exercise practitioners can assist exercisers in developing effective, individualized imagery-intervention programs. Giacobbi et al. (2003) provided some useful suggestions to consider when designing these programs. First, practitioners should briefly explain to their clients the results of scientific studies that demonstrate the potential benefits of mental imagery in exercise settings. In other words, practitioners should attempt to "sell" the imagery "product" to them by explaining the benefits in an appropriate, clear, and succinct manner. Further research may help determine the most effective way to disseminate this information to various subgroups of exercisers (for example, males versus females, older versus younger exercisers, and participants in various forms of physical activity).

Giacobbi et al. (2003) also suggested that exercisers should be encouraged to regularly imagine their goals, especially during down times or rest periods. Mental-imagery programs do not, however, need to be structured and follow a set routine. In fact, Giacobbi et al. found that "positive cognitive and motivational benefits can result from the use of fleeting mental images in the car, at work, or at night" (p. 174). They also proposed that goals should be written down and discussed with an exercise practitioner, friend, relative, or exercise partner. They encouraged exercisers to find fun and creative ways to imagine exercise behavior and exercise goals, both in and outside of the exercise environment, in order to ensure that the imagery-intervention program is effective and individualized.

Based on the available research, exercisers and practitioners are strongly encouraged to incorporate some form of exercise imagery into physical-activity programs. The suggested outcomes of exercise-imagery interventions include, but are not limited to, increased self-efficacy, exercise behavior, and exercise adherence. Research and anecdotal evidence has shown that the use of imagery in the sport setting is an important part of an athlete's training and competition program, the benefits of which are numerous and varied. With further research into the applications of imagery in exercise settings, many more benefits and contexts for imagery use are likely to be identified, which will lead to its increasing importance in promoting participation in physical activity.

CONCLUSIONS

Because only a limited number of studies have investigated exercise imagery, the scope for future research is substantial. The current findings that suggest links between exercise imagery and increased exercise motivation and adherence constitute a strong rationale for continued study.

Hall (1995), Hausenblas et al. (1999), and Giacobbi et al. (2003) all proposed that exercise imagery might be a useful intervention for increasing exercise participation and adherence. Further research needs to continue to investigate these ideas (Hausenblas et al. 1999). For example, longitudinal studies with large sample sizes, conducted on exercisers of varying ages, activity types, and fitness levels, could determine further links between exercise imagery and exercise adherence. Investigating the effects of using exercise imagery to encourage people to begin an exercise program, as well as its effects on exercise motivation and adherence, may also prove interesting. In addition, the effects of exercise imagery on self-efficacy and other psychological factors (such as motivation and anxiety), and the links between self-efficacy and exercise adherence warrant further research.

Gammage et al. (2000) suggested that examining imagery in relation to measures of exercise behavior other than frequency of exercise, such as duration of participation in an exercise program or the number of hours spent on exercise per week, may be informative. Different patterns of imagery use may be noticed among people who have been exercising for different lengths of time or who invest differing amounts of time per week into exercise programs.

A large, important, and relevant task for future researchers is to determine how to make exercise imagery work better and in more situations (Hall 2001). For example, addressing how imagery works in various physical activities for different people and understanding how exercise imagery can be applied most effectively to fitness training programs is important. Practitioners need advice on the important elements of exercise-imagery delivery, and exercisers require more information on the "hows" and "whys" of incorporating imagery into their physical-activity programs.

In their study of female exercisers, Giacobbi et al. (2003) found that appearance-related images served important motivational purposes that were linked to sustaining exercise behavior. They also proposed that there might be links between appearance-related imagery and body dissatisfaction in the exercise setting. This proposition does appear possible from their data, but further research is required before any substantial claims can be made.

So far, all the research on the uses of exercise imagery, the relationship of exercise imagery to self-efficacy, and the links between exercise imagery and both intention to exercise and actual exercise behavior has been conducted with relatively high-level exercisers. We have mentioned that in most developed countries, people who are sedentary or who do too little physical activity to generate health benefits constitute major physical and psychological health concerns. We cannot assume that exercise imagery would have the same motivational effects on people who do no physical activity as it does on those who participate at high levels. Nor can it be taken for granted that the effect of exercise imagery on low-level exercisers will lie somewhere between its impact on high-level exercise participants and those who do no physical activity other than work and household duties. This appears to be a critical and urgent area for research.

Perhaps the examination of the effect of exercise frequency on exercise imagery conducted by Gammage et al. (2000) can provide some clues about how low-level exercisers and nonexercisers might employ imagery for exercise, or not. (Even the low-level exercise group in their study was quite active in absolute terms.) Extrapolating from that study, it would seem likely that nonexercisers would do little or no exercise imagery. But the more pertinent question for improved community health is whether exercise-imagery interventions would produce increased levels of physical activity in sedentary people or low-level exercisers. Once again, based on cautious extrapolation of research information on relatively active people, it appears that exercise-imagery scripts aimed to increase activity levels in sedentary or low-active people need to be individualized. For example, in the study by Giacobbi et al. (2003), people who were involved in different activities used exercise imagery for different purposes; for example, runners used imagery for competitive outcomes, and aerobics participants used it to rehearse routines and experience aspects of the exercise context. Although accessing active exercisers is easy, and accessing exercisers within university communities is even easier for university-based researchers, research on exercise imagery must be quickly expanded to include sedentary and low-active people of all ages, both genders, and a wide range of educational, occupational, social, and economic demographics.

The recent development of research on imagery in the context of exercise has important implications. Because many developed countries share great concern about the large proportion of the population that does not undertake sufficient, regular physical activity to gain widely recognized health benefits, any techniques that can enhance physical-activity participation will be of great value. The theoretical arguments that Hall (1995) rehearsed and the research reported in this chapter suggest that imagery might have the potential to increase self-efficacy or self-confidence for physical activity, motivation and intention to exercise, and exercise behavior. It is important that the research on imagery for exercise is urgently applied to individuals who are sedentary or have a low level of physical activity, because these are the people who are at highest risk for physical and mental health problems. Given the recent rapid development of exercise psychology, the limited success of encouraging people to initiate and maintain healthy levels of physical activity (Buckworth and Dishman 2002) suggests that effective techniques are much sought after. Great opportunities are available for research on imagery related to physical activity, especially in sedentary individuals. We look forward to seeing a great deal of interest in this field during the next few years.

CHAPTER 13

FUTURE DIRECTIONS IN RESEARCH AND PRACTICE

In this book we have explored the diverse aspects of imagery examined by researchers in the context of sport and exercise and pointed out the substantial breadth of application of the imagery process as a means to enhance sport performers' experiences and performance. We have tried to present a comprehensive picture of the research and practice of imagery in sport; nonetheless, imagery has been examined from so many angles and in such a range of contexts that it would be a mighty challenge to cover every element of it. Similarly, its applications in sport are so diverse that we can give only a broad-brush reflection of the scope of imagery practice, with apologies to those sport psychology practitioners who have developed exciting, powerful imagery programs that are not included here.

A massive challenge still awaits researchers, and opportunities abound to apply imagery in new ways and to new aspects of sport and exercise. Although discussions of future research directions and practical applications of imagery in sport at specific levels end each chapter, it is time to consider both these issues in a consolidated way, often on a more global or generic level. In this chapter we explore some of the issues regarding research and directions for practice of imagery in sport that we consider relevant for the immediate future. The propositions and suggestions that follow depend more on our own perspectives than has much of the material in the previous 12 chapters. If only a few of these ideas spark some research or trigger ideas for new programs or approaches to practice, or if they stimulate debate about what should be studied or how we should do imagery in sport and exercise, the chapter will have served its purpose.

FUTURE DIRECTIONS IN IMAGERY RESEARCH

Imagery is a widely practiced psychological skill (Gould, Tammen, Murphy, and May 1989; Jowdy, Murphy, and Durtschi 1989) that has been the subject of much research in motor behavior and sport psychology. Although the research on imagery is quite extensive and varied and provides a strong basis for the use of imagery in sport and exercise, we have noted weaknesses and gaps in it. This section discusses some suggestions for future research on imagery in sport and exercise.

In general, imagery research demonstrates that it can enhance sport performance, but little is known about the processes involved in imagery. Research has tended to ask *if* imagery works, rather than *how* and *why* it works. Basic research is needed to clarify the mechanisms underlying the imagery process, determine more precisely the concomitants of effective imagery, and provide future research with measures that are reliable, valid, and that address the richness of imagery. Table 13.1 summarizes future directions for research on imagery in sport and exercise. These directions, issues, methodological considerations, and more are discussed in greater detail in later sections of this chapter.

ISSUES FOR FUTURE RESEARCH

This section discusses potential areas and issues to investigate in research on imagery in sport.

DEVELOPMENT AND TESTING OF THEORETICAL MODELS

Future research should attempt to develop and test theoretical models of imagery effects in the sport and exercise domain. Various theories have been applied to explain the effects of imagery in sport over the years, some of which have been adapted from general psychology and others from the motor domain. After 60 years, the psychoneuromuscular and symbolic learning theories are still the major perspectives in the area of learning and performance of motor and sport skills, but little more is known about them. Psychologists have proposed other explanations, such as Lang's (1977) bioinformational theory and Ahsen's (1984) triple-code theory, but they have not rigorously tested them in sport. Well-designed studies are needed to clarify the role of muscular innervation and symbolic representation as proposed by psychoneuromuscular and symbolic learning theories. For instance, no sound study has measured muscle innervation in muscle groups during imagery of both a task and performance. These theories seem to apply largely to what Murphy (1990)

Table 13.1 Future Directions for Research on Imagery in Sport and Exercise

Research direction	Explanation
Issues for future research	
Develop and test theoretical models	Research is needed to clarify understanding of how imagery operates in sport and exercise.
Study imagery functions other than skill learning or performance enhancement	Imagery is used for functions other than mental practice and skill acquisition; research on these uses, which include the development of motivation, confidence, or concentration, is required.
Examine imagery of expert skills in highly skilled performers	Research investigating how imagery operates with high-level performers and whether this is different from beginner or novice participants is important.
Explore psychophysiological processes associated with imagery in sport	Increased knowledge of the psychophysiological processes associated with imagery in sport may increase understanding of how imagery operates and enhance the efficacious use of imagery.
Examine the learning of imagery skills in children	To increase understanding of how children acquire and develop imagery skills.
Examine imagery development using longitudinal methods	To investigate whether imagery training brings about changes in the long-term in imagery ability and performance.
Investigate imagery ability and sense modality	Imagery ability and imagery modality should be considered as moderators in imagery use and effectiveness.
Investigate aspects of imagery perspective	To explore imagery-perspective issues (e.g., the effect of the nature of the sport skill, imagery-perspective development, differences in psychophysiological responses, and influence on aspects other than performance, such as motivation and confidence).

(continued)

Table 13.1 *(continued)*

Research direction	Explanation
Explore exercise imagery	Exercise imagery issues include the type of imagery associated with exercise and exercise imagery's impact on adopting and maintaining physical activity participation.
Methodological considerations	
Performance assessment and alternative variables	Consideration of the performance measures used and the role of factors such as confidence, motivation, skill level, and nature of imagery in imagery research.
Provide adequate descriptions of imagery treatments used in studies	Studies need to describe the imagery protocol used so that it can be replicated and compared with other studies.
Use manipulation checks	Researchers need to verify that athletes are imagining what they were instructed to.
Use well-developed imagery-measurement approaches	Imagery measures should be used in research and should consider various aspects of imagery ability and use.
Use skilled performers in research	Much imagery research has used lower-level performers; more could be learned about imagery use with elite-level athletes.
Include psychophysiological measures in imagery studies	Measurement of psychophysiological changes that occur during imagery may increase our understanding of imagery. Brain-scanning approaches could be especially useful.
Use longitudinal research methods	Longitudinal research approaches may provide information about long-term changes in performance or affective states due to imagery or changes in imagery use. Most studies have been short-term.

and Murphy and Martin (2002) referred to as the mental practice (MP) model; they are explanations of the effects of MP on skill learning. The central issue for the MP model is how to explain the process by which mental practice can mimic the effects of physical practice. This means that until recently, psychologists have largely ignored other functions of imagery in sport and exercise. However, imagery is used for more than skill learning in sport; therefore these theories do not adequately describe the scope of imagery's application in sport.

Alternative models on the working of imagery in sport have been slow to develop, although over the last decade some models that consider imagery as it functions in sport and exercise have appeared. Recent ones, such as the Applied Model of Imagery Use in Sport (AMIUS; Martin, Moritz, and Hall 1999), the Physical, Environment, Task, Timing, Learning, Emotion, and Perspective elements model (PETTLEP; Holmes and Collins 2001), the four Ws of imagery use (4W; Munroe, Giacobbi, Hall, and Weinberg 2000), the three-level model of imagery use in sport (Murphy and Martin 2002), and the hierarchical model of imagery ability in sport (SIAM; Watt and Morris 1998a, b, 1999a, b, 2000, 2001; Watt, Morris, and Andersen, 2004) provide conceptualizations of how imagery works in sport.

As yet, few of these models have undergone rigorous empirical analysis, but the support they receive from applied sport psychologists suggests that they have some merit. Research on these models is beginning to be reported in the literature, but more study is encouraged. For researchers, the models present several implications that are only beginning to be explored. For instance, the AMIUS model, which incorporates motivational and cognitive imagery functions (CS, CG, MS, MG-M, MG-A), predicts that desired outcomes are best achieved by using the specific functions of imagery. This would suggest that self-efficacy should increase more when a motivational function of imagery (MG-M) rather than a cognitive form of imagery (CS) is used. In addition, these models need to be refined as we progress. For instance, other types of imagery may be added to the models (Martin, Moritz, and Hall 1999). A study by Munroe, Giacobbi, Hall, and Weinberg (2000) suggested that CG imagery can be further distinguished as strategy development and execution.

So far the research on these models has focused primarily on imagery use. More research on other aspects, such as the impact of imagery ability, sport situation, or sport type as a moderator, would help clarify the models. The SIAM model addresses imagery ability as opposed to imagery functions; it may add to the imagery-use models. In addition, imagery modality, as investigated in the SIAM model, could be added to the imagery-use models since it can have an impact on the effectiveness of imagery. That is, CS imagery for skill acquisition may benefit more from kinesthetic imagery, whereas olfactory imagery, for example, may provide additional benefit to motivational imagery by enriching the scene.

The recent models, except for the PETTLEP, have also not included imagery perspective. It could be that perspective mediates the effectiveness of imagery for different functions. In line with the PETTLEP model, which proposes a functional equivalence between imagery and motor preparation, research that investigates whether imagery and motor preparation are functionally equivalent is needed in sport. This has been a hot topic in cognitive neuroscience, but so far researchers have investigated only simple movement skills rather than complex sport skills.

One issue concerning the imagery-use models is the temporal sequencing of imagery use and motivational and cognitive aspects of performance (Martin, Moritz, and Hall 1999); in other words, which comes first? Many of the studies on the models so far have investigated imagery use but not related it to outcome. Even if a relationship between imagery use and performance exists, it is not known whether it is causal. For instance, if athletes used motivational imagery extensively and showed high levels of motivation, did the imagery cause an increase in motivation or were the athletes using more motivational imagery because they were motivated in the first place?

Imagery Functions Other Than Skill Learning and Performance Enhancement

In the last decade or so imagery research and models have begun to explore imagery functions beyond those of the MP model, such as strategy learning, concentration, motivation, and confidence. Even though it seems that applied sport psychologists often use imagery for these functions, little research explores these uses in sport or exercise. Future research could give more focus to these functions of imagery rather than utilizing performance as the dependent variable. In terms of the motivational function of imagery, flow is a motivational variable that has not been directly investigated as an outcome of imagery, even though athletes often report using imagery to get into a certain mode or automated state (Munroe, Giacobbi, Hall, and Weinberg 2000).

Expert Imagery Skills in Highly Skilled Performers

The research on imagery and MP has focused largely on studies using novice or beginner performers learning new skills; consequently less is known about imagery with high-level performers. Research that investigates how imagery operates with high-level performers, and whether this is different than with beginner or novice participants, would increase our understanding of imagery with highly skilled athletes.

PSYCHOPHYSIOLOGICAL PROCESSES ASSOCIATED WITH IMAGERY IN SPORT

Much work can be done in an attempt to understand how imagery and physiological processes interact in sport and exercise. Research that investigates physiological changes due to imagery training would be of great interest to the field in understanding the processes associated with imagery in sport. Perhaps it would also provide some guidelines for how to use these psychophysiological processes to gain the greatest advantage from imagery training.

LEARNING OF IMAGERY SKILLS IN CHILDREN

Few sport psychology studies have investigated the development of imagery in children. Imagery is a basic memory system that is probably activated before infants start to use language to remember things (Simons 2000). In fact, for many centuries, people have recognized imagery as an effective way of remembering information (Reed 1996). Still, we do not have an in-depth understanding of how young athletes acquire and develop imagery skills (Murphy and Martin 2002), for example, in terms of imagery perspective development (see Morris and Spittle 2001).

IMAGERY DEVELOPMENT USING LONGITUDINAL METHODS

Studies that investigate whether imagery training brings about changes in imagery ability over time are also warranted. Although the term "imagery ability" is used, imagery is generally seen as a skill that can be improved with practice. Limited research has been done on the development of imagery skills over extended periods of time, to determine whether they change in addition to performance. If athletes' imagery skills are being developed, that means their future imagery practice should be more effective than their first exposure to imagery training. If children are taught imagery skills as junior athletes, would it give them an advantage over their opponents once they are adults?

IMAGERY ABILITY AND SENSE MODALITY

Sport psychologists and psychologists in general have devoted more research to visual imagery than other sensory modalities. The kinesthetic sense is often described as important in imagery of sport skills (Murphy and Martin 2002; Orlick 1990) but has attracted much less research than visual imagery. In addition, athletes do report imagining their surroundings, especially the competition venue (Munroe, Giacobbi, Hall, and Weinberg 2000). What they report could depend on what researchers ask or what athletes think is important. If athletes do not image contextual factors, then imagery that uses a wider range of senses, such as tactile, auditory, olfactory, and gustatory modalities, may be beneficial.

Perhaps this will be addressed by research using the SIAM model (Watt et al. 2003). Based on suggestions that imagery that is more realistic (Lang 1977) will produce more change in behavior, cognition, or affect, we could predict that imagery that utilizes a wider range of sensory modalities, with a higher degree of clarity, will produce greater change. Studies that measure imagery modality, using instruments such as the SIAM, could compare imagery ability and outcome to assess the effects of sense modality.

In terms of imagery ability or skill, the speed of generation and duration of imagery have not been adequately investigated. Most studies on imagery ability have focused on clarity and controllability, but the speed of generation of images and ability to hold them may be more sensitive indicators of imagery skill and may have a bigger impact on outcome. Research that involves initial assessment of the dimensional components of imagery ability and then compares outcomes in relation to those dimensions over a long-term imagery program could significantly increase our understanding of the impact of those dimensions.

ASPECTS OF IMAGERY PERSPECTIVE

Many problems have contributed to mixed findings in the imagery perspective literature: the confounding of internal and external imagery with kinesthetic and visual imagery, the poor quality of instructions used in studies, random assignment of participants without considering perspective use or preference, the use of questionable scales in the measurement of internal and external imagery, lack of manipulation checks to verify adherence to imagery instructions, absence of description of training protocols, large differences between imagery practice conditions, and, until recently, the lack of consideration of aspects of the task.

The confounding of internal and external imagery with kinesthetic and visual imagery abounds in the literature; as a consequence, many studies have not actually compared internal and external imagery. The random assignment of participants without considering initial perspective use or preference might be problematic in many studies. Preference has been reported as being important to imagery-perspective use, but no systematic research has investigated whether it actually exists. Many studies have not used manipulation checks to assess whether participants have complied with the imagery instructions or training. Researchers have also relied on objective physical performance scores to assess training programs rather than determining whether imagery-perspective training actually taught participants to use one.

Until relatively recently, researchers have failed to recognize that the tasks being imaged and performed in their studies might mediate the relationship between imagery perspective and performance enhancement, with the result that one perspective is not superior in all situations

(Glisky, Williams, and Kihlstrom 1996; Hardy and Callow 1999; Spittle and Morris 1999a, b, 2000; White and Hardy 1995). The research on task type suggests that different tasks influence the efficacy of perspective use; however, this relationship is still unclear. Clearly, more research is needed on the influence of imagery perspectives on performance of sport skills, specifically to address issues of task type, imagery-perspective preference, the interaction of external and kinesthetic imagery, and imagery-training effects on perspective use. One issue that has not been adequately addressed is comparison of the impact of internal and external imagery on cognition, affect, and motivation rather than performance (Hardy, Jones, and Gould 1996). This might help clarify the role of imagery perspective in imagery-use models.

Research that examines the default hypothesis of imagery-perspective use would add much to the understanding of perspective preference in sport and exercise (Morris and Spittle 2001). The default hypothesis is based on the idea that internal imagery may be the default perspective and the extent to which an athlete uses external imagery depends on experience, particularly during childhood. Certain predictions flow from the default hypothesis, which could be tested in future research. An obvious prediction is that younger people will favor the internal perspective. Another prediction is that experience will influence perspective use. Studies could explore the sport experience of adolescents and adults and compare it with imagery-perspective use.

EXERCISE IMAGERY

Exercise imagery has received some recent research interest, and with good reason. Given the difficulties in adopting and maintaining exercise and physical activity, imagery could prove to be an effective intervention in the exercise setting. Once again, research is needed. Imagery can serve motivational, confidence, and performance functions that might help in exercise participation, and these are beginning to be investigated. Variables involved in the imagery and exercise field could also be isolated, to investigate whether exercise imagery has a direct effect or influences participation through factors such as motivation or self-efficacy (Hall 2001).

METHODOLOGICAL CONSIDERATIONS

In this section we discuss issues related to the design and conduct of research on imagery in sport, to guide future investigation. These include how we assess performance changes following imagery, the need for adequate description of imagery treatments in research reports, the importance of using manipulation checks to ensure that the imagery treatment was carried out as planned, the development and use of sport and exercise imagery measures, the involvement of skilled performers in imagery research, the inclusion of psychophysiological measures to enhance our understanding of brain and bodily processes associated with imagery use, and the application of longitudinal research designs.

PERFORMANCE ASSESSMENT AND ALTERNATIVE VARIABLES

Some researchers have suggested that performance assessment in imagery and MP is a potential problem in considering the efficacy of such interventions (Feltz and Landers 1983; Suinn 1983). Performance measures of high-level athletes may not be sensitive enough to small changes in performance, yet at the elite level such changes are incredibly important. Other performance measures, such as consistency or secondary task measures (e.g., effort), might be useful (Budney, Murphy, and Woolfolk 1994). Single-subject designs, such as those utilized by Kendall, Hrycaiko, Martin, and Kendall (1990), Kearns and Crossman (1992), Callery and Morris (1993, 1997a, b, c), and Shambrook and Bull (1996) are useful because they may be able to pick up performance changes for an elite athlete and graph consistency over time. Also, graphical analyses of individual performance can counter Hawthorne or placebo effects by providing intra-subject control.

Thoughtful examination of those factors that appear to influence the operation of imagery is another direction for future research. Major concomitants of imagery include, again, the role of motivation, expectancy, or belief in the imagery process and the interaction between skill level and the nature of the imagery presented. The precise role of imagery ability in successful imagery is another issue, along with benefits to the practitioner's capability to design effective programs based on the measurement of imagery-ability parameters. The role of relaxation is still relevant, not as a necessary condition for imagery but as a factor that might enhance the experience greatly in some circumstances (and merely add time to the session in others). Another problem highlighted by Murphy (1990) is that researchers have largely neglected differences between participants' imagery styles, assuming that all participants will benefit from MP. An issue that needs investigation is whether certain people would benefit from imagery while others would gain more from another kind of intervention because of their imaginal style. Such research adopts more of an individual-differences approach rather than a traditional experimental one.

Meta-analysis has overcome some of the problems of the imagery and MP literature and has been useful in interpreting MP's effects on performance. The Feltz and Landers (1983), Feltz, Landers, and Becker (1988), and Hinshaw (1991) meta-analyses are widely cited to describe the efficacy of MP and imagery, but an exploration of MP effects compared to physical practice (PP) effects, using meta-analysis, has not been published (Goginsky and Collins 1996).

ADEQUATE DESCRIPTIONS OF IMAGERY TREATMENTS USED IN STUDIES

A problem with research on imagery has been a lack of adequate description of imagery or MP protocols and instructions used in studies. Lack of consistency in, or description of, the timing of instruction, the nature and type of instructions, the number and length of sessions, and the timing of posttests has made it difficult to replicate studies and confidently compare the results. For example, a 6-week, 3-sessions-per-week program of 30 minutes per session is likely to have different effects than a single practice session on the day of testing, so these conditions need to be reported. In addition, if an imagery variable was manipulated, researchers should provide information on how this was achieved. For instance, studies on imagery perspective and stimulus and response propositions should describe how these were manipulated.

MANIPULATION CHECKS

Many studies in the imagery literature have failed to use manipulation checks to find out what participants actually imagine. In many cases, researchers have assumed that participants followed the instructions or imagined according to the assigned condition. Yet it has been found that participants can change or vary the imagery script (e.g., Collins, Smith, and Hale 1998; Harris and Robinson 1986; Jowdy and Harris 1990; Spittle and Morris 2000). Very few studies have measured what participants actually *report* imagining, as opposed to what the researchers *told* them to imagine. This has created a problem with ensuring the success of independent variable manipulation in the imagery literature.

Generally, manipulation checks are self-reports that ask participants about their imagery. Investigating what athletes are doing during imagery may also be achieved through creative experimental approaches, such as dual-task procedures. For example, based on functional-equivalence views of imagery, interference should occur when participants need to perform two tasks that use the same sense modality (Moran 2002). This being the case, if an athlete is engaging in kinesthetic imagery, performance on a concurrent task that relies on the kinesthetic sense should be affected, but a visual or auditory task should not deteriorate so much.

WELL-DEVELOPED IMAGERY-MEASUREMENT APPROACHES

The imagery and MP literature reports the use of various measurement approaches, often with imagery measures that were not specifically designed for research in sport or exercise. A major problem across imagery studies has been the lack of control and measurement of imagery or MP quality. Psychologists have suggested that imagery ability is important to the effectiveness of imagery (Feltz and Landers 1983; Weinberg

1982), yet it has not been systematically measured in studies. When researchers have done so, usually they have measured only vividness and controllability; however, many other dimensions of imagery could be investigated. To assume that control and vividness are the only important dimensions of imagery is a narrow view. The efficacy of imagery in some tasks could be associated with other factors or dimensions, such as intensity and reality of the image, ease and speed of image generation, duration of image, sense modalities used, imagery perspective employed, and image content.

Recent developments in models have produced more applicable assessment approaches. The development of a promising measure of imagery use in sport, the Sport Imagery Questionnaire (SIQ; Hall, Mack, Paivio, and Hausenblas 1998); a measure of imagery use in exercise, the Exercise Imagery Questionnaire (EIQ; Hausenblas, Hall, Rodgers, and Munroe 1999); and a measure of imagery ability in sport, the Sport Imagery Ability Measure (SIAM, Watt et al. 2003) have opened up new areas for research. These include the moderating roles that imagery use and ability might play in the effective application of imagery, especially when it is used to enhance performance. Alternative approaches for imagery measurement might also be considered, including verbalization protocols to monitor actual imagery content (Spittle and Morris 1999a, b) or psychophysiological approaches, especially using central brain mapping procedures such as PET and rCBf, which are described in chapter 7.

SKILLED PERFORMERS IN RESEARCH

The research on imagery and MP has focused largely on studies using novice or beginner performers learning new skills. It has demonstrated that imagery is effective at enhancing motor learning but is difficult to translate to the use of imagery with skilled or high-level performers in sport. Additional descriptive and exploratory research on how high-level athletes use imagery is needed, but more important, we need experimental approaches that investigate whether these different uses of imagery are effective with high-level athletes.

PSYCHOPHYSIOLOGICAL MEASURES IN IMAGERY STUDIES

The psychophysiology of imagery has been a hot topic in other areas, such as neuroscience, and many papers are being published about brain activity during motor imagery and motor preparation. In sport psychology, the psychophysiological research to date has largely been limited to peripheral-measures studies, such as those examining heart rate and EMG. Central studies that utilize measures such as positron emission tomography (PET) and magnetic resonance imaging (MRI) to investigate sport and exercise skills would add much to our understanding of imagery in these areas. These techniques could also be applied to imagery variables, such as internal and external imagery or motivational imagery versus cognitive imagery, to ascertain any differences in activation patterns for various types of imagery.

LONGITUDINAL RESEARCH METHODS

Longitudinal research approaches may provide information about long-term changes in performance or affective states due to imagery or changes in imagery use. So far studies have generally been short-term and so have provided information only on short-term changes; thus we know little about the long-term effects of imagery training in sport and exercise.

FUTURE DIRECTIONS IN IMAGERY PRACTICE

Given that the possible applications of imagery are as varied as the creative imaginations of those who use this highly flexible technique, speculations could run wild in this section. To provide some structure to the discussion, we consider two kinds of future direction in the practice of imagery in sport. First we address the application of imagery *to* new aspects of sport and related activities. As well as examining the use of imagery in new sport contexts, we also raise the possibility of applying approaches developed in sport psychology to cognate fields. Second, we reflect on the application *of* new imagery techniques and procedures. We propose wider use of new techniques and the application of new elements in programs. The future directions of imagery application are presented in table 13.2.

APPLICATION TO NEW ASPECTS OF SPORT

In the past, the primary area of application for imagery has been the enhancement of sport-skills performance (e.g., Morris, Spittle, and Perry 2004; Vealey and Greenleaf 2001). Imagery is typically included in psychological-skills training programs for athletes, alongside goal setting, stress management, building confidence, and enhancing concentration (e.g., Morris and Thomas 2004). Morris et al. (2004) presented examples of this application, citing reports of imagery programs that were designed to enhance performance in major sports, such as baseball (She and Morris 1997), basketball (Carter and Kelly 1997; Shambrook and Bull 1996), soccer (Hale and Whitehouse 1998), and golf (Beauchamp, Bray, and Albinson 2002; Taylor and Shaw 2002), and minor sports like kayaking (Millard, Mahoney, and Wardrop 2001), Australian Rules football (Callery and Morris 1997a, b, c), and Gaelic football (O'Donoghue and Ormsby 2002).

Table 13.2   Future Directions for Application of Imagery in Sport and Exercise

Area of application	Explanation
Applications to new aspects of sport	
Recently established areas of application of imagery in sport	Moving beyond performance enhancement to personal development, well-being, and enjoyment
New areas of application of imagery in sport	Increasing use of imagery to enhance motivation in sport, rehabilitation from injury, and recovery from heavy training
Future areas of application of imagery	Developing imagery use in areas like coping skills, flow enhancement, and motivation for physical activity
Application of imagery to related fields	Applying knowledge about imagery in sport to fields like the performing arts and business
Application of new imagery techniques and procedures	
Dos and don'ts in the application of imagery to sport	Guidelines for applying imagery exist, but the dos and don'ts of imagery change as research and applied experience dictate.
New applications of technical aids to imagery in sport	Technical aids like biofeedback and flotation are in use, but new technologies can alter their application. Examining ways to make current applications work optimally is essential.
New procedures for the application of imagery in sport	Ways to expand imagery use and make it more effective (e.g., use of minivideo camcorders or phone camcorders for video modeling on site and development of effective assessment to help customize imagery programs).

NEW AND RECENTLY ESTABLISHED AREAS OF APPLICATION

Recently, sport psychologists have begun to apply imagery in other ways that are associated with personal development, psychological well-being, and enjoyment of sport but that also affect performance (Morris et al. 2004). The reduction of stress and anxiety is one application that many sport performers would readily choose in order to enhance the positive (or reduce the negative) experience of competition. Whereas various relaxation techniques have been used to decrease anxiety, imagery of a pleasant place or of effective coping and imagery done in the flotation environment are effective and increasingly popular ways to manage stress and anxiety (see chapters 10 and 11). Similarly, imagery of handling difficult situations well and imagery of success have been shown to be effective in developing confidence (Morris et al. 2004). Imagery exercises that involve focusing on a specific object or thought can enhance concentration, and imagery of scenes in which many things are happening can broaden attention (e.g., Bond and Sargent 2004).

Although the imagery applications just mentioned are relatively new and growing, they are well established. Perhaps the newest applications for imagery in regard to thoughts, feelings, and behavior, which sport psychologists are starting to implement, are to enhance motivation, facilitate rehabilitation from injury, and support recovery from heavy training. Hall and his colleagues (e.g., Hall 2001; Hall et al. 1998; Munroe et al. 2000) have been examining imagery use in sport for more than 10 years, distinguishing between imagery for cognitive and motivational purposes as proposed earlier still by Paivio (1985). Nonetheless, the application of imagery to enhance motivation is in its infancy. Martin and Hall (1995) reported on the use of imagery to enhance motivation in soccer. Gaskin and Morris (2002) proposed more general applications for imagery enhancement of intrinsic motivation. Their proposal for applying imagery to develop intrinsic motivation was based on the self-determination theory (Deci and Ryan 1985). The application of that theory involves imagery exercises that focus on the experience of self-determination, or the feeling of being in control, in the sport context as well as imagery scripts that aim to build the athlete's perceived competence regarding the activity. According to Deci and Ryan, the perception of being self-determining and the perception of being competent are the two precursors of intrinsic motivation. Given the importance of intrinsic motivation for effort and persistence, especially in the face of initial failure, this imagery approach has great potential application to sport.

Like the proposal that imagery can enhance motivation, the idea that it can facilitate rehabilitation from injury is not new (Green 1993; Ievleva and Orlick 1991), but this kind of imagery use has not been widely reported in the literature. One reason could be that practitioners want to have a sound basis for it, given the risks associated with inappropriate treatment of injury. At the same time, as chapter 11 reveals, research on the application of imagery for injury rehabilitation has been slow to emerge, perhaps because of the difficulty of gaining access to appropriate samples for such research. Serious athletes who have been injured during the season are usually in no mood to volunteer for research in which they "imagine their injury getting better." Ironically, the existing research shows that imagery has a range of uses, each of which can smooth the path to recovery (see chapter 11). Thus, the application of imagery in injury rehabilitation appears to be a promising direction for the future.

The demands of heavy training schedules continue to plague elite sport, leading to high stress levels, overtraining, and burnout in performers who have only recently attained elite status and, in some cases, those who are still striving for that goal. The latest thinking is that it is not so much a problem of *overdoing* practice and performance as it is a result of *underestimating* the recovery time needed between bouts of heavy training (Kellman 2002). Imagery can be applied to the effects of heavy training in many of the same ways it is used in injury rehabilitation. We do not claim that imagery can substitute for rest between practice sessions, but athletes could employ healing imagery to enhance recovery in fatigued muscles, pleasant-place imagery to reduce the effects of stress associated with heavy training, and positive-outcome imagery to increase motivation and confidence concerning practice (see chapter 11). Imagery in flotation offers particular advantages in this context. Floating in body-temperature water is proposed to have physical benefits (Suedfeld, Turner, and Fine 1990) and has been shown to be deeply relaxing (Aldridge et al. 2003). Further, imagery of the type just described can be carried out in an environment with few distractions. Athletes based at the Australian Institute of Sport have taken advantage of the imagery-and-flotation option for some time (Bond 1987). Nonetheless, imagery for recovery from heavy training is included among those areas that have great potential for substantially expanded use in high-level sport because it has not been widely reported.

FUTURE AREAS OF IMAGERY IN SPORT

Some of the areas in which imagery has been implicated in theoretical or research papers suggest the potential for new areas of application, such as to develop coping skills, enhance the experience of flow in sport, and enhance motivation for exercise and physical activity. As noted in chapter 8, Weinberg and Gould (2003) recently advocated the use of imagery to cope with high-pressure performance situations.

Noh, Morris, and Andersen (2002, 2003, in press) have reported a set of studies that included an imagery script as part of a coping intervention in the performance context of dance. Based on life stress, coping skills, and social-support questionnaires, Noh et al. (in press) found that Korean ballet dancers experienced high levels of stress during practice and performance and typically reported limited coping skills in those situations. Further, regression analysis indicated that the strongest predictor of injury among the dancers was inadequate coping skills. In-depth interviews supported this picture, with many dancers resorting to inappropriate eating behavior and alcohol consumption as coping strategies to handle the substantial stress (Noh et al. 2002). Noh et al. (2003) devised an intervention in which imagery of effective coping with the specific stressors experienced by the Korean ballet dancers was combined with positive self-talk. This intervention produced an increase in self-reported coping skills and a reduction in the incidence of injury, compared to a control group and an autogenic-training intervention. Noh and Morris (in press) emphasized that the questionnaire and interview studies provided information that permitted the intervention's imagery script to focus on specific stressful elements of the study population's performance environment. Such information can be gathered by assessment in each sport or performance environment, preferably using a mix of questionnaire and interview techniques. This approach seems to have great potential, but, as Noh and Morris pointed out, studies are needed that examine the results of effective-coping imagery scripts as the sole intervention technique, rather than in combination with other techniques.

We consider it surprising that finding research or applications in which imagery is employed to enhance the occurrence of the flow state is difficult (Csikszentmihalyi 1990). Jackson and Csikszentmihalyi (1999) described flow as a psychological state that is associated with positive affect, increased intrinsic motivation, and peak experiences. They proposed that enhancing the experience of flow in a task or activity, such as sport performance, can lead to increased effort, persistence, and performance. They described nine antecedents of flow in sport, which are also the basis for measures of dispositional flow (Dispositional Flow Scale-2; Jackson and Ecklund 2002) and flow state (Flow State Scale-2; Jackson and Ecklund 2002) developed by Jackson. Jackson and Csikszentmihalyi proposed that flow is more likely to arise when (a) athletes' skills match the challenge imposed by the task; (b) their awareness merges with their actions; (c) they have clear goals; (d) they receive unambiguous feedback about their performance; (e) their concentration is focused totally on the task at hand; (f) they experience a sense of control over the situation; (g) they experience a loss of self-consciousness; (h) they experience a transformation in time (often time seems to be slowed down, so that there is plenty of time for performance); and (i) they have an "autotelic" experience (they seem to do things automatically, without having to think about them).

Throughout this book, imagery has been shown to enhance most of the nine antecedents; thus it seems reasonable to propose that imagery, which is specifically directed at the antecedents in a particular sport context, should enhance the experience of flow. In addition to this indirect evidence, the limited research on flow in sport offers some evidence that it can be enhanced by imagery. That evidence largely depends on the acknowledged similarity between hypnosis and imagery (e.g., Liggett 2000). Grove and Lewis (1996) found that people who were more readily hypnotizable (as measured by a self-report hypnotic-susceptibility scale) reported higher levels of flow. Pates and colleagues (Pates and Maynard 2000; Pates, Cummings, and Maynard 2002; Pates, Oliver, and

Maynard 2003) found that "hypnosis" interventions, which essentially comprised relaxation, imagery, and deepening components, enhanced flow and performance in golf chipping, basketball three-point shooting, and golf putting, respectively. Sport psychologists are now beginning to realize the benefits that can be gleaned from enhancing flow (e.g., Jackson and Csikszentmihalyi 1999; Pates et al. 2003), such as greater enjoyment, higher frequency and duration of participation, greater effort and persistence (especially in the face of failure), and peak experiences, as well as the possibility of improved performance.

The growing interest in flow as a positive experience that can assist sport performers means that the rich and various ways that imagery could be used to enhance the antecedents of flow present great possibilities for the field. We might even revisit much of the previous research on imagery and performance to explore the proposition that flow is a mediator in that relationship. In the past, researchers have not measured flow when they have examined imagery's effect on performance, let alone explored the causal connections between imagery, flow, and performance.

We have observed that practitioners have started to use imagery to enhance motivation for sport performance; Hall and Martin (1995) presented the first research evidence of this in the context of intrinsic motivation. In chapter 12, we reported on the research that Hall and his colleagues conducted on the possible role of imagery in the context of exercise and physical activity (e.g., Hausenblas et al. 1999; Gammage et al. 2000). Although we questioned the strong emphasis placed on Paivio's (1985) motivational function of imagery for exercise compared to his proposal about cognitive function, the application of imagery to enhance motivation for exercise does appear to be a major future direction of imagery practice. Imagery scripts that emphasize successful completion of exercise programs have the potential to enhance self-efficacy, while the achievement of desired outcomes, such as greater health and fitness or weight loss, should enhance outcome expectancy. A focus in imagery scripts on pleasant experiences during physical activity should also enhance motivation to perform the exercise. In fact, perhaps practitioners and researchers should consider the links between flow and motivation for physical activity.

APPLICATION OF IMAGERY TO SPORT- AND EXERCISE-RELATED FIELDS

Sport and exercise psychology has relied on mainstream psychology to a large extent for its theoretical frameworks and research methods. In its relatively short history, however, this subdiscipline of psychology has developed practical programs and procedures that have proved to be attractive outside sport. Morris and Thomas (2004) have discussed the growing trend of application of sport and exercise psychology in the business world (e.g., Jones 2002) and in the performing arts (e.g., Hays 2000). People who strive to attain the highest levels of performance in nonsport activities are turning to sport psychologists for assistance, and consequently, we can expect that proven imagery applications in sport will be modified for use in those fields. In business, a major focus is on team building, including developing commitment to the group and its goals and cultivating motivation to strive hard. In the arts, especially music and singing, drama, and dance, motivation and goal setting, stress management, confidence building, and focusing attention are critical to optimizing performance.

The research by Noh and colleagues (Noh et al. 2003; in press) on enhancing coping skills and reducing stress in dance exemplified one way to employ imagery. In dance, and ballet in particular, where injuries are frequent, the impact of the imagery and self-talk intervention on injury also has noteworthy implications. Many other jobs and activities involve performing complex skills in high-pressure conditions, including those of surgeons, pilots, physical therapists, and dentists. People in these fields can benefit from the application of imagery programs in ways that are similar to their use in sport.

APPLICATION OF NEW IMAGERY TECHNIQUES AND PROCEDURES

Although the application of imagery in sport is a relatively recent development, imagery research has a long history. Based on what was already known about imagery, writers like Vealey (1986) were able to present substantial lists of guidelines for the application of imagery to sport, and imagery was included in early psychological-skills training programs (e.g., Martens 1987; Orlick 1980). As research on imagery practice in sport has expanded, those guidelines have been refined (e.g., Gould, Damarjian, and Greenleaf 2002; Murphy and Jowdy 1992; Murphy and Martin 2002; Perry and Morris 1995; Vealey and Greenleaf 2001). Much of what we know about procedures to deliver imagery programs effectively is reviewed in chapter 8. Nonetheless, the quality of imagery training and practice can still be enhanced in some areas.

DOS AND DON'TS IN APPLYING IMAGERY

In chapter 8, we presented guidelines for implementing imagery and identified thought processes and behaviors to avoid during imagery practice. Those guidelines were based on current best practice, which derives from research and experience in applied settings. Sport psychology researchers and practitioners are continually refining the "dos" and "don'ts" of imagery application, so anyone who aims to employ imagery must be conversant with the latest research and applied writing. Imagery is a ubiquitous process, but one that is not yet directly observable. Having written a book on what we *do* know about imagery, we must acknowledge that we don't know how much we *don't* know.

We also realize that much remains to learn about how to apply imagery optimally. An example is the issue of imagining incorrect skill production. Based on the research to date (e.g., Taylor and Shaw 2002; Woolfolk et al. 1985), we advise athletes not to perform imagery of incorrect skill production. The one exception is when imagery is being used for problem solving, but we stress that this use should be only occasional and should be a separate process from imagery rehearsal for skill performance. This exception is based on intuition; we know of no research that has shown that imagery of incorrect skill production does not have a negative effect on actual skill performance, even if it is isolated from regular imagery practice.

Further, the use of different terms in the literature creates considerable confusion. Here we have carefully specified "incorrect skill production." Some writers refer to "negative performance" as opposed to positive performance. This is a less precise term because the meaning of "negative" is unclear in this context. What is negative in one situation can be positive in other circumstances, and what is negative for one person is often positive for another. The word "performance" is also imprecise. Performance has many aspects. The term could refer to skill production or strategy; it could relate to how individuals manage their emotions, or it might concern physical aspects of behavior, such as power or endurance. To add to this fuzziness, we often distinguish between performance, in the sense of doing the activity, and outcome, which refers to the end product. For example, in the context of golf putting, which was the task examined by Woolfolk et al., performance would be the act of swinging the putter through the ball, and the outcome would be where the ball ended up, in the cup or perhaps short and to the left of the hole. We recommend that imagery should involve both *correct* performance, or skill production (e.g., a club swing through the ball), and a *positive* outcome (e.g., the ball goes into the hole). Although only correct skill-production imagery directly affects actual movements, imagery of successful outcomes enhances confidence, which indirectly affects skill production. More specific research is needed on the components of "positive" imagery before we can be confident about our advice to sport psychology practitioners and athletes.

The need for more research applies to most of the field of imagery. Other examples include real-speed versus slow-motion imagery, the use of relaxation with imagery, the benefit of imagery training on nonsport content, and the appropriate amount of imagery practice. We believe that the advice in this book is the best available today, but some of it will change tomorrow. Be prepared!

NEW APPLICATIONS OF TECHNICAL AIDS TO IMAGERY

The potential for technical aids to facilitate imagery is now well established from research, and they are employed in conjunction with imagery practiced in locations that have the resources to provide them, such as the Australian Institute of Sport and the United States Olympic Training Center. Use of biofeedback and video modeling (relatively portable techniques) in combination with imagery could be expanded beyond those kinds of environments to general use in practice and competition. However, the use of flotation is limited to a controlled environment, so the issues relating to its optimal use as an adjunct to imagery concern the transfer of effects from the flotation laboratory to the sport venue.

Small, portable GSR units that present a tone through an ear piece have been used by sport psychologists to provide biofeedback during relaxation training for many years. Visual information about heart rate (HR) on wristwatch-style receivers, used for a similar purpose, has also been available for quite some time. These devices can serve the same function when imagery, rather than progressive muscle relaxation, autogenic training, or the relaxation response, is used to induce the relaxed state. Right now, athletes can use this equipment in biofeedback training with imagery, which starts at the training venue and moves to the competition arena once the athlete is comfortable and in control. No doubt miniature EMG and EEG devices will be available before too long; we have seen the first models, but they are not yet highly reliable. More reliable versions of these devices will permit imagery to be applied to the control of muscle activity and brainwaves away from the laboratory. At the very least, those athletes who feel comfortable with imagery work could use pleasant-place or coping imagery, supported by reliable miniature GSR or HR devices, instead of other techniques to induce relaxation.

Flotation has been shown to be a powerful adjunct to imagery (see chapter 10). Its biggest limitation is that it requires an expensive laboratory setup and lacks portability. Nonetheless, the transfer of the effect of imagery in the flotation environment to actual task production, such as basketball free-throw shooting or even competition performance, has been demonstrated (e.g., Lee and Hewitt 1987; Suedfeld and Bruno 1990). By exploring factors in the imagery and flotation experience that affect transfer, we can optimize the transfer of imagery benefits gained in flotation to the competition context. For example, examining the effect on actual performance of including imagery of the competition context prior to performance imagery during flotation would be interesting. Further, would piping crowd or other noises typical of competition venues into the restricted sensory environment of the flotation tank assist transfer of flotation effects to the performance imagery in competition? We are not aware of any research that has studied techniques that can be used between flotation and performance to enhance the effectiveness of imagery in flotation. Does imagery in flotation, followed by imagery sessions at the practice or competition venue, lead to greater benefits than imagery practice in flotation only? Investigation of these issues could considerably change the procedures used to support imagery during and after the powerful experience of imagery in flotation.

NEW PROCEDURES FOR THE APPLICATION OF IMAGERY

Video modeling may be given a new lease on life by the recent development of mini video recorders, smaller than a hand, and the ongoing mobile-telephone revolution. Telephones that can record and replay video material are already being sold by the thousands. Both these types of devices make the use of video modeling on competition sites feasible, as a method of cueing imagery of an ideal, or at least excellent, performance. Although we propose these practices as new directions for the application of imagery in sport, the application of such technology needs to be approached with caution. We must do further research to examine the strengths and weaknesses of video modeling using this technology as portable adjuncts to imagery. In particular, we need to study the impact of imagery that is based on portable video-modeling devices in circumstances in which video recorders and monitors have not been available until now, such as on site and during travel. This should lead to the development of guidelines for the effective use of these devices in supporting imagery practice by athletes.

Practitioners who use imagery effectively customize imagery scripts for the needs of individual athletes. Little research has examined this approach, especially from the perspective of advising applied sport psychologists about the best way to determine what to include in a customized script. The research on coping skills in dance reported earlier in this chapter provides some support for this approach. In that research, two studies examined the factors that were important for the population of interest, namely Korean high-level ballet dancers. The first study, using questionnaires and regression analysis, identified coping skills as needing development (Noh et al., in press). In the second study, Noh et al. (2002) identified the main stressors that Korean ballet dancers had to manage: dance directors' criticism, the pressure of intense practice and competition, rivalry between training colleagues and friends for leading roles, and the need for stringent dieting to attain and maintain the ideal body. Imagery and self-talk interventions, which were designed specifically to address those stressors, enhanced coping skills and reduced the incidence of injury (Noh et al. 2003). In the Noh et al. intervention study, the imagery script was customized to Korean ballet dancers as a whole rather than to each individual dancer. Also, the imagery script's design was based on research, when it would typically evolve from the practitioner's assessment of the performer. Nonetheless, the principle was demonstrated. Customized imagery scripts that are designed on the basis of thorough assessment of athletes' individual needs are likely to be particularly effective; however, we still need to develop guidelines for efficient, reliable ways to conduct those assessments. Imagery script design that is based on the outcomes of such assessment is another area that requires more thought, research, and guidance.

CONCLUSIONS

Imagery is a ubiquitous process that most people experience almost all the time. In sport and exercise, imagery has many functions, which has led to a great deal of research. Unfortunately, much of that research has not been systematic; often, it is as if we have opened the door to a room full of interesting things, glanced in, and then closed the door and glanced into another room, then another. We need to identify the most critical issues relating to the imagery process in the context of sport and exercise and establish major research programs to study them in detail. In this chapter, we have given our views about some of those issues in two ways. First, regarding future research related to imagery in sport, we have discussed some of the major issues concerning imagery that have been addressed in other chapters. Second, we have looked at the future of the application of imagery in sport and noted some of the major questions that research must answer to improve the use of imagery in practice. We have left in abeyance the important task of prioritizing imagery research. A challenge for the future is to get imagery researchers to discuss this issue, let alone come to some agreement about the appropriate focuses of research, when it is the very richness of the imagery process that makes it so fascinating.

The richness of imagery is also a major factor in the consideration of its application. Imagery can be used in almost every aspect of human experience. We can imagine actions, emotions, and even biological processes of healing (as discussed in chapter 12). In chapters 9, 10, 11, and 12, we presented some of the areas in which imagery has already been applied. Here we have suggested some additional directions for the future, but we acknowledge that new, unforeseen approaches will undoubtedly arise tomorrow, based on the needs of athletes and the creativity of sport psychologists. Equally important to the topics to which we can apply imagery are the principles that help us use best-practice imagery procedures with athletes. We addressed some of these in chapter 8 and discussed some approaches that are specific to technical aids, rehabilitation from injury, and exercise in chapters 10, 11, and 12, respectively. In this chapter we have made suggestions about future directions in the development of techniques and procedures to apply imagery effectively. We present no sensational insights about the practice of imagery in sport, but perhaps some of the suggestions will stimulate practitioners to explore new approaches that will benefit the field.

In the future, practitioners might, through their experience of delivering programs, identify critical components that are not evident to imagery experts. Researchers might derive new techniques from their studies' findings. Often discoveries that change the direction of scientific research and practice arise by serendipity or as by-products of work that has other focuses. Although we await such a momentous development in imagery research or practice, we must continue to develop aspects of the application of imagery to sport and exercise in a rather piecemeal fashion. On one point, there is little question: Imagery is a powerful tool, which we are only beginning to use effectively and efficiently in sport. We look forward to reading about the new discoveries that emanate from research and the original approaches that practitioners find effective in using imagery in sport and exercise.

REFERENCES

Abma, C.L., M.D. Fry, Y. Li, and G. Relyea. 2002. Differences in imagery content and imagery ability between high and low confident track and field athletes. *Journal of Applied Sport Psychology* 14 (2): 67-75.

Adrian, E.D., and B.H.C. Matthews. 1934. The Berger Rhythm: Potential changes from the occipital lobes in man. *Brain* 57: 335-385.

Ahsen, A. 1984. ISM: The triple-code model for imagery and psychophysiology. *Journal of Mental Imagery* 8: 15-42.

———. 1985. Unvividness parodox. *Journal of Mental Imagery* 9(4) 1-18.

———. 1993. A commentary on imagery tests. *Journal of Mental Imagery* 17(1 and 2): 153-196.

———. 1995. Self-report questionnaires: New directions for imagery research. *Journal of Mental Imagery* 19(3 & 4) 107-123.

———. 1997. Visual imagery and performance during multisensory experience, synaesthesia and phosphenes. *Journal of Mental Imagery* 21(3 and 4): 1-40.

Aldridge, T. 2002. Flotation REST and imagery of basketball free-throw shooting: An investigation of the relaxation-imagery relationship. Master's thesis. Victoria University of Technology, Melbourne, Australia.

Aldridge, T., T. Morris, and M.B. Andersen. 2003. A comparison of flotation and autogenic relaxation for the facilitation of imagery of basketball shooting. In *New approaches to exercise and sport psychology: Theories, methods and applications. Proceedings of the 11th European Congress of Sport Psychology,* ed. R. Stelter. CD-ROM (three-page full paper). Copenhagen, Denmark: University of Copenhagen.

Allers, R., and F. Scheminsky. 1926. Über Aktionsstrome der Muskeln bei motorischen und verwandten Vorgangen. *Pflugers Archiv für die gesamte Physiologie* 212: 169-182.

Anastasi, A., and S. Urbina. 1997. *Psychological testing.* 7th ed. Engelwood Cliffs, NJ: Prentice Hall.

Anderson, J.R. 1980. *Cognitive psychology and its implications.* New York: W.H. Freeman.

———. 1983. *The architecture of cognition.* Cambridge, MA: Harvard University Press.

Anderson, M.P. 1981a. Assessment of imaginal processes: Approaches and issues. In *Cognitive assessment,* ed. T.V. Merlussi, C.R. Glass, and M. Genest, 149-187. New York: Guilford Press.

———. 1981b. Imagery assessment through content analysis. In *Imagery. Vol. 2, Concepts, results, and applications,* ed. E. Klinger, 93-101. New York: Plenum Press.

Annett, J. 1986. On knowing how to do things. In *Generation and modulation of action patterns,* ed. H. Heuer and C. Fromm, 187-200. Berlin: Springer.

———. 1995. Imagery and motor processes: Editorial overview. *British Journal of Psychology* 86: 161-167.

———. 1996. On knowing how to do things: A theory of motor imagery. *Cognitive Brain Research* 3: 65-69.

Annett, J., B. Cripps, and H. Steinberg. 1995. *Exercise addiction: Motivation for participation in sport and exercise.* Leicester, England: British Psychological Society.

Ashton, R., and White, K. 1974. Factor analysis of the Gordon test of visual imagery control. *Perceptual and Motor Skills* 38: 945-946.

———. 1980. Sex differences in imagery vividness: An artifact of the test. *British Journal of Psychology* 71: 35-38.

Atienza, F., I. Balaguer, and M.L. Garcia-Merita. 1994. Factor analysis and reliability of the Movement Imagery Questionnaire. *Perceptual and Motor Skills* 78: 1323-1328.

———. 1998. Video modeling and imagery training on performance of tennis service of 9- to 12-year-old children. *Perceptual and Motor Skills* 87(2): 519-529.

Babin, L.A., and A.C. Burns. 1998. A modified scale for the measurement of communication-evoked mental imagery. *Psychology and Marketing* 15: 261-278.

Bakker, F.C., M.S.J. Boschker, and T. Chung. 1996. Changes in muscular activity while imagining weightlifting using stimulus or response propositions. *Journal of Sport and Exercise Psychology* 18: 313-324.

Bandura, A. 1969. *Principles of behavior modification.* New York: Holt, Reinhart, & Winston.

———. 1977a. Self-efficacy: Toward a unifying theory of behavioral change. *Psychological Review* 84: 191-215.

———. 1977b. *Social learning theory.* New York: Holt, Rinehart, & Winston.

———. 1986. *Social foundations of thought and actions: A social cognitive theory.* Englewood Cliffs, NJ: Prentice Hall.

Barabasz, A.F., and M. Barabasz. 1989. Effects of restricted environmental stimulation: Enhancement of hypnotizability in experimental and clinical pain control. *International Journal of Clinical and Experimental Hypnosis* 37: 217-231.

Bar-Eli, M. 2002. The effect of mental training with biofeedback on the performance of young swimmers. *Applied Psychology: An International Review* 51: 567-581.

Barr, K.A., and C.R. Hall. 1992. The use of imagery by rowers. *International Journal of Sport Psychology* 23: 243-261.

Bauer, R.M., and W.E. Craighead. 1979. Psychophysiological responses to the imagination of fearful and neutral situations: The effects of imagery instructions. *Behavior Therapy* 10: 389-403.

Beauchamp, M.R., S.R. Bray, and J.G. Albinson. 2002. Pre-competition imagery, self-efficacy, and performance in collegiate golfers. *Journal of Sports Sciences* 20: 697-705.

Beilock, S.L., J.A. Afremow, A.L. Rabe, and T.H. Carr. 2001. "Don't miss!" The debilitating effects of suppressive imagery on golf putting performance. *Journal of Sport and Exercise Psychology* 23: 200-221.

Bennett, G.K., H.G. Seashore, and A.G. Wesman. 1966. *Differential aptitude tests.* New York: Psychological Corporation.

Berthoz, A. 1996. The role of inhibition in the hierarchical gating of executed and imagined movements. *Cognitive Brain Research* 3: 101-113.

Besteiner, R., P. Hollinger, P. Lindinger, G. Lang, and A. Berthoz. 1995. Mental representations of movements: Brain potentials associated with imagination of hand movements. *Electroencephalography and Clinical Neurophysiology* 96: 183-193.

Betts, G.H. 1909. *The distribution and functions of mental imagery.* New York: Columbia University Press.

Bexton, W.H., W. Heron, and T.H. Scott. 1954. Effects of decreased variation in the sensory environment. *Canadian Journal of Psychology* 8: 70-76.

Beyer, L., T. Weiss, E. Hansen, A. Wolf, and A. Seidel. 1990. Dynamics of central nervous activation during motor imagination. *International Journal of Psychophysiology* 9: 75-80.

Bird, A.M., and B.K. Cripe. 1986. *Psychology and sport behavior.* St. Louis: Times Mirror/Mosby College Publishing.

Bird, E.I. 1984. EMG quantification of mental practice. *Perceptual and Motor Skills* 59: 899-906.

Bird, K.D., and D. Hadzi-Pavlovic. 1983. Simultaneous test procedures and the choice of a test statistic in MANOVA. *Psychological Bulletin* 93: 167-178.

Blair, A., C. Hall, and G. Leyshon. 1993. Imagery effects on the performance of skilled and novice soccer players. *Journal of Sports Sciences* 11(2): 95-101.

Blakeslee, T.R. 1980. *The right brain.* New York: Anchor Press.

Blumenstein, B. 2002. Biofeedback applications in sport and exercise: Research findings. In *Brain and body in sport and exercise: Biofeedback applications in performance enhancement,* ed. B. Blumenstein, M. Bar-Eli, and G. Tenenbaum, 37-55. Chichester, England: Wiley.

Blumenstein, B., M. Bar-Eli, and D. Collins. 2002. Biofeedback training in sport. In *Brain and body in sport and exercise: Biofeedback applications in performance enhancement,* ed. B. Blumenstein, M. Bar-Eli, and G. Tenenbaum, 55-76. Chichester, England: Wiley.

Blumenstein, B., M. Bar-Eli, and G. Tenenbaum. 1995. The augmenting role of biofeedback: Effects of autogenic, imagery and music training on physiological indices and athletic performance. *Journal of Sports Sciences* 13: 343-354.

———. 1997. A five-step approach to mental training incorporating biofeedback. *Sport Psychologist* 11(4): 440-453.

————. 2002. *Brain and body in sport and exercise: Biofeedback applications in performance enhancement.* Chichester, England: Wiley.

Blumenstein, B., I. Breslav, M. Bar-Eli, and G. Tenenbaum. 1995. Regulation of mental states and biofeedback techniques: Effects on breathing pattern. *Biofeedback and Self-Regulation* 20(2): 169-183.

Bohan, M., J.A. Pharmer, and A.F. Stokes. 1999. When does imagery practice enhance performance on a motor task? *Perceptual and Motor Skills* 88: 651-658.

Bond, J.W. 1987. Flotation therapy: Theoretical concepts. *Sports Science and Medicine Quarterly* 4: 2-4.

Bond, J., and G. Sargent. 1995. Concentration skills in sport: An applied perspective. In *Sport psychology: Theory, applications and issues,* ed. T. Morris and J. Summers, 386-419. Brisbane, Australia: Wiley.

————. 2004. Concentration skills in sport: An applied perspective. In *Sport psychology: Theory, applications and issues,* second edition, ed. T. Morris and J. Summers, 388-422. Brisbane, Australia: Wiley.

Bonnet, M., J. Decety, M. Jeannerod, and J. Requin. 1997. Mental simulation of an action modulates the excitability of spinal reflex pathways in man. *Cognitive Brain Research* 5: 221-228.

Boschker, M.S.J., F.C. Bakker, and M.B. Rietberg. 2000. Retroactive interference effects of mentally imagined movement speed. *Journal of Sports Sciences* 18: 593-603.

Brewer, B.W. 2001. Psychology of sport injury rehabilitation. In *Handbook of sport psychology,* 2nd ed., ed. R.N. Singer, H.A. Hausenblas, and C.M. Janelle, 787-810. New York: Wiley.

Brewer, B.W., K.E. Jeffers, A.J. Petipas, and J.L. Van Raalte. 1994. Perceptions of psychological interventions in the context of sport injury rehabilitation. *Sport Psychologist* 8: 176-188.

Bryan, A. 1987. Single-subject designs for evaluation of sport psychology interventions. *Sport Psychologist* 1: 283-292.

Buckworth, J., and R.K. Dishman. 2002. *Exercise psychology.* Champaign, IL: Human Kinetics.

Budney, A.J., S.M. Murphy, and R.L. Woolfolk. 1994. Imagery and motor performance: What do we really know? In *Imagery in sports and physical performance,* ed. A.A. Sheikh and E.R. Korn, 97-120. Amityville, NY: Baywood Publishing.

Bull, S.J. 1991. *Sport psychology: A self-help guide.* Marlborough, England: Crowood Press.

Caird, S.J.A., A. McKenzie, and G. Sleivert. 1999. Biofeedback and relaxation techniques improve running economy in sub-elite long-distance runners. *Medicine and Science in Sports and Exercise* 321: 717-722.

Callery, P., and T. Morris. 1993. The effect of mental practice on the performance of an Australian Rules football skill. In *Proceedings of VIII World Congress of Sport Psychology,* ed. S. Serpa, J. Alves, V. Ferreira, and A. Paula-Brito, 646–651. Lisbon: ISSP.

———. 1996. Imagery, self-efficacy, and performance of a football skill. *Proceedings of the Australian Council for Health, Physical Education, and Recreation National Conference.* Melbourne: ACHPER.

———. 1997a. Imagery, self-efficacy, and goal-kicking performance. In *Proceedings of the IX World Congress of Sport Psychology,* ed. R. Lidor and M. Bar-Eli, 169-171. Netanya, Israel: ISSP.

———. 1997b. Modeling imagery, self-efficacy, and performance. In *Proceedings of the IX World Congress of Sport Psychology,* ed. R. Lidor and M. Bar-Eli, 172-174. Netanya, Israel: ISSP.

———. 1997c. The effects of an imagery program on self-efficacy and performance of an Australian Rules Football skill. In *Proceedings of the IX World Congress of Sport Psychology,* ed. R. Lidor and M. Bar-Eli, 175-177. Netanya, Israel: ISSP.

Callow, N., and L. Hardy. 1997. Types of imagery associated with high sport confidence and self-efficacy. In *Proceedings of the IX World Congress of Sport Psychology,* ed. R. Lidor and M. Bar-Eli, 178-180. Netanya, Israel: ISSP.

———. 2001. Types of imagery associated with sport confidence in netball players of varying skill levels. *Journal of Applied Sport Psychology* 13: 1-17.

———. 2004. The relationship between the use of kinesthetic imagery and different visual imagery perspectives. *Journal of Sports Sciences* 22: 167-177.

Calmels, C., and J.E. Fournier. 2001. Duration of physical and mental execution of gymnastic routines. *Sport Psychologist* 15: 142-150.

Campos, A., and M.J. Perez. 1988. Vividness of Movement Imagery Questionnaire: Relations with other measures of mental imagery. *Perceptual and Motor Skills* 67: 607-610.

———. 1990. A factor analytic study of two measures of mental imagery. *Perceptual and Motor Skills* 71: 995-1001.

Carpenter, W.B. 1894. *Principles of mental physiology.* 4th ed. New York: Appleton.

Carpinter, P.J., and B.J. Cratty. 1983. Mental activity, dreams, and performance in team sport athletes. *International Journal of Sport Psychology* 14: 186-197.

Carroll, D., J.S. Mazillier, and S. Merian. 1982. Psychophysiological changes accompanying different types of arousing and relaxing imagery. *Psychophysiology* 19: 75-82.

Carter, J.E., and A.E. Kelly. 1997. Using traditional and paradoxical imagery interventions with reactant intramural athletes. *Sport Psychologist* 11: 175-189.

Chara, P.J., and D.A. Hamm. 1989. An inquiry into the construct validity of the Vividness of Visual Imagery Questionnaire. *Perceptual and Motor Skills* 69: 127-136.

Chartrand, J.M., D.P. Jowdy, and S.J. Danish. 1992. The Psychological Skills Inventory for Sports: Psychometric characteristics and applied implications. *Journal of Sport and Exercise Psychology* 14(4): 405-413.

Chi, L. 2004. Achievement goal theory. In *Sport psychology: Theory, applications, and issues,* 2nd ed., ed. T. Morris and J. Summers, 152-174. Brisbane, Australia: Wiley.

Chi, K., and J.L. Duda. 1995. Multi-sample confirmatory factor analysis of the Task and Ego Orientation in Sport Questionnaire. *Research Quarterly for Exercise and Sport* 66: 1-8.

Clark, H. 1916. Visual imagery and attention. *American Journal of Psychology* 27: 461-492.

Clark, L.V. 1960. Effect of mental practice on the development of a certain motor skill. *Research Quarterly* 31: 560-569.

Cochin, S., C. Barthelemy, S. Roux, and J. Martineau. 1999. Observation and execution of movement: Similarities demonstrated by quantified electroencephalography. *European Journal of Neuroscience* 11: 1839-1842.

Cohen, J. 1990. Things I have learned (so far). *American Psychologist* 45: 1304-1312.

———. 1994. The earth is round (*p* < .05). *American Psychologist* 49: 997-1003.

Cohn, P.J. 1990. Pre-performance routines in sport: Theoretical support and practical applications. *Sport Psychologist* 4: 301-312.

Coker, C.A. 2004. *Motor learning and control for practitioners.* New York: McGraw-Hill.

Collins, D. 1995. Psychophysiology and sport performance. In *European perspectives on exercise and sport psychology,* ed. S.J.H. Biddle, 154-178. Champaign, IL: Human Kinetics.

Collins, D., and B.D. Hale. 1997. Getting closer . . . but still no cigar! Comments on Bakker, Boschker, and Chung (1996). *Journal of Sport and Exercise Psychology* 19: 207-212.

Collins, D.J., D. Smith, and B.D. Hale. 1998. Imagery perspectives and karate performance. *Journal of Sports Sciences* 16(1): 103-104.

Conroy, D.E., R.W. Motl, and E.G. Hall. 2000. Progress toward construct validation of the Self-Presentation in Exercise Questionnaire (SPEQ). *Journal of Sport and Exercise Psychology* 22: 21-38.

Corbin, C.B. 1967a. Effects of mental practice on the development of a certain mental skill. *Research Quarterly* 31: 560-569.

———. 1967b. The effects of covert rehearsal on the development of a complex motor skill. *Journal of General Psychology* 76: 143-150.

———. 1972. Mental practice. In *Ergogenic aids and muscular performance,* ed. W.P. Morgan, 94-118. New York: Academic Press.

Cornoldi, C., B. Bertuccelli, P. Rocchi, and B. Sbrana. 1993. Processing capacity limitations in pictorial and spatial representations in the totally congenitally blind. *Cortex* 29: 675-689.

Costello, C.G., and P. McGregor. 1957. The relationship between some aspects of visual imagery and the alpha rhythm. *Journal of Mental Science* 103: 786-795.

Cox, R.H. 1998. *Sport psychology: Concepts and applications.* 4th ed. Boston: McGraw-Hill.

———. 2002. *Sport psychology: Concepts and applications.* 5th ed. Boston: McGraw-Hill.

Cremades, J.G. 2002. Hemispheric activation differences in experts and novices during imagery performance: An EEG study. Abstract in *Journal of Sport and Exercise Psychology* 24: S48.

Crews, D. 1994. Animal sexuality. *Scientific American* (November): 108-114.

Csikszentmihalyi, M. 1990. *Flow: The psychology of optimal experience.* New York: Harper Collins.

Cumming, J., C. Hall, C. Harwood, and K. Gammage. 2002. Motivational orientations and imagery use: A goal perspective. *Journal of Sports Sciences* 20: 127-136.

Cumming, J.L., and D.M. Ste-Marie. 2001. The cognitive and motivational effects of imagery training: A matter of perspective. *Sport Psychologist* 15: 276-288.

Cunnington, R., R. Iansek, J.L. Bradshaw, and J.G. Phillips. 1996. Movement-related potentials associated with movement preparation and motor imagery. *Experimental Brain Research* 111: 429-436.

Cupal, D.D. 1998. Psychological interventions in sport injury prevention and rehabilitation. *Journal of Applied Sport Psychology* 10: 103-123.

Cupal, D.D., and B.W. Brewer. 2001. Effects of relaxation and guided imagery on knee strength, reinjury anxiety, and pain following anterior cruciate ligament reconstruction. *Rehabilitation Psychology* 46: 28-43.

Cuthbert, B.N., S.R. Vrana, and M.M. Bradley. 1991. Imagery: Function and physiology. *Advances in Psychophysiology* 4: 1-42.

Daniels, F.S., and D.M. Landers. 1981. Biofeedback and shooting performance: A test of disregulation and systems theory. *Journal of Sport Psychology* 3: 271-282.

Davidson, R.J., and G.E. Schwartz. 1977. Brain mechanisms subserving self-generated imagery: Electrophysiological specificity and patterning. *Psychophysiology* 14: 598-602.

Dean, G.M., and P.E. Morris. 2003. The relationship between self-reports of imagery and spatial ability. *British Journal of Psychology* 94(2): 245-273.

Decety, J. 1996a. The neurological basis of motor imagery. *Behavioural Brain Research* 77: 45-52.

———. 1996b. Do imagined and executed actions share the same neural substrate? *Cognitive Brain Research* 3: 87-93.

Decety, J., and D.H. Ingvar. 1990. Brain structures participating in mental stimulation of motor behavior: A neurophysiological interpretation. *Acta Psychologica* 73: 13-31.

Decety, J., M. Jeannerod, D. Durozard, and G. Baverel. 1993. Central activation of autonomic effectors during mental simulation of motor actions. *Journal of Physiology* 461: 549-563.

Decety, J., M. Jeannerod, M. Germain, and J. Pastene. 1991. Vegetative response during imagined movement is proportional to mental effort. *Behavioural Brain Research* 42: 1-5.

Decety, J., M. Jeannerod, and C. Prablanc. 1989. The timing of mentally represented actions. *Behavioural Brain Research* 34: 35-42.

Decety, J., and M. Lindgren. 1991. Sensation of effort and duration of mentally executed actions. *Scandinavian Journal of Psychology* 32: 97-104.

Decety, J., D. Perani, M. Jeannerod, V. Bettinardi, B. Tadary, R. Woods, J.C. Mazziotta, and F. Fazio. 1994. Mapping motor representations with PET. *Nature* 371: 600-602.

Decety, J., B. Philippon, and D.H. Ingvar. 1988. rCBF landscapes during motor performance and motor ideation of a graphic gesture. *European Archives of Psychiatric Neurological Science* 238: 33-38.

Decety, J., H. Sjoholm, E. Ryding, G. Stenberg, and D. Ingvar. 1990.The cerebellum participates in mental activity: Tomographic measurements of regional cerebral blood flow. *Brain Research* 535: 313-317.

Deci, E.I., and R.M. Ryan. 1985. *Intrinsic motivation and self-determination in human behavior.* New York: Plenum Press.

Deecke, L. 1996. Planning, preparation, execution, and imagery of volitional action. *Cognitive Brain Research* 3: 59-64.

DeFrancesco, C., and K.L. Burke. 1997. Performance enhancement strategies used in a professional tennis tournament. *International Journal of Sport Psychology* 28: 185-195.

Deiber, M.P., V. Ibanez, M. Honda, N. Sadato, R. Raman, and M. Hallett. 1998. Cerebral processes relate to visuomotor imagery and generation of simple finger movement studies with positron emission tomography. *Neuroimaging* 7: 73-85.

Deiber, M.P., R.E. Passingham, J.G. Colebatch, K.J. Friston, P.D. Nixon, and R.S.J. Frackowiak. 1991. Cortical areas and the selection of movement: A study with positron emission tomography. *Experimental Brain Research* 84: 393-402.

Denis, M. 1985. Visual imagery and the use of mental practice in the development of motor skills. *Canadian Journal of Applied Sport Science* 10: 45-165.

Deschaumes-Molinaro, C., A. Dittmar, and E. Vernet-Maury. 1991. Relationship between mental imagery and sporting performance. *Behavioural Brain Research* 45: 29-36.

De Witt, D.J. 1980. Cognitive and biofeedback training for stress reduction with university athletes. *Journal of Sport Psychology* 2: 288-294.

Di Vesta, F.J., G. Ingersoll, and P. Sunshine. 1971. A factor analysis of imagery tests. *Journal of Verbal Learning and Verbal Behavior* 10: 471-479.

Dowling, P. 1973. Validation of the Vividness of Visual Imagery Questionnaire. Unpublished manuscript, University of Queensland, Brisbane, Australia. Cited in K. White, P.W. Sheehan, and R. Ashton, 1977, Imagery Assessment: A survey of self-report measures. *Journal of Mental Imagery* 1: 145-170.

Doyle, L.A., and D.M. Landers. 1980. Psychological skills in elite and sub-elite shooters. Unpublished manuscript.

Driskell, J.E., C. Copper, and A. Moran. 1994. Does mental practice enhance performance? *Journal of Applied Psychology* 79: 481-492.

Driscoll, K., and L. Wood. 2001, May. *Directions for physical activity. Victorian Health Promotion Foundation (VicHealth) discussion document.* Retrieved November 15, 2003, from http://www.vichealth.vic.gov.au.

Duda, J.L. 1989. The relationship between task and ego orientation and perceived purpose of sport among male and female high school athletes. *Journal of Sport and Exercise Psychology* 11: 318-335.

———. 1992. Sport and exercise motivation: A goal perspective analysis. In *Motivation in sport and exercise,* ed. G. Roberts, 57-91. Champaign, IL: Human Kinetics.

Duda, J.L., and S.A. White. 1992. The relationship of goal perspectives to beliefs about success among elite skiers. *Sport Psychologist* 6: 334-343.

Dworetsky, J.P. 1988. *Psychology.* 3rd ed. St. Paul: West Publishing.

Eddy, K.A.T., and S.D. Mallalieu. 2003. Mental imagery in athletes with visual impairments. *Adapted Physical Activity Quarterly* 20: 347-368.

Ehrsson, H.H., S. Geyer, and E. Naito. 2003. Imagery of voluntary movement of fingers, toes, and tongue activates corresponding body-part specific motor representations. *Journal of Neurophysiology* 90: 3304-3316.

Elko, K., and A.C. Ostrow. 1992. The effects of three mental-preparation strategies on strength performance of young and older adults. *Journal of Sport Behavior* 15: 34-41.

Engelkamp, J., and R.L. Cohen. 1991. Current issues in memory of action events. *Psychological Research* 53: 175-182.

Epstein, M.L. 1980. The relationship of mental imagery and mental rehearsal to performance on a motor task. *Journal of Sport Psychology* 2: 211–220.

Ericsson, K.A., and H.A. Simon. 1993. *Protocol analysis: Verbal reports as data.* Rev. ed. Cambridge, MA: MIT Press.

Ernest, C.H. 1977. Imagery ability and cognition: A critical review. *Journal of Mental Imagery* 2: 181-216.

Etnier, J.L., and D.M. Landers. 1996. The influence of procedural variables on the efficacy of mental practice. *Sport Psychologist* 10: 48-57.

Eton, D.T., F.H. Gilner, and D.C. Munz. 1998. The measurement of imagery vividness: A test of the reliability and validity of the Vividness of Visual Imagery Questionnaire and the Vividness of Movement Imagery Questionnaire. *Journal of Mental Imagery* 22: 125-136.

Evans, L., L. Hardy, and S. Fleming. 2000. Intervention strategies with injured athletes: An action research study. *Sport Psychologist* 14, 188-206.

Eysenck, M.W. 2002. *Simply psychology.* 2nd ed. Sussex, England: Psychology Press.

Facchini, S., W. Muellbacher, F. Battaglia, B. Boroojerdi, and M. Hallett. 2002. Focal enhancement of motor cortex excitability during motor imagery: A transcranial magnetic stimulation study. *Acta Neurologica Scandinavia* 105: 146-151.

Farah, M.J. 1984. The neurological basis of mental imagery: A componential analysis. *Cognition* 18: 245-272.

———. 1989. The neural basis of mental imagery. *Trends in Neurosciences* 12: 395-399.

Farah, M.J., F. Peronnet, M.A. Gonon, and M.H. Giard. 1988. Electrophysiological evidence for a shared representational medium for visual images and visual percepts. *Journal of Experimental Psychology: General* 117: 248-257.

Farahat, E., A. Ille, and B. Thon. 2004. Effect of visual and kinesthetic imagery on the learning of a patterned movement. *International Journal of Sport Psychology* 35: 119-132.

Farthing, C.W., M. Venturino, and S.W. Brown. 1983. Relationship between two different types of imagery vividness questionnaire items and three hypnotic susceptibility scale factors: A brief communication. *International Journal of Clinical and Experimental Hypnosis* 31(1): 8-13.

Feltz, D.L. 1982. Path analysis of the causal elements of Bandura's theory of self-efficacy and an anxiety-based model of avoidance behavior. *Journal of Personality and Social Psychology* 42: 764-781.

Feltz, D.L., and D.M. Landers. 1983. The effect of mental practice on motor-skill learning and performance: A meta-analysis. *Journal of Sport Psychology* 2: 211-220.

Feltz, D.L., D.M. Landers, and B.J. Becker. 1988. A revised meta-analysis of the mental practice literature on motor-skill learning. In *Enhancing human performance: Issues, theories, and techniques,* ed. D. Druckman and J. Swets, 1-65. Washington, DC: National Academy Press.

Feltz, D.L., and C.D. Lirgg. 2001. Self-efficacy beliefs of athletes, teams, and coaches. In *Handbook of sport psychology,* 2nd ed., ed. R.N. Singer, H.A. Hausenblas, and C.M. Janelle, 340-361. New York: Wiley.

Feltz, D.L., and D.A. Mugno. 1983. A replication of the path analysis of the causal elements in Bandura's theory of self-efficacy and the influence of autonomic perception. *Journal of Sport Psychology* 5: 263-277.

Feltz, D.L., and C.A. Reissinger. 1990. Effects of in-vivo emotive imagery and performance feedback on self-efficacy and muscular endurance. *Journal of Sport and Exercise Psychology* 12: 132-143.

Fernandez, E., and D.C. Turk. 1986, August. *Overall and relative efficacy of cognitive strategies in attenuating pain.* Paper presented at the 94th annual convention of the American Psychological Association, Washington, DC.

Fery, Y.A. 2003. Differentiating visual and kinesthetic imagery in mental practice. *Journal of Experimental Psychology* 57: 1196-1961.

Fery, Y.A., and P. Morizot. 2000. Kinesthetic and visual image in modeling closed motor skills: The example of the tennis serve. *Perceptual and Motor Skills* 90: 707-722.

Finke, R.A. 1980. Levels of equivalence of mental images and perception. *Psychological Review* 87: 113-132.

———. 1985. Theories relating mental imagery to perception. *Psychological Bulletin* 98: 236-259.

———. 1989. *Principles of mental imagery.* Cambridge, MA: MIT Press.

Finke, R.A., and R.N. Shephard. 1986. Visual functions of mental imagery. In *Handbook of perception and human performance,* ed. K.R. Boff, L. Kaufman, and J.P. Thomas, 37-55. New York: Wiley.

Fitts, P., and M.I. Posner. 1967. *Human performance.* Belmont, CA: Brooks/Cole.

Fogarty, L.A., and T. Morris. 2003. *Aspects of imagery in sports. Proceedings of the XI European Congress of Sport Psychology,* 60. Copenhagen, Denmark.

Foster, J. and K. Porter. 1987. *Mental training for healing athletic injury.* Unpublished manuscript.

Fox, P.T., J.J. Pardo, S.E. Peterson, and M.E. Raichle. 1987. Supplementary motor and premotor responses to actual and imagined hand movements with positron emission tomography. *Society for Neuroscience Abstracts* 13: 1433.

Frederick-Racascino, C.M., and T. Morris. 2004. Intrinsic and extrinsic motivation in sport and exercise. In *Sport psychology: Theory, applications, and issues,* ed. T. Morris and J. Summers, 121-151. Brisbane, Australia: Wiley.

Freedman, R. 1991. Psychophysiological mechanisms of temperature feedback. *Biofeedback and Self-Regulation* 16: 95-115.

Gabriele, T.E., C.R. Hall, and T.D. Lee. 1989. Cognition in motor learning: Imagery effects on contextual interference. *Human Movement Science* 8: 227-245.

Gabriele, T.E., T.D. Lee, and C.R. Hall. 1991. Contextual interference in movement timing: Specific effects in retention and transfer. *Journal of Human Movement Studies* 20: 177-188.

Gammage, K.L., C.R. Hall, and W.M. Rodgers. 2000. More about exercise imagery. *Sport Psychologist* 14: 348-359.

Garza, D.L., and D.L. Feltz. 1998. Effects of selected mental practice on performance, self-efficacy, and competition confidence of figure skaters. *Sport Psychologist* 12: 1-15.

Gaskin, C., and T. Morris. 2002. Using imagery to enhance intrinsic motivation. In *Readings in sport psychology in Nigeria,* ed. P.B. Ikulayo and G.C. Ilogu, 227-244. Lagos, Nigeria: Phil-Chel Educational & Consultancy Services.

Gates, S.C., M.T. DePalma, and G.A. Shelley. 2003. An investigation of the relationship between visual imagery perspectives, kinesthetic imagery and locus of control. *Applied Research in Coaching and Athletics Annual* 18: 145-164.

Gauvin, L., and S.J. Russell. 1993. Sport-specific and culturally adapted measures in sport and exercise psychology research: Issues and strategies. In *Handbook of research on sport psychology,* ed. R.N. Singer, M. Murphy, and L.K. Tennant, 891-900. New York: Macmillan.

Gentile, A.M. 1972. A working model of skill acquisition with application to teaching. *Quest* (monograph) 17: 3-23.

———. 1987. Skill acquisition: Action, movement, and neuromotor processes. In *Movement science: Foundations for physical therapy in rehabilitation,* ed. J.H. Carr, R.B. Shepherd, J. Gordon. A.M. Gentile, and J.M. Hinds, 93-154. Rockville, MD: Aspen.

———. 2000. Skill acquisition: Action, movement, and neuromotor processes. In *Movement science: Foundations for physical therapy,* 2nd ed., ed. J.H. Carr and R.B. Shepherd, 111-187. Rockville, MD: Aspen.

George, L. 1986. Mental imagery enhancement training in behavior therapy: Current status and future prospects. *Psychotherapy: Theory, Research, Practice, Training* 23(1): 81-92.

Georgopoulos, A.P., and J.T. Massey. 1987. Cognitive spatial motor processes. *Experimental Brain Research* 65: 361-370.

Giacobbi, P.R., Jr., H.A. Hausenblas, E.A. Fallon, and C.R. Hall. 2003. Even more about exercise imagery: A grounded theory of exercise imagery. *Journal of Applied Sport Psychology* 15: 160-175.

Gill, D.L. 2000. *Psychological dynamics of sport and exercise,* 2nd ed. Champaign, IL: Human Kinetics.

Glisky, M.L., J.M. Williams, and J.F. Kihlstrom. 1996. Internal and external mental imagery perspectives and performance on two tasks. *Journal of Sport Behavior* 19(1): 3-18.

Godin, G., J. Jobin, and J. Bouillon. 1986. Assessment of leisure-time exercise behavior by self-report: A concurrent validity study. *Canadian Journal of Public Health* 77: 359-362.

Goginsky, A.M., and D. Collins. 1996. Research design and mental practice. *Journal of Sports Sciences* 14: 381-392.

Goldenberg, G., I. Podreka, M. Steiner, K. Willmes, E. Suess, and L. Deecke. 1989. Regional cerebral blood flow patterns in visual imagery. *Neuropsychologia* 27: 641-664.

Golla, F., E.L. Hutton, and W.G. Walter. 1943. The objective study of mental imagery: 1 Physiological concomitants. *Journal of Mental Science* 89: 216-223.

Gordon, R. 1949. An investigation into some of the factors that favour the formation of stereotyped images. *British Journal of Psychology, 39,* 156-167.

Gordon, S., R. Weinberg, and A. Jackson. 1994. Effect of internal and external imagery on cricket performance. *Journal of Sport Behavior* 17: 60-75.

Goss, S., C. Hall, E. Buckolz, and G. Fishburne. 1986. Imagery ability and the acquisition and retention of movements. *Memory and Cognition* 14: 469-477.

Gough, D. 1989. Improving batting skills with small college baseball players through guided visual imagery. *Coaching Clinic* 27: 1-6.

Gould, D., and N. Damarjian. 1996. Imagery training for peak performance. In *Exploring sport and exercise psychology,* 1st ed., ed. J.L. Van Raalte and B. Brewer, 25-50. Washington, DC: American Psychological Association.

Gould, D., N. Damarjian, and C. Greenleaf. 2002. Imagery training for peak performance. In *Exploring sport and exercise psychology,* 2nd ed., ed. J.L. Van Raalte and B.W. Brewer 49-74. Washington, DC: American Psychological Association.

Gould, D., V. Tammen, S.M. Murphy, and J. May. 1989. An examination of the U.S. Olympic sport psychology consultants and the services they provide. *Sport Psychologist* 3: 300-312.

Grafton, S.T., M.A. Arbib, L. Fadiga, and G. Rizzolatti. 1996. Localization of grasp representations in humans by positron emission tomography: 2. Observation compared with imagination. *Experimental Brain Research* 112: 103-111.

Gray, J.J., M.J. Haring, and N.M. Banks. 1984. Mental rehearsal for sport performance: Exploring the relaxation imagery paradigm. *Journal of Sport Behavior* 7: 68-78.

Gray, S.W. 1990. Effect of visuomotor rehearsal with videotaped modeling on racquetball performance of beginning players. *Perceptual and Motor Skills* 70(2): 379-385.

Gray, S.W., and S.J. Fernandez. 1990. Effects of visuomotor behavior rehearsal with videotaped modeling on basketball shooting performance. *Psychology: A Journal of Human Behavior* 26(4): 41-47.

Green, L.B. 1993. The use of imagery in the rehabilitation of injured athletes. In *Psychological bases of sport injuries,* 1st ed., ed. D. Pargman, 199-218. Morgantown, WV: Fitness Information Technology.

———. 1999. The use of imagery in the rehabilitation of injured athletes. In *Psychological bases of sport injuries,* 2nd ed., ed. D. Pargman, 235-251. Morgantown, WV: Fitness Information Technology.

Gregory, W., R. Cialdini, and K. Carpenter. 1982. Self-reliant scenarios as mediators of likelihood estimates and compliance: Does imagining make it so? *Journal of Personality and Social Psychology* 43: 89-99.

Grouios, G. 1992. Mental practice: A review. *Journal of Sport Behavior* 15(1): 42-59.

Grove, J.R., and M.A.E. Lewis. 1996. Hypnotic susceptibility and the attainment of flowlike states during exercise. *Journal of Sport and Exercise Psychology* 18: 380-391.

Hale, B.D. 1982. The effects of internal and external imagery on muscular and occular concomitants. *Journal of Sport Psychology* 4: 379–387.

———. 1986. Application of Lang's bioinformational theory of emotional imagery to sport psychology. In *Sport psychology in theory and practice,* ed. L. Unestahl, 172-178. Orebro, Sweden: Veje Publishing Inc.

———. 1994. Imagery perspectives and learning in sports performance. In *Imagery in sports and physical performance,* ed. A.A. Sheikh and E.R. Korn, 75-96. Amityville, NY: Baywood Publishing.

———. 1998. *Effect of mental imagery of a motor task on the Hoffman reflex.* Eugene, OR: Microform Publications.

Hale, B.D., P. Holmes, D. Smith, N. Fowler, and D. Collins. 2003. Give those men a cigar (but no light): A reply to Slade, Landers, and Martin. *Journal of Sport and Exercise Psychology* 25: 402-409.

Hale, B.D., J.S. Raglin, and D.M. Koceja. 2003. Effect of mental imagery of a motor task on the Hoffman reflex. *Behavioral Brain Research* 142: 81-88.

Hale, B.D., and A. Whitehouse. 1998. The effects of imagery-manipulated appraisal on intensity and direction of competitive anxiety. *Sport Psychologist* 12: 40-51.

Hall, C.R. 1985. Individual differences in the mental practice and imagery of motor-skill performance. *Canadian Journal of Applied Sport Sciences* 10(4): 17S-21S.

———. 1995. The motivational function of mental imagery for participation in sport and exercise. In *Exercise addiction: Motivation for participation in sport and exercise,* ed. J. Annett, B. Cripps, H. Steinberg, 15-21. Leicester, England: British Psychological Society.

———. 1997. Lew Hardy's third myth: A matter of perspective. *Journal of Applied Sport Psychology* 9: 310-313.

———. 1998. Measuring imagery abilities and imagery use. In *Advances in sport and exercise psychology measurement,* ed. J.L. Duda, 165-172. Morgantown, WV: Fitness Information Technology.

———. 2001. Imagery in sport and exercise. In *Handbook of research on sport psychology,* 2nd ed., ed. R.N. Singer, H.A. Hausenblas, and C.M. Janelle, 529-549. New York: Wiley.

Hall, C.R., L. Bernoties, and D. Schmidt. 1995. Interference effects of mental imagery on a motor task. *British Journal of Psychology* 86: 181-190.

Hall, C., E. Buckolz, and G. Fishburne, 1989. Searching for a relationship between imagery ability and memory of movements. *Journal of Human Movement Studies* 17: 89-100.

Hall, C., D. Mack, and A. Paivio. 1995. Imagery use by athletes: The development of an imagery use by athletes questionnaire. Paper presented at the annual meeting of the Canadian Society for Psychomotor Learning and Sports Psychology, Hamilton, Canada.

Hall, C.R., D.E. Mack, A. Paivio, and H.A. Hausenblas. 1998. Imagery use by athletes: Development of the Sport Imagery Questionnaire. *International Journal of Sport Psychology* 29: 73-89.

Hall, C.R., and K.A. Martin. 1997. Measuring movement imagery abilities: A revision of the movement imagery questionnaire. *Journal of Mental Imagery* 21: 143-154.

Hall, C., and J. Pongrac. 1983. *Movement Imagery Questionnaire.* London, Canada: University of Western Ontario.

Hall, C.R., C. Pongrac, and E. Buckolz. 1985. The measurement of imagery ability. *Human Movement Science* 4: 107-118.

Hall, C.R., and W.M. Rodgers. 1989. Enhancing coaching effectiveness in figure skating through a mental-skills training program. *Sport Psychologist* 4: 1-10.

Hall, C.R., W.M. Rodgers, and K.A. Barr. 1990. The use of imagery by athletes in selected sports. *Sport Psychologist* 4: 1-10.

Hall, C., D. Schmidt, M. Durand, and E. Buckolz. 1994. Imagery and motor skills acquisition. In *Imagery in sports and physical performance,* ed. A.A. Sheikh and E.R. Korn, 121-134. Amityville, NY: Baywood Publishing Co.

Hall, C., J. Toews, and W. Rodgers. 1990. Les aspects motivationnels de l'imagerie en activités motrices. *Revue des Sciences et Techniques des Activités Physiques et Sportives* 22: 27-32.

Hall, E.G., and E.S. Erffmeyer. 1983. The effect of visuomotor behavior rehearsal with videotaped modeling on free-throw accuracy of intercollegiate female basketball players. *Journal of Sport Psychology* 5: 343-346.

Hall, E.G., and C.J. Hardy. 1991. Ready, aim, fire . . . Relaxation strategies for enhancing marksmanship. *Perceptual and Motor Skills* 72: 775-786.

Hallett, M., J. Fieldman, L.G. Cohen, N. Sadato, and A. Pascual-Leone. 1995. Involvement of primary motor cortex in motor imagery and mental practice. *Behavioral and Brain Sciences* 17: 210.

Hamberger, K., and J. Lohr. 1980. Relationship of relaxation training to the controllability of imagery. *Perceptual and Motor Skills* 51: 103-110.

Hanrahan, S.J. 1998. Practical considerations for working with athletes with disabilities. *Sport Psychologist* 12: 346-357.

Hardy, L. 1996. Three myths about applied consultancy work. *Journal of Applied Sport Psychology* 9: 107-118.

———. 1997. The Coleman Robert Griffiths Address: Three myths about applied consultancy work. *Journal of Applied Sport Psychology* 9: 277-294.

Hardy, L., and N. Callow. 1999. Efficacy of external and internal visual imagery perspectives for the enhancement of performance on tasks in which form is important. *Journal of Sport and Exercise Psychology* 21: 95-112.

Hardy, L., G. Jones, and D. Gould. 1996. *Understanding psychological preparation for sport: Theory and practice of elite performers.* West Sussex, England: Wiley.

Harris, D.V. 1986. A comment to a comment . . . Much ado about nothing. *Journal of Sport Psychology* 8: 349.

Harris, D.V., and B.L. Harris. 1984. *The athlete's guide to sports psychology: Mental skills for physical people.* New York: Leisure Press.

Harris, D.V., and W.J. Robinson. 1986. The effects of skill level on EMG activity during internal and external imagery. *Journal of Sport Psychology* 8: 105–111.

Harwood, C., J. Cumming, and C. Hall. 2003. Imagery use in elite youth sport participants: Reinforcing the applied significance of achievement goal theory. *Research Quarterly for Exercise and Sport* 74: 292-300.

Hashimoto, R., and J.C. Rothwell. 1999. Dynamic changes in corticospinal excitability during motor imagery. *Journal of Brain Research* 125: 75-81.

Hausenblas, H.A., C.R. Hall, W.M. Rodgers, and K.J. Munroe. 1999. Exercise imagery: Its nature and measurement. *Journal of Applied Sport Psychology* 11: 171-180.

Hays, K.F. 2000. Breaking out: Doing sport psychology with performing artists. In *Doing sport psychology,* ed. M.B. Andersen, 261-274. Champaign, IL: Human Kinetics.

Hayward, S. 1997. *Biopsychology: Physiological psychology.* Hampshire, England: MacMillan.

Haywood, K.M., and N. Getchell. 2001. *Life-span motor development.* 3rd ed. Champaign, IL: Human Kinetics.

Hecker, J.E., and L.M. Kaczor. 1988. Application of imagery theory to sport psychology: Some preliminary findings. *Journal of Sport and Exercise Psychology* 10: 363-373.

Heil, J. 1984. Imagery for sports: Theory, research, and practice. In *Cognitive sport psychology,* ed. W.F. Straub and J.M. Williams, 245-252. Lansing, NY: Sport Science Associates.

———. 1993. Mental training in injury management. In *Psychology of sport injury,* ed. J. Heil, 151-174. Champaign, IL: Human Kinetics.

Heron, W. 1957. The pathology of boredom. *Scientific American* 196: 52-56.

Highlen, P., and B. Bennett. 1979. Psychological characteristics of successful and non-successful elite wrestlers: An exploratory study. *Journal of Sport Psychology* 1: 123-137.

Hinshaw, K.E. 1991. The effects of mental practice on motor skill performance: Critical evaluation and meta-analysis. *Imagination, Cognition and Personality* 11: 3-35.

Hird, J.S., D.M. Landers, J.R. Thomas, and J. Horan. 1991. Physical practice is superior to mental practice in enhancing cognitive and motor performance. *Journal of Sport and Exercise Psychology* 13: 281-293.

Hiscock, M. 1978. Imagery assessment through self-report: What do imagery questionnaires measure? *Journal of Consulting and Clinical Psychology* 46: 223-230.

Hodge, K. 1994. Mental toughness in sport: lessons for life. The pursuit of personal excellence. *Journal of Physical Education New Zealand* 27: 12-16.

Holmes, P.S., and D. Collins. 2001. The PETTLEP approach to motor imagery: A functional equivalence model for sport psychologists. *Journal of Applied Sport Psychology* 13: 60-83.

———. 2002. Functional equivalence solutions for problems with motor imagery. In *Solutions in Sport Psychology,* ed. I.M. Cockerill, 120-140. London: Morgan.

Howe, B.L. 1991. Imagery and sport performance. *Sports Medicine* 11: 1-5.

Huberty, C.J., and J.D. Morris. 1989. Multiple analysis versus multiple univariate analyses. *Psychological Bulletin* 105: 302-308.

Huck, S.W., and R.A. McLean. 1975. Using repeated measures ANOVA to analyze the data from a pretest–post-test design: A potentially confusing task. *Psychological Bulletin* 82: 511-518.

Hugdahl, K. 1995. *Psychophysiology: The mind–body perspective.* Cambridge, MA: Harvard University Press.

Humara, M., and R.L. Willard. 2002. Disabled athletes and mind power. *Psyched.* [Online]. 2(3): 10 paragraphs. Available: www.psychedonline.org/Articles/Vol2Iss3/Disabledathletes.htm..

Hung, C.L., T.M. Hung, Y.K. Chang, D.Y. Fong, J.F. Kao, L.C. Lo, et al. 2002. The relationship between imagery ability and EEG activity. Abstract in *Journal of Sport and Exercise Psychology* 24: S72-S73.

Hutchison, M. 1984. *The book of floating.* New York: Morrow.

Ievleva, L., and T. Orlick. 1991. Mental links to enhanced healing: An exploratory study. *Sport Psychologist* 5: 25-40.

———. 1999. Mental paths to enhanced recovery from a sports injury. In *Psychological bases of sport injuries,* 2nd ed., ed. D. Pargman, 199-220. Morgantown, WV: Fitness Information Technology.

Ingvar, D.H., and L. Philipson. 1977. Distribution of the cerebral blood flow in the dominant hemisphere during motor ideation and motor performance. *Annals of Neurology* 2: 230-237.

Isaac, A. 1992. Mental practice—does it work in the field? *Sport Psychologist* 6: 192-198.

Isaac, A.R., and D.F. Marks. 1994. Individual differences in mental imagery experience: Developmental changes and specialization. *British Journal of Psychology* 85: 479-500.

Isaac, A.R., D.F. Marks, and D.G. Russell. 1986. An instrument for assessing imagery of movement: The Vividness of Movement Imagery Questionnaire (VMIQ). *Journal of Mental Imagery* 10: 23-30.

Jackson, P.L., M.F. LaFleur, F. Malouin, C.L. Richards, and J. Doyon. 2003. Functional cerebral reorganization following motor sequence learning through mental practice with motor imagery. *Neuroimage* 20: 1171-1180.

Jackson, S.A., and M. Csikszentmihalyi. 1999. *Flow in sports.* Champaign, IL: Human Kinetics.

Jackson, S.A., and R.C. Eklund. 2002. Assessing flow in physical activity: The Flow State Scale-2 and Dispositional Flow Scale-2. *Journal of Sport and Exercise Psychology* 24: 133-150.

Jacobson, E. 1930a. Electrical measurements of neuromuscular states during mental activities: Part 1. Imagination of movement involving skeletal muscle. *American Journal of Physiology* 91: 567-606.

———. 1930b. Electrical measurements of neuromuscular states during mental activities: Part 2. Imagination and recollection of various muscular acts. *American Journal of Physiology* 94: 27-34.

———. 1930c. Electrical measurements of neuromuscular states during mental activities: Part 3. Visual imagination and recollection. *American Journal of Physiology* 95: 694-702.

———. 1930d. Electrical measurements of neuromuscular states during mental activities: Part 4. Evidence of contraction of specific muscles during imagination. *American Journal of Physiology* 95: 703-712.

————. 1931a. Electrical measurements of neuromuscular states during mental activities: Part 5. Variation of specific muscles contracting during imagination. *American Journal of Physiology* 96: 115-121.

————. 1931b. Electrical measurements of neuromuscular states during mental activities: Part 6. A note on mental activities concerning an amputated limb. *American Journal of Physiology* 96: 122-125.

————. 1931c. Electrical measurements of neuromuscular states during mental activities: Part 7. Imagination, recollection, and abstract thinking involving the speech musculature. *American Journal of Physiology* 97: 20-209.

Janssen, J.J., and A.A. Sheikh. 1994. Enhancing athletic performance through imagery: An overview. In *Imagery in sports and physical performance,* ed. A.A. Sheikh and E.R. Korn, 1-22. Amityville, NY: Baywood Publishing.

Jeannerod, M. 1994. The representing brain: Neural correlates of motor intention and imagery. *Behavioral and Brain Sciences* 17: 187-202.

————. 1995. Mental imagery in the motor context. *Neuropsychologia* 33: 1419-1432.

————. 1997. *The cognitive neuroscience of action.* Oxford, England: Blackwell.

————. 1999. Mental imaging of motor imagery in humans. *Current Opinion in Neurobiology* 9: 735-739.

Johnson, P. 1982. The functional equivalence of imagery and movement. *Quarterly Journal of Experimental Psychology* 34A: 349-365.

Johnson, U. 2000. Short-term psychological intervention: A study of long-term-injured athletes. *Journal of Sport Rehabilitation* 9: 207-218.

Jones, G. 2002. Performance excellence: A personal perspective on the link between sport and business. *Journal of Applied Sport Psychology* 14, 268-281.

Jones, L., and G. Stuth. 1997. The uses of mental imagery in athletics: An overview. *Applied and Preventative Psychology* 6: 101-115.

Jones, M.V., S.R. Bray, R.D. Mace, A.W. MacRae, and C. Stockbridge. 2002. The impact of motivational imagery on the emotional state and self-efficacy levels of novice climbers. *Journal of Sport Behavior* 25: 57-73.

Jopson, L., K. Henschen, and B. Schultz. 1989. Imagery and gymnastics. *Journal of Applied Research in Coaching and Athletics* 4: 272-281.

Jowdy, D.P., and D.V. Harris. 1990. Muscular responses during mental imagery as a function of motor-skill level. *Journal of Sport and Exercise Psychology* 12: 191-201.

Jowdy, D.P., S.M. Murphy, and S. Durtschi. 1989. An assessment of the use of imagery by elite athletes: Athlete, coach, and psychologist perspectives. (Report). Colorado Springs: U.S. Olympic Committee.

Juhasz, J.B. 1972. On the reliability of two measures of imagery. *Perceptual and Motor Skills* 35: 874.

Kamyia, J. 1968. Conscious control of brainwaves. *Psychology Today* 1(11): 56-60.

Kaplan, R.M., and D.P. Saccuzzo. 1997. *Psychological testing: Principles, applications, and issues.* 4th ed. Pacific Grove, CA: Brooks/Cole.

Kasai, T., S. Kawai, M. Kawanishi, and S. Yahagi. 1997. Evidence for facilitation of motor-evoked potentials (MEPs) induced by motor imagery. *Brain Research* 744: 147-150.

Katz, A.N. 1983. What does it mean to be a high? In *Imagery, memory, and cognition: Essays in honor of Allan Paivio,* ed. J.C. Yuille, 39-63. Hillsdale, NJ: Erlbaum.

Kearns, D.W., and J. Crossman. 1992. Effects of a cognitive intervention package on the free-throw performance of varsity basketball players during practice and competition. *Perceptual and Motor Skills* 75: 1243-1253

Kellman, M., ed. 2002. *Enhancing recovery: Preventing underperformance in athletes.* Champaign, IL: Human Kinetics.

Kendall, G., D. Hrycaiko, G.L. Martin, and T. Kendall. 1990. The effects of an imagery rehearsal, relaxation, and self-talk package on basketball game performance. *Journal of Sport and Exercise Psychology* 12: 157-166.

Kenitzer, R.F., and W.B. Briddell. 1991. Effect of mental-imagery strategies on swimming performance. *Applied Research in Coaching and Athletics Annual* 259-273.

Kerlinger, F.N. 1986. *Foundations of behavioral research.* 3rd ed. New York: Holt, Rinehart, & Winston.

Kerr, G., and L. Leith. 1993. Stress management and athletic performance. *Sport Psychologist* 7: 221-231.

Kihlstrom, J.F., M.L. Glisky, M.A. Peterson, E.M. Harvey, and P.M. Rose. 1991. Vividness and control of mental imagery: A psychometric analysis. *Journal of Mental Imagery* 15: 133-142.

Kline, P. 1993. *The handbook of psychological testing.* London: Routledge.

Kohl, R.M., and D.L. Roenker. 1980. Bilateral transfer as a function of mental imagery. *Journal of Mental Imagery* 12: 197-206.

———. 1983. Mechanism involvement during skill imagery. *Journal of Motor Behaviour* 15: 179-190.

Kolonay, B.J. 1977. The effects of visuomotor behavior rehearsal on athletic performance. Master's thesis, City University of New York, Hunter College.

Kolt, G.S. 2000. Doing sport psychology with injured athletes. In *Doing sport psychology,* ed. M.B. Andersen, 223-236. Champaign, IL: Human Kinetics.

Korn, E.R. 1994. Mental imagery in enhancing performance: Theory and practical exercises. In *Imagery in sport and physical performance,* ed. A.A. Sheikh and E.R. Korn, 201-230. Amityville, NY: Baywood Publishing Co.

Kosslyn, S.M. 1980. *Image and mind.* Cambridge, MA: Harvard University Press.

———. 1994. *Image and brain.* Cambridge, MA: MIT Press.

Kosslyn, S.M., N.M. Alpert, W.L. Thompson, V. Maljkovic, S.B. Weise, C.F. Chabris, S.E. Hamilton, S.L. Rauch, and F.S. Buonanno. 1993. Visual mental imagery activates topographically organized visual cortex: PET investigations. *Journal of Cognitive Neuroscience* 55: 263-287.

Kosslyn, S.M., G. Ganis, and W.L. Thompson. 2001. Neural foundations of imagery. *Nature Reviews Neuroscience* 2: 635-642.

Kress, J., J. Schroeder, J.A. Potteiger, M. Haub. 1999. The use of psychological skills training to increase 10 km cycling performance: An exploratory investigation. *International Sports Journal* 3: 44-54.

Kremer, P.J., and J.L. Pressing. 1998. A test of the bioinformational theory of mental imagery in sport. Paper presented at the 33rd Australian Psychological Society Conference (October), Melbourne, Australia.

Kuhtz-Buschbeck, J.P., C. Mankopf, C. Holznecht, H. Siebner, S. Umer, and O. Jansen. 2003. Effector-independent representations of simple and complex imagined finger movements: A combined fMRI and TMS study. *European Journal of Neuroscience* 18(12): 3375-3393.

Kwekkeboom, K.L. 2000. Measuring imaging ability: Psychometric testing of the Imaging Ability Questionnaire. *Research in Nursing and Health* 23(4): 301-309.

LaFleur, M.F., P.L. Jackson, F. Malouin, C.L. Richards, A.C. Evans, and J. Doyon. 2002. Motor learning produces parallel dynamic functional changes during the execution and imagination of sequential foot movements. *Neuroimage* 16: 142-157.

Landers, D.M. 1999. Mental practice/imagery and performance: Research findings guiding application. *Proceedings of the Asian-South Pacific Association of Sport Psychology, Wuhan, China* 3: 1-8.

———. 2003. Thanks anyway, but I'm not smoking what you're smoking: A reply to Hale, Holmes, Smith, Fowler, and Collins. *Journal of Sport and Exercise Psychology* 25: 410-413.

Lane, J.B. 1977. Problems in assessment and control of imagery. *Perceptual and Motor Skills* 45: 363-368.

Lang, P.J. 1977. Imagery in therapy: An informational processing analysis of fear. *Behavior Therapy* 8: 862-886.

———. 1979a. A bioinformational theory of emotional imagery. *Psychophysiology* 16: 495-512.

———. 1979b. Language, image, and emotion. In *Advances in the study of communication and affect: Perception of emotion in self and others,* ed. K. Kliner, K.R. Blankenstein, and I.M. Speigal, 107-117. New York: Plenum Press.

Lang, P.J., M. Kozac, G.A. Miller, D.N. Levin, and A. McLean. 1980. Emotional imagery: Conceptual structure and pattern of somato-visceral response. *Psychophysiology* 17: 179-192.

Lang, P.J., D.N. Levin, G.A. Miller, and M.H. Kozak. 1983. Fear behavior, fear imagery, and the psychophysiology of emotion: The problem of affective response integration. *Journal of Abnormal Psychology* 92: 276-306.

Lang, P.J., B.G. Melamed, and J.A. Hart. 1970. A psychophysiological analysis of fear modification using an automated desensitization procedure. *Journal of Abnormal Psychology* 76: 229-234.

Lang, W, D. Cheyne, P. Hollinger, W. Gerschlager, and G. Lindinger. 1998. Electric and magnetic fields accompanying internal simulation of movement. *Cognitive Brain Research* 3: 125-129.

Larner, C., and T. Morris. 1997. Imagery, video modeling, and diving performance. In *Innovations in Sport Psychology: Linking Theory to Practice. Proceedings of the IX World Congress of Sport Psychology,* 414-416. Netanya, Israel: ISSP.

Latash, M.L. 1998. *Neurophysiological basis of movement.* Champaign, IL: Human Kinetics.

Lavallee, D., J. Kremer, A.P. Moran, and M. Williams. 2004. *Sport psychology: Contemporary themes.* Basingstoke, Hampshire, England: Palgrave MacMillan.

Lawther, K.S. 1968. *The learning of physical skills.* Englewood Cliffs, NJ: Prentice Hall.

Lee, A.B., and J. Hewitt. 1987. Using visual imagery in a flotation tank to improve gymnastic performance and reduce physical symptoms. *International Journal of Sport Psychology* 18: 223-230.

Lee, C. 1990. Psyching up for a muscular endurance task: Effects of image content on performance and mood state. *Journal of Sport and Exercise Psychology* 12: 66-73.

LeBoutillier, N., and D.F. Marks. 2003. Mental imagery and creativity: A meta-analytic review study. *British Journal of Psychology* 94(1): 29-44.

Leonard, C.T. 1998. *The neuroscience of human movement.* St. Louis: Mosby.

Lequerica, A., L. Rapport, B.N. Axelrod, K. Telmet, and R.D. Whitman. 2002. Subjective and objective assessment methods of mental imagery control: Construct validation of self-report measures. *Journal of Clinical and Experimental Neuropsychology* 24(8): 1103-1116.

LeUnes, A.D., and J.R. Nation. 2002. *Sport psychology: An introduction.* 3rd ed. Pacific Grove, CA: Brooks/Cole Thomson Learning.

Li, S., M. Latash, and V. Zatsiorsky. 2004. Effects of motor imagery on finger-force responses to transcranial magnetic stimulation. *Cognitive Brain Research* 20(2): 273-291.

Lidor, R. 1997. Effectiveness of a structured learning strategy on acquisition of game-related gross motor tasks in school settings. *Perceptual and Motor Skills* 84: 67-80.

Lidor, R., and R.N. Singer. 2000. Teaching performance routines to beginners. *Journal of Physical Education, Recreation and Dance* 71: 34-36, 52.

Liggett, D.R. 2000. *Sport hypnosis.* Champaign, IL: Human Kinetics.

Likert, R., and W.H. Quasha. 1970. *Revised Minnesota Paper Form Board Test.* New York: Psychological Corporation.

Lilly, J.C. 1956. Mental effects of reduction of ordinary levels of physical stimuli on intact, healthy persons. *Psychiatric Research Reports* 5: 1-9.

———. 1977. *The deep self.* New York: Simon and Schuster.

Livesay, J.R., and M.R. Samaras. 1998. Covert neuromuscular activity of the dominant forearm during visualization of a motor task. *Perceptual and Motor Skills* 86: 371-374.

Li-Wei, Z. 1991. EMG and EEG patterns in juvenile table-tennis players during imagery practice. *Sport Science* (Beijing) 11(486): 3-65.

Li-Wei, Z., M. Qi-Wei, T. Orlick, and L. Zitzelsberger. 1992. The effect of mental-imagery training on performance enhancement with 7-10-year-old children. *The Sport Psychologist* 6: 230-241.

Lorh, B.A., and Scogin, F. 1998. Effects of self-administered visuomotor behavioral rehearsal on sport performance of collegiate athletes. *Journal of Sport Behavior* 21: 206-218.

Lorenz, C., and U. Neisser. 1985. Factors of imagery and event recall. *Memory and Cognition* 13: 494-500.

Lotze, M., P. Montoya, M. Erb, E. Hulsman, H. Flor, U. Klose, N. Birbaumer, and W. Grodd. 1999. Activation of cortical and cerebellar motor areas during executed and imagined hand movements: An fMRI study. *Journal of Cognitive Neuroscience* 14: 491-501.

Lotze, M., G. Scheler, H.R.M. Tan, C. Braun, and N. Birbaumer. 2003. The musician's brain: Functional imaging of amateurs and professionals during imagery and performance. *NeuroImage* 20: 1817-1830.

Lovell, G., and D. Collins. 2001. Speed of image manipulation, imagery ability, and motor skill acquisition. *International Journal of Sport Psychology* 32(4): 355-368.

Lutz, R.S. 2001. IR, learning, and performance of motor tasks: Relationships and mediating processes. *Dissertation Abstracts International* 62: 2528.

———. 2003. Covert muscle excitation is outflow from the central generation of motor imagery. *Behavioral Brain Research* 140: 149-164.

Lutz, R., and D.E. Lindner. 2001. Does electromyographic activity during motor imagery predict performance? A test of bioinformational theory and functional equivalence. *Journal of Sport and Exercise Psychology* 23: s63.

Lynch, J. and Scott, W. 1999. *Running within: A guide to mastering the body-mind-spirit connection for ultimate training and racing.* Champaign, IL: Human Kinetics.

MacKay, D.G. 1981. The problem of rehearsal or mental practice. *Journal of Motor Behavior* 13: 274-285.

Maeda, F., and A. Pascual-Leone. 2003. Transcranial magnetic stimulation: Studying motor neurophysiology of psychiatric disorders. *Psychopharmacology* 168: 359-376.

Magill, R.A. 2004. *Motor control and learning: Concepts and applications.* 7th ed. Dubuque, IA: McGraw-Hill.

Mahoney, M.J. 1989. Psychological predictors of elite and non-elite performance in Olympic weightlifting. *International Journal of Sport Psychology,* 20: 1-12.

Mahoney, M.J., and M. Avener. 1977. Psychology of the elite athlete: An exploratory study. *Cognitive Therapy and Research* 3: 361-366.

Mahoney, M.J., and M. Epstein. 1981. The assessment of cognition in athletes. In *Cognitive assessment,* ed. T.V. Merluzzi, C.R. Glass, and M. Genest, 439-451. New York: Guilford Press.

Mahoney, M.J., T.J. Gabriel, and T.S. Perkins. 1987. Psychological skills and exceptional athletic performance. *Sport Psychologist* 1: 181-199.

Malouin, F., C.L. Richards, P.L. Jackson, F. Dumas, and J. Doyon. 2003. Brain activations during motor imagery of locomotor-related tasks: A PET study. *Human Brain Mapping* 19: 47-62.

Markland, D., and L. Hardy. 1993. The Exercise Motivations Inventory: Preliminary development and validity of a measure of individuals' reasons for participation in regular physical exercise. *Personality and Individual Differences* 15: 289-296.

Marks, D.F. 1973. Visual imagery differences in recall of pictures. *British Journal of Psychology* 64: 17-24.

Marks, D.F., and A. Isaac. 1995. Topographical distribution of EEG activity accompanying visual and motor imagery in vivid and non-vivid imagers. *British Journal of Psychology* 86: 271-282.

Marschark, M., and R.R. Hunt. 1989. A reexamination of the role of imagery in learning and memory. *Journal of Experimental Psychology: Learning, Memory, and Cognition* 15: 710-720.

Marsh, H.W. 1998. Foreword. In *Advances in Sport and Exercise Psychology Measurement,* ed. J.L. Duda. Morgantown, WV: Fitness Information Technology.

Martens, R. 1982. *Imagery in sport.* Paper presented at the conference on Medical and Scientific Aspects of Elitism in Sport, Brisbane, Australia.

———. 1987. *Coaches Guide to Sport Psychology.* Champaign, IL: Human Kinetics.

———. 2004. *Successful Coaching.* 3rd ed. Champaign, IL: Human Kinetics.

Martens, R., D. Burton, R.S. Vealey, L. Bump, and D.E. Smith. 1990. Development and validation of the Competitive State Anxiety Inventory-2. In *Competitive anxiety in sport,* ed. R. Martens, R.S. Vealey, and D. Burton, 117-232. Champaign, IL: Human Kinetics.

Martin, K., and C. Hall. 1995. Using mental imagery to enhance intrinsic motivation. *Journal of Sport and Exercise Psychology* 17: 54-69.

Martin, K.A., S.E. Moritz, and C.R. Hall. 1999. Imagery use in sport: A literature review and applied model. *Sport Psychologist* 13: 245-268.

Martinez, R.K. 2000. Changes in the frequency power spectrum of the human EEG during visual and kinesthetic imagery. *Dissertation Abstracts International* 61: 545.

Mastrich, J. 2002. A guide to sports psychology for parents and coaches. In *Really winning: Using sports to develop character and integrity in our boys,* ed. J. Mastrich, 80-115. New York: St. Martins Press.

Matlin, M. W. 1989. *Cognition,* 2nd ed. New York: Holt Rhinehart & Winton.

Mayo, R.J. 1977. *The development and construct validation of a measure of intrinsic motivation.* PhD diss., Purdue University.

McAleney, P.J., A. Barabasz, and M. Barabasz. 1990. Effects of flotation-restricted environmental stimulation on intercollegiate tennis performance. *Perceptual and Motor Skills* 71: 1023-1028.

McAuley, E. 1985. Modeling and self-efficacy: A test of Bandura's model. *Journal of Sport Psychology* 7: 283-295.

———. 1992. Understanding exercise behavior: A self-efficacy perspective. In *Motivation in sport and exercise,* ed. G.C. Roberts, 107-128. Champaign Il: Human Kinetics.

McBride, E.R., and A.L. Rothstein. 1979. Mental and physical practice and the learning and retention of open and closed skills. *Perceptual and Motor Skills* 49: 359-365.

McCullagh, P., and M.R. Weiss. 2001. Modeling: Learning, developmental, and social psychological considerations. In *Handbook of research on sport psychology,* 2nd ed., ed. R.N. Singer, M. Murphy, and L.K. Tennant, 106-125. New York: MacMillan.

———. 2002. Observational learning: The forgotten psychological method in sport psychology. In *Exploring sport and exercise psychology,* 2nd ed., ed. J.L. Van Raalte, 131-149. Washington, DC: American Psychological Association.

McKelvie, S.J., and P.P. Gingras. 1974. Reliability of two measures of visual imagery. *Perceptual and Motor Skills* 39: 417-418.

McKelvie, S.J. 1994. Guidelines for judging psychometric properties of imagery questionnaires as research instruments: A quantitative proposal. *Perceptual and Motor Skills* 79: 1219-1231.

———. 1995. The VVIQ as a psychometric test of individual differences in visual imagery vividness: A critical quantitative review and plea for direction. *Journal of Mental Imagery* 19(3-4): 1-106.

McKenzie, A.D., and B.L. Howe. 1997. The effect of imagery on self-efficacy for a motor skill. *International Journal of Sport Psychology* 28: 196-210.

McLean, N., and A. Richardson. 1994. The role of imagery in perfecting already learned physical skills. In *Imagery in sports and physical performance,* ed. A.A. Sheikh and E.R. Korn, 59-73. Amityville, NY: Baywood Publishing.

Meakin, F. 1903. Mutual inhibition of memory images. *Psychological Review Monographs* 4: 207-305.

Meichenbaum, D. 1977. *Cognitive behavior modification.* New York: Plenum Press.

———. 1985. *Stress inoculation training.* New York: Permagon Press.

Mellet, E., L. Petit, B. Mazoyer, M. Denis, and N. Tzourio. 1998. Reopening the mental imagery debate. Lessons from functional anatomy. *Neuroimage* 8: 129-139.

Mermecz, D.A., and B.G. Melamed. 1984. The assessment of emotional imagery training in children. *Behaviour Therapy* 15: 156-172.

Meyers, A.W., C.J. Cooke, J. Cullen, and L. Liles 1979. Psychological aspects of athletic competitors: A replication across sports. *Cognitive Therapy and Research* 3: 361-366.

Millard, M., C. Mahoney, and J. Wardrop. 2001. A preliminary study of mental and physical practice on the kayak wet exit skill. *Perceptual and Motor Skills* 92: 977-984.

Miller, G.A., D.N. Levin, M.J. Kozak, E.W. Cook, A. McLean, J. Carroll, and P.J. Lang. 1981. Emotional imagery: Individual differences in imagery ability and physiological responses. *Psychophysiology* 18: 196.

Minas, S.C. 1980. Mental practice of a complex perceptual-motor skill. *Journal of Human Movement Studies* 4: 102-107.

Moran, A. 1993. Conceptual and methodological issues in the measurement of mental imagery skills in athletes. *Journal of Sport Behavior* 16: 156-170.

———. 2002. In the mind's eye. *Psychologist* 15: 414-415.

———. 2004. *Sport and exercise psychology: A critical introduction.* Hove, England: Routledge.

Moran, A., and T. MacIntyre. 1998. "There's more to an image than meets the eye": A qualitative study of kinesthetic imagery among elite canoe-slalomists. *Irish Journal of Psychology* 19: 406-423.

Moritz, S.E., C.R. Hall, K.A. Martin, and E. Vadocz. 1996. What are confident athletes imaging? An examination of image content. *Sport Psychologist* 10: 171-179.

Morris, P.E., and P.J. Hampson. 1983. *Imagery and consciousness.* London: Academic.

Morris, T. 1997. *Psychological skills training in sport: An overview.* 2nd ed. Leeds: National Coaching Foundation.

Morris, T., H. Clayton, H. Power, and Han Jin-song. 1995. Gender and motives for participation in sport and exercise. *Proceedings of the FEPSAC IX European Congress of Sport Psychology* 364-373. Brussels: FEPSAC.

Morris, T., and S. Koehn. 2004. Self-confidence in sport and exercise. In *Sport psychology: Theory, applications, and issues,* 2nd ed., ed. T. Morris and J. Summers, 175-209. Brisbane, Australia: Wiley.

Morris, T., and M. Spittle. 2001. Internal and external imagery: A case of default theory? In *Proceedings of the X World Congress of Sport Psychology*, vol. 5, ed. A. Papaioannou, M. Goudas, and Y. Theodorakis, 11-13. Athens, Greece: ISSP.

Morris, T., M. Spittle, and C. Perry. 2004. Mental imagery in sport. In *Sport psychology: Theory, applications, and issues,* 2nd ed., ed. T. Morris and J. Summers, 344-383. Brisbane, Australia: Wiley.

Morris, T., and P. Thomas. 2004. Applied sport psychology. In *Sport psychology: Theory, applications and issues,* ed. T. Morris and J. Summers, 236-277. Brisbane, Australia: Wiley.

Morrisett, L.N. 1956. *The role of implicit practice in learning.* PhD diss., Yale University.

Morrison, P.R., and K.D. White. 1984. Imagery control: What is really being measured? *Journal of Mental Imagery* 8(2): 13-18.

Mumford, P., and C. Hall. 1985. The effects of internal and external imagery on performing figures and figure skating. *Canadian Journal of Applied Sport Sciences* 10: 171-177.

Munroe, K., P.R. Giacobbi, C.R. Hall, and R. Weinberg. 2000. The four *W*s of imagery use: Where, when, why, and what. *Sport Psychologist* 14: 119-137.

Munroe, K., C. Hall, S. Simms, and R. Weinberg. 1998. The influence of type of sport and time of season on athletes' use of imagery. *Sport Psychologist* 12(4): 440-449.

Munzert, J., and D. Hackfort. 1999. Individual preconditions for mental training. *International Journal of Sport Psychology* 30: 41-62.

Murphy, K.R., and C.O. Davidshofer. 1994. *Psychological testing: Principles and applications.* 3rd ed. Englewood Cliffs, NJ: Prentice Hall.

Murphy, S.M. 1990. Models of imagery in sport psychology: A review. *Journal of Mental Imagery* 14: 153-172.

―――. 1994. Imagery interventions in sport. *Medicine and Science in Sports and Exercise* 26: 486-494.

Murphy, S.M., and D.P. Jowdy. 1992. Imagery and mental practice. In *Advances in sport psychology,* ed. T.S. Horn, 221-250. Champaign, IL: Human Kinetics.

Murphy, S.M., and K.A. Martin. 2002. The use of imagery in sport. In *Advances in sport psychology,* 2nd ed., ed. T.S. Horn, 405-439. Champaign, IL: Human Kinetics.

Murphy, S.M., R.L. Woolfolk, and A.J. Budney. 1988. The effects of emotive imagery on strength performance. *Journal of Sport and Exercise Psychology* 10: 334–345.

Murray, J.M. 1989. *Competitive anxiety as a positive effect.* PhD diss., University of Virginia.

Naito, E., and M. Matsumura. 1994. Movement-related slow potentials during motor imagery and motor suppression in humans. *Cognitive Brain Research* 2: 131-137.

Neisser, U. 1976. *Cognition and reality: Principles and implications of cognitive psychology.* San Francisco: W.H. Freeman.

Nicol, M. 1993. Hypnosis in the treatment of repetitive strain injury. *Australian Journal of Clinical and Experimental Hypnosis* 21: 121-126.

Nideffer, R.M. 1985. *Athletes' guide to mental training.* Champaign, IL: Human Kinetics.

Noel, R.C. 1980. The effect of visuomotor behavior rehearsal on tennis performance. *Journal of Sport Psychology* 2: 221-226.

Noh, Y.E., and T. Morris. In press. Using research to design targeted coping interventions in dance. *Medical Aspects of Dance.*

Noh, Y.E., T. Morris, and M.B. Andersen. 2002. *Sources of stress and coping strategies of Korean ballet dancers.* Paper presented at Association for the Advancement of Applied Psychology (AAASP), Tucson, Arizona.

———. 2003, June. Psychological interventions for coping with stress in dancers. In *Seeking values of life through exercise and sport,* 4th ASPASP International Congress, 403-407. Seoul, Korea.

———. In press. Psychosocial factors in ballet injuries. *International Journal of Sport and Exercise Psychology.*

Norlander, T., H. Bergman, and T. Archer. 1999. Primary process in competitive archery performance: Effects of flotation REST. *Journal of Applied Sport Psychology* 11: 194-209.

Nowlis, D.P., and J. Kamyia. 1970. The control of electroencephalographic alpha rhythms through auditory feedback and the associated mental activity. *Psychophysiology* 6(4): 476-484.

Nunnally, J.C. 1978. *Psychometric theory.* 2nd ed. New York: McGraw-Hill.

O'Connor, E. 2003. Sports skills applied to rehabilitation: Relaxation and imagery. *SportEx Medicine* 15: 7-8.

O'Donoghue, P.G., and D. Ormsby. 2002. The effectiveness of mental-imagery training in enhancing of free kicks in Gaelic football. *Journal of Sports Sciences* 20: 70.

O'Halloran, A.M., and L. Gauvin. 1994. The role of preferred cognitive style in the effectiveness of imagery training. *International Journal of Sport Psychology* 25: 19-31.

Oishi, K., T. Kasai, and T. Maeshima. 2000. Autonomic response specificity during motor imagery. *Journal of Physiological Anthropology and Applied Human Science* 19: 255-261.

Oishi, K., M. Kimura, M. Yasukawa, T. Yoneda, and T. Maeshima. 1994. Amplitude, reduction of H-reflex during mental movement simulation in elite athletes. *Behavioral Brain Research* 62: 55-61.

Onestak, D.M. 1997. The effect of Visuomotor Behavior Rehearsal (VMBR) and videotaped modeling (VM) on the free-throw performance of intercollegiate athletes. *Journal of Sport Behavior* 20(2): 185-198.

Orliaguet, J.P., and Y. Coello. 1998. Differences between actual and imagined putting movements in golf: A chronometric analysis. *International Journal of Sport Psychology* 29: 157-169.

Orlick, T. 1980. *In pursuit of excellence: How to win in sport and life through mental training.* 1st ed. Champaign, IL: Human Kinetics.

———. 1990. *In pursuit of excellence: How to win in sport and life through mental training.* 2nd ed. Champaign, IL: Human Kinetics.

———. 2000. *In pursuit of excellence: How to win in sport and life through mental training.* 3rd ed. Champaign, IL: Human Kinetics.

Orlick, T., and N. McCaffrey. 1991. Mental training with children for sport and life. *Sport Psychologist* 5: 322-334.

Orlick, T., and J. Partington. 1988. Mental links to excellence. *Sport Psychologist* 2: 105-130.

Ostrow, A.C., ed. 1996. *Directory of psychological tests in the sport and exercise sciences.* 2nd ed. Morgantown, WV: Fitness Information Technology.

Page, S.J., W. Sime, and K. Nordell. 1999. The effects of imagery on female college swimmers' perceptions of anxiety. *Sport Psychologist* 13: 458-469.

Paivio, A. 1971. *Imagery and verbal processes.* New York: Holt, Rinehart, and Winston.

———. 1975. Coding distinctions and repetition effects in memory. In *Psychology of learning and motivation,* vol. 9, ed. G.H. Bower. Orlando, FL: Academic Press.

———. 1985. Cognitive and motivational functions of imagery in human performance. *Canadian Journal of Applied Sport Science* 10: 22S-28S.

———. 1986. *Mental representations: A dual coding approach.* Oxford: Clarendon Press.

Paivio, A., and R. Harshman. 1983. Factor analysis of a questionnaire on imagery and verbal habits and skills. *Canadian Journal of Psychology* 37: 461-483.

Parrott, C.A., and K.T. Strongman. 1985. Utilization of visual imagery in creative performance. *Journal of Mental Imagery* 9: 53-66.

Parsons, L.M., and P.T. Fox. 1998. The neural basis of implicit movements used in recognizing hand shape. *Cognitive Neuropsychology* 15: 583-615.

Partington, J. 1990. *Personal knowledge in imagery: Implications for novice gymnasts, figure skaters, and their coaches.* Paper presented at the Conference of the Canadian Society for Psychomotor Learning and Sport Psychology, Windsor, Ontario.

Pates, J., A. Cummings, and I. Maynard. 2002. The effects of hypnosis on flow states and three-point shooting performance in basketball players. *Sport Psychologist* 16: 34-47.

Pates, J., and I. Maynard. 2000. Effects of hypnosis on flow states and golf performance. *Perceptual and Motor Skills* 91: 1057-1075.

Pates, J., R. Oliver, and I. Maynard. 2003. The effects of hypnosis on flow states and golf-putting performance. *Journal of Applied Sport Psychology* 13: 341-354.

Pedhazur, E.J., and L.S. Schmelkin. 1991. *Measurement, design, and analysis: An integrated approach.* Hillsdale, NJ: Lawrence Erlbaum Associates.

Peper, E., and A. Schmid. 1983. Fifteen-month follow-up with asthmatics utilizing EMG/incentive inspirometer feedback. *Biofeedback and Self-Regulation* 17: 143-151.

Perkins, D., G.V. Wilson, and J.H. Kerr. 2001. The effects of elevated arousal and mood on maximal strength performance in athletes. *Journal of Applied Sport Psychology* 13: 239-259.

Peronnet, F., and M.J. Farah. 1989. Mental rotation: An event-related potential study with a validated mental-rotation task. *Brain and Cognition* 9: 279-288.

Perry, C., and T. Morris. 1995. Mental imagery in sport. In *Sport psychology: Theory, applications and issues,* ed. T. Morris and J. Summers, 339-385. Brisbane, Australia: Wiley.

Petipas, A., and S.J. Danish. 1995. Caring for injured athletes. In *Sport psychology interventions,* ed. S.M. Murphy, 255-281. Champaign, IL: Human Kinetics.

Petrie, T.A., and F. Perna. 2004. Psychology of injury: Theory, research, and practice. In *Sport psychology: Theory, applications, and issues,* 2nd ed., ed. T. Morris and J. Summers, 547-571. Brisbane, Australia: Wiley.

Pfurtscheller, G., and C. Neuper. 1997. Motor imagery activates primary sensorimotor area in humans. *Neuroscience Letters* 239: 65-68.

Pickenhain, L. 1976. Die Bedeutung innerer Ruckkoppelungskreise für den Lernvorgang. *Zeitschrift für Psychologie* (Leipzig) 184: 551-561.

Pickenhain, L., and L. Beyer. 1979. Beziehungen zwischen den hieracisch organisierten Ruckmeldekreisen und der Ergebnisruckmeldubg als wesentlicher Faktor für die Ausbildung innerer Modelle von Arbeitshandlungen. In *Arbeits- und Ingenieurpsychologie und Intensivierung,* ed. F. Felix and K.P. Timp. Berlin: Deutscher Verlag der Wissenchaften.

Poretta, D.L., P.R. Surburg, and M. Gillespie. 1999. Use of various instructional methods for enhancing gross motor skill acquisition in students with moderate mental retardation. *Clinical Kinesiology* 53: 63-68.

Porro, C.A., M.P. Francescato, V. Cettelo, M.E. Diamond, P. Baraldi, C. Zuiani, M. Bazzocchi, and P.E. di Prampero. 1996. Primary motor and sensory cortex activation during motor performance and motor imagery: A functional magnetic resonance study. *Journal of Neuroscience* 16: 7688-7698.

Powell, G.E. 1973. Negative and positive practice on motor skill acquisition. *Perceptual and Motor Skills* 37: 312.

Price, F.L., and M.B. Andersen. 2000. Into the maelstrom: A five-year relationship from college ball to the NFL. In *Doing sport psychology,* ed. M.B. Andersen, 193-206. Champaign, IL: Human Kinetics.

Pylyshyn, Z.W. 1973. What the mind's eye tells the mind's brain: A critique of mental imagery. *Psychological Bulletin* 80: 1-24.

———. 1979. The rate of mental rotation of images: A test of a holistic analogue hypothesis. *Memory and Cognition, 7,* 19-28.

Quilter, S.M., J.P. Band, and G.M. Miller. 1999. Measuring mental imagery with visual analogue scales. *Journal of Mental Health Counseling* (American Mental Health Counselors Association) 21: 161.

Ram, N., and P. McCullagh. 2003. Self-modeling: Influence on psychological responses and physical performance. *Sport Psychologist* 17: 220-241.

Reed, S.K. 1996. *Cognition.* 4th ed. Pacific Grove, CA: Brooks/Cole.

Reid, M.R., P.D. Drummond, and L.T. Mackinnon. 2001. The effect of moderate aerobic exercise and relaxation on secretory immunoglobulin A. *International Journal of Sports Medicine* 22(2): 132-137.

Reise, S.P., N.G. Waller, and A.L. Comrey. 2000. Factor analysis and scale revision. *Psychological Assessment* 12(3): 287-297.

Richardson, A. 1967. Mental practice: A review and discussion. Part 2. *Research Quarterly* 38: 263-273.

———. 1969. *Mental imagery.* New York: Springer.

———. 1977. The meaning and measurement of memory imagery. *British Journal of Psychology* 68: 28-43.

———. 1983. Imagery: Definitions and types. In *Imagery: Current theory, research, and application,* ed. A.A. Sheikh, 1-34. New York: Wiley.

———. 1994. *Individual differences in imaging: Their measurement, origins, and consequences.* Amityville, NY: Baywood.

Richardson, J.T.E. 1988. Vividness and unvividness: Reliability, consistency, and validity of subjective imagery ratings. *Journal of Mental Imagery* 12: 115-122.

———. 1999. *Imagery.* Hove, England: Psychology Press.

Rodgers, W.M., and L. Gauvin. 1998. Heterogeneity of incentives for physical activity and self-efficacy in high-active and moderately active women exercisers. *Journal of Applied Social Psychology* 28: 1016-1029.

Rodgers, W.M., C.R. Hall, C.M. Blanchard, and K.J. Munroe. 1999. The relationship between imagery and obligatory exercise. Paper presented at the Canadian Psychomotor Learning and Sport Psychology Society Conference, Edmonton, Canada.

———. 2001. Prediction of obligatory exercise by exercise-related imagery. *Psychology of Addictive Behaviors* 15: 152-154.

Rodgers, W., C.R. Hall, and E. Buckolz. 1991. The effect of an imagery training program on imagery ability, imagery use, and figure skating performance. *Journal of Applied Sport Psychology* 3: 109-125.

Rodgers, W.M., K.J. Munroe, and C.R. Hall. 2002. Relations among exercise imagery, self-efficacy, exercise behavior, and intentions. *Imagination, Cognition, and Personality* 21: 55-65.

Rodgers, W.M., and M.J.L. Sullivan. 2001. Task, coping, and scheduling self-efficacy in relation to frequency of physical activity. *Journal of Applied Social Psychology* 31: 741-753.

Rogers, H., and T. Morris. 2003. An overview of the development and validation of the Recreational Exercise Motivation Measure (REMM). In *New approaches to exercise and sport psychology: Theories, methods, and applications. Proceedings of the 11th European Congress of Sport Psychology,* ed. R. Stelter. CD-ROM. 3-page full paper. Copenhagen, Denmark: University of Copenhagen.

Roland, P.E., and L. Friberg. 1985. Localization of cortical areas activated by thinking. *Journal of Neurophysiology* 53: 1219-1243.

Roland, P.E., B. Larsen, N.A. Lassen, and E. Shinhoj. 1980. Supplementary motor area and other cortical areas in organization of voluntary movements in man. *Journal of Neurophysiology* 43: 118-136.

Roland, P.E., E. Shinhoj, N.A. Lassen, and B. Larsen. 1980. Different cortical areas in man in organization of voluntary movement of extrapersonal space. *Journal of Neurophysiology* 43: 137-150.

Romero, D.H., M.G. Lacourse, K.E. Lawrence, S. Schandler, and M.J. Cohen. 2000. Event-related potentials as a function of movement parameter variations during motor imagery and isometric contraction. *Behavioral Brain Research* 117: 83-96.

Rose, D.J. 1997. *A multilevel approach to the study of motor control and learning.* Needham Heights, MA: Allyn and Bacon.

Rosenbaum, D.A. 1991. *Human motor control.* London: Academic Press.

Rosler, F., M. Heil, and U. Glowalla. 1993. Memory retrieval from long-term memory by slow event-related brain potentials. *Psychophysiology* 30: 170-182.

Ross, J.S., J. Tkach, P. Ruggieri, M. Lieber, and E. Lapresto. 2003. The mind's eye: Functional MR imaging evaluation of golf motor imagery. *American Journal of Neuroradiology* 24: 1036-1044.

Ross, M.J., and R.S. Berger. 1996. Effects of stress inoculation training on athletes' postsurgical pain and rehabilitation after orthopedic injury. *Journal of Consulting and Clinical Psychology* 64: 406-410.

Rotella, B., B.A. Boyce, B. Allyson, and J. Savis. 1998. *Case studies in sport psychology.* Boston: Jones and Bartlett.

Rotella, R.J., B. Gansneder, D. Ojala, and J. Billing. 1980. Cognitions and coping strategies of elite skiers: An exploratory study of young developing athletes. *Journal of Sport Psychology* 2: 350-354.

Roth, M., J. Decety, M. Raybaudi, R. Massarelli, C. Delon-Martin, C. Segebarth, et al. 1996. Possible involvement of primary motor cortex in mentally simulated movement: A functional magnetic resonance imaging study. *NeuroReport* 7: 1280-1284.

Roure, R., C. Collet, C. Deschaumes-Molinaro, G. Delhomme, A. Dittmar, and E. Vernet-Maury. 1999. Imagery quality estimated by autonomic response is correlated to sporting performance enhancement. *Physiology and Behavior* 66: 63-72.

Roure, R., C. Collet, C. Deschaumes-Molinaro, A. Dittmar, H. Rada, G. Delhomme, and E. Vernet-Maury. 1998. Autonomic nervous system responses correlate with mental rehearsal in volleyball training. *European Journal of Applied Physiology and Occupational Physiology* 78: 99-108.

Rushall, B.S. 1991. *Imagery training in sports: A handbook for athletes, coaches, and sport psychologists.* Spring Valley, CA: Sports Science Associates.

———. 1992. *Mental-skills training for sports.* Canberra, Australia: Sports Science Associates.

———. 1995. *Mental skills training for sports: A manual for athletes, coaches, and sport psychologists.* 2nd ed. Spring Valley, CA: Sports Science Associates.

Rushall, B.S., and L.G. Lippman. 1998. The role of imagery in physical performance. *International Journal of Sport Psychology* 29: 57-72.

Russell, W.D. 2000. Coping with injuries in scholastic athletics. *Journal of Physical Education, Recreation and Dance* 71: 41-47.

Ryan, D.E., T. Blakeslee, and M. Furst. 1986. Mental practice and motor skill learning: An indirect test of the neuromuscular feedback hypothesis. *International Journal of Sport Psychology* 17: 60-70.

Ryan, E.D., and J. Simons. 1981. Cognitive demand imagery and frequency of mental practice as factors influencing the acquisition of mental skills. *Journal of Sport Psychology* 4: 35-45.

———. 1982. Efficacy of mental imagery in enhancing mental practice of motor skills. *Journal of Sport Psychology* 4: 41-51.

————. 1983. What is learned in mental practice of motor skills: A test of the cognitive motor hypothesis. *Journal of Sport Psychology* 5: 419-426.

Ryan, R.M., C.M. Frederick, D. Lepes, N. Rubio, and K.M. Sheldon. 1997. Intrinisc motivation and exercise adherence. *International Journal of Sport Psychology* 28: 335-354.

Ryding, E., J. Decety, H. Sjoholm, G. Stenberg, and D.H. Ingvar. 1993. Motor imagery activates the cerebellum regionally. A SPECT rCBf study with 99m TcHMPAO. *Cognitive Brain Research* 2: 94-99.

Sack, A.T., and D.E.J. Linden. 2003. Combining transcranial magnetic stimulation and functional imaging in cognitive brain research: Possibilities and limitations. *Brain Research Reviews* 43: 41-56.

Sackett, R.S. 1934. The influences of symbolic rehearsal upon the retention of a maze habit. *Journal of General Psychology* 10: 376-395.

Salmon, J., C. Hall. and I. Haslam. 1994. The use of imagery by soccer players. *Journal of Applied Sport Psychology* 6: 116-133.

Sargent, G. 1996. Developing a mental skills training program 3. *Sports Coach* 8: 26-27.

————. 1997. Developing a mental skills training program 4. *Sports Coach* 9: 32-33.

Savoy, C., and P. Beitel. 1996. Mental imagery for basketball. *International Journal of Sport Psychology* 27: 454-462.

Scherzer, C.B., B.W. Brewer, A.E. Cornelius, J.L. Van Raalte, A.J. Petipas, J.H. Sklar, M.H. Pohlman, R.J. Krushell, and T.D. Ditmar. 2001. Psychological skills and adherence to rehabilitation after reconstruction of the anterior cruciate ligament. *Journal of Sport Rehabilitation* 10: 165-172.

Schmidt, R.A. 1982. *Motor control and learning: A behavioral emphasis.* Champaign, IL: Human Kinetics.

Schmidt, R.A., and T.D. Lee. 1999. *Motor control and learning: A behavioral emphasis.* 3rd ed. Champaign, IL: Human Kinetics.

Schmidt, R.A., and C.A. Wrisberg. 2004. *Motor learning and performance: A problem-based learning approach.* 3rd ed. Champaign, IL: Human Kinetics.

Schnitzler, A., S. Salenius, R. Salmelin, V. Jousamki, and R. Hari. 1997. Involvement of primary motor cortex in motor imagery: A neuromagnetic study. *Neuroimage* 6: 201-208.

Schunk, D.H., A.R. Hanson, and P.D. Cox. 1987. Peer-model attributes and children's achievement behavior. *Journal of Educational Psychology* 79: 54-61.

Schutz, R.W. 1998. Assessing the stability of psychological traits and measures. In *Advances in sport and exercise psychology measurement,* ed. J.L. Duda, 393-408. Morgantown, WV: Fitness Information Technology.

Schutz, R.W., and M.E. Gessaroli. 1993. Use, misuse, and disuse of psychometics in sport psychology research. In *Handbook of research on sport psychology,* ed. R.N. Singer, M. Murphy, and L.K. Tennant, 901-917. New York: Macmillan.

Screws, D.P., and P.R. Surburg. 1997. Motor performance of children with mild mental disabilities after using mental imagery. *Adapted Physical Activity Quarterly* 14: 119-130.

Seabourne, T.G., R. Weinberg, and A. Jackson. 1984. Effect of individualized practice and training of visuo-motor behavior rehearsal in enhancing karate performance. *Journal of Sport Behavior* 7: 58-67.

Seabourne, T.G., R.S. Weinberg, A. Jackson, and R.M. Suinn. 1985. Effect of individualized, nonindividualized, and package intervention strategies on karate performance. *Journal of Sport Psychology* 7: 40-50.

Shaffer, D.R. 2000. *Social and personality development.* 4th ed. Belmont, CA: Wadsworth.

Shaffer, S.M., and D.M. Wiese-Bjornstal. 1999. Psychosocial intervention strategies in sports medicine. In *Counseling in sports medicine,* ed. R. Ray and D.M. Wiese-Bjornstal, 41-54. Champaign, IL: Human Kinetics.

Shambrook, C.J., and S.J. Bull. 1996. The use of a single-case research design to investigate the efficacy of imagery training. *Journal of Applied Sport Psychology* 8: 27-43.

Shaw, W.A. 1938. The distribution of muscular action-potentials during imaging. *Psychological Record* 2: 195-216.

———. 1940. The relation of muscular action potentials to imaginal weightlifting. *Archives of Psychology* 247: 50.

She, W., and T. Morris. 1997. Imagery, self-confidence, and baseball hitting. In *Proceedings of the IX World Congress of Sport Psychology,* ed. R. Lidor and M. Bar-Eli, 626-628. Netanya, Israel: ISSP.

Sheehan, P.W. 1967a. A shortened version of Betts' Questionnaire upon Mental Imagery. *Journal of Clinical Psychology* 23: 386-389.

———. 1967b. Reliability of a short test of imagery. *Perceptual and Motor Skills* 25: 744.

Sheehan, P.W., R. Ashton, and K. White. 1983. Assessment of mental imagery. In *Imagery: Current theory, research, and application,* ed. A.A. Sheikh, 189-221. New York: Wiley.

Sheikh, A.A., and E.R. Korn (eds.) 1994. *Imagery in sports and physical performance.* Amityville, NY: Baywood.

Shick, J. 1970. Effects of mental practice on selected volleyball skills for college women. *Research Quarterly* 41: 88-94.

Short, P.L. 1953. The objective study of mental imagery. *British Journal of Psychology* 44: 38-51.

Short, S.E., J. Afremow, and L. Overby. 2001. Using mental imagery to enhance children's motor performance. *Journal of Physical Education, Recreation and Dance* 72: 19-23.

Short, S.E., J.M. Bruggeman, S.G. Engel, T.L. Marback, L.J. Wang, A. Willadsen, and M.W. Short. 2002. The effect of imagery function and imagery direction on self-efficacy and performance on a golf-putting task. *Sport Psychologist* 16: 48-67.

Shumway-Cook, A., and M.H. Woollacott. 2001. *Motor control: Theory and practical applications.* 2nd ed. Baltimore: Lippincott, Williams, & Wilkins.

Simons, J. 2000. Doing imagery in the field. In *Doing Sport Psychology,* ed. M.B. Andersen, 77-92. Champaign, IL: Human Kinetics.

Singer, R.N. 1986. *Peak performance: And more.* Ithaca, NY: Movement Publications.

———. 1988. Strategies and metastrategies in learning and performing self-paced athletic skills. *Sport Psychologist* 2: 49-68.

Slade, J.M., D.M. Landers, and P.E. Martin. 2002. Muscular activity during real and imagined movements: A test of inflow explanations. *Journal of Sport and Exercise Psychology* 24: 151-167.

Slaughter, J.W. 1902. Behavior of mental images. *American Journal of Psychology* 13: 526-549.

Slee, J.A. 1988. Vividness as a descriptor and index of imagery. *Journal of Mental Imagery* 12: 123-132.

Smith, D. 1987. Conditions that facilitate the development of sport imagery training. *Sport Psychologist* 1: 237-247.

Smith, D., P. Holmes, L. Whitemore, D. Collins, and T. Devonport. 2001. The effect of theoretically based imagery scripts on field hockey performance. *Journal of Sport Behavior* 24: 408-419.

Smith, M. 1998. *Mental skills for the artistic sports: Developing emotional intelligence.* Red Deer, Alta.: Johnson Gorman Publishers.

Smyth, M.M., and A. Waller. 1998. Movement imagery in rock climbing: Patterns of interference from visual, spatial, and kinesthetic secondary tasks. *Applied Cognitive Psychology* 12: 145-157.

Solso, R. L. 1991. *Cognitive Psychology,* 3rd ed. Boston: Allyn & Bacon.

Sordoni, C., C. Hall, and L. Forwell. 2000. The use of imagery by athletes during injury rehabilitation. *Journal of Sport Rehabilitation* 9: 329-338.

———. 2002. The use of imagery in athletic injury rehabilitation and its relationship to self-efficacy. *Physiotherapy Canada* 177-185.

Speed, H.D., and M.B. Andersen. 2000. What exercise and sport scientists don't understand. *Journal of Science and Medicine in Sport* 3(1): 84-92.

Spielberger, C.D., R.L. Gorsuch, and R.E. Lushene. 1970. *STAI manual for the State Trait Anxiety Inventory.* Palo Alto, CA: Consulting Psychologists.

Spittle, M., and T. Morris. 1997. Concentration skills for cricket bowlers. *Sports Coach* 20(2): 32.

———. 1998. Examination of internal and external imagery of open and closed sports skills using concurrent verbalization. Paper presented at the Australian Psychological Society Annual Conference (September), Melbourne, Australia.

———. 1999a. Training of imagery perspectives. *Proceedings of the 5th International Olympic Committee World Congress on Sport Sciences,* 142. Sydney, Australia.

————. 1999b. State and trait measurement of imagery perspectives. *Proceedings of the 3rd International Congress of the Asian South Pacific Association of Sport Psychology,* 327-329. Wuhan, China: ASPASP.

————. 2000. Imagery perspective preferences and motor performance. *Australian Journal of Psychology* 52S: 112.

Starkes, J.L., W. Helsen, and R. Jack. 2001. Expert performance in sport and dance. In *Handbook of sport psychology,* 2nd ed., ed. R.N. Singer, H.A. Hausenblas, and C.M. Janelle, 174-201. New York: Wiley.

Start, K.B., and A. Richardson. 1964. Imagery and mental practice. *British Journal of Education Psychology* 34: 280-284.

Stephan, K.M., G.R. Fink, C.D. Frith, and R.S.J. Frackowiak. 1993. Functional anatomy of mental representation of hand movements in healthy subjects. Abstract in *International Union of Psychological Sciences* (Glasgow), 497.

Stephan, K.M., G.R. Fink, R.E. Passingham, D. Silbersweig, A.O. Ceballous-Bauman, C.D. Frith, and R.S.J. Frackowiak. 1995. Functional anatomy of the mental representation of upper extremity movements in healthy participants. *Journal of Neurophysiology* 73: 373-386.

Sthalekar, H.A. 1993. Hypnosis for relief of chronic phantom pain in a paralyzed limb: A case study. *Australian Journal of Clinical Hypnotherapy and Hypnosis* 14: 75-80.

Stinear, C.M., and W.D. Byblow. 2004. Modulation of corticospinal excitability and intracortical inhibition during motor imagery is task-dependent. *Experimental Brain Research* 157: 351-358.

Strauss, A., and J. Corbin. 1990. *Basics of qualitative research: Grounded theory procedures and techniques.* Newbury Park, CA: Sage.

Stuss, D.T., F.F. Sarazin, E.E. Leech, and T.W. Picton. 1983. Event-related potentials during naming and mental rotation. *Electroencephalography and Clinical Neurophysiology* 56: 133-146.

Suedfeld, P. 1980. *Restricted environmental stimulation: Research and clinical applications.* New York: Wiley.

Suedfeld, P., and T. Bruno. 1990. Flotation REST and imagery in the improvement of athletic performance. *Journal of Sport and Exercise Psychology* 12: 82-85.

Suedfeld, P., D. Collier, and B. Hartnett. 1993. Enhancing perceptual-motor accuracy through flotation REST. *Sport Psychologist* 7: 151-159.

Suedfeld, P., J.W. Turner Jr., and T.H. Fine. 1990. *Restricted environmental stimulation: Theoretical and empirical developments in flotation REST.* New York: Springer-Verlag.

Suinn, R.M. 1972a. Behavior rehearsal training for ski racers. Letter to the editor in *Behavior Therapy* 3: 519-520.

————. 1972b. Removing emotional obstacles to learning and performance by visuo-motor behavior rehearsal. *Behavior Therapy* 3: 308-310.

————. 1976a. Visual motor behavior rehearsal for adaptive behavior. In *Counseling methods,* ed. J. Krumboltz and C. Thoresen, 360-366. New York: Holt, Rinehart & Winston.

———. 1976b. Body thinking: Psychology for Olympic champs. *Psychology Today* 10(2): 38-43.

———. 1977. Behavioral methods at the Winter Olympic Games. Letter to the editor in *Behavior Therapy* 8: 283-284.

———. 1983. Imagery and sports. In *Imagery: Current theory, research, and application,* ed. A.A. Sheikh, 507-534. New York: Wiley.

———. 1984. Imagery and sports. In *Cognitive sport psychology,* ed. W.F. Straub and J.M. Williams, 253-272. Lansing, NY: Sport Science Associates.

———. 1993. Imagery. In *Handbook of research on sport psychology,* ed. R.N. Singer, M. Murphey, and L.K. Tennant, 492-510. New York: Macmillan.

———. 1996. Imagery rehearsal: A tool for clinical practice. *Psychotherapy in Private Practice* 15(3): 27-31.

———. 1997. Mental practice in sport psychology: Where have we been, where do we go? *Clinical Psychology: Science and Practice* 4(3): 189-207.

Suinn, R.M., and Andrews, F.A. 1981. *Psychological strategies of professional competitors.* Unpublished manuscript.

Surburg, P.R. 1991. Preparation process facilitation of a motor task through imagery practice with adolescents who have mental retardation. *American Journal on Mental Retardation* 95: 428-434.

Surburg, P.R., D.L. Poretta, and V. Sutlive. 1995. Use of imagery practice for improving a motor skill. *Adapted Physical Activity Quarterly* 1: 217-227.

Surgent, F.S. 1991. Using your mind to beat injuries. *Running and FitNews* 9: 4-5.

Switras, J. 1978. An alternate-form instrument to assess vividness and controllability of mental imagery in seven modalities. *Perceptual and Motor Skills* 46: 379-384.

Syer, J., and C. Connolly. 1987. *Sporting body, sporting mind: An athlete's guide to mental training.* London: Simon & Schuster.

Taylor, J.A., and D.F. Shaw. 2002. The effects of outcome imagery on golf-putting performance. *Journal of Sports Sciences* 20: 607-613.

Taylor, J., and S. Taylor. 1997. *Psychological approaches to sports injury rehabilitation.* Gaithersburg, MD: Aspen.

Tenenbaum, G., M. Corbett, and A. Kitsantas. 2002. Biofeedback: Applications and methodological concerns. In *Brain and body in sport and exercise: Biofeedback applications in performance enhancement,* ed. B. Blumenstein, M. Bar-Eli, and G. Tenenbaum, 101-122. Chichester, England: Wiley.

Tenenbaum, G., and G. Fogarty. 1998. Application of the Rasch analysis to sport and exercise psychology measurement. In *Advances in sport and exercise psychology measurement,* ed. J.L. Duda, 409-422. Morgantown, WV: Fitness Information Technology.

Thomas, P.R., and G.J. Fogarty. 1997. Psychological skills training in golf: The role of individual differences in cognitive preferences. *Sport Psychologist* 11: 86-106.

Thompson, J.K., and L. Pasman. 1991. The Obligatory Exercise Questionnaire. *Behavioral Assessment Review* (May): 137.

Tinti, C., D. Galati, M.G. Vecchio, R. De Beni, and C. Cornoldi. 1999. Interactive auditory and visual images in persons who are totally blind. *Journal of Visual Impairment and Blindness* 93: 579-583.

Toates, F. 2001. *Biological psychology: An integrative approach.* Essex, England: Pearson.

Tokumaru, O., C. Mizumoto, Y. Takada, H. Ashida. 2003. EEG activity of aviators during imagery flight training. *Clinical Neurophysiology* 114: 1926-1935.

Tower, R.B. 1981. Imagery measurement in clinical settings: Matching the method to the question. In *Imagery.* Vol. 2, *Concepts, results, and applications,* ed. E. Klinger, 79-9. New York: Plenum Press.

Travis, C.A., and M.L. Sachs. 1991. Applied sport psychology and persons with mental retardation. *Sport Psychologist* 5: 382-391.

Tremblay, F., L. Tremblay, and D.E. Colcer. 2001. Modulation of corticospinal excitability during imagined knee movements. *Journal of Rehabilitation Medicine* 33: 230-234.

Turner, J.W., Jr., and T.H. Fine. 1983. Effects of relaxation associated with brief restricted environmental stimulation therapy (REST) on plasma cortisol, ACTH, and LH. *Biofeedback and Self-regulation* 8: 115-126.

Ungerleider, S. 1996. *Mental training for peak performance: Top athletes reveal the mind exercises they use to excel.* Emmaus, PA: Rodale Press.

Ungerleider, S., and J.M. Golding. 1991. Mental practice among Olympic athletes. *Perceptual and Motor Skills* 72: 1007-1017.

United States Olympic Committee. 1998. [Online]. *Sport psychology: An introduction to imagery and simulation.* Available: www.midtools.com/imginto.html. [May 25, 1999].

Vadocz, E.A., C.R. Hall, and S.E. Moritz. 1997. The relationship between competitive anxiety and imagery use. *Journal of Applied Sport Psychology* 9: 241-253.

Vandenberg, S., and A.R. Kuse. 1978. Mental rotations: A group test of three-dimensional spatial visualization. *Perceptual and Motor Skills* 47: 599-604.

Van Gyn, G.H., H.A. Wenger, and C.A. Gaul. 1990. Imagery as a method of enhancing transfer from training to performance. *Journal of Sport and Exercise Psychology* 12: 366-375.

Vealey, R.S. 1986. Imagery training for performance enhancement. In *Applied sport psychology: Personal growth to peak performance,* 1st ed., ed. J.M. Williams, 209-231. Mountain View, CA: Mayfield.

Vealey, R., and C.A. Greenleaf. 1998. Seeing is believing: Understanding and using imagery in sport. In *Applied sport psychology: Personal growth to peak performance,* 3rd ed., ed. J.M. Williams, 247-283 Mountain View, CA: Mayfield.

Vealey, R.S., and C.A. Greenleaf. 2001. Seeing is believing: Understanding and using imagery in sport. In *Applied sport psychology: Personal growth to peak performance,* 4th ed., ed. J.M. Williams, 247-288. Mountain View, CA: Mayfield.

Vealey, R.S., and S.M. Walter. 1993. Imagery training for performance enhancement and personal development. In *Applied sport psychology: Personal growth to peak performance,* 2nd ed., ed. J.M. Williams, 200-224. Mountain View, CA: Mayfield.

Vecchi, T., M.L. Monticelli, and C. Cornoldi. 1995. Visuo-spatial working memory: Structures and variables affecting a capacity measure. *Neuropsychologia* 33: 1549-1564.

Victorian Government Department of Human Services. Victorian Population Health Survey 2002, selected findings. Retrieved November 15, 2003, from www.dhs.vic.gov.au/phd/healthsurveillance/downloads/vphs2002.pdf.

Vigus, T.L., and J.M. Williams. 1985. The physiological correlates of internal and external imagery. Unpublished manuscript.

Vogt, S. 1995. On relations between perceiving, imagining, and performing in the learning of cyclical movement sequences. *British Journal of Psychology* 86: 191-216.

Wagaman, J.D, A.F. Barabasz, and M. Barabasz. 1991. Flotation REST and imagery in the improvement of collegiate basketball performance. *Perceptual and Motor Skills* 79: 119-122.

Wang, Y., and W.P. Morgan. 1992. The effect of imagery perspectives on the psychophysiological responses to imagined exercise. *Behavioural Brain Research* 52: 167-174.

Wann, D.L. 1997. *Sport psychology.* Upper Saddle River, N.J.: Prentice Hall.

Watt, A. 2003. *Development and validation of the Sport Imagery Ability Measure.* PhD diss., Victoria University, Melbourne, Australia.

Watt, A.P., and T. Morris. 1998a. *The Sport Imagery Ability Measure: Development and reliability analysis.* Paper presented at the 33rd Australian Psychological Society Conference (October), Melbourne, Australia.

———. 1998b. *Information manual for the Sport Imagery Ability Measure.* Melbourne, Australia: Victoria University of Technology.

———. 1999a. Reliability, factor structure, and criterion validity of the Sport Imagery Ability Measure (SIAM). *Proceedings of the 3rd International Congress of the Asian South Pacific Association of Sport Psychology,* 330-332. Wuhan, China: ASPASP.

———. 1999b. Convergent and discriminant validity of the Sport Imagery Ability Measure (SIAM). Paper presented at the 5th International Olympic Committee World Congress on Sport Sciences (November), Sydney, Australia.

———. 2000. The qualitative analysis of sport-oriented mental imagery. Paper presented at "The Brain Games," 35th Annual Conference of the Australian Psychological Society in Association with the International Society of Sport Psychology (October), Canberra, Australia.

———. 2001. Criterion validity of the Sport Imagery Ability Measure (SIAM). In *Proceedings of the 10th World Congress of Sport Psychology,* Vol. 2 (May), ed. A. Papaioannou, M. Goudas, and Y. Theodorakis, 60-62. Skiathos, Greece.

Watt, A.P., T. Morris, and M.B. Andersen. 2004. Issues in the development of a measure of imagery ability in sport. *Journal of Mental Imagery* 28 (3): 149-180.

Watt, A.P., T. Morris, T. Lintunen, T. Elfving, and D. Riches. 2001. Confirmatory factor analysis of the Sport Imagery Ability Measure (SIAM). In *Proceedings of the 10th World Congress of Sport Psychology,* Vol. 4 (May), ed. A. Papaioannou, M. Goudas, and Y. Theodorakis, 167-169. Skiathos, Greece.

Watt, A.P., M. Spittle, T. Jaakkola, and T. Morris. 2003. Structural equation models of measures of imagery ability and imagery use. Paper published in *Proceedings of the XI European Congress of Sport Psychology* (July), Copenhagen.

Watt, A.P., M. Spittle, and T. Morris. 2002. Evidence related to the evaluation of measures of sport imagery. *Proceedings of the Science and Medicine in Sport Conference* (October), Melbourne, Australia.

Wehner, T., S. Vogt, and M. Stadler. 1984. Task-specific characteristics during mental training. *Psychological Research* 46: 389-401.

Weinberg, R. 1981. The relationship between mental preparation strategies and motor performance. *Quest* 33: 195-213.

———. 1982. The relationship between mental strategies and motor performance: A review and critique. *Quest* 32: 195-213.

———. 1988. *The mental advantage.* Champaign, IL: Leisure Press.

Weinberg, R., J. Butt, B. Knight, K.L. Burke, and A. Jackson. 2003. The relationship between the use and effectiveness of imagery: An exploratory investigation. *Journal of Applied Sport Psychology* 15: 26-40.

Weinberg, R., and D. Gould. 1999. *Foundations of sport and exercise psychology.* 2nd ed. Champaign, IL: Human Kinetics.

———. 2003. *Foundations of sport and exercise psychology.* 3rd ed. Champaign, IL: Human Kinetics.

Weinberg, R., T. Seabourne, and A. Jackson. 1981. Effects of visuo-motor behavior rehearsal, relaxation, and imagery on karate performance. *Journal of Sport Psychology* 3: 228-238.

———. 1982. Effects of visuo-motor behavior rehearsal on state-trait anxiety and performance: Is practice important? *Journal of Sport Behavior* 5: 209-219.

———. 1987. Arousal and relaxation instructions prior to the use of imagery. *International Journal of Sport Psychology* 18: 205-214.

Weiss, M.R. 1991. Psychological skill development in children and adolescents. *Sport Psychologist* 5: 335-354.

White, A., and L. Hardy. 1995. Use of different imagery perspectives on the learning and performance of different motor skills. *British Journal of Psychology* 86: 169-180.

White, A., and L. Hardy. 1998. An in-depth analysis of the uses of imagery by high-level slalom canoeists and artistic gymnasts. *Sport Psychologist* 12(4): 387-403.

White, K., and Ashton, R. 1976. Correlational study of the relationship between Betts' and QMI and Gordon's test. Unpublished Manuscript. Department of Psychology, University of Queensland. Cited in K. White, P.W. Sheehan, and R. Ashton, 1977, Imagery assessment: A survey of self-report measures. *Journal of Mental Imagery* 1: 145-170.

————. 1977. Visual imagery control: One dimension or four? *Journal of Mental Imagery* 1: 245-252.

White, K.D., R. Ashton, and R.M.D. Brown. 1977. The measurement of imagery vividness: Normative data and their relationship to sex, age, and modality differences. *British Journal of Psychology* 68: 203-211.

White, K., R. Ashton, and H. Law. 1974. Factor analysis of the shortened form of Betts' Questionnaire upon Mental Imagery. *Australian Journal of Psychology* 26: 183-190.

————. 1978. The measurement of imagery vividness: Effects of format and order on the Betts' Questionnaire upon Mental Imagery. *Canadian Journal of Behaviour Science* 10: 68-78.

White, S.A. 1993. The relationship between psychological skills, experience, and practice commitment among collegiate male and female skiers. *Sport Psychologist* 7(1): 49-57.

Wichman, H., and P. Lizotte. 1983. Effects of mental practice and locus of control on performance of dart throwing. *Perceptual and Motor Skills* 56: 807-812.

Wiese, D.M., M.R. Weiss, and D.P. Yukelson. 1991. Sport psychology in the training room: A survey of athletic trainers. *Sport Psychologist* 5: 25-40.

Wiese-Bjornstal, D.M., D.M. Gardetto, and S.M. Shaffer. 1999. Effective interaction skills for sports medicine professionals. In *Counseling in sports medicine,* ed. R. Ray and D.M. Wiese-Bjornstal, 55-74. Champaign, IL: Human Kinetics.

Wijers, A.A., L.J. Otten, S. Feenstra, G. Mulder, and L.J.M. Mulder. 1989. Brain potentials during selective attention, memory search, and mental rotation. *Psychophysiology* 26: 452-467.

Williams, J.D., G. Rippon, B.M. Stone, and J. Annett. 1995. Psychophysiological correlates of dynamic imagery. *British Journal of Psychology* 86: 283-300.

Williams, J.M., R.J. Rotella, and C.B. Scherzer. 2001. Injury risk and rehabilitation: Psychological considerations. In *Applied sport psychology: Personal growth to peak performance,* 4th ed., ed. J.M. Williams, 456-479. Mountain View, CA: Mayfield.

Williams, L.R.T., and A. Isaac. 1991. Skill differences associated with movement performance: II. Imagery and kinesthesis. *Journal of Human Movement Studies* 21: 129-136.

Wolmer, L., N. Laor, and P. Toren. 1999. Image control from childhood to adolescence. *Perceptual and Motor Skills* 89: 471-485.

Woods, B. 1998. *Applying psychology to sport.* London: Hodder & Stoughton.

Woolfolk, R.L., S.M. Murphy, D. Gottesfeld, and D. Aitken. 1985. Effects of mental rehearsal of task motor activity and mental depiction of task outcome on motor skill performance. *Journal of Sport Psychology* 7: 191-197.

Woolfolk, R.L., W. Parrish, and S.M. Murphy. 1985. The effects of positive and negative imagery on motor skill performance. *Cognitive Therapy and Research* 9: 335-341.

Wrisberg, C.A. 2001. Levels of performance skill: From beginners to experts. In *Handbook of Sport Psychology,* 2nd ed., ed. R.N. Singer, H.A. Hausenblas, and C.M. Janelle, 3-19. New York: Wiley

Wrisberg, C.A., and M.R. Ragsdale. 1979. Cognitive demand and practice level: Factors in the mental rehearsal of motor skills. *Journal of Human Movement Studies* 5: 201-208.

Wuyam, B., S.H. Moosavi, J. Decety, L. Adams, R.W. Lansig, and A. Guz. 1995. Imagination of dynamic exercise produced ventilatory responses which were more apparent in competitive sportsmen. *Journal of Physiology* 482: 713-724.

Yahagi, S., and T. Kasai. 1998. Facilitation of motor evoked potentials (MEPs) in first dorsal interosseous (FDI) muscle is dependent on different motor images. *Electroencephalographic Clinical Neurophysiology* 109: 409-417.

Yahagi, S., K. Shimura, and T. Kasai. 1996. An increase in cortical excitability with no change in spinal excitability during motor imagery. *Perceptual and Motor Skills* 83: 288-290.

Yue, G., and K.J. Cole. 1992. Strength increases from the motor program: Comparison of training with maximal voluntary and imagined muscle contractions. *Journal of Neurophysiology* 67: 1114-1123.

Young-Overby, L. 1990. A comparison of novice and experienced dancers' imagery ability. *Journal of Mental Imagery* 14: 173-184.

Zaichkowsky, L.D., and C.Z. Fuchs. 1988. Biofeedback applications in exercise and athletic performance. *Exercise and Sport Sciences Reviews* 16: 381-421.

Ziegler, S. 1987. Comparison of imagery styles and past experience in skills performance. *Perceptual and Motor Skills* 64: 579-586.

Zubek, J.P., ed. 1969. *Sensory deprivation: Fifteen years of research.* Englewood Cliffs, NY: Appleton-Century-Crofts.

INDEX

Note: The italicized *f* and *t* following page numbers refer to figures and tables, respectively.

About the Authors

Tony Morris, PhD, is a professor of sport and exercise psychology at Victoria University in Victoria, Australia. Morris has published widely on imagery in sport and is known as the leading researcher on the topic. He has authored numerous book chapters on imagery in sport and is the author of one of the leading texts on sport and exercise psychology as well as an authoritative reference text on the status of sport psychology around the world. He has held numerous positions with national and international sport psychology associations, including president of the Asian South Pacific Association of Sport Psychology since 1999 and treasurer of the International Society of Sport Psychology since 2001.

Michael Spittle, PhD, is a lecturer in motor behavior at the University of Ballarat in Victoria, Australia. His current teaching includes motor learning, motor control, sport and exercise psychology, measurement and evaluation in human movement, and cricket, as well as supervision of several postgraduate students. Spittle has a Physical Education and honors degree from Victoria University, a postgraduate degree in psychology from Deakin University, and a PhD from Victoria University in the area of imagery perspectives and performance of open and closed motor skills. He has participated in and enjoys many sports and activities including cricket, Australian Rules football, soccer, surfing, running, and fitness training.

Anthony Watt, PhD, is a lecturer in physical education at Victoria University in Victoria, Australia. Under Dr. Morris he completed his PhD work in 2003 in the area of assessment of imagery ability in sport. In addition to his lecturing, he cosupervises doctoral students working in the area of imagery use in sport. Watt has extensive background in physical education and sport, in which imagery has been examined.

About the Contributing Authors

Scott Fletcher

Scott studied Applied Psychology and Sport Studies at the undergraduate and graduate diploma level at the University of Canberra, before doing a masters degree by research at the University of Otago in New Zealand, where he studied the experience of flow in rugby. Since 2002, Scott has been studying for a PhD in the School of Human Movement, Recreation and Performance at Victoria University. His thesis examines the role of coaches in the pre-match psychological preparation of basketball players. Scott has also been involved in research on anxiety and goal attainment. He has participated in cricket as a player and a coach.

Cadeyrn Gaskin

After studying for undergraduate, honours, and masters qualifications in sports management and coaching at Massey University in New Zealand, Cadeyrn has been researching physical activity and psychosocial functioning in people with cerebral palsy for his PhD at Victoria University. Cadeyrn has also been involved in research on coaching and has written about imagery and intrinsic–extrinsic motivation. Cadeyrn is an avid exerciser, who rarely misses a day at the gym. He has also been a keen coach of cricket and soccer, and has participated in soccer refereeing in New Zealand.

Michelle Walsh

Michelle completed undergraduate and honours degrees in psychology at Melbourne University prior to undertaking a professional masters degree in sport psychology at Victoria University. Michelle is now conducting research on exercise and depression in people who have recently experienced heart problems for her PhD in the School of Human Movement, Recreation and Performance at Victoria University. Michelle is involved in practice in the area of weight management and exercise, and she also does some individual and group exercise training. She is a keen social exerciser, and enjoys playing tennis, netball, and going to the gym.